Reformed Historical Theology

Edited by
Herman J. Selderhuis

In co-operation with
Emidio Campi, Irene Dingel, Benyamin F. Intan,
Elsie Anne McKee, Richard A. Muller, and Risto Saarinen

Volume 76

Ryan M. McGraw (ed.)

Charles Hodge

American Reformed Orthodox Theologian

Vandenhoeck & Ruprecht

Bibliographic information published by the Deutsche Nationalbibliothek:
The Deutsche Nationalbibliothek lists this publication in the Deutsche Nationalbibliografie; detailed bibliographic data available online: https://dnb.de.

Typesetting: le-tex publishing services, Leipzig
Cover design: SchwabScantechnik, Göttingen
Printed and bound: Hubert & Co. BuchPartner, Göttingen
Printed in the EU

Vandenhoeck & Ruprecht Verlage | www.vandenhoeck-ruprecht-verlage.com

ISSN 2198-8226
ISBN 978-3-525-56089-1

Table of Contents

Acknowledgements

Several streams converged, resulting in this project. First, Crossway asked me to contribute a chapter on Princeton on original sin in their academic line to a forthcoming volume entitled, *Ruined Sinners to Reclaim.* Being surprised by what I found, this led me to see the need for studying broader continuities and discontinuities between Reformed orthodoxy and "Old Princeton" theology. I thank Johnny and David Gibson for pressing me out of my comfort zone to participate in this project.

Second, I served as a critical reader for Scott Cook's ThM thesis at Greenville Presbyterian Theological Seminary. Scott treated shifts in defining God's attributes in nineteenth century American Presbyterian thought, sometimes contrasting authors like Hodge with earlier Reformed orthodox precedents. This led me to see once again the need for larger trajectories in the history of ideas related to figures like Hodge. As Scott pulled his research into a larger PhD project, I not only wanted to expand his research into other areas, but I wanted him on the team to write a chapter in this book, which turned into a chapter and a half, due to our common interest in the Trinity. Scott both spurred on the idea for this book and contributed much to its pages.

Third, I regularly teach a course on Prolegomena and I always felt a bit hazy in my understanding of the shift on historical treatments of theology as a science, all of which seemed to hover around post-Enlightenment contexts. Astute students asking good questions pressed me to seek greater clarity and understanding on this issue, leading to my chapter on theology as a science in this volume.

Fourth, C. N. Willborn, who knows far more nineteenth-century American theology than I do, introduced me to the primary Reformed authors from the time period, including many off the beaten path, roughly twenty years ago. Nick gave me food for thought, which ruminated in the back of my mind as I researched and wrote primarily on John Owen, Reformed Scholasticism, and other Reformed orthodox related themes over the past decade. He provoked in me enough interest in and familiarity with American Reformed theology to develop the seed thoughts of this present volume.

Now that this book has taken shape, thanks are due to many people. First, I thank the contributors for their patience with me as a brutal editor, often adding to their already heavy workloads. All the authors worked very hard in bringing their expertise to bear on their given topics, patiently wading through my comments and often stretching themselves beyond their fields of expertise at various points. It has been a joy and blessing to work with you all.

Second, editors always need critical feedback as well. This is how we learn in research and writing. John Fesko graciously lent his time as a brutal editor in his own right to give me exactly the kind of criticism on my own material in this book. John sent my chapter on Theology as a Science bleeding with comments and exclamation marks. In the end, we may not see eye to eye on some of my conclusions about Hodge's views and the reasons behind them. However, this is what has made my friendship with John so fruitful over the years. We love and respect each other as brothers and friends in the Lord, and as historians and systematic theologians. I have likely learned much more from John than he has from me over the years, but I thank him for being a diligent student of history and a friend willing to help me make my own work better more times than I can count. I dedicate this volume to him as a small token of thanks.

Third, I thank Herman Selderhuis for his early interest in this project. Herman is always a pleasure to work with and a great encouragement. I am also an admirer of his own voluminous historical writing, and I have developed a greater appreciation for him in relation to how many books he edits.

Fourth, thanks are due to Fred Sanders for his interest and feedback on the chapter on the Trinity. Fred has brought more clarity to the doctrine of the Trinity in recent years, both on academic and popular levels, likely than anyone else I know. Though this is not a work on systematic theology, I hope that historical studies like this one will continue to give systematic theologians food for thought by putting more big picture options on the table.

Fifth, Jehona Kicaj with Brill shepherded the transition from V&R to Brill in bringing this volume to print. Jehona helped greatly in keeping the project on track and settling a final deadline for the chapters, for which I and the other authors are profoundly grateful.

Lastly, I thank my wife and children, who always listen to me talk through my projects. A book like this one is far more academic and complex than many other things that I write, which are geared towards the church primarily rather than the scholarly world. Krista in particularly always makes living life in communion with the Triune God an even greater joy, and my children (Owen, Calvin, Jonathan, and Callie) take an increasing interest in my work as Krista and I grow into more adult-like friendships with them. Owen and Calvin even bravely took my Reformed Scholasticism course in 2022, which I hope opened to them a new world. At the very least, they now understand why dad worked for so many years on his Hodge book. I thank the Lord for them all, and there are no other people with whom I would rather share life, fellowship, and worship.

Ryan M. McGraw
Greenville Presbyterian Theological Seminary 2022

Introduction

Charles Hodge (1797–1878) was one of the most important American Reformed theologians of the nineteenth-century, representing a benchmark in the "Old Princeton" theological tradition. He lived during a time of seismic change, affecting cultural, social, and scientific ideas, through a period including the American Civil War and its aftermath. As professor of Systematic Theology at Princeton Seminary, he influenced an inter-denominational group of ministers and missionaries, extending his influence far beyond the Presbyterian Church in the United States of America. Studying Hodge's life and theology provides a snapshot of a pivotal period of development in American history and culture. He also identified himself both as an American and as a Reformed theologian.

The primary thesis of this volume is that Charles Hodge was an American theologian who self-consciously sought to defend and transmit Reformed orthodoxy into an American context, reflecting the persistence and change of ideas. This is important because most studies of Hodge, and other Princeton theologians, highlight their American context at length while neglecting how tightly they wove Reformed orthodox ideas into their thought. Hodge's theology is marked by the persistence of Reformed orthodoxy as well as by changes resulting from issues that arose within nineteenth-century America. Hodge was aware of some of these American influences on his theology, but other issues affected him of which he was unaware, or at least less aware. Following a historical introduction bv Paul Gujhar, the areas chosen for this study include Hodge's use of philosophy (Aza Goudriaan) his definition of theology as a science (Ryan McGraw), his doctrine of God (Scott Cook), his use of personhood language in relation to the Trinity (Cook and McGraw) his treatment of the imputation of Adam's sin (C. N. Willborn), his delineation of church offices (Alan Strange), the controversy in which he debated the validity of Roman Catholic baptism (Mark Herzer), and his conception of Christ's presence in the Lord's Supper (Stefan Lindholm).

Each of these areas illustrate a clear point of continuity with Reformed orthodox teaching as well as a distinctively American twist in Hodge's ideas. The first two chapters establish Hodge's historical and philosophical contexts, stressing both his Reformed orthodoxy and his engagement with a wide range of early modern and modern philosophers. Remaining chapters treat targeted areas of Hodge's theology that illustrate persistence with Reformed orthodoxy and change in nineteenth century America. His definition and method of theology drew from medieval and early Reformed authors, while adjusting his evaluation of theology as a science in light of post-enlightenment definitions of science and scientific progress. His explanation of the divine attributes both built upon and altered historic Reformed orthodox ideas at key points. Hodge's treatment of the Trinity broadly retained the catholic Christian doctrine, while reflecting shifting definitions of personhood in the nineteenth century, and using "subordination" langue that was relatively unusual in earlier church history. Retaining the imputation of Adam's sin as grounded in high Reformed orthodox views of the covenant of works, he redefined the nature of imputation in light of American controversies, especially related to New England theology and fears of pantheism. While Hodge's church polity had historic precedent in Presbyterianism, American debates over the nature and number of church offices, and the grounds on which he defended the validity of Roman Catholic baptism reflected some new avenues of thought. Lastly, both picking up and rejecting strands of earlier Reformed thought and melding them with the Westminster Standards, his description of Christ presence in the Lord's Supper and his debates with John Williamson Nevin were colored by his concerns with modern pantheistic theologies.

The purpose of each chapter is primarily historical rather than dogmatic, aiming to understand Hodge's ideas in context. Spanning between Reformed orthodoxy and nineteenth century America broadens this context, attempting to build large-scale trajectories in Reformed thought and helping to fill a relative vacuum in this area of studies. Believing that historians can seek to be objective without claiming to be neutral, we have adopted the method of trying to "see things their way" by stressing historical contexts and explanations more than contemporary uses and categories. Most of the authors here are connected to the Reformed tradition in some way, and many disagree with each other at points regarding the degree of continuity and discontinuity between Hodge and his Reformed predecessors. Many more of us would have even more disagreements over whether we regard Hodge's ideas on each point treated good or bad. All of us have sought to understand and explain Hodge's ideas better with an eye to nineteenth century American and the early modern sources on which he relied so heavily. Regardless of what opinions readers hold currently about Hodge, they should approach this material with open minds as they wade through the difficult philosophical, scientific, political, and religious issues that contributed to who Hodge was, what he did, and why. Due to the complexity of topics treated, some of these chapters are better able to illustrate the fact that things were different in nineteenth century America than why they were so.

Every scholar invited to contribute to this volume either has expertise in Reformed orthodoxy, nineteenth-century America, or some combination of the two. Seeking to press authors to wed these two fields, the editor has provided contributors with a set of issues and questions necessary to bridge the gap between Reformed orthodox and American theological studies in relation to Hodge's self-identification with both. The goal is to provide a comparison between Hodge's views and earlier Reformed thought to explain the transmission and transformation of ideas more clearly. All authors were required to contextualize their subjects in order to furnish readers with the widest context possible, both for Hodge, and for the ideas that he built upon or modified. As such, this project both drew from the expertise of each author and pressed them beyond it either into later or earlier centuries.

Hoping to break fresh ground by connecting two rarely intersecting fields of historical Reformed theology, the editor hopes to shed light on broader developments and trajectories in the history of ideas. Only by recovering the Reformed orthodox background from which Hodge drew can we truly appreciate how his post-Enlightenment American context affected his thought. This broad approach to investigating American Reformed theology indicates the importance of a constructing a more complex and far-reaching context for Hodge's thought than many have attempted up to this point. Expanding this context will better help readers understand how older ideas both carried over and shifted in nineteenth century America. The field for further research along these lines is currently wide open, and we hope that this volume will serve as a starting point in the conversation. Beginning with this volume, the emerging picture is that Charles Hodge was both an American and a Reformed orthodox theologian.

Ryan M. McGraw
Editor

Contributors

Scott Cook, Part-Time Faculty of History and Apologetics, Greenville Presbyterian Theological Seminary

Aza Goudriaan, Guest Professor of Historical Theology, ETF Leuven, and Associate Professor of Church History, PThU, Amsterdam/Groningen

Paul C. Gutjahr, Associate Dean for Arts and Humanities and Undergraduate Education; Ruth Halls Professor, English University of Indiana

Mark Herzer, Pastor of Christ Covenant Presbyterian Church, Warminster PA

Stefan Lindholm, Lecturer in Systematic Theology, Johannelund School of Theology, Uppsala, Sweden

Ryan McGraw, Morton H. Smith Professor of Systematic Theology, Greenville Presbyterian Theological Seminary

Alan D. Strange, Professor of Church History, Mid-America Reformed Seminary

C. N. Willborn, Adjunct Professor of Church History, Greenville Presbyterian Theological Seminary

Paul C. Gutjahr

1. Reflections on the Life and Thought of Charles Hodge

1.1 Foundations

Theologians and their theologies do not spring from a vacuum. They are born of a complex mixture of cultural, historical and personal factors. Such is the case of Charles Hodge, perhaps America's most important nineteenth-century Reformed theologian. This chapter seeks to tease out some of the dialogical interplay between Hodge the man and the times in which he lived, in order to better understand his pivotal role in helping to craft a highly influential, and often uniquely American, brand of Reformed theology.

The Hodges of Philadelphia were a distinguished and affluent family for much of the eighteenth century. Immigrating to the American colonies from Ireland in the 1730s, three Hodge brothers had quickly established themselves as successful sea merchants in one of the colonies busiest port cities.[1] Andrew, the most successful of the brothers, bought a number of ships, began a provisioning business for sea-going vessels, built a large warehouse, established a prosperous store, and controlled his own dock on the Philadelphia waterfront. In the years leading up to the American Revolution, he became one of the city's wealthiest and most important citizens, and many of his sons rose to become influential businessmen and sea captains tied to Philadelphia's maritime economy.[2]

Charles Hodge was the son of Hugh Hodge, the eighth child of Andrew Hodge. By the time Charles was born on December 27, 1797, the once influential and aristocratic Hodge family of Philadelphia was in decline. The diminished state of the Hodge family's merchant trade due to the war for independence from Britain was at least partly responsible for Huge Hodge's decision to move away from the well-worn commercial paths of his family.[3] Hugh leaned into his keen interest in science to pursue the profession of medicine. It was a career choice that would lead to his death in 1798. While treating patients during a series of devastating Yellow Fever outbreaks that ravaged Philadelphia, Hugh ultimately succumbed to the disease. Charles was barely six months old when his father died.

---

1 A. A. Hodge, *Life of Charles Hodge* (New York: Charles Scribner's Sons, 1880), 1.

2 Frank Willing Leach, "The Philadelphia of our Ancestors," *North American*, Sunday, June 14, 1908, 1.

3 Hugh L. Hodge, *Memoranda of Family History Dictated by Hugh L. Hodge* (n. p.: 1903), 20–21.

Thus, Hodge spent his earliest years cared for by his mother, Mary, and a circle of Philadelphia family and friends. Descended from French Huguenot stock, Mary was renowned for her Christian piety and unusually keen intellect.[4] Hodge's lifelong commitment to education can be traced, at least in part, to his mother's own immense intellectual giftedness and lifelong love of learning. Throughout his life, Hodge recounted vivid memories of his mother's penchant to recite lines from Dryden and Pope, and she took a profound interest in every phase of her sons' educations. Mary made significant sacrifices to see that her sons were educated. In order to pay for their primary and secondary schooling, she took boarders into her home and undertook small paying jobs.[5] At one point, due to a series of financial stresses culminating in the government embargos enacted during the War of 1812 and their effect on the last remnants of her family holdings tied to the once great Hodge sea trade, Mary had to sell her family home and commence a pattern of frequent moves within and around Philadelphia in order to continue to care for, and educate, Hodge and his elder brother, Hugh.

In Hodge's ancestry and formative years, one finds key pillars of his lifelong character and inclinations. The devout Protestant nature of his mother and the deep Presbyterian roots of the Hodge family would be a continual guide in his ecclesiastical and theological thinking. Hodge not only joined the Presbyterian Church upon his conversion in 1815, but spent the remainder of his life developing into one of its most important leaders. One wonders if the peripatetic existence that Mary and her sons in Hodge's earliest years found its answer in Hodge's later contentment in residing for almost his entire life in the small town of Princeton, New Jersey. The economic vicissitudes that so battered his family in his youth made him keenly aware of property rights and markers of social standing, sensitivities that would have great bearing on his own thinking when it came to his Federalist-leaning political views and issues such as slavery. His attachment to the forms and doctrines of Presbyterianism and his highly structured, largely unchanging, theological hermeneutic raise the distinct possibility that Hodge found in such a structured religious tradition a means of stabilizing his world when that world had started off with such vast gulfs of vulnerability and uncertainty.

1.2 Education

Hodge became an undergraduate at Princeton College in 1812. By the time he entered the College, its curriculum had been deeply influenced by the teaching and

4 Hodge, *Life of Charles Hodge*, 8.

5 Hodge, *Memoranda of Family History Dictated by Hugh L. Hodge*, 24–25.

intellectual commitments of John Witherspoon. When Witherspoon took over the presidency of Princeton College in 1768, he ushered in a new era in the school's history. He put a pronounced emphasis on preparing men not only for the ministry, but also for professions in the realms of law, politics, education, medicine, and business. He also brought a new philosophical orientation to the College, a thorough commitment to Scottish Common Sense Realism. This philosophical commitment would become the dominant intellectual school of thought in American higher education up through the Civil War, and it also became an absolute bulwark in Hodge's own theological thinking.[6]

Founded on the writings of Francis Hutcheson, Thomas Reid, and Dugald Stewart, Scottish Common Sense Philosophy highlighted the serious Enlightenment engagement with science without losing science and philosophy's connection to religious belief.[7] At its core, this school of philosophical thought held out two central truths. First, it taught that some basic truths were self-evident. Being a careful and patient observer made truth accessible to anyone through one's ordinary "common" sense, and thus the sense could be trusted to provide a sound basis for all scientific, philosophical, and theological endeavors. For those who believed in Common Sense Realism, all of God's manifold work and his very presence in the world was a fact available and verifiable to all thoughtful observers. This notion of the observable nature of truth was refined and popularized for Common Sense Realists by the seventeenth-century scientist and natural philosopher, Francis Bacon, who pursued such observable truth through developing structured methods of inductively investigating natural and intellectual phenomena so as to be able to separate truth from fallacy.[8] Second, Scottish Realism contained a pronounced ethical dimension; it taught that all people in addition to their five senses had a common moral sense that allowed them to distinguish between good and evil. It was the Common Sense belief in self-evident truth, and the mind's ability to systematically and thoroughly investigate that truth, which would come to define Hodge's own theological thinking.

By the time Hodge entered Princeton College, Witherspoon had been dead for nearly two decades, and the archly conservative Ashbel Green held the College's presidency. Green's tenure was marked by a clear emphasis on training young

---

6 Lawrence A. Cremin, *American Education: The National Experience 1783–1876* (New York: Harper and Row, 1980), 27.

7 A helpful overview of Scottish Common Sense philosophy in America is found in Mark A. Noll, "Common Sense Traditions and American Evangelical Thought," *American Quarterly* 37, no. 2 (1985): 220–225.

8 The importance of Bacon in Scottish Common Sense and Presbyterian thought finds its fullest treatment in Theodore Dwight Bozeman, *Protestants in an Age of Science: The Baconian Ideal and Antebellum Religious Thought* (Chapel Hill, NC: University of North Carolina Press, 1977).

men for the ministry. He instituted a reactionary curriculum for the time, moving away from Witherspoon's practical and commerce-friendly course of study in areas touching on science, modern languages, and mathematics. Instead, Green placed renewed emphasis on the classical languages and the study of the Bible. Hodge entered Princeton College as Green turned back the school's curriculum to content that had been popular in higher education a century earlier. Such a religious focus was further accented by the fact that Princeton Theological Seminary was founded during Green's presidency, and many of the College's students went on to do their ministerial training at the College's neighboring seminary. Thus, Hodge's undergraduate experience was marked by Green's return to traditional, eighteenth-century Presbyterian notions of higher education, which along with classical language work and biblical studies once again foregrounded Witherspoon's lectures on moral philosophy, a curriculum that had withered in the years after Witherspoon's death, as well as the mandatory reading of William Paley's writings on natural philosophy.[9]

Amid Green's focus on raising up the country's next generation of clergy, Hodge spent the majority of his undergraduate years doing everything he could to be prepared for pursuing a career in medicine. Hodge not only followed his father in his career aspirations, but also in enjoying a deep and abiding interest in all things scientific.[10] Throughout his life, Hodge never tired of reading about the newest scientific developments, and he proved unfailing in willingness to converse with faculty and students both at Princeton College and Princeton Theological Seminary about how science buttressed Christian belief. His interest in science and scientific methodologies would constantly inflect his theological writings in the decades to come.[11]

Green's emphasis on the making religion a prominent part of life at Princeton College bore its most notable fruit in a revival that swept through the institution in the winter of 1815. This revival brought forty of the College's 105 students to

---

9 Mark A. Noll, *Princeton and the Republic, 1768–1822* (Princeton, NJ: Princeton University Press, 1989), 275. Darrel Guder, "History of Belles Lettres at Princeton" (Ph.D. diss., University of Hamburg, 1964): 227; 234. The most comprehensive treatment of the use of Paley's works in American colleges is Wilson Smith, "William Paley's Theological Utilitarianism in America," WMQ 11:2 (Apr. 1954): 402–424.

10 Ronald L. Numbers, "Charles Hodge and the Beauties and Deformities of Science," in *Charles Hodge Revisited: A Critical Appraisal of His Life and Work*, eds. John W. Stewart and James H. Moorhead (Grand Rapids, MI: William B. Eerdmans Publishing Co., 2002), 77. This essay provides a good overview of Hodge's lifelong interest in the connections between theology and science.

11 E. Brooks Holifield, *Theology in America: Christian Thought from the Age of the Puritans to the Civil War* (New Haven, CT: Yale University Press, 2003), 379–381. Walter H. Conser, Jr. *God and the Natural World: Religion and Science in Antebellum America* (Columbia, SC: University of South Carolina Press, 1993), 65–74. Bozeman, *Protestants in an Age of Science*, 154–159.

a profession of faith. Hodge was one such convert, and his profession of faith prompted him to decide near the end of his senior year to swerve away from an intended medical career to pursue the ministry instead. As a result, at the age of eighteen Hodge began his studies at Princeton Theological Seminary, putting himself under the tutelage and care of the Seminary's two founding faculty members: Archibald Alexander and Samuel Miller. Hodge would become particularly close to Alexander, who would take on a father role for the fatherless Hodge.

The training of Alexander and Miller at the Seminary highlighted a brand of Reformed, Calvinist theology that placed a premium on exalting God's glory through stressing his omnipotence and absolute sovereignty.[12] Central to their thinking was the conviction that it was God who orchestrated every aspect of his creation and that he was the pivotal catalyst in human salvation. Such a stress on God's absolute control over all aspects of humanity would become the hallmark attribute of the theology that would be taught at the Seminary throughout the nineteenth century and would later come to be called more colloquially "The Princeton Theology."[13]

Alexander and Miller shaped the Seminary's curriculum primarily around the Westminster Confession (1646), but they also incorporated thinking found in the confessional statements of the Second Helvetic Confession (1566) and the Canons of Dort (1619). Although bearing some differences, each of these confessions clearly upheld firm doctrinal statements on the sovereignty of God and the totally depraved nature of humanity. To knit together the strands running through all three of these confessional statements, they turned most notably to the apologetic work of Swiss Reformed Theologian Francis Turretin and the emphasis on systematic, inductive reasoning and notions of self-evident truth found in Witherspoon's brand of Scottish Common Sense philosophy.[14] Other important religious thinkers in Alexander and Miller's seminary curriculum included the English politician and writer Soame Jenyns, the natural philosopher and English clergyman William Paley, and English Presbyterian Puritan John Flavel.[15] At Princeton Seminary, students were taught an unwavering view of God's sovereignty and a firm conviction that God's sovereignty was self-evident both in the natural truths found in God's creation and the revealed truths found in the Holy Scriptures.[16]

Such confessional statements, along with Turretin's three-volume *Institutes of Elenctic Theology* (1679–1685), formed the basis for Hodge's own systematic ap-

---

12 Holifield, *Theology in America*, 11.

13 David F. Wells, ed., *The Princeton Theology* (Grand Rapids, MI: Baker Book House, 1989), 17–24.

14 Mark A. Noll, ed., *The Princeton Theology, 1812-1921* (Grand Rapids, MI: Baker Book House, 1983), 13; 27–33.

15 Lefferts A. Loetscher, *Facing the Enlightenment and Pietism* (Westport, CT: Greenwood Press, 1983), 17–26. Holified, *Theology in America*, 379–380.

16 Holifield, *Theology in America*, 378–387.

proach to Christian doctrine in the years to come. Hodge was so thoroughly tied to Turretin in his own teaching that he had the Swiss theologian's *Institutes* translated from Latin into English, with the purpose of widening Turretin's influence among American Christians.[17] When it later came time for Hodge to compose his own course of lectures on systematic theology at the Seminary that eventuated in his magisterial *Systematic Theology*, many points of the work's organization can be seen to largely, if not entirely, echo Turretin's *Institutes* in his commitment to addressing the central topics found in the Westminster Confession.

1.3 Influence

Hodge had originally intended to go into the Presbyterian pastorate, but a year after his graduation he was offered a one-year lectureship position in biblical languages at the Seminary. His natural linguistic ability made him a good fit for this position, and his decision to accept this lectureship led to joining the Seminary's faculty for the remainder of his life. At first, Hodge struggled with the idea of staying at the Seminary, fearing that he might be missing more exciting and consequential frontline ministry opportunities either pastoring his own church or taking a post on a mission field. In the end, however, he accepted the lectureship because he believed it to be the place where he might be able to exercise the most influence. In pastoring a congregation, he would touch the lives of that single congregation. In teaching ministers, he had the opportunity to touch the lives of countless congregations.

This issue of influence would be a central theme throughout Hodge's life. He was a man driven by the need to make the most of his gifts and the most of his time. Forever echoing in his mind was a biblical refrain often repeated by his mother: "To whom much is given, much will be required."[18] In the years that followed, Hodge would pursue his quest for influence in three basic ways: through his teaching at the Seminary, through his publishing the premier Presbyterian journal of his day along writing with several books, and finally through his leadership in different associations such as the Presbyterian General Assembly and its numerous committees, various mission boards, and the Board of Trustees at Princeton College.

His long tenure as a professor of the seminary is perhaps his most recognized avenue of influence. During his fifty-six-year career, he taught over three thousand seminarians. No American professor of the era would teach a greater number of

---

17 J. Mark Beach, "Francis Turretin's *Institutes of Elenctic Theology*," in *The Oxford Handbook of Reformed Theology*, eds. Michael Allen and Scott R. Swain (New York: Oxford University Press, 2020), 291–292.

18 Mary Hodge to Hugh and Charles Hodge, January 13, 1810, Charles Hodge Papers, Firestone Library, Princeton University, Box 7, Folder 4.

graduate students. His students would make their own marks as pastors, publishers, missionaries, educators, politicians, and seminary and college professors.

Another widely recognized avenue of influence for Hodge was the vast reach of his various publishing endeavors. Hodge was immensely savvy in recognizing early the power of print in the United States, a country which enjoyed the world's highest literacy rates in the early nineteenth century.[19] Such literacy rates led to an antebellum culture that one print historian has aptly characterized as one where "reading became a necessity of life."[20] Beginning in the 1820s, America's burgeoning print culture was unrivaled around the world for its volume and reach. America as a young democracy had come to hold an almost sacred belief in the power of print.[21] Print and the truth it could convey was one of the surest paths to an informed citizenry, and an informed citizenry was one of the surest paths to the kind of virtue needed to sustain a democratic form of government.[22]

Antebellum Christians fully embraced the promise offered through publishing, exhibiting an almost messianic faith in the power of the press. Whereas spreading God's word had once primarily been the realm of preachers, an unprecedented increase in the production and consumption of printed material in the opening decades of the nineteenth century led countless Protestants to believe that publishing's unrivaled reach would usher in a new age of mass conversions to Christ. Such Protestants were jubilant in their conviction that "types of lead and sheets of paper may be the light of the World."[23] Such optimism was fueled by the rise of several powerful Christian publishing enterprises, including the American Bible Society (1816), the American Sunday School Union (1824), and the American Tract Society (1825).[24] By the middle of the century, the output of these three societies accounted for approximately sixteen percent of all books produced in the United States.[25]

---

19 Ronald J. Zboray, *A Fictive People: Antebellum Economic Development and the American Reading Public* (New York: Oxford University Press, 1993), 196–201. Lee Soltow and Edward Stevens, *The Rise of Literacy and the Common School in the United States: A Socioeconomic Analysis to 1870* (Chicago, IL: University of Chicago Press, 1981), 53, 56, 155–176, 189.

20 William J. Gilmore, *Reading Becomes a Necessity of Life: Material and Cultural Life in New England, 1780–1835* (Knoxville, TN: University of Tennessee Press, 1989), xxi.

21 Candy Gunther Brown, *The Word in the World: Evangelical Writing, Publishing, and Reading in America* (Chapel Hill, NC: University of North Carolina Press, 2004), 1–2.

22 Derek H. Davis, *Religion and the Continental Congress, 1774–1789: Contributions to Original Intent* (New York: Oxford University Press, 2000) 196.

23 Quoted in Joan Brumberg, *Mission for Life: The Judson Family and American Evangelical Culture* (New York: New York University Press, 1984), 67.

24 The best overview of religious publishing in this period can be found in David P. Nord, *Faith in Reading: Religious Publishing and the Birth of Mass Media in America, 1790–1860* (New York: Oxford University Press, 2004).

25 Brown, *The Word in the World*, 51.

Hodge was an early adopter of this move toward religiously didactic publishing as can be seen in his founding of the *Biblical Repertory* (later the *Biblical Repertory and Princeton Review*) in 1825, a quarterly theological journal he directed for nearly five decades. By editing over one hundred and twenty issues and contributing more than two hundred articles to its pages, Hodge established himself as a major voice in nearly every important religious controversy of his day. In addition to his articles for the *Repertory*, Hodge wrote several longer book-length works: Commentaries on four New Testament books (1835, 1856, 1857, 1859), a major history of the American Presbyterian Church (1839–40), the immensely popular devotional *The Way of Life* (1841), a landmark critique of Darwinism (1874), and his magnum opus, his *Systematic Theology* (1872–73). These writings gave Hodge's influence an international scope as he became one of the best known and most widely respected American theologians in Europe.

Hodge was also involved in a wide range of associations and governing bodies throughout his life. Through his leadership in these organizations, he was able to exercise great influence over the bodies they governed. Three groupings of governance bodies were particularly important to Hodge. The first of these was found in area of missionary activity. In the earliest years of Hodge's time on the Seminary faculty, he spent two years studying in Europe to better his understanding of German Higher biblical criticism and work on his ancient languages. Both endeavors were tied to his own desire to accurately interpret the Bible and teach methods of accurate biblical interpretation. While in Europe, Hodge gained a global view of Protestantism, and through that view he had become convinced of the vital importance of the United States in the efforts of world evangelization.

While in Europe, Hodge formulated a theory that vital Christian belief underwent certain cycles: "During one age, there are many revivals of religion, and a general prevalence of evangelical spirit and exertion; to this succeeds a period of coldness and declension; and to this either a period of revival or of open departure from the faith."[26] In contrast to the lack of religious fervor he witnessed in France and Germany, Hodge saw the massive and ubiquitous revivals happening in America as a sign that the United States was near the apex of its religious cycle. Such cresting religious fervor gave America an unrivaled ability at the time to spread the message of God grace throughout the world. Hodge never wavered in his desire to take advantage of America enjoying its high-water mark in terms of religious influence. Throughout his life, he never doubted that American missionary activity would be the means of converting innumerable unbelievers to the Christian faith.[27] He

---

26 Charles Hodge, "Lecture Addressed to the Students of the Theological Seminary," *Biblical Repertory: A Journal of Biblical Literature and Theological Review* 1, no. 1 (January 1829): 93.

27 Hodge had a particular bond with missionary activity in France. The best single account of this bond can be found in Richard Gardiner, "Princeton and Paris: An Early Nineteenth Century Bond

showed this conviction as he served from the mid-1840s to 1870 on both the Presbyterian Board of Foreign Missions and the Presbyterian Board of Domestic Missions. He even served for two years as the president of the Board of Foreign Missions (1868–1870).[28]

The second governing body where he sought to extend his influence was the General Assembly of the Presbyterian Church. Beginning in 1842, Hodge became a regular delegate to the General Assembly, representing the Seminary's needs and accomplishments to his Presbyterian brethren. He stretched the breadth of his influence in national Presbyterianism by remaining active in a number of national committees and boards sponsored by the General Assembly. In 1846, he was elected to the post of General Assembly's moderator. While his time as moderator was not particularly troubled, he did have to help the Assembly navigate two potentially divisive issues: the abolition of slavery and the establishment of Presbyterian parochial schools. For the former, he helped the Assembly take the middle ground of hoping the regrettable practice of slavery might eventually be abolished but not advocating any stance that held it unscriptural and thereby worthy of immediate elimination. When it came to Presbyterian parochial schools, Hodge favored establishing such a common school system sponsored by the denomination, wishing to establish such schools next to every Presbyterian Church in the nation. The initiative never gained the widespread support it needed to come into existence, but it was a cause Hodge spent his life supporting.[29]

Finally, Hodge exercised influence through helping to guide Princeton College as one of its trustees. Throughout his life, Hodge was a devoted alumnus of his *alma mater,* and in 1850 he was invited to take a seat on the College's board of trustees. He quickly established himself as one of its most respected members. He played a particularly important role when he was called upon to help the College choose a new president. Hodge's college classmate, John Maclean Jr., who had joined the College faculty at the age of twenty-three as a chemistry professor and had spent the next thirty-five years in the service of the College was being considered for the position when several trustees thought him too ordinary for the august position. Hodge played a pivotal role in changing their minds. John Maclean Jr. became Princeton's tenth president in 1854.

Perhaps Hodge's greatest contribution to the College while trustee, however, came in his unwavering commitment to "the religious character of the College," which he

---

of Mission" (senior thesis, Princeton Theological Seminary, 1994). His missionary commitment within Presbyterianism is recounted in David Calhoun, "Last Command: Princeton Theological Seminary and Missions (1812–1862)," (PhD diss., Princeton Theological Seminary, 1983), 208.

28 Hodge, *Life of Charles Hodge*, 384.

29 Charles Hodge, "General Assembly, 1846," *Biblical Repertory and Princeton* Review 18, no. 3 (July 1846): 435.

believed was the "first great aim of its administration."[30] While a trustee, he took a great interest in seeing that faculty who were appointed were both committed Christians and outstanding scholars in their disciplines. He also was largely responsible for the College maintaining its firm commitment to a liberal arts education that stressed the role of religion in learning. He championed a curriculum that avoided any overt professionalization and narrowness by stressing an educational regimen that eschewed the teaching of "science without literature, or literature without science."[31]

1.4 Scripture

While Hodge undertook various leadership roles, it is important to understand certain central beliefs that provided the engine that drove his influence. Perhaps the most fundamental of these beliefs was his view of Scripture. Hodge was a distinct product of, and advocate for, the Reformed tradition's stress on the importance of the Bible, and in no country was the Bible more prized as a religious and cultural cornerstone than in America. In the seventeenth and eighteenth centuries, education laws were put in place in the colonies with the express purpose of enabling European Americans to read the Bible.[32] By the nineteenth century, copies of the Bible were widely circulated by various Christian societies with the goal of placing a copy of the Bible in every American household.[33]

High American literacy rates, coupled with the ability of these readers to gain access to the Bible, created a profound culture of individual biblical interpretation. The potential chaos of such individual interpretation needed to be controlled, and at Princeton that control came to center in a new view of the Bible itself. The centuries-long Christian tradition of biblical interpretation found in the Catholic Church, and even in early Protestantism had tended to emphasize the divine inspiration of the Bible's various interpreters. The Reformed centerpiece of *Sola Scriptura* changed this equation. Instead of emphasizing the divine inspiration of the Bible's interpreters, Princeton Seminary's faculty increasingly stressed the divine inspiration

---

30 Hodge, *Life of Charles Hodge*, 386.

31 Trustee Bound Volumes, 1868–1878, Seeley G. Mudd Manuscript Library, Princeton University Archives, Department of Rare Books and Special Collections, Princeton University Library, 5:649–650.

32 Robert E. Brown, "The Bible in the Seventeenth Century," in *The Oxford Handbook of the Bible in America*, ed. Paul C. Gutjahr (New York: Oxford University Press, 2017), 80–82.

33 Paul C. Gutjahr. *An American Bible: A History of the Good Book in the United States, 1777–1880* (Stanford, CA: Stanford University Press, 1999), 32–33.

and infallibility of the Bible itself.[34] In their minds, the Bible's core text was such that its divinely-inspired nature gave it a kind of stability that would help guide and control its interpretation.

Hodge played a pivotal role in espousing the stability of the text, especially in light of the rise of modern textual criticism. Leaning heavily on his belief in Scottish Common Sense philosophy, Hodge argued that the Bible could help control its own interpretation because it was an absolutely reliable text which the common reader could study to be led by its divinely inspired self-evident and self-enforcing truths.[35] Hodge used his commitment to Scottish Common Sense to proclaim that the Bible was "a plain book", readily accessible with its clear truths to every person of normal intellect.[36] This emphasis mirrored earlier Reformed approaches to the perspicuity of Scripture, such as that represented by Turretin, but Hodge reoriented the doctrine line light of modern philosophy. In his Common Sense approach to biblical interpretation, he offered a useful philosophical underpinning to help Christians sort out for themselves the truest biblical interpretations as they were confronted with myriad options offered them by competing preachers and denominations. He, and other more conservative Protestants of this period, tirelessly advocated a view that the Bible could be readily and rightly understood by the common reader.[37] This was standard historic Reformed emphasis, but presented in a new way.

Thus, for Hodge and countless others in this period, the plain, self-evident, and stable Bible came to take on the character of a giant repository of fixed truths and proof texts available to anyone. Such an approach was relatively new as earlier Reformed authors tended to present the Bible as an unfolding message about knowing God. For Hodge, Scripture was a scientific textbook full of data. Perhaps most famously, Hodge captured this Common Sense view of the Scriptures at the outset of his *Systematic Theology*. Here, Hodge stated that the Bible was a magnificent "store-house of facts."[38] Furthermore, he argued that it was the duty of every Christian "to ascertain, collect, and combine all the facts which God has revealed concerning himself and our relation to him. These facts are all in the Bible. . . . It is in this sense that 'The Bible, and the Bible alone, is the religion of the

---

34 Jerry Wayne Brown, *The Rise of Biblical Criticism in America, 1800–1870* (Middletown, CT: Wesleyan University Press, 1969), 5.

35 Mark A. Noll, "Common Sense Traditions and American Evangelical Thought," in *American Quarterly* 37 (Summer 1985): 220–5.

36 Charles Hodge, "The Inspiration of Holy Scripture," *Biblical Repertory and Princeton* Review 29, no. 4 (October 1857): 664.

37 Mark Noll, *America's God: From Jonathan Edwards to Abraham Lincoln* (New York: Oxford University Press, 2005), 93–103.

38 Charles Hodge, *Systematic Theology*, vol. 1, (New York: Charles Scribner's Sons, 1872), 10.

Protestants.'"[39] In this way, Hodge held that the teachings of the Bible were not available to only a select few, but to all who took time to carefully investigate its content.

Hodge's Common Sense approach to the Bible became particularly important as German Higher Criticism increasingly came to influence various ways American clergy and laypeople read the Bible. Higher Criticism sought to rise above the mere examination of words and sentence structures to consider a biblical book's authorship, literary tradition and historical setting. In Protestant Germany, the study of the Bible had moved outside the confines of Church structures and found a home in German universities. This also reflected the fact, that in contrast to preceding centuries, theology was no longer the primary focus and purpose of European universities. Here, scholars increasingly treated the Bible like any other ancient literary text, often stressing its form and function, rather than its divine nature. Thus, one of the great challenges facing the Bible as it entered the nineteenth century centered on how scholars at leading American universities began to treat the book not as solely a product of divine authorship, but of human authorship as well.[40] Many influential American biblical scholars came to view the Bible's stories as they would any story from ancient Middle Eastern source material.[41] As Higher Critics began to use different literary and historical approaches to the biblical text, they posited new theories concerning the authorship of various biblical books. Debates arose surrounding the belief that Moses wrote the Pentateuch, with many Higher Critics arguing that a number of different authors had composed books such as Genesis.[42] Higher Criticism came to argue against a host of traditional beliefs about the Bible, which in the minds of many conservative American Protestants destabilized a firm belief in a divinely-inspired Bible. This type of reasoning raised questions as to how classic Protestant views of Scripture could persist in light of contemporary scholarship. Hodge sought both to retain and develop standard Reformed approaches to Scripture in this light.

German philosophy in general and the type of historicism encouraged by Higher Criticism in particular led to new ideas about human language that challenged traditional views that words had eternally fixed meanings as determined by God and transmitted through the Scriptures. Adopting and adapting the views of German Idealists like Immanuel Kant, Johann Ficte, Friedrich Schelling, and G. W. F. Hegel, Higher Critics held to a more fluid view of language, arguing that words were simply

39 Charles Hodge, *Systematic Theology*, vol. 1, (New York: Charles Scribner's Sons, 1872), 10–11.

40 Philip F. Gura, *American Transcendentalism: A History* (New York: Hill & Wang, 2007), 31.

41 Debby Applegate, *The Most Famous Man in America: The Biography of Henry Ward Beecher* (New York: Doubleday, 2006), 120.

42 Gura, *American Transcendentalism: A History*, 25.

arbitrary markers for ideas.[43] Eschewing the type of clear empiricism championed by Hodge and Scottish Common Sense philosophy, Higher Critics propounded that the meaning of words could change over time and in different cultural settings.

Central to German idealism was the belief that humans had an innate, often emotional, intuitive faculty that allowed them to make sense of their world. German Idealism as practiced among liberal American Christians such as William Ellery Channing, Theodore Parker, and Ralph Waldo Emerson cut against the beliefs taught by Scottish Common Sense by unsettling the conviction that the mind was the court of first and last resort in understanding both language and the physical world.[44] For such thinkers, the heart was a necessary, and often a superior, means of understanding the world. By the middle of the nineteenth century, such views were gaining ground among American Trinitarian Protestants. Leading Congregational figures such as Horace Bushnell, Edwards Amasa Park, and Henry Ward Beecher championed the notion that there was an intuitive, heart-centered faculty that was essential to understanding the Scriptures.[45]

Park, in particular, became a leading voice for more Romantic notions of scriptural interpretation when he argued that biblical language was best interpreted by using different modes of understanding. According to Park, the intellect or "logical consciousness" was the best means of understanding matters expressed in the language of propositional and literal truths.[46] On the other hand, he believed that the heart or the "'intuitive consciousness" was the best means of understanding God's truth as it was communicated in emotion-evoking images through figurative language.[47] Park saw figurative language as appealing to one's affections, making it more elastic and less precise in its meanings.[48] He taught that not every passage in the Bible was "intended for logical proof; they may have been designed for passionate appeals and figure into the shape of argument, not to convince the reason but to carry the heart by a strong assault."[49]

Of course, more conservative Christians such as Hodge thought such double-mindedness in biblical interpretation was nonsense. Disturbed by Park's musings

---

43 Jurgen Herbst, *The German Historical School in American Scholarship* (Ithaca, NY: Cornell University Press, 1965), 73–97.

44 Gura, *American Transcendentalism: A History*, 50–53; 66–67.

45 Barbara M. Cross, *Horace Bushnell: Minister to a Changing America* (Chicago, IL: University of Chicago Press, 1958), 109. Applegate, *The Most Famous Man in America: The Biography of Henry Ward Beecher*, 133.

46 Edwards Amasa Park, *The Theology of the Intellect and of the Feelings* (Andover, MA: Warren F. Draper, 1850), 4.

47 Charles Hodge, "The Theology of the Intellect and that of the Feelings," *Biblical Repertory and Princeton Review* 22, no. 4 (October 1850), 646.

48 Park, *The Theology of the Intellect and of the Feelings*, 6.

49 Park, *The Theology of the Intellect and of the Feelings*, 9.

about interpretative elasticity and different modes of apprehending truth, Hodge entered into a two-year titanic periodical battle against Park during which the two men exchanged a series of essays published in Hodge's *Biblical Repertory* and Park's own journal *Bibliotheca Sacra*. Throughout, Hodge held fast to the traditional Reformed line of reasoning, which argued the Bible was a wholly reliable document and it taught only "one definite form of faith."[50] The Bible's contents were fully comprehensible through a commonsense use of reason. Hodge, and those like him, were particularly aggrieved by Park's German Idealist school of thought, which held that theology derived from reason alone often found itself antiquated by scientific advances, whereas theology interpreted through the heart need not "always accommodate itself to scientific changes, but may often use its old statements, even if, when literally understood, they be incorrect, and it thus abides as permanent as are the main impressions of truth."[51] Hodge found this denigration of Scriptural truth fantastically dangerous. For him, any truth revealed in Scripture always held up amid scientific scrutiny because the truths of science always agreed with the truths found in the Bible.

In this way, Hodge laid the groundwork for later Princeton theologians to establish a view of inerrant scriptures that would be widely adopted by conservative American Christians throughout the twentieth and twenty-first centuries. Perhaps the most famous of these inerrant defenses came in 1881 from Hodge's son, Archibald Alexander, and the formidable Presbyterian theologian Benjamin Warfield. The younger Hodge and Warfield gave no quarter to scientific attacks on the content of the Bible or romantic notions of the language it contained. They argued for the total trustworthiness of the Christian Scriptures, stating that "the Scriptures not only contain, but ARE THE WORD OF GOD, and hence that all their elements and all their affirmations were absolutely errorless, and binding the faith and obedience of men."[52] It was a view Hodge himself held close for his entire life.[53]

50 Hodge, "The Theology of the Intellect and that of the Feelings," 659.

51 Park, *The Theology of the Intellect and of the Feelings*, 10.

52 Archibald Alexander Hodge and Benjamin B. Warfield, "Inspiration", *Presbyterian Review* 2 (April 1881): 237.

53 David L. Kelsey, "Charles Hodge as Interpreter of Scripture," in *Charles Hodge Revisited: A Critical Appraisal of His Life and Work*, eds. John W. Stewart and James H. Moorhead (Grand Rapids, MI: William B. Eerdmans Publishing Co., 2002), 218.

1.5 Hermeneutic

As important as it was to his thinking, Hodge's firm commitment to an errorless text does not fully illuminate how he chose to interpret that text. His manner of interpreting the Bible – or his hermeneutic – needs further explication in order to not only understand what he taught and published, but also how his theological thinking was later adopted by other biblical expositors who followed in his footsteps. Hodge's biblical hermeneutic was built on the twin pillars of Scottish Commonsense Philosophy and a commitment to the Reformed tradition as it was articulated in the Westminster Confession and by such figures as Francis Turretin and John Calvin. His interpretations would often toggle between these twin pillars, stressing one more than the other depending on the particular passages studied, or issues being addressed. Benjamin Warfield, the Princeton theologian who came to dominate the Seminary's intellectual life after Hodge's death, wrote of his predecessor that "few men could equal" Hodge in his ability to capture a passage's "general flow of thought," while he saw Hodge as having little patience for "the technicalities of exegesis."[54] Warfield saw Hodge's biblical interpretations as often guided by a "theological predilection," which rose out of the teachings of famous Reformers and the history of the Church.[55] It should also be remembered that Hodge was not immune to having his biblical hermeneutic influenced by his own personal history as well, as his life experience can sometimes be detected in his expositions of Scripture.

The power of a Common Sense-inflected hermeneutic is seen not only in his view that the Bible was full of readily accessible self-evident truths, but also in the way Hodge approached ascertaining those truths. One of the clearest examples of his thinking in this regard comes across in his biblical arguments supporting slavery. In an article simply entitled "Slavery" and published in the 1836 *Biblical Repertory*, Hodge offered what he hoped would be a straightforward, and thus, universally embraced articulation of the Bible's teaching on the topic of slavery. His central, Common Sense point was simple: Slavery had existed in the time of Christ and nowhere does Jesus or any other biblical author condemn it. He asked if the emancipation of slaves was such a clear Christian mandate, why did Christ and his apostles never posit such a position. Furthermore, why had Paul and other biblical authors offered instructions to slave owners without ever advocating widespread emancipation?[56] Hodge was strongly in favor of gradual emancipation, for he saw slavery as a flawed social institution that denigrated the dignity of both men and

54 Hodge, *Life of Charles Hodge*, 589.

55 Hodge, *Life of Charles Hodge*, 590.

56 Charles Hodge, "Slavery," *Biblical Repertory and Theological* Review 8, no. 2 (April 1836): 277.

women, but he argued there was no biblical precedent for categorically forbidding it.[57]

Hodge's views on the issue of slavery are also a place where one can detect the inflection of his own life experience on his interpretative practice. Since the poverty of his nomadic youth, Hodge was personally interested and invested in notions of social stability and individual property rights. The government's actions during the Revolution and the War of 1812 had helped wipe out the fortunes of his family, so he was acutely aware what sweeping national policies could do to the welfare of individual (in this case, white) citizens. He had also owned two slaves, and he was firmly convinced that he had been entrusted with their care to help better their lives.[58] These life experiences influenced his thinking about slavery. He justified the institution by making a crucial distinction between slaveholding and slave laws.[59] Slaveholding was not condemned by Scripture, but how slaveholding was enacted through slave laws was subject to biblical teaching on how God commanded people to treat one another. In Hodge's eyes, slavery only became a sin when the laws that governed it ran counter to the commands of God.[60]

Hodge's hermeneutic and its dependence on historical precedent finds one of its best examples in how he chose to argue against the tidal wave of anti-Catholic sentiment in his day to defend Roman Catholic baptism. Hodge stood firm in his defense of the efficacy of Catholic baptism, a stance that made him immensely unpopular with many of his Presbyterian brethren when, in 1845, he refused to join the Presbyterian General Assembly in denouncing the efficacy of Roman Catholic baptism. When he heard of the General Assembly's vote in that year to not recognize the spiritual efficacy of Roman Catholic baptism, Hodge stood amazed that his Presbyterian brethren could have declared "Calvin, Luther, and all the men of that generation, as well as thousands who with no other than Romish baptism" who had long "been received into the Protestant churches, to have lived and died unbaptized."[61] In viewing the long history of the Christian Church from the time of Christ to his own day, this position against Roman Catholic baptism was incomprehensible to him. In this way, Hodge's concerns over Roman Catholic baptism reflected both his Reformed orthodox commitments and his American

---

57 Hodge, "Slavery," 302.

58 David Torbett, *Theology and Slavery: Charles Hodge and Horace Bushnell* (Macon, GA: Mercer University Press, 2006), 70–71,

59 Hodge, "Slavery," 278. See also David Neil Murchie, "Morality and Social Ethics in the Thought of Charles Hodge" (PhD diss., Drew University, 1980), 294–308.

60 Hodge, "Slavery," 293.

61 Charles Hodge, "General Assembly of 1845," *Biblical Repertory and Princeton Review* 17, no. 3 (July 1845): 444.

context. As a subsequent chapter will show, he also reshaped classic defenses of this practice.

Hodge spent roughly two-thirds of his customary annual *Repertory* article summarizing the proceedings of each year's General Assembly meeting by questioning the 1845 gathering's vote to invalidate Catholic baptism. Although he used the Bible to help make his case, he mainly relied on various historical precedents to argue against the Assembly's vote. Like many Protestants, Hodge believed that the Catholic Church was "corrupted and overlaid by false and soul-destroying abuses and errors," but he also held that it was still a body of believers that professed the essential elements of true Christianity as laid forth in the Bible.[62] This was a slight modification of standard Reformed orthodox approaches to the subject, which generally treated the Roman Catholic Church as a false church. In the end, Hodge had no doubt that while the Catholics may have perverted certain aspects of the practice of baptism, they still executed the sacrament with the clear "intention of complying with the command of Christ, and of doing what he requires to be done, by those who accept the covenant of grace."[63]

1.6 Sovereignty

While Hodge held dearly to the Westminster Confession's first chapter on the centrality of Scripture as a trustworthy guide for life, he was no less committed to the Westminster Confession's second chapter on the character and omnipotent sovereignty of God.[64] His commitment to God's sovereignty comes across in some of his earliest and most influential writings, many of which were born out of the factionalism over religious revivalism that came to define the Old and New Schools of Presbyterianism.[65] Like many other denominations, Presbyterians were confronted by the reality that thousands were converting to Christianity in the opening decades of the nineteenth century. How was one to explain such widespread revival? New School Presbyterians argued that humans played a key role in choosing salvation, while their Old School brethren held that human nature was so depraved that it was only through God's initiating salvific action that anyone could be drawn to faith in Christ.

---

62 Hodge, *Life of Charles Hodge*, 340.

63 Hodge, "General Assembly of 1845," 448.

64 *The Westminster Confession of Faith* (Lawrenceville, GA: The Presbyterian Orthodox Church, 2007), 1–12.

65 Key theological differences between the Old and New School are neatly encapsulated in Isaac Van Arsdale Brown, *A Historical Vindication of the Abrogation of the Plan of Union* (Philadelphia, PA: Wm. S. & Alfred Martien, 1855), 288–308.

New School Presbyterians found justification for their views in the teachings of the Yale Seminary professor Nathaniel Taylor. Positing a collection of theological positions that would later come to be commonly called the New Haven Theology, Taylor placed the responsibility for sin squarely on the shoulders of each individual. In so doing, Taylor positioned the ability to accept Christ as one's Lord and Savior as primarily an act of personal agency, not a result of an omnipotent God's predestined choice. [66] For Taylor and his followers, choosing salvation was mainly a matter of personal, not divine, agency.

For Hodge, and the other more traditional Calvinists who came to make up the Old School, the root issue came down to the traditional, sometimes ambiguous Augustinian doctrine of imputation. This doctrine held that the responsibility (and thus the punishment) for Adam's initial sin in Eden was *imputed* to all future generations of humanity. This traditional view of imputation held that Adam chose to sin in Eden and both he and his posterity were punishable for that choice. That first choice – the Original Sin – laid the responsibility for humanity's sinful nature at Adam's feet. Such a view of imputation was critically important because it undergirded the consequent belief that it was only in Jesus's – the new Adam – death on the cross to satisfy God's righteous justice that humanity's sin could be taken away. [67] Central to this belief in imputation was the fact that humanity could not choose to save itself. By their very nature, humans were too sinful to choose such a salvific path. Only Christ's intervention could bring humanity back into right relationship with its creator. Hodge subtly redefined imputation in terms of inherent corruption, moral inability, and liability to punishment, which a chapter below addresses. The main point here is that for Hodge and the Old School, the agency bound up in regeneration was not human; it was entirely divine.

Two important Protestant apologists of the era joined their voices to Taylor's as the controversy over imputation and its implications for various views of human nature began to grow. Moses Stuart, the highly respected Andover professor, and Albert Barnes, the immensely popular head pastor of the Philadelphia's large and affluent First Presbyterian Church, both wrote widely-read commentaries on the biblical Book of Romans. Stuart published the first edition of his *A Commentary on the Epistle to the Romans* in 1832 and Barnes followed it with his own *Notes on Romans* in 1834. Both volumes moved away from the traditional Calvinist view

66 For good treatments of the New Haven Theology and its influence in the early nineteenth century, see: Earl A. Pope, "The Rise of the New Haven Theology," *Journal of Presbyterian History* 44, no. 1 (1966) 24–44; and Earl A. Pope, "The Rise of the New Haven Theology II," *Journal of Presbyterian History* 44, no. 2 (1966): 106–121.

67 For a good overview of the issues at stake in the imputation controversy, see Charles Hodge, "Review of an Article in the June number of the *Christian Spectator*, entitled, 'Inquiries respecting the Doctrine of Imputation,'" *Biblical Repertory and Theological Review* 2, no. 3 (July 1830): 425–472.

that placed Original Sin as something only God's initiating action could overcome. Instead, Stuart and Barnes placed themselves in a line of thinking that Hodge and his fellow Princetonians considered heretical in the mode of the fourth-century schismatic Pelagius, who taught "that man was born without sin; and that he could be saved by his own exertions."[68] Such thinking ran directly counter to Turretin and his Augustinian and Calvinist-rooted thinking, making God far less central to the process of salvation.[69]

It was the imputation controversy and its practical application for such issues as revivalism that moved Hodge to write the first of what would become several New Testament commentaries. He decided to match Stuart and Barnes's writings with his own *A Commentary on the Epistle to the Romans* (1835). For all three men, the issue of imputation was most clearly articulated in the fifth book of Romans, and it was to this book that both Hodge and Stuart dedicated the greatest amount of exposition in their works.[70] One verse in the fifth book stood out as particularly important in the thinking of both sides:

> Wherefore, as by one man sin entered into the world, and death by sin;
> and so death passed upon all men, for that all have sinned (Rom. 5:12, KJV).

As in so many theological controversies, this one came down to a matter of emphasis. Hodge stressed the traditional Augustinian and Calvinist line of reasoning that used as its fulcrum the phrase "by one man," arguing that one man (Adam) stood as a fountainhead for the sin that so marked all of human existence after the expulsion from Eden. Stuart most clearly articulated an interpretation of this verse that weighted the last three words of the verse: "all have sinned." In so doing, Stuart stressed humanity's moral choices – not the choice of Adam – as the pivotal point of consideration. In Stuart's eyes, men had chosen sin, and they could just as easily choose salvation. Hodge never wavered from a much more traditional Reformed stance, namely that since the Fall, only the sovereign will of God could bring about salvation by changing human hearts. Humans could receive such salvation, but only as God enabled them to do so.

---

68 Archibald Alexander, "The Early History of Pelagianism," *Biblical Repertory and Theological Review* 2, no. 1 (January 1830): 89.

69 J. Mark Beach, "Francis Turretin's *Institutes of Elenctic Theology*," in *The Oxford Handbook of Reformed Theology*, eds. Michael Allen and Scott R. Swain (New York: Oxford University Press, 2020), 287. Francis Turretin, *Institutes of Elenctic Theology*, vol. 1 (Phillipsburg, NJ: P&R Publishing, 1992), 462–464; 629–636.

70 Mark A. Noll, "Charles Hodge," in *Reading Romans through the Centuries*, eds. Jeffrey P. Greenman and Timothy Larsen (Grand Rapids, MI: Brazos Press, 2005), 182.

The importance of God's sovereignty can be seen in other elements of Hodge's thinking as well. Particularly noticeable in this regard was Hodge's love of, and lifelong engagement with, matters of science. Since his earliest premedical days at Princeton College, Hodge had an unflagging interest in scientific developments. It was an interest that he carried to the end of his life, and becomes readily apparent in his final published book, a theological and scientific critique of Darwinism. By the 1870s, Hodge had become convinced that Darwin's thoughts on evolution posed the greatest single challenge to traditional Christian belief. So, in the winter of 1873 when the Princeton Club, a local association of Princeton's most prominent men, asked him to address the topic of Darwinism, Hodge eagerly took the chance to begin setting down his thoughts on the topic. His talk at the Princeton Club was so well received that Hodge moved away from feeling that he would write no more book-length works and composed his last extended treatise, his widely-read and hugely influential *What is Darwinism? (*1874).

Hodge used his *What is Darwinism?* to set down his final thoughts on the importance of seeking a crucial harmony between science and religion. He had long held that the fields of science and theology were absolutely complementary in nature, holding that "the Bible cannot contradict science, neither can science contradict the Bible."[71] Earlier, in his *Systematic Theology*, he had argued against Darwinism because he felt it "a mere hypothesis" hopelessly weakened by the reality that it could not take into account countless facts that opposed it.[72] Even worse, Darwin's theories could not be proved, an unforgivable sin in Hodge's mind when it came to scientific claims.[73] In the end, however, Hodge summarized his answer to the question found in his book's title by declaring that Darwinism was but atheism, and he based this view firmly on his bedrock conviction in the utter and total sovereignty of God.[74] Darwinism was atheism, not because it advocated a particular view of evolution or even that humans might be descended from apes (although he intensely disagreed with this point of view), but because "by far the most important and only distinctive element of his theory" was the idea that natural selection was "without design, being conducted by unintelligent physical causes." [75] Darwinism was atheism because it excluded any notion of an absolutely sovereign God who stood as the agent who had designed, created, and sustains the world.

---

71 Charles Hodge, "Scripture and Science," *New York Observer*, March 26, 1863, 98–99.

72 Charles Hodge, *Systematic Theology*, vol. 2 (New York: Charles Scribner's Sons, 1871), 12–24.

73 Charles Hodge, "The Testimony of Modern Science to the Unity of Mankind," *Biblical Repertory and Princeton Review* 31, no. 1 (January 1859): 107.

74 Charles Hodge, *What is Darwinism?* (New York: Scribner, Armstrong, & Co., 1874), 177.

75 Hodge, *What is Darwinism?*, 2.

1.7 Culmination

Hodge's desire to bring science and religion into harmony was but a piece of his thoroughly synthetic theological thinking. Hodge had always sought to put all elements in God's creation – both natural and revealed – into harmonious relationship. His quest for such harmony may well have found its initial inspiration during his trip to Europe when he was able to attend the lectures of the great naturalist, geographer, and explorer Alexander Von Humboldt at Berlin University. Humboldt's Berlin lectures on "Physical Geography" covered an extraordinary breadth of topics ranging from geology to global climate to botany to biology. Through it all, Humboldt sought organizing principles that brought together and stressed the connections between these varied phenomena. His connective thinking would reach its apex of expression in his titanic, multivolume *Cosmos* (1845–1858), in which he sought to set down grander general theories about how all nature was organized and interrelated. It was his attempt to bring order to the seeming chaos of natural phenomena.

Nearly twenty-five years after the appearance of *Cosmos's* first volume, Hodge attempted his own project on harmonizing every aspect of God's creation. In 1867 at the age of seventy, Hodge began writing his *Systematic Theology* (1871–1872). Refusing simply to cobble together earlier writings and lecture notes, Hodge composed his *Systematic* anew, wishing the multi-volume work to stand as a single organic whole. In the end, it would take Hodge five years to complete his three-volume *Systematic*. When it was finished, it stood as the longest published systematic theology ever to come from an American.

Integrative thinking is the hallmark of the systematic theology enterprise, and Hodge called such work "the brightest form of theology – as isolated truths assume a higher form when seen in their harmonious dependence."[76] He likened interlinked biblical truths to "the columns of a Grecian temple each symmetrical & beautiful" as they stand alone, but "something more & something higher, when seen as parts of a beautiful whole."[77] Hodge's masterwork stands apart for the way in which it not only sought to harmonize various biblical teachings with each other, but also sought to reveal the myriad linkages between God's revealed word and his creation. Consequently, no topic stood outside Hodge's consideration as he sought to reveal the Bible's relationship to such diverse fields as medicine, psychology, law, geology, astronomy, political science, and philosophy.

---

76 Charles Hodge, "The Study of Theology," (lecture, August 27, 1847), Charles Hodge Manuscript Collection, Princeton Theological Seminary, Library Special Collections, Speer Library, Box 11, Folder 5, 18.

77 Hodge, "The Study of Theology."

At its core, Hodge's *Systematic Theology* was a grand apologia for the omnipotence and benevolence of a merciful God. His emphasis on God's omnipotence comes across in his continued commitment to traditional Reformed views on imputation. His stance on imputation that he had advocated so strongly in his thirties, he now revisited in his seventies. The importance he put on the topic and his views of the doctrine itself remained unchanged throughout his life. Hodge dedicated almost 150 pages of his *Systematic's* second volume to a discussion of imputation and sin, while his *Systematic's* largest single chapter, "The Means of Grace," is a nearly 250-page discussion of God as sole arbiter in matters of salvation.[78]

Hodge's stress on God's benevolence comes across in the indomitable optimism that pervades his *Systematic.* He firmly believed in the goodness of his God and the wondrous nature of His creation. In one of his last talks given to his students, he showed the optimism that so marked his *Systematic* when he stated that he believed "that the vast majority of the human race were to share the beatitudes and glories of his Lord's redemption."[79] Perhaps one of Hodge's greatest contributions to American Reformed Theology was this optimistic outlook, tempering the dour contours of early American Puritan variations of Calvinism that had in some cases held such a high view of God that people were encouraged toward a willingness to be damned for His greater glory.[80]

Hodge was not only optimistic about God's pervasive mercy and global plans of salvation, but he was also optimistic about humanity's ability to understand the divine. Thoroughly committed to the Common Sense Enlightenment ideal that believed the human mind could approach an accurate understanding of God as revealed in the Scriptures and in nature, Hodge stood against a rising tendency found in post-Civil War theologies influenced by German Romanticism that held the mind could have no hope of fully understanding God. Such a Romantic understanding of the divine, as the famous Brooklyn preacher Henry Ward Beecher was fond of stating, came not from the cold calculation of biblical passages and doctrine, but through a "heart that breathes kindness and love."[81] German Romantics and those they influenced argued that God could only be truly understood by turning from the head to the heart.[82]

---

78 Charles Hodge, *Systematic Theology*, vol. 2 (New York: Charles Scribner's Sons, 1871), 130–276; Charles Hodge, *Systematic Theology*, vol. 3 (New York: Charles Scribner's Sons, 1872), 466–709.

79 Hodge, *Life of Charles Hodge*, 532.

80 Williston Walker, *Ten New England Leaders* (New York: Silver, Burdett, 1901), 346. Samuel Hopkins, *Works of Samuel Hopkins, D.D.*, vol. 2 (Boston, Mass.: Doctrinal Tract and Book Society, 1854), 756.

81 Henry Ward Beecher, "The True Religion," in *Sermons, Preached in Plymouth Church, Brooklyn, New York* (London: Richard D. Dickinson, 1871), 207.

82 James Turner, *Without God, Without Creed: The Origins of Unbelief in America* (Baltimore, MD: The Johns Hopkins University Press, 1985), 196–197.

Hodge's *Systematic* was a forceful rebuttal to such thinking. Holding fast to his Scottish Common Sense philosophical roots, Hodge trumpeted the intellectual nature of theological study by arguing that theology was, in fact, a science. In his aptly named first chapter, "Theology as a Science," he carefully and relentlessly made the case for the rational nature of theological study, a type of study that was the most fruitful when it was marked by the same rigorous methods of investigation, factual collation, and postulate formulation found in the best science of his day.[83] This stood in partial contrast to earlier Reformed models, which understood theology as spiritual wisdom rather than science. Hodge took emerging views of scientific method, importing them into his definition and approach to theology as a whole. At the same time, Hodge never strayed from God's sovereign action even in the act of biblical interpretation. Ultimately, it was God who revealed all truth through the Holy Spirit.[84]

When Hodge passed away at the age of 81 in 1878, he died having never wavered in his firm commitment to the Westminster Confession and its high view of Scripture and the Sovereignty of God. Upon his death, one eulogist wrote that "no Protestant divine in our day has done more than he in the elucidation and defence of the doctrines set forth in our Confession and Catechism."[85] For Hodge, God's word was an utterly reliable documentation of His action in the world, and understanding the self-evident truths of that documentation was available to everyone who pursued such understanding by making "use of ordinary means" of thinking.[86] In Hodge's mind, God had revealed Himself most fully in the words of Scripture, and those words were not far off, but available to everyone who took the time to carefully and prayerfully study them.

Works Cited

Alexander, Archibald. "The Early History of Pelagianism." *Biblical Repertory and Theological Review* 2, no. 1 (January 1830): 77:113.

Applegate, Debby. *The Most Famous Man in America: The Biography of Henry Ward Beecher*. New York: Doubleday, 2006.

Beach, J. Mark. "Francis Turretin's *Institutes of Elenctic Theology*." In *The Oxford Handbook of Reformed Theology*, edited by Michael Allen and Scott R. Swain, 280–294. New York: Oxford University Press, 2020.

83 Charles Hodge, *Systematic Theology*, vol. 1 (New York: Charles Scribner's Sons, 1872), 1.

84 Charles Hodge Charles Hodge, "The Study of Theology," (lecture, August 27, 1847), Charles Hodge Manuscript Collection, Princeton Theological Seminary, Library Special Collections, Speer Library, Box 11, Folder 5, 5.

85 "The Late Dr. Hodge," *New York Observer and Chronicle*, July 4, 1878, 211.

86 Charles Hodge, *Systematic Theology*, vol. 1 (New York: Charles Scribner's Sons, 1872), 152.

Beecher, Henry Ward. "The True Religion." In *Sermons, Preached in Plymouth Church, Brooklyn, New York,* 205–235. London: Richard D. Dickinson, 1871.

Bozeman, Theodore Dwight. *Protestants in an Age of Science: The Baconian Ideal and Antebellum Religious Thought.* Chapel Hill, NC: University of North Carolina Press, 1977.

Brown, Candy Gunther. *The Word in the World: Evangelical Writing, Publishing, and Reading in America, 1789–1880.* Chapel Hill, NC: University of North Carolina Press, 2004.

Brown, Isaac Van Arsdale. *A Historical Vindication of the Abrogation of the Plan of Union.* Philadelphia: Wm. S. & Alfred Martien, 1855.

Brown, Jerry Wayne. *The Rise of Biblical Criticism in America, 1800–1870.* Middletown, CT: Wesleyan University Press, 1969.

Brown, Robert E. "The Bible in the Seventeenth Century." In *The Oxford Handbook of the Bible in America,* edited by Paul C. Gutjahr, 79–95. New York: Oxford University Press, 2017.

Brumberg, Joan. *Mission for Life: The Judson Family and American Evangelical Culture.* New York: New York University Press, 1984.

Calhoun, David. "Last Command: Princeton Theological Seminary and Missions (1812–1862)." PhD dissertation, Princeton Theological Seminary, 1983.

Conser, Walter, H., Jr. *God and the Natural World: Religion and Science in Antebellum America.* Columbia, SC: University of South Carolina Press, 1993.

Cremin, Lawrence A. *American Education: The National Experience, 1783–1876.* New York: Harper & Row, 1980.

Cross, Barbara M. *Horace Bushnell: Minister to a Changing America.*

Chicago: University of Chicago Press, 1958.

Davis, Derek H. *Religion and the Continental Congress, 1774–1789: Contributions to Original Intent.* New York: Oxford University Press, 2000.

Gardiner, Richard. "Princeton and Paris: An Early Nineteenth Century Bond of Mission. Senior thesis, Princeton Theological Seminary, 1994.

Gilmore, William J. *Reading Becomes a Necessity of Life: Material and Cultural Life in New England, 1780–1835.* Knoxville, TN: University of Tennessee Press, 1989.

Darrel Guder. "History of Belles Lettres at Princeton," Ph.D. diss., University of Hamburg, 1964.

Gura, Philip. *American Transcendentalism: A History.* New York: Hill & Wang, 2007.

Gutjahr, Paul C. *An American Bible: A History of the Good Book in the United States, 1777 1880.* Stanford, CA: Stanford University Press, 1999.

Herbst, Jurgen. *The German Historical School in American Scholarship.* Ithaca, NY: Cornell University Press, 1965.

Hodge, A. A. *Life of Charles Hodge.* New York: Charles Scribner's Sons, 1880.

Hodge, Archibald Alexander and Benjamin B. Warfield. "Inspiration." *Presbyterian Review* 2 (April 1881): 225–260.

Hodge, Charles. "General Assembly of 1845." *Biblical Repertory and Princeton Review* 17, no. 3 (July 1845): 428–471.

———. "General Assembly, 1846." *Biblical Repertory and Princeton Review* 18, no. 3 (July 1846): 418–456.

———. "The Inspiration of Holy Scripture." *Biblical Repertory and Princeton Review* 29, no. 4 (October 1857): 660–698.

———. "Lecture Addressed to the Students of the Theological Seminary." *Biblical Repertory A Journal of Biblical Literature and Theological Review* 1, no. 1 (January 1829): 75–98.

———. "Review of an Article in the June number of the *Christian Spectator,* entitled, 'Inquiries respecting the Doctrine of Imputation.'" *Biblical Repertory and Theological Review* 2, no. 3 (July 1830): 425–472.

———. "Scripture and Science." *New York Observer,* March 26, 1863.

———. "Slavery." *Biblical Repertory and Theological Review* 8, no. 2 (April 1836): 268–305.

———. *Systemic Theology.* Three volumes. New York: Charles Scribner's Sons, 1871–2.

———. "The Testimony of Modern Science to the Unity of Mankind." *Biblical Repertory and Princeton Review* 31, no. 1 (January 1859): 103–149.

———. "The Theology of the Intellect and That of the Feelings." *Biblical Repertory and Princeton Review* 22, no. 4 (October 1850): 642–674.

———. *What is Darwinism?* New York: Scribner, Armstrong, & Co., 1874.

Hodge, Hugh L. *Memoranda of Family History Dictated by Hugh L. Hodge.* N. p.: n. p., 1903.

Holifield, E. Brooks. *Theology in America: Christian Thought from the Age of the Puritans to the Civil War.* New Haven, CT: Yale University Press, 2003.

Hopkins, Samuel. *Works of Samuel Hopkins, D. D.* Volume two. Boston: Doctrinal Tract and Book Society, 1854.

"The Late Dr. Hodge." *New York Observer and Chronicle,* July 4, 1878.

Leach, Frank Willing. "The Philadelphia of Our Ancestors." *North American,* June 14, 1908.

Lefferts A. Loetscher. *Facing the Enlightenment and Pietism: Archibal Alexander and the Founding of Princeton Theological Seminary.* Westport, CT: Greenwood Press, 1983.

Murchie, David Neil. "Morality and Social Ethics in the Thought of Charles Hodge." PhD dissertation, Drew University, 1980.

Noll, Mark A. *America's God: From Jonathan Edwards to Abraham Lincoln.* New York: Oxford University Press, 2005.

———. "Charles Hodge." In *Reading Romans Through the Centuries,* edited by Jeffrey P. Greenman and Timothy Larsen, 169–186. Grand Rapids, MI: Brazos Press, 2005.

———. "Common Sense Traditions and American Evangelical Thought." *American Quarterly* 37, no. 2 (1985): 216–238.

______. *Princeton and the Republic, 1768–1822.* Princeton, NJ: Princeton University Press, 1989.

———, ed. *The Princeton Theology, 1812–1921.* Grand Rapids, MI: Baker Book House, 1983.

Nord, David Paul. *Faith in Reading: Religious Publishing and the Birth of Mass Media in America, 1790–1860.* New York: Oxford University Press, 2004.

Park, Edwards Amasa. *The Theology of Intellect and of the Feelings.* Andover, MA: Warren F. Draper, 1850.

Pope, Earl A. "The Rise of New Haven Theology." *Journal of Presbyterian History* 44, no. 1 (1966): 24–44.

———. "The Rise of New Haven Theology II." *Journal of Presbyterian History* 44, no. 2 (1966): 106–121.

Wilson Smith, "William Paley's Theological Utilitarianism in America," *William and Mary Quarterly* 11:2 (Apr. 1954): 402–424.

Soltow, Lee and Edward Stevens. *The Rise of Literacy and the Common School in the United States: A Socioeconomic Analysis to 1870.* Chicago, IL: University of Chicago Press, 1981.

Stewart, John W. and James H. Moorhead, eds. *Charles Hodge Revisited: A Critical Appraisal of His Life and Works.* Grand Rapids, MI: William B. Eerdmans Publishing Co., 2002. See esp. "Charles Hodge and the Beauties and Deformities of Science" and "Charles Hodge as Interpreter of Scripture."

Torbett, David. *Theology and Slavery: Charles Hodge and Horace Bushnell.* Macon, GA: Mercer University Press, 2006.

Turner, James. *Without God, Without Creed: The Origins of Unbelief in America.* Baltimore: The Johns Hopkins University Press, 1985.

Turretin, Francis. *Institutes of Elenctic Theology.* Volume 1. Phillipsburg, NJ: P & R Publishing, 1992.

Walker, Williston. *Ten New England Leaders.* New York: Silver, Burdett, 1901.

Wells, David F., ed. *The Princeton Theology.* Grand Rapids, MI: Baker Book House, 1989. *The Westminster Confession of Faith.* Lawrenceville, GA: The Presbyterian Orthodox Church, 2007.

Zboray, Ronald J. *A Fictive People: Antebellum Economic Development and the American*

Aza Goudriaan

2. Modern Philosophers in the *Systematic Theology* of Charles Hodge

For Charles Hodge philosophy was very important. This was a conviction he shared with many representatives of the Reformed tradition before him. Philosophy has a certain "common ground" with theology; it pursues reliable and relevant knowledge, but it must yield to the authority of the Bible.[1] In this essay, Hodge's relation to modern philosophy is considered from the angle of how he interacted, in his *Systematic Theology*, with a number of philosophers. Being selective by necessity, we start in the early modern period with René Descartes (1596–1650), who has often been considered the "father of modern philosophy," and then focus on his use of Spinoza (1632–1677) and Leibniz (1646–1716). Taking an early starting point allows for continuities to emerge between Hodge and the Reformed orthodox of the early modern era, who responded in their own ways the philosophers of their day, and a continuity between early modern philosophy and the modern thinking with which Hodge interacted. Spinoza, for example, figured prominently in nineteenth-century German philosophy and theology, with factored heavily

1 Charles Hodge, *Systematic Theology* [henceforth *ST*], 3 vols. (n.p.: Hendrickson, 1999), 1: 55–58. For this essay, I have also used the searchable text that is available at https://www.ccel.org/ccel/hodge. For a bibliography of Hodge, see e.g. John W. Stewart, "Bibliography of the Works by and about Charles Hodge," in *Charles Hodge Revisited. A Critical Appraisal of His Life and Works*, ed. John W. Stewart and James H. Moorhead (Grand Rapids: Eerdmans, 2002), 335–375. On Hodge and philosophy, see Peter Hicks, *The Philosophy of Charles Hodge. A 19th Century Evangelical Approach to Reason, Knowledge and Truth* (Lewiston: Edwin Mellen, 1997); Owen Anderson, *Reason and Faith in the Theology of Charles Hodge. American Common Sense Realism* (New York: Pelgrave Macmillan, 2014); Bruce Kuklick, "The Place of Charles Hodge in the History of Ideas in America," in *Charles Hodge Revisited. A Critical Appraisal of His Life and Work*, ed. John W. Stewart and James H. Moorhead (Grand Rapids: Eerdmans, 2002), 63–76; Paul C. Gutjahr, *Charles Hodge. Guardian of American Orthodoxy* (Oxford: Oxford University Press 2012); Charles D. Cashdollar, *The Transformation of Theology, 1830–1890. Positivism and Protestant Thought in in Britain and America* (Princeton: Princeton University Press, 1989), index s.v. Hodge; John C. Vander Stelt, *Philosophy and Scripture. A Study in Old Princeton and Westminster Theology* (PhD dissertation, VU Amsterdam) (Marlton NJ: Mack Publishing, 1978), 120–147. On Reformed orthodoxy and early modern philosophy, see e. g. David Sytsma, *Richard Baxter and the Mechanical Philosophers* (New York: Oxford University Press, 2017); Aza Goudriaan, *Reformed Orthodoxy and Philosophy, 1625–1750: Gisbertus Voetius, Petrus van Mastricht, and Anthonius Driessen* (Leiden 2006); Richard A. Muller, *Post-Reformation Reformed Dogmatics. The Rise and Development of Reformed Orthodoxy, ca. 1520 to ca. 1725*, vol. 1 (Grand Rapids: Baker Academic, 2003), chapter 8.

into Hodge's thinking.[2] Next, we will consider a number of modern philosophers: Immanuel Kant (1724–1804), the founder of critical philosophy, Georg Wilhelm Friedrich Hegel (1770–1831), whom Hodge considered a major representative of modern philosophical pantheism, and William Hamilton (1788–1856), who combined elements of modern German philosophy with the tradition of Scottish Common Sense philosophy.

As noted above, this essay will focus primarily on the three volumes of Hodge's *Systematic Theology.* Representing his mature thought and covering the broad field of Christian doctrine, studying the *Systematic Theology* provides clear insight into how philosophers played a role in Hodge's explanation of the Christian faith. The investigation will reveal the theological topics where conversations with philosophers took place, which may provide some indication of how substantial may have been the contribution of any given philosopher to the shape of Hodge's theology. As such, Hodge's sustained attention to the intersection between theology and philosophy marks continuity with earlier Reformed thought, while his nineteenth-century American context necessarily brought discontinuity as Hodge interacted with new ideas.

2.1 René Descartes

René Descartes has often been considered the "father of modern philosophy."[3] When tracing Hodge's interaction with modern philosophers a consideration of Descartes is not out of scope, and Descartes also serves a bridge between philosophical shifts under Reformed orthodoxy and the modern context in which Hodge lived and wrote. Descartes was not very important for Hodge on the whole, but he nonetheless quoted him from a seventeenth-century Latin edition of the *Meditations* and Descartes's *Responsiones* to the objections against the *Meditations* (Amsterdam 1685).[4] Hodge mentioned Descartes a few times in passing, and several times he discussed a theoretical viewpoint that Descartes had defended. He noted that Descartes "was a sincere Catholic, and died in communion with the Church" and

---

2 On Hodge's studies in Germany and their impact, see e. g. Andrew W. Hoffecker, *Charles Hodge: The Pride of Princeton* (Phillipsburg: P&R, 2011), part 2; cf. Gutjahr, *Charles Hodge*, chapters 17–19, and B.A. Gerrish, "Charles Hodge and the Europeans," in *Charles Hodge Revisited. A Critical Appraisal of His Life and Works*, ed. John W. Stewart and James H. Moorhead (Grand Rapids: Eerdmans, 2002), 129–158.

3 Cf. Hans Peter Schütt, *Die Adoption des "Vaters der modernen Philosophie." Studien zu einem Gemeinplatz der Ideengeschichte* (Frankfurt/Main: Vittorio Klostermann, 1998).

4 *ST* 1: 205, 377, 409.

he appreciated Descartes's view that God and matter are "substances distinct from our minds"—not one single substance, as Spinoza thought.[5]

Hodge does not seem to have had a first-hand acquaintance with the seventeenth-century Reformed discussions about Descartes. In the Dutch theological landscape of the seventeenth century, for example, Cartesianism was integrated in theology by such divines as Abraham Heidanus, Frans Burman, and Christoph Wittich, whereas others, such as Gisbertus Voetius, Jacobus Revius, Petrus van Mastricht, and Melchior Leydekker, opposed the new philosophy on various accounts. The critics covered a wide field that included objections against Cartesian doubt, the denial of substantial forms, various aspects of the Cartesian body-soul distinction, the notion of an "idea of God" in the human mind that served as a starting point for proving God's existence (as opposed to arguing from creation), and so on.[6] Even without having studied the seventeenth-century debates, however, Hodge seems to have sided with basic convictions of the earlier anti-Cartesians.

One of the Cartesian views that Hodge discussed was the ontological argument for God's existence. He did not differentiate, however, between the argument from the third meditation (the argument from causes) and that of the fifth meditation (the so-called ontological argument), but he considered both arguments to be essentially one argument.[7] Hodge here seems to gloss over the minutiae of the Cartesian argument. It is very clear, however, that he was not convinced by the Cartesian argument, but rather accepted the Kantian criticism of the ontological argument according to which "if the predicate be removed, the subject is removed" and real existence is something not included in the idea of any subject.[8] Generally, Hodge preferred *a posteriori* arguments for God's existence to the kind of *a priori* method involved in various forms of the ontological argument.[9] In this respect, his thinking was in line with earlier anti-Cartesians.

Hodge also quoted Descartes on the issue of the limitations of human knowledge of God. Here he cited a passage from a letter, probably written to Marin Mersenne in 1630, in which the philosopher emphasized that God, being infinite and omnipotent, must remain incomprehensible to a finite intellect, but can only be touched (or

---

5 *ST* 1: 331.

6 *Cf.* Aza Goudriaan, "Descartes, Cartesianism, and Early Modern Theology," in *The Oxford Handbook of Early Modern Theology, 1600–1800*, ed. Ulrich L. Lehner, Richard A. Muller, A.G. Roeber (New York: OUP, 2016), 533–549, and references.

7 *ST* 1: 205. Hodge verbally quoted Descartes, *Secundae responsiones*, prop. 2 (AT 7: 167,17–22), which is essentially the argument of the third meditation, and he juxtaposes this with the argument involving the three angles of a triangle equaling two right angles, which is a feature of the "ontological" argument of the fifth meditation (cf. AT 7: 64, 66–69).

8 *ST* 1: 205–6.

9 Chapter 4 of this present volume explores this theme in more detail.

apprehended) by human thinking, thus taking up an ancient Augustinian distinction between 'comprehending' and 'touching something with our thinking.'[10] By taking this emphasis on God's incomprehensibility as characteristic of Descartes's thinking, Hodge left unmentioned other elements of Cartesian philosophy that some seventeenth-century representatives of Reformed orthodoxy had considered too audacious pretentions of knowing God. Descartes, after all, was only able to escape from universal doubt thanks to the *cogito ergo sum* and, crucially, an 'idea of God' that he found in his thinking mind, a mental image of God that he considered exceedingly 'clear and distinct' and that therefore could serve to prove the existence of God, its only possible Cause. Critics saw various problems here, including some overreach in the claimed quality of the natural knowledge of God.[11]

Hodge also cited Descartes as the author who defended a notion of absolute power in the sense that three angles of a triangle are equal to two right angles only because God willed this to be so, not because this could not be otherwise.[12] Hodge then seemed to distance himself from Descartes's radical view—as seventeenth-century theologians usually did before him[13]—by stating that God's "will is limited by his nature" and that He cannot do what is impossible. At this point, however, Hodge did not cite the traditional view that impossibility is that which involves inherent contradiction.[14] However, he retained here the common Christian idea that while no divine truth is contrary to reason, some divine truths were above reason, requiring divine revelation.

Hodge mentioned Descartes's *cogito* explicitly in his *Systematic Theology*. Adapting the idea to an extent, Hodge was convinced that human consciousness involved the awareness of individual existence, as being distinct from what is not myself. Here Descartes's "I think, therefore I am" served as an apt illustration of what he meant by self-consciousness, since Descartes, as Hodge quoted him, had also stated that *cogito ergo sum* did not involve a syllogism.[15] Here Hodge agreed with Henry Longeville Mansel, whose interpretation of the *cogito* he had also cited before.[16]

---

10 *ST* 1: 338, quoting Descartes from a 1682 edition of the correspondence. Descartes to [Mersenne], [27 May 1630], AT 1: 152,10–19 (French text; Hodge quoted the passage in Latin). On the distinction between *comprehendere* and *attingere cogitatione*, cf. Aza Goudriaan, *Philosophische Gotteserkenntnis bei Suárez und Descartes, im Zusammenhang mit der niederländischen Theologie und Philosophie des 17. Jahrhunderts* (Leiden: Brill, 1999), 216–217.

11 Cf. Goudriaan, *Philosophische Gotteserkenntnis*, 212–213.

12 *ST* 1: 409, with reference to Descartes, *Responsiones sextae*, § 6; AT 7: 432.

13 *Cf.* Goudriaan, "Descartes, Cartesianism, and Early Modern Theology," 541–542.

14 *ST* 1: 409. Still, Hodge agreed with the traditional definition, see 1: 51: "That is impossible which involves a contradiction…" He attacked the Scottish philosopher William Hamilton for asserting that faith may need to believe what the mind understands to be impossible (see below).

15 *ST* 1: 377–378, there 377 a reference to Descartes, *Secundae responsiones*, AT 7: 140,18–23.

16 *ST* 1: 361. On Mansel, see below.

Thus, Hodge's cautious evaluation of Descartes illustrates both elements of continuity and discontinuity with earlier Reformed though. Continuity in the sense that Hodge used Descartes against monism, had reservations about Descartes's ontological argument, emphasized the limitations of the natural knowledge of God, and rejected the notion of a radical divine arbitrariness. A basic discontinuity appears in the fact that Hodge seems to have developed his assessment independently from the seventeenth-century Reformed debates, probably based on his appropriation of Scottish Common Sense Realism.[17]

2.2 Baruch Spinoza

In Hodge's *Systematic Theology*, Spinoza is mentioned repeatedly, as is Spinozism – "Cartesianism run wild," as Hodge liked to cite Leibniz as saying.[18] The more substantial references are concerned with pantheism, sin or evil, the knowledge of God, and miracles.[19] Hodge considered Spinoza's philosophy the main cause for "[t]he revival of Pantheism since the Reformation."[20] In fact, Spinoza's legacy at this point had been debated intensively in eighteenth- and early nineteenth- century philosophy and theology. The *Pantheismusstreit* between Jacobi and Mendelssohn is a major example of the continuing presence of Spinoza and pantheism as topics of debate in German intellectual life. In his discussion of pantheism Hodge devoted a section to Spinoza.[21] Spinoza admitted just one substance. What really exists is the Infinite, of which "nothing can be affirmed," since every determination is a negation (*omnis determinatio est negatio*).[22] Thus "god" was not merely in everything, but he was everything. Hodge's concern with Spinoza fit into his broader obsession with various forms of nineteenth-century pantheism, which also appeared alongside of his persistent criticisms of nineteenth-century German theology. Thus, the ideas of

---

17 Chapter 4 below explores Common Sense Realism more overtly. More or less, Hodge used this philosophical method to argue that God implanted certain self-evident truths in human consciousness, securing the universal consent of mankind. This meant that the "testimony of consciousness" served for him as a source of evidence, providing building blocks for theological truths by providing their basic premises.

18 *ST* 1: 331, 593 (here specifically connected with pantheism: "the pantheism of Spinoza, which Leibnitz calls Cartesianism *en outre*".

19 Hodge also quoted Spinoza's rejection of final causality (*ST* 1: 227, cf. *Ethica* 1, appendix), a point on which Spinoza followed Descartes. In an argument against equating necessity with certainty, Hodge pointed at the unacceptable consequences, one of which was that it would place "Luther into the category with Spinoza; all Augustinians into the same class with the French materialists" (*ST* 2: 285).

20 *ST* 1: 330.

21 *ST* 1: 330–332.

22 *ST* 1: 331, cf. 382.

a seventeenth century philosopher spilled over and blended into Hodge's nineteenth century concerns with the effects of these ideas on American theology.

Hodge repeatedly cited the Latin text of Spinoza based on the edition of Spinoza's *oeuvre* by theologian Heinrich Eberhard Gottlob Paulus.[23] On Spinoza's pantheism, Hodge also cited the *Essay on Pantheism* that the Church of England divine John Hunt published in 1866.[24] As an illustration of the pantheists' claim that the Absolute has no intellect or will, Hodge quoted Spinoza's *Ethics* 5.40, where Spinoza wrote that "all minds together constitute the eternal and infinite intellect of God."[25] Moreover, according to Spinoza, "the human mind is a part of the infinite intellect of God," and as a "determined mode of thinking" it is not free. The human mind itself has "no absolute faculty of understanding, desiring, loving, etc."[26] As Hunt had summarized, Spinoza acknowledged in God a "free necessity," but denied freedom to humans.[27] Hodge quoted Spinoza directly on the topic of freedom and necessity. Liberty, as Spinoza defined it, admitted no external determination, but existed merely "by the necessity of its nature."[28] In a letter to Hendrik Oldenburg, Spinoza wrote that God was not subjected to Fate but "all things follow with inevitable necessity from the nature of God."[29] This necessity, and the identity of God and nature implied the impossibility of miracles, as explained in the *Tractatus theologico-politicus* (1670). Hodge quoted Spinoza extensively on this point, showing the denial of miracles as a consequence of pantheism.[30] In Hodge's mind, the pantheistic denial of miracles via Spinoza was eerily similar to ways in which modern German and American theologians conceived of the relationship between God and the world.[31] While

---

23 Paulus's edition, volume 1 (1802) is quoted in *ST* 1: 338, 412; volume 2 (1803) in *ST* 1: 301n., 303n, 305n; 335n, 394n; 2:133n. Heinrich Eberhard Gottlob Paulus (ed.), *Benedicti de Spinoza opera quae supersunt omnia*, 2 vols. (Jena: Bibliopolus academicus, 1802–1803). On Paulus (1761–1851), see Friedrich Wilhelm Graf, "Paulus, Heinrich Eberhard Gottlob," *RGG*, fourth ed., 8 vols. (Tübingen: Mohr Siebeck, 1998–2005), 6: 1065–1066.

24 London: Longmans et al., 1866, cited in *ST* 1: 303–306. On Hunt, see Philipp Schaff and Samuel Macauley Jackson (eds.), *Encyclopedia of Living Divines and Christian Workers of All Denominations* (New York: Funk and Wagnalls, 1887), 106.

25 *ST* 1: 301, quoting Spinoza, *Ethica*, 5.14, schol.

26 *ST* 1: 303, quoting Spinoza, *Ethica*, 2.11, coroll., and 2.48, demonstratio and scholium. In a section discussing how pantheism "Precludes the possibility of Knowledge in God" (393), Hodge gave a somewhat puzzling quotation from the scholium of *Ethica* 1.17, where Spinoza stated that the divine intellect is totally different from that of humans (394).

27 *ST* 1: 303, citing John Hunt, *An Essay on Pantheism*, 231.

28 *ST* 1: 412, quoting *Ethica* 1, definitio 7.

29 *ST* 1: 412, citing Epistola 23 = 75.

30 *ST* 1: 626–627, quoting *Tractatus theologico-politicus*, chapters 3 and 6.

31 James Turner, "Charles Hodge in the Intellectual Weather of the Nineteenth Century," in *Charles Hodge Revisited. A Critical Appraisal of His Life and Works*, ed. John W. Stewart and James H. Moorhead (Grand Rapids: Eerdmans, 2002), 41–61, there 56–57.

sharing a common opponent with Reformed orthodoxy,[32] he pulled the discussion into modern concerns.

As far as the human body was concerned, Hodge concluded that from Spinoza's idea that the body is a mode of God's being or extension, it followed that the body had its "divine rights as well as the soul" and should follow its pursuits and inclinations.[33] Blurring the distinction between the Creator and his creatures also eroded moral standards that Hodge wanted to uphold.

Hodge also mentioned Spinoza as a pantheist in the context of a discussion of Friedrich Schleiermacher's Christology. Here the reference was entirely indirect, that is, based on an analysis of Ferdinand Christian Baur. Baur had argued, in his work on the Trinity and the atonement, that Schleiermacher's view on the relation between God and the world was essentially Spinozist. Baur agreed with David Friedrich Strauss, who had asserted that Schleiermacher's *Glaubenslehre* was essentially Spinozist, and that in Schleiermacher the distinction between God and world was not stronger than Spinoza's differentiation between the aspects of nature (*natura naturans, natura naturata*).[34] Hodge used Baur and Strauss in support of the claim that Schleiermacher was influenced by Spinozan pantheism, which again highlighted the fresh philosophical and religious challenges that Hodge faced in his own context.

When discussing a number of "anti-Christian" theories of sin, Hodge quoted Spinoza as a representative of the second such theory, which declares sin to be "a mere Limitation of Being."[35] Hodge cited specifically *Ethics* 4.20, where Spinoza wrote that as things seek what is useful to them, namely their self-preservation, they are more virtuous. The equivalence of power and virtue specifically led to the consideration, wrote Hodge, that "the want of virtue, or evil, is weakness, or limitation of being."[36] This was a position that Hodge found also in Hegelian theologian Ferdinand Christian Baur, the eclectic philosopher Victor Cousin, and writer Thomas Carlyle.[37] Moreover, on this topic he quoted Hegel as saying that

---

32 See, for example, Bernhardinus de Moor, *Commentarius perpetuus in Johannis Marckii Compendium theologiae christianae didactico-elencticum*, vol. 2 (Leiden: Johannes Hasebroek, 1763), 460–464.

33 *ST* 1: 308.

34 *ST* 3: 444–445; citing, there 444, Ferdinand Christian Baur, *Die Lehre von der Dreieinigkeit und Menschwerdung Gottes in ihrer geschichtlichen Entwicklung*, vol. 3, Die neueste Geschichte des Dogma, von der Reformation bis in die neueste Zeit (Tübingen: Osiander, 1843), 842 and 850. Hodge (445n2) mentions in addition that, according to Baur (*Lehre von der Dreieinigkeit*, 858–859), Eduard Zeller, too, had argued that Schleiermacher's concept of God was essentially Spinozistic.

35 *ST* 2: 133; cf. 1: 305.

36 *ST* 2: 133; 1: 305. The logic of this notion, Hodge wrote, led to the conclusion that "there is no such thing as moral obligation; no such thing as right or wrong" (306).

37 *ST* 2: 133–134.

"The manifestation of the nothingness of the finite as power, is justice"[38]—which, to Hodge, was a philosophical phrasing of the view that "Might is Right."[39] The connection between evil and finite being was linked with the issue of pantheism: if humans are a mode or part of God, a redefinition of evil as 'limited being' instead of moral sin is not surprising. Hence, the issues of evil and pantheism being related, Hodge mentioned also in his discussion of pantheism Spinoza's statement, in *Ethics* 4.20, on the correlation between being, power, and goodness.[40] In older Reformed thinking, stretching back to authors like Augustine and Boethius, sin had no independent ontological existence. Sin was a privation, a lack of moral perfection that should have existed in persons that were otherwise created good. If Hodge wanted to uphold this classical position, he had to oppose the definition of sin in terms of limited being, for that view turned sin into an ontological category and denied the goodness of created beings that are, by definition, finite.

Spinoza is also cited twice on the subject of the knowability of God. Hodge mentioned him, together with Hegel, Schelling, and Cousin for holding the view that God can be known as well as any other being. Hodge cited *Ethica* 2.46 where Spinoza claimed an "adequate and perfect" knowledge of God.[41] This line of thinking may be one reason why Hodge categorized the philosophy of Spinoza as "mysticism," which in his definition meant either the notion of an "identity of God and the soul, or the immediate intuition of the infinite."[42] On the other hand, however, Hodge quoted a passage from a letter in which "even Spinoza" admitted that he did "not know God entirely" but "some of His attributes, but not all, nor for the most part."[43] Hodge may have quoted the latter passage as a text in which Spinoza expressed, *malgré lui*, the truth that God is known only imperfectly. In any case, Hodge shared his opposition against Spinoza's claim of having an "adequate" knowledge of God

---

38 *ST* 1: 417. Hodge, who provided no reference, may have read the sentence, in this form, in Karl Hase, *Lehrbuch der evangelischen Dogmatik*, 2nd ed. (Leipzig: Breitkopf & Härtel, 1838), 163 note R (with reference to "Hegel, Ph.d.Rel. Bd. II, S. 47"): "Die Manifestation der Nichtigkeit des Endlichen als Macht ist die Gerechtigkeit: darin wird den endlichen Dingen ihr Recht angethan." This sentence seems an abbreviated version of what Hegel wrote: "Die Manifestation der Nichtigkeit, Idealität dieses Endlichen, daß das Seyn nicht wahrhafte Selbständigkeit ist, diese Manifestation als Macht ist die *Gerechtigkeit*: darin wird den endlichen Dingen ihr Recht angethan"; *Georg Wilhelm Friedrich Hegel's Vorlesungen über die Philosophie der Religion, nebst einer Schrift über die Beweise vom Daseyn Gottes*, ed. Philipp Marheineke [*Georg Wilhelm Friedrich Hegel's Werke*, vol. 12] (2nd ed., Berlin: Duncker & Humblot, 1840), 56. On Hodge's direct use of this edition of Hegel's works, see below.

39 *ST* 1: 417.

40 The section on pantheism: *ST* 1: 299–334, there 305.

41 *ST* 1: 335.

42 *ST* 1: 61–62.

43 *ST* 1: 338, quoting Epistola 60 = 56.

with Reformed orthodoxy,[44] but he updated his evaluation of Spinoza's pantheism in his own way in light of modern concerns.

2.3 Gottfried Wilhelm Leibniz

Hodge cited several theological positions of Gottfried Wilhelm Leibniz, whose philosophy, as he noted repeatedly, was applied to theology by Christian Wolff (1679–1754).[45] Hodge read various works of Leibniz in different editions (he quoted from both the eighteenth-century edition by Louis Dutens and the nineteenth-century edition by Johann Eduard Erdmann) and he mentioned the philosopher more often than he did either Descartes or Spinoza. Adopting a mostly critical stance, he mentioned Thomas Reid (1710–1796) as "one of the most able opponents"[46] of Leibniz, but he also had a positive appreciation of some of the philosopher's views. Reid was one of the primary constructors of the Common Sense Realism Hodge found so helpful, as mediated through William Hamilton (1788–1856). On one occasion, Hodge recommended specifically the discussion on the relationship between faith and reason ("Discours préliminaire de la conformité de la foy avec la raison") that was the opening text of the *Essai de théodicée*. This introductory treatise, Hodge said, was one of the works that "deserve the careful perusal of the theological student."[47] Nonetheless, Hodge was quite critical about several of Leibniz's philosophical positions.

Thus, he rejected the definition of God's justice as "benevolence guided by wisdom."[48] On that definition, defended by Leibniz and others— Hodge wrote that in the United States "the same view has been extensively adopted"[49]—the present world is the best possible one, and God's permission of sin results from His benevolence.[50] Hodge, however, defended the idea that justice and benevolence are distinct, and that justice involves the notion that sin deserves punishment. For this reason, collapsing justice and benevolence was theologically impossible. He explained

44 In 1676, for example, the University Curators and Burgomasters of Leiden publicly prohibited the teaching of, among other things, the notion that "Homines habere ideam adaequatam de Deo." P.C. Molhuysen, *Bronnen tot de geschiedenis der Leidsche Universiteit*, vol. 3 ('s-Gravenhage: Martinus Nijhoff, 1918), 320.

45 *ST* 1: 5, 419. Cf., on Leibnizian-Wolffian philosophy, 2: 591, 728; 3: 76. On Leibniz as a theologian, see e. g. Irena Backus, *Leibniz: Protestant Theologian* (Oxford: Oxford University Press, 2016).

46 *ST* 2: 302, 305.

47 *ST* 1: 44. Cf. the quotation in volume 3: 62.

48 *ST* 1: 419; 2: 489–490.

49 *ST* 1: 419.

50 *ST* 1: 419–420.

this in his discussion of justice as a distinct divine attribute, and repeated it in his discussion of Christ's satisfaction.[51]

Another point of disagreement was linked with the doctrine of providence. Hodge quoted Leibniz's citation of a passage in which Pierre Bayle stated that God does everything that occurs and denied the existence of secondary causes—a position that Hodge strongly contradicted, in line with Reformed orthodoxy generally, which had defended secondary causality against some early modern philosophers.[52] According to Hodge, "[w]e are forced by the constitution of our nature to believe in the external world and in the reality of second causes."[53] "Constitution of our nature" reflected Common Sense Realism by arguing that secondary causation was recognized universally and unavoidably by humanity. This was, after all, the presupposition of all sciences, including theology.[54] Accordingly, Hodge could not endorse the occasionalist model of causality, on which he cited Leibniz's description, noting that Nathanael Emmons (1745–1840) took the same position.[55] In the chapter on providence, he addressed Leibniz's theory of pre-established harmony.[56] Here he seems to have mocked the idea that the physical motion of a body is not caused by any mental volition: "Leibnitz's hand would have written all his wonderful books, mathematical and philosophical, and conducted all his controversies with

---

51 *ST* 1: 419–424; 2: 489–493.

52 *ST* 1: 580, referring to G.W. Leibniz, *Essais de théodicée,* third part, § 386; cf. C.J. Gerhardt, ed., *Die philosophischen Schriften von Gottfried Wilhelm Leibniz*, vol. 6 (Berlin: Weidmann, 1885), 344. Hodge here quoted from the Erdmann's edition of Leibniz's *Opera*, 1840. On the Reformed defence of secondary causality, see e. g. J.A. van Ruler, *The Crisis of Causality. Descartes and Voetius on God, Nature and Change* (Leiden: Brill, 1995); Goudriaan, *Reformed Orthodoxy and Philosophy*, chapter 3. Hodge, however, was aware of the fact that even in the Reformed tradition a few thinkers had gone in the direction of supporting the notion of divine mono-causality (e. g. Huldrych Zwingli: "causas secundas non rite causas vocari," *ST* 1: 592). Incidentally, Hodge feared that Jonathan Edwards' view that providence was a continual creation ran the risk of denying secondary causation, thus sliding into another form of pantheism.

53 *ST* 1: 580.

54 For more detail, see chapter 3 below on Hodge's views of theology as a science.

55 *ST* 1: 594, quoting Leibniz, *De ipsa natura sive de vi insita actionibusque creaturarum*, § 10; cf. C.J. Gerhard, ed., *Die philosophischen Schriften von Gottfried Wilhelm Leibniz*, vol. 4 (Berlin: Weidmann, 1880), 509, where Leibniz referred to thinkers such as Robert Fludd, Nicolas Malebranche (cf. Hodge, *ST* 1: 593), and to Cartesians generally. Without providing a specific reference, Hodge also quoted from Nathanael Emmons, *Systematic Theology*, in *The Works of Nathanael Emmons*, vol. 2, ed. Jacob Ide (Boston: Congregational Board of Publication, 1860), 435 (i. e. "Sermon XXX. Divine and Human Agency Inseparably Connected"). Cf. Bruce Kuklick, *A History of Philosophy in America, 1720–2000* (Oxford: Clarendon, 2001), 41–42.

56 *ST* 1: 597–598; cf. 2: 45–46, where Hodge called the theory "unsatisfactory" (45); 1: 58. Cf. Nathan J. Archer, "Inscrutable Providence: The Doctrine of Divine Concurrence in the Thought of Charles Hodge," PhD dissertation, Calvin Theological Seminary (Grand Rapids, 2015), 176–177. I thank Stefan Lindholm for kindly providing me with the text of this dissertation.

Bayle, Clarke, and Newton, though his soul had never been created."[57] This objection would also apply to the occasionalist model. A problem noted by earlier Protestant critics was that this model deprived the soul of moral responsibility for the actions of the body.[58]

In Hodge there is also a mild parallel to the earlier theological criticism that Leibniz subjected God to necessity. Hodge quoted Leibniz's view that God's benevolence implied a moral necessity (*une nécessité morale*) for Him to create the universe.[59] Hodge did not devote much time to this issue, but simply declared that God was entirely independent from creation and that He was completely free when He decided to create the universe.[60] A related element in Leibniz's idea of a "best possible world" that God created was that sin was inevitable. Hodge disagreed with the theory, for it limited the infinite power of God.[61] He rejected the idea of the "father of optimism"—referring to the idea that the present world is the best possible one—according to whom "sin is the necessary means of the greatest good."[62] Moreover, according to Hodge, Leibniz's idea that sin was bound up with human imperfection as such, failed to do justice to "the real nature of sin," which was morally culpable opposition to God and his law.[63]

Hodge quoted Leibniz on various other subjects as well, including the human will,[64] and the "great truth" of the analogy between the human mind and God. The idea was that good properties of the human soul are in God in an infinite way.[65] According to Leibniz, this was also applicable to the Trinity. Hodge cited from the *Remarques sur le livre d'un Antitrinitaire Anglois,* a brief text dating from 1693–4, where Leibniz argued that the reflexivity of the human mind, when it was thinking about itself, was some sort of shadow of two substances being individually in one

---

57 *ST* 1: 598. Hodge quoted from Samuel Clarke's argument against Leibniz in *ST* 2: 295.

58 Thus, for example, the Groningen theologian Anthonius Driessen on the system of pre-established harmony, *Lumen et doctrina conscientiae, per Scripturam S. illustratae et pseudophilosophis nostri et praeteriti temporis oppositae* (Groningen: Cost & Groenewout, 1728), 73: "Mutilatam sic animam capitis praesertim damnant, LIBERTATE privant, machinam fatalium consecutionum faciunt, nostram a Deo dependentiam moralem, Relligionis fundamentum omne (o quam velim ut inscii!) subruentes"; cf. Goudriaan, *Reformed Orthodoxy and Philosophy*, 255–256.

59 *ST* 1: 556, with reference to Leibniz, *Théodicée*, second part, § 201 (ed. Gerhardt, vol. 6, 236).

60 *ST* 1: 556.

61 *ST* 1: 433.

62 *ST* 2: 287.

63 *ST* 2: 142–143.

64 *ST* 2: 286.

65 *ST* 1: 374.

substance and yet distinct from one another by their mutual relations.[66] Here Hodge mentioned Leibniz as one among several thinkers who defended philosophical analogies for the divine Trinity—attempts that he thought had some value, though not much: "The most they can do, is to show that in other spheres and in relation to other subjects, we find a somewhat analogous triplicity in unity." Hodge's reticence with respect to the "vestiges of the Trinity" seem to reflect quite well the majority view among the earlier Reformed orthodox.[67]

2.4 Immanuel Kant

During his stay in Germany as a student, Hodge translated into English an article by Philipp Albert Stapfer on the life of Kant. It was published in 1828 in the *Biblical Repertory.*[68] At that time, Hodge wrote, hardly anyone in Germany was still willing to consider himself a Kantian. Nonetheless, the influence of the philosophy of Kant continued to be felt.[69] In the *Systematic Theology,* Kant is mentioned quite a few times, but he is rarely cited directly.[70] One direct quote is taken from the *Kritik der praktischen Vernunft* as edited by Karl Rosenkranz in 1838 in *Immanuel Kant's Sämmtliche Werke*, but the English translation that he gives seems to be taken from Mansel.[71] The same edition of Kant's collected works is the source for another direct quotation, this time from the *Kritik der reinen Vernunft,*[72] a work that Hodge

66 *ST* 1: 480, quoting from Leibniz, *Remarques sur le livre d'un Antitrinitaire Anglois*, in *Gothofredi Guillielmi Leibnitii … opera omnia*, ed. Louis Dutens, vol. 1 (Geneva: De Tournes, 1768), 24–27, there 27.

67 Richard A. Muller, *Post-Reformation Reformed Dogmatics. The Rise and Development of Reformed Orthodoxy, ca. 1520 to 1725*, vol. 4, The Triunity of God (Grand Rapids: Baker Academic, 2003), 157–167.

68 Hicks, *The Philosophy of Charles Hodge*, 45–48.

69 Ibid., 46.

70 Hoffecker, *Charles Hodge*, chapter 10, noted that "Only seven references .. mention Kant's thought in the index to Hodge's *ST*." The index, however, is by no means exhaustive and could have given about 27 references.

71 *ST* 1: 343, referring to volume 8 of *Immanuel Kant's Sämmtliche Werke*, ed. Karl Rosenkranz & Friedrich Wilhelm Schubert (Leipzig: Leopold Voss, 1838), 282. Hodge indicated that Mansel quoted this passage, he repeats Mansel's translation verbally, but adds to Mansel's reference the relevant volume number of the collected works (Henry Longeville Mansel, *The Limits of Religious Thought, Examined in Eight Lectures Delivered Before the University of Oxford in the Year MDCCCLVIII* (Boston: Gould & Lincoln, 1859), 241 and note 2 there).

72 *ST* 1: 377, citing *Immanuel Kant's Sämmtliche Werke*, ed. Karl Rosenkranz & Friedrich Wilhelm Schubert, vol. 2 (Leipzig: Leopold Voss, 1838), 173 (=B 250).

later also cited in the English translation by J.M.D. Meiklejohn.[73] In most cases, a Kantian view is merely mentioned or summarized. In comparison, there are many more direct quotations of Leibniz than of Kant in Hodge's *Systematic Theology.*

Hodge seems to have expressed some ambivalence about Kant. On one hand he writes about "the anti-theistic principles of Kant"[74] but on the other hand he saw Kant as a theist: "Kant, although a theist, regards all as unphilosophical enthusiasts who assume that God hears or answers prayer."[75] Hodge noted that Kant "undertook to show that reason is incompetent to prove any religious truth" and instead accepted "our moral consciousness" as "the only foundation for religion."[76] For Kant, noted Hodge, religion was "observance of the moral law as a divine institution."[77] Still, even with respect to morality, Hodge mentioned the view of Friedrich Julius Stahl ("perhaps the greatest living authority on the philosophy of law"[78]) that Kant *ignored* God while his followers denied Him.[79] Hodge himself similarly noted that Kant's pupils took his thinking a step further downhill: "When Kant proved that there was no rational evidence of the existence of God, and fell back from the speculative to the practical reason (*i. e.* from reason to faith), his followers universally gave up all faith in a personal God."[80]

Kant's criticism of philosophical arguments for God's existence (the ontological, cosmological, and physico-theological arguments) left little room for negotiation,[81] but Hodge noted Kant's esteem for the teleological argument (Kant called it physico-theological): "Even Kant, although denying its conclusiveness, says that the teleological argument should always be treated with respect. It is, he says, the oldest, the clearest, and the best adapted to the human mind."[82] In a discussion of "the moral nature of man" Hodge noted that Kant and a philosopher such as his

---

73 *ST* 3: 46, quoting J.M.D. Meiklejohn (trans.), *Critique of Pure Reason, Translated from the German of Immanuel Kant* (London: Henry G. Bohn, 1855), 498.

74 *ST* 1: 363. Hicks, *The Philosophy of Charles Hodge*, 191n85: "This was the first time Hodge specifically branded Kant anti-theistic."

75 *ST* 3: 695, with reference, *inter alia*, to the biography ("Von Kant selbst genau revidirt und berichtigt") by Ludwig Ernst Borowski, *Darstellung des Lebens und Characters Immanuel Kant's* (Königsberg: Nicolovius, 1804), 199.

76 *ST* 1: 43.

77 *ST* 1: 21.

78 *ST* 3: 260.

79 *ST* 3: 261, referring to Friedrich Julius Stahl, *Philosophie des Rechts*, vol. 2.1, Rechts- und Staatslehre auf der Grundlage christlicher Weltanschauung, 4th edition (Heidelberg: J.C.B. Mohr, 1870), 74: Grotius provided "der erste Keim der Lossagung von der Religion, die bei Kant als Ignorirung und bei der jüngsten Schule als Läugnung Gottes sich entfaltet."

80 *ST* 1: 343.

81 Cf. *ST* 1: 203, 205, 210, 228–229, cf. 408.

82 *ST* 1: 226. No reference is provided; see Kant, *Kritik der reinen Vernunft*, B 651 (ed. Wilhelm Weischedel [Darmstadt: Wissenschaftliche Buchgesellschaft, 1983], 550).

esteemed William Hamilton, "while denying the validity of all other arguments for the existence of God, admit that our nature forces us to believe that He is, and that He is a person."[83] This appeal to "our nature" fit well into Hodge's Common Sense Realist appeal to the universal testimony of consciousness. The moral argument went beyond the confines of the *Critique of Pure Reason,* but even there Kant asserted that human reason as such needs the concept the idea of God as a real substance—even though God's existence, according to Kant, cannot be proven by speculative reason.[84]

Hodge mentioned Kant in passing at several other points, though without devoting much attention to him.[85] He cited, among others, Kant's distinction between opinion, faith, and knowledge, as illustration of a common distinction between faith and knowledge that had some plausibility, but, nonetheless, was not satisfactory.[86] In Kant's view, redemption was "a purely natural process,"[87] as was justification, which was based on "our own natural moral character and conduct" attempting to conform to Christ as "the ideal of humanity."[88] Still, Kant's philosophy had its merits: it was "in some aspects salutary." The context suggests that Hodge was thinking of the fact that Kant did not allow an isolated consideration of happiness, but strictly joined happiness and goodness together, implying that humans are happy "in exact proportion to their goodness, and miserable in proportion as they are wicked." This also meant that sin deserved punishment.[89]

Hodge's interaction with Kant was largely muted. This fact is interesting in that Kant introduced seismic shifts in the knowledge of God previously unknown to Reformed orthodox authors. Yet as important as Kant's ideas were historically, Hodge viewed them as passé, Kant's agnostic thought largely being displaced by German and American pantheism.

---

83 *ST* 1: 239.

84 The point has been emphasized by Wolfhart Pannenberg, *Systematische Theologie*, vol. 1 (Göttingen: Vandenhoeck & Ruprecht, 1988), 102–103; *Theologie und Philosophie. Ihr Verhältnis im Lichte ihrer gemeinsamen Geschichte* (Göttingen: Vandenhoeck & Ruprecht, 1996), 181–182. Cf. Kant, *Kritik der reinen Vernunft*, B 697–730.

85 E. g. *ST* 1: 58, 36, 377, 381; *ST* 2: 272, 444.

86 *ST* 3: 46–49, there 46.

87 *ST* 2: 451.

88 *ST* 3: 135.

89 *ST* 3: 196–197.

2.5 Georg Wilhelm Friedrich Hegel

In 1872, noting the transitoriness of human speculation, Hodge wondered: "Who is now a Hegelian? Forty years ago, who was not?"[90] The philosophy of Hegel had been very influential and Hodge still mentioned it repeatedly, especially in connection with "idealistic pantheism."[91] Yet only very rarely did he cite Hegel's works directly. On one occasion, he cited the volume of Hegel's *Werke* that gives the text of the *Vorlesungen über die Philosophie der Religion,* edited by Philipp Marheineke.[92] The quoted passage expressed Hegel's idea that human knowledge of God is actually God's knowledge of Himself and of the human being. Another reference to Hegel includes ideas seeming to make God dependent on humans, treating them as essential one in being. This citation came via Mansel: according to Hegel, God exists only insofar He is being known, and to deny the knowability of the infinite God is, according to the philosopher, sin against the Holy Spirit.[93] Hodge also quoted philosophical historiography on Hegel, but this, too, occurred rarely.[94] Hodge's primary interest in Hegel played into his larger project of opposing pantheism of every variety.

In addition to the major issue of pantheism, another area in which Hodge criticized Hegel concerned the relationship between Christianity and philosophy, and especially the Hegelian claim to understanding reality. Schelling and Hegel, according to Hodge, presented philosophy in the clothes of Christian terms. What actually happened, however, was that "Christian ideas were entirely excluded, while the

90 *ST* 3: 661.

91 *ST* 1: 58, 75, cf. 118, 331; 2:428; cf. 1: 356, and 2:731: "the Hegelian dictum, 'What God does I do, and what I do God does.'" A precursor of Hegelian pantheism, according to Hodge, was the medieval thinker John Scotus Erigena; *ST* 1:75; 2: 584.

92 *ST* 1: 336, quoting—in what is apparently Hodge's English translation—*Georg Wilhelm Friedrich Hegel's Vorlesungen über die Philosophie der Religion, nebst einer Schrift über die Beweise vom Daseyn Gottes*, ed. Philipp Marheineke [*Georg Wilhelm Friedrich Hegel's Werke*, vol. 12] (2nd ed., Berlin: Duncker & Humblot, 1840), 496: "Daß der Mensch von Gott weiß, ist nach der wesentlichen Gemeinschaft ein gemeinschaftliches Wissen, — d.i. der Mensch weiß nur von Gott, insofern Gott im Menschen von sich selbst weiß, dieß Wissen ist Selbstbewußtseyn Gottes, aber ebenso ein Wissen desselben vom Menschen, und dieß Wissen Gottes vom Menschen ist Wissen des Menschen von Gott."

93 *ST* 1: 335, citing Henry Longeville Mansel, *The Limits of Religious Thought, Examined in Eight Lectures Delivered Before the University of Oxford in the Year MDCCCLVIII* (Boston: Gould & Lincoln, 1859), 301. Mansel considered the comment on the sin against the Holy Ghost an "awful charge" lacking serious motivation.

94 *ST* 1: 302, freely translating Carl Ludwig Michelet, *Geschichte der letzten Systeme der Philosophie in Deutschland von Kant bis Hegel*, vol. 2 (Berlin: Duncker & Humblot, 1838), 646 (the reference to 647 is an error), on Hegel's view that God "is the only true personal Being" that absorbs within Himself the other of Himself.

language of the Bible was retained."[95] Still, according to Hodge, it was Hegel's belief that Christianity could be translated into philosophy that led the philosopher to the conviction that Christianity was "the absolute religion." Hodge rejected this idea: instead, Christianity was meant to be believed by children without being reserved for philosophers.[96] The philosophy of Hegel, in turn, had become a starting point for new theologies. Hodge regretted that theological systems based on thinkers such as Hegel "almost superseded the old biblical systems."[97] He did not elaborate Hegel's distinction between the religious representation (*Vorstellung*), with its spatio-temporal limitations, and the philosophical concept that understands what the representation means and brings its true content on the level of the philosophical *Begriff*. Hodge quoted, however, Carl Gottlieb Bretschneider's biting summary, in a discussion of *Religionsgeheimnisse*, of a Hegelianism that pretends to know it all: "there are mysteries in religion only for those who have not raised themselves to the Hegelian grade of knowledge. For the latter all is clear; all is knowledge; and Christianity is the solution, and therefore the revelation of all mysteries." This, wrote Hodge, was "the insanity of presumption."[98]

According to Hodge, Schelling, Hegel, and Schleiermacher, with their pantheistic ideas, stood at the basis of modern Christology.[99] The main reason why Hodge considered this Christology pantheistic is because it asserted generically the oneness of God and humans: "Hegel says that what the Bible teaches of Christ is not true of an individual, but only of mankind as a whole..."[100] Hodge quoted how Fredinand Christian Baur summarized the views of Schleiermacher and Hegel: "the divine nature is the truth of humanity, and human nature the reality, or existence-form (die Wirklichkeit) of the divine nature."[101] These thinkers maintained the classical terminology of different divine and human natures, but their main point obviously was the ontological oneness of these natures—a claim that Hodge rejected as pantheistic.

---

95 *ST* 1: 71.

96 *ST* 3: 208.

97 *ST* 3: 76.

98 *ST* 3: 78, citing Carl Gottlieb Bretschneider, *Systematische Entwickelung aller in der Dogmatik vorkommenden Begriffe, nach den symbolischen Schriften der evangelisch-lutherischen und reformirten Kirche und den wichtigsten dogmatischen Lehrbüchern ihrer Theologen*, 4th ed. (Leipzig: Barth, 1841), 163–164 (§ 29). Incidentally, the quoted sentences were new to the fourth edition of 1841; they take the place of what was, in the third edition of 1825, a totally different comment on idealism.

99 *ST* 2: 428, cf. 1: 118–119 and 3: 182, 655 note.

100 *ST* 2: 429.

101 *ST* 3: 182, with reference to Ferdinand Christian Baur, *Die christliche Lehre von der Versöhnung in ihrer geschichtlichen Entwicklung, von der ältesten Zeit bis auf die neueste* (Tübingen: C.F. Osiander, 1838), 330 note.

2.6 William Hamilton

Previous sections have explored the significance of continental European philosophy to Hodge. This is in line with findings of recent research on Hodge's indebtedness to German thinking.[102] Furthermore, Hodge's overt appropriation of the Scottish philosophy of common sense is well known and beyond dispute. It is persistently visible in the *Systematic Theology,* where representatives of Common Sense Realism such as Thomas Reid,[103] Dugald Stewart,[104] and James McCosh[105] are cited a few times. However, Hodge quoted William Hamilton far more frequently, his name even figuring in several section headings: those concerned with the knowledge of God, and the relation between faith and knowledge.[106] Hamilton was a somewhat ambivalent thinker, who integrated Kantian ideas into a philosophy of common sense. McCosh regretted that Hamilton reached beyond Reid's philosophical heritage, whose works Hamilton edited.[107]

As was probably unsurprising for a Princeton theologian at the time, Hodge had a first-hand knowledge of Hamilton's works. In the *Systematic Theology,* he quoted from Hamilton's *Discussions on Philosophy and Literature, Education and University Reform* (1853),[108] the *Lectures on Metaphysics and Logic,* which were posthumously edited by Henry Longueville Mansel and John Veitch (1859–1860),[109] O.W. Wight's edition of *Philosophy of Sir William Hamilton* (1853),[110] and from Hamilton's edition of the works of Thomas Reid.[111]

The radical shift in Hamilton's reputation among Princeton Presbyterians—a change from positive appreciation to firm rejection that occurred "almost overnight" in 1860—has been extensively analyzed by Peter Hicks.[112] According to Hicks, two main reasons motivated the Princetonians' rupture with Hamilton: he taught "an

102 See e. g. Hicks, *The Philosophy of Charles Hodge*, chapter 2; Annette G. Aubert, "Old Princeton and European Scholarship," in *The Oxford Handbook of Calvin and Calvinism*, ed. Bruce Gordon and Carl Trueman (Oxford: Oxford University Press, 2021), 457–474.

103 *ST* 1: 209, 231; 2: 286, 290, 294, 300, 303, 305; 3: 43.

104 *ST* 1: 209; 2: 287, 303, 305, 307.

105 *ST* 1: 209–210, 359; 3: 55.

106 *ST* 1: 346, 349, 351, 352; 3: 80.

107 A. Ryan, "Hamilton, Sir William Stirling, baronet (1788–1856)," *Oxford Dictionary of National Biography*, https://doi.org/10.1093/ref:odnb/12144.

108 *ST* 1: 304, 346–348, 351, 365, 555.

109 *ST* 1: 365, 555; 3: 55.

110 *ST* 1: 340.

111 *ST* 1: 210; 2: 306; 3: 48.

112 Hicks, *The Philosophy of Charles Hodge*, 1–35, there 1.

unknowable impersonal God," and he considered human reason unable to find truth in religion.[113] The disagreement is also reflected in Hodge's *Systematic Theology*.

Hodge, nonetheless, valued Hamilton's "invaluable service to the cause of truth" in defending the philosophy of common sense, a philosophy that Hodge summarized in four main points. (1) The teachings of consciousness are self-evidently true and beyond doubt; (2) what our nature by its inherent laws leads us to believe is true and must be taken as such; (3) the previous point applies to all faculties: senses, reason, and conscience—otherwise God would not be trustworthy; (4) if the statements of conscience or reason are universal and necessary, then we are not bound by arbitrary assertions of individuals, but by necessary universally recognized truths.[114] Hodge appreciated the impressive erudition with which Hamilton had shown how these principles were maintained by major philosophers throughout the centuries.[115]

Hodge particularly expressed appreciation for Hamilton's support of common sense philosophy in a chapter on "the knowledge of God."[116] In the same chapter he mentioned another "great service ... to the cause of truth" that Hamilton provided, which consisted in showing "the utter futility" of the assertion of modern philosophers that God is knowable immediately and adequately, without any reliance upon experience or human nature.[117] Hamilton had argued that since the nature of our faculty of knowing shapes our knowledge, our finite mind limits what we can know of the infinite God, which Hodge found to be a strong argument against the notion that God could be "fully" known as He is in Himself.[118] He viewed this as a classic expression of divine incomprehensibility without denying God's knowability. A similar line of thought had been followed, for example, in the seventeenth century by Reformed thinkers who contested Descartes's notion that the "idea of God" in the human mind was "most clear and distinct." As Jacobus Revius wrote: "if we know in a finite manner Him who is infinite, we do not know Him clearly and distinctly as He is."[119] In other words, Descartes's claim to have a clear and distinct knowledge of God seemed incompatible with the finitude of the human mind. Hodge, sharing the concerns of his Reformed predecessors, maintained both God's incomprehensibility and knowability.

---

113 Ibid., 27.

114 *ST* 1: 360–361. Cf. 1: 279, 340, 343.

115 *ST* 1: 360–361.

116 *ST* 1: 335–365.

117 *ST* 1: 345–346, there 346.

118 *ST* 1: 346.

119 Jacobus Revius, *Suarez repurgatus, sive syllabus disputationum metaphysicarum Francisci Suarez, societatis Jesu Theologi, cum notis* (Leiden: Frans Heger, 1644), 576: "si enim finite cognoscimus eum qui infinitus est, non cognoscimus eum clare et distincte sicut est."

Hamilton, however, radicalized the notion of divine incomprehensibility in a way that went clearly beyond what seventeenth-century anti-Cartesians intended and what Hodge was willing to admit. Since, in Hamilton's view, knowing implies limitating, he concluded that the Infinite could not be known, nor could the Infinite or Absolute possess knowledge, for as such the Infinite/Absolute does not allow the finiteness and conceptual distinctions that are implied in knowing.[120] The way in which Hamilton conducted the argument, in Hodge's eyes, made him similar to Samson who wrecked the Philistines by losing his own life. In his view, Hamilton's argument destroyed indeed "the stupendous systems of pantheistic atheism" and the modern notion that the Infinite can be fully known directly, but he denied theism in the process.[121] According to Hamilton, God cannot be known; He is "incogitable." Hodge read in Hamilton and Mansel that the infinite God "cannot be a person; cannot know, cannot be cause, cannot be conscious, cannot be the subject of any moral attributes."[122] However, being a theist, Hamilton claimed that what is unthinkable nonetheless needs to be believed.[123] Hodge disagreed strongly and took the classical view that the contradictory cannot be believed. Echoing the old Reformed and medieval adage, he maintained that some truths were above reason, but no divine truth was inherently contradictory. In his argument, Hodge took up the core tenet of the common sense philosophy, namely, that the natural faculties of the human being are basically reliable and that all people know this by the testimony of human consciousness. The mind, moreover, is a unity. Hence, to surmise that a person "must think one way and believe another; that the laws of his reason force him to regard as false what his conscience or senses force him to regard as true is to destroy his rationality."[124] Hamilton's adherence to the principles of the common sense philosophy was contradicted by his view of the knowledge of God, which denies "the veracity of consciousness," is in fact "suicidal" and leads to skepticism.[125]

Hamilton, whom Hodge mentioned routinely in the same breath with Mansel, started from a wrong Hegelian definition of the Unconditioned ,or Infinite, according to which it "must include all modes of being."[126] By contrast, Hodge maintained the classical concept, according to which the Infinite has attributes that are both

---

120 *ST* 1: 347.

121 *ST* 1: 348–349, the quotation on 349.

122 *ST* 1: 351; cf. 356, 393–394.

123 *ST* 1: 352; cf. 239.

124 *ST* 1: 352–353, there 353.

125 *ST* 1: 362–363; cf. 340: "he did not adhere to his own principle, 'That what is by nature necessarily believed to be, truly is.'"

126 *ST* 1: 356.

unlimited and totally independent.[127] In addition, Hamilton and others defined knowledge as comprehension or as forming a mental image of the thing known, which Hodge considered a "wrong definition." Knowledge was rather "the perception of the truth."[128]

In the context of creation, Hodge again noted Hamilton's adoption of a notion of God that seemed to be monistic, verging on pantheism. Hamilton assumed, writes Hodge, "'an absolute identity of existence in the effect and in the complement of its causes – between the *causatum* and the *causa,*' and therefore 'an absolute identity of existence' between God and the world."[129] Hodge rejected this view, a position that had been resisted, he wrote, throughout the history of the Church because it assumes the divisibility of the divine substance.[130] He did not use the term pantheism in this context, but pantheism seems to have been his primary concern. In fact, Hodge mentioned Hamilton as one example of "many Theistic and even Evangelical writers of our day," that is around 1871, who favor "the Monistic theory," which viewed "all things as modifications of the substance of God."[131] The case of Hamilton showed that, from Spinoza through Hegel and others, pantheism had even entered the thinking of those who were sympathetic to the Scottish philosophy of common sense. Hodge's nineteenth-century context resulted in a preoccupation with pantheism that went beyond Reformed orthodox concerns even though Spinoza's pantheism had been an issue in the last decades of the seventeenth century already.

In Hodge's *Systematic Theology,* Hamilton was quoted in passing on other topics as well.[132] One of these concerned the relation between reason and faith. In his edition of the works of Thomas Reid, Hamilton mentioned Augustine's statement that knowledge is based on reason, while faith rests on authoritative testimony. Hamilton admitted the accuracy of this view, but he added that ultimately reason itself is also based on authority. Human reason accepts data beyond itself, so that "belief is the primary condition of reason, and not reason the ultimate ground of belief." Not "the proud *Intellige ut credas* of Abelard," but rather "the humble *Crede*

127 *ST* 1: 357.

128 *ST* 1: 360–361.

129 *ST* 1: 554–555, there 555, quoting William Hamilton, *Discussions on Philosophy and Literature, Education and University Reform* (New York: Harper, 1853), 575–576. Hodge also cited a parallel passage in William Hamilton, *Lectures on Metaphysics and Logic,* ed. Henry Longeville Mansel & John Veitch, vol. 1 (Boston: Gould & Lincoln, 1859), 533.

130 Yet chapter 4 below shows that Hodge himself conceived of the divine attributes as real distinctions in God, modifying traditional Christian views of divine simplicity.

131 *ST* 1: 554.

132 *ST* 1: 193, 209, 301, 304, 381, 408; 2: 306.

ut intelligas of Anselm" set both reason and faith on the right foundation.[133] Hodge agreed. Human reasoning presupposes "primary truths" that are "beliefs" and "are taken on trust"—a classical, though often underplayed, position that can be traced back at least to Aristotle's view on first principles, as explained in his *Posterior analytics*.[134]

Hodge diverged, however, from Hamilton's view that 'knowledge' concerns the present only, whereas memory of past events is 'belief.' Hodge, by contrast, argued that memory is no less a knowledge of the past than "other forms of consciousness are a knowledge of the present."[135] In the end, it seems fair to say that Hodge's defense, against Hamilton, of the knowability and transcendence of God stood in clear continuity with basic convictions of Reformed orthodoxy. The case with respect to the four points of the common sense philosophy that Hodge appreciated in Hamilton is less straightforward. Still, insofar as the defense of the basic reliability of the human senses and intellectual faculties resisted radical skepticism, there may be continuity at this point as well. The theological responses to Cartesian doubt, not only by the Reformed but also by thinkers from other confessional backgrounds, may provide relevant material for comparison. The Dutch theologian Revius, for example, defended the basic reliability of the human senses by referring to the many appeals made to the senses in the Bible: these would be wrong if the senses were basically unreliable.[136]

2.7 Conclusion

This brief survey of the way in which Hodge in his *Systematic Theology* interacted with several modern philosophers could easily be expanded. Hodge, for example, quoted Victor Cousin frequently, not only as a historian of philosophy, but also as a systematic philosopher in his own right. Moreover, he devoted a section to a critical examination of the positivism of Auguste Comte.[137] These are just two examples of modern philosophers—two French thinkers, in this case—of which

133 *ST* 3: 48, citing William Hamilton, ed., *The Works of Thomas Reid, D.D., Now Fully Collected, With Selections from His Unpublished Letters*, 2nd ed. (Edinburgh: Maclachlan, 1849), 760b. See also *ST* 3: 60.

134 *ST* 3: 48.

135 *ST* 3: 55–56, there 55, citing Hamilton, *Lectures on Metaphysics and Logic*, 1: 152–153.

136 Jacobus Revius, *Methodi cartesianae consideratio theologica* (Leiden: Hieronymus de Vogel, 1648), chapter 10, also in *Jacobus Revius, A Theological Examination of Cartesian Philosophy. Early Criticisms (1647)*, ed. Aza Goudriaan (Leiden: Brill, 2002).

137 *ST* 1: 254–262. See also 1: 408; 2: 16; 3: 346.

Hodge had a first-hand knowledge. However, what we have seen thus far illustrates important characteristics of Hodge's interaction with modern philosophy.

Hodge's reception of the philosophers discussed above shows the significance of continental European philosophy for his thinking, even though he rejected most of the positions that the philosophers argued for. Hodge mostly cited primary works in German, French, or Latin, occasionally using translations. He could also summarize a philosopher's views as common knowledge at times. The pervasiveness of continental European thinking appears perhaps most clearly in the case of the Scottish philosopher William Hamilton, who came from the common sense tradition that Hodge supported, but Hamilton integrated elements of Kantian and idealist thinking—elements that Hodge considered wrongheaded and unconvincing.

Hodge's citations also reveal a few major themes on which Hodge interacted with the philosophers. These are the knowledge of God and the concept of God. The first theme involves the issue of the arguments for God's existence (Descartes, Kant, Hamilton), and the question whether God can be known by human reason (Kant, Hegel, Hamilton, to some extent also Leibniz), and to what extent: fully and adequately, or only in a limited manner (Descartes, Spinoza, Hegel, Hamilton). The other major issue concerned the contrast between theism and pantheism. Pantheist thinking was found in Spinoza, Hegel, and in theologians who adopted their way of thinking, including in their Christology. The pervasiveness of "monism" appeared also in Hodge's discussion of Hamilton and, for example, in an anecdote dating back from Hodge's time in Germany that he related to illustrate how "many Theistic and even Evangelical writers of our day" were affected by monistic thinking: he cited the *Erweckungstheologe* Friedrich Tholuck as asking a number of students at his dinner table "'Is this knife the substance of God?' and they all answered, 'Yes.'"[138] Against such pantheistic thinking, Hodge defended the transcendence of God. The issue of pantheism has a bearing on the concept of evil in general (Spinoza, Hegel), though in relation to sin specifically Hodge mentioned other philosophers as well (Leibniz, Kant). Leibniz was quoted quite often, mostly related to providence (pre-established harmony, optimism). Hodge's references to modern philosophers were mostly critical but he also expressed agreement with elements of Descartes, Leibniz, Kant, and Hamilton. In his reception of early modern philosophers, Hodge did not refer to Reformed thinkers of the era of Protestant orthodoxy. His evaluations, however, reveal a high degree of continuity with basic positions taken by earlier generations on the philosophies of Descartes, Spinoza, and Leibniz. They, too, defended a natural finite human knowledge of a transcendent God who is entirely free. Like his Reformed orthodox predecessors, Hodge treated philosophy in the service of theology, which meant that some philosophical ideas were useful and

138 *ST* 1: 554.

others were not. Ultimately, for Hodge, philosophy was useful only insofar as it helped defend and explain biblical truth.[139]

Works Cited

Anderson, Owen. *Reason and Faith in the Theology of Charles Hodge. American Common Sense Realism* (New York: Pelgrave Macmillan, 2014).

Archer, Nathan J. "Inscrutable Providence: The Doctrine of Divine Concurrence in the Thought of Charles Hodge," PhD dissertation, Calvin Theological Seminary (Grand Rapids, 2015).

Aubert, Annette G. "Old Princeton and European Scholarship," in *The Oxford Handbook of Calvin and Calvinism*, ed. Bruce Gordon and Carl Trueman (Oxford: Oxford University Press, 2021), 457–474.

Backus, Irena. *Leibniz: Protestant Theologian* (Oxford: Oxford University Press, 2016).

Baur, Ferdinand Christian. *Die christliche Lehre von der Versöhnung in ihrer geschichtlichen Entwicklung, von der ältesten Zeit bis auf die neueste* (Tübingen: C.F. Osiander, 1838)

Baur, Ferdinand Christian. *Die Lehre von der Dreieinigkeit und Menschwerdung Gottes in ihrer geschichtlichen Entwicklung,* vol. 3, Die neueste Geschichte des Dogma, von der Reformation bis in die neueste Zeit (Tübingen: Osiander, 1843).

Borowski, Ludwig Ernst. *Darstellung des Lebens und Characters Immanuel Kant's* (Königsberg: Nicolovius, 1804).

Bretschneider, Carl Gottlieb. *Systematische Entwickelung aller in der Dogmatik vorkommenden Begriffe, nach den symbolischen Schriften der evangelisch-lutherischen und reformirten Kirche und den wichtigsten dogmatischen Lehrbüchern ihrer Theologen,* 4th ed. (Leipzig: Barth, 1841).

Cashdollar, Charles D. *The Transformation of Theology, 1830–1890. Positivism and Protestant Thought in in Britain and America* (Princeton: Princeton University Press, 1989).

Descartes, René. *Oeuvres de Desartes,* ed. Charles Adam & Paul Tannery [AT], 11 vols. (Paris: Vrin, 1996).

Driessen, Anthonius. *Lumen et doctrina conscientiae, per Scripturam S. illustratae et pseudophilosophis nostri et praeteriti temporis oppositae* (Groningen: Cost & Groenewout, 1728).

Emmons, Nathanael. *Systematic Theology,* in *The Works of Nathanael Emmons,* vol. 2, ed. Jacob Ide (Boston: Congregational Board of Publication, 1860).

Gerrish, B.A. "Charles Hodge and the Europeans," in *Charles Hodge Revisited. A Critical Appraisal of His Life and Works,* ed. John W. Stewart and James H. Moorhead (Grand Rapids: Eerdmans, 2002), 129–158.

139 Chapters 3–5 below illustrate how modern philosophical ideas such as "science," time and eternity, and "person" shifted meaning in Christian theology at key points to some extent.

Goudriaan, Aza. *Reformed Orthodoxy and Philosophy, 1625–1750: Gisbertus Voetius, Petrus van Mastricht, and Anthonius Driessen* (Leiden: Brill, 2006).

Goudriaan, Aza. *Philosophische Gotteserkenntnis bei Suárez und Descartes, im Zusammenhang mit der niederländischen Theologie und Philosophie des 17. Jahrhunderts* (Leiden: Brill, 1999), 216–217.

Goudriaan, Aza. "Descartes, Cartesianism, and Early Modern Theology," in *The Oxford Handbook of Early Modern Theology, 1600–1800*, ed. Ulrich L. Lehner, Richard A. Muller, A.G. Roeber (New York: OUP, 2016), 533–549.

Graf, Friedrich Wilhelm. "Paulus, Heinrich Eberhard Gottlob," *RGG*, fourth ed., 8 vols. (Tübingen: Mohr Siebeck, 1998–2005), 6: 1065–1066.

Gutjahr, Paul C. *Charles Hodge. Guardian of American Orthodoxy* (Oxford: Oxford University Press 2012).

Hamilton, William. *Discussions on Philosophy and Literature, Education and University Reform* (New York: Harper, 1853).

Hamilton, William. *Lectures on Metaphysics and Logic*, ed. Henry Longeville Mansel & John Veitch, vol. 1 (Boston: Gould & Lincoln, 1859).

Hamilton, William, ed. *The Works of Thomas Reid, D.D., Now Fully Collected, With Selections from His Unpublished Letters*, 2nd ed. (Edinburgh: Maclachlan, 1849).

Hase, Karl. *Lehrbuch der evangelischen Dogmatik*, 2nd ed. (Leipzig: Breitkopf & Härtel, 1838).

Hegel, Georg Wilhelm Friedrich. *Gottfried Wilhelm Friedrich Hegel's Vorlesungen über die Philosophie der Religion, nebst einer Schrift über die Beweise vom Daseyn Gottes*, ed. Philipp Marheineke [*Georg Wilhelm Friedrich Hegel's Werke*, vol. 12] (2nd ed., Berlin: Duncker & Humblot, 1840).

Hicks, Peter. *The Philosophy of Charles Hodge. A 19th Century Evangelical Approach to Reason, Knowledge and Truth* (Lewiston: Edwin Mellen, 1997).

Hodge, Charles. *Systematic Theology* [henceforth *ST*], 3 vols. (n.p.: Hendrickson, 1999), cf. https://www.ccel.org/ccel/hodge.

Hoffecker, Andrew W. *Charles Hodge: The Pride of Princeton* (Phillipsburg: P&R, 2011).

Hunt, John. *Essay on Pantheism* (London: Longmans et al., 1866).

Kant, Immanuel. *Immanuel Kant's Sämmtliche Werke*, vol. 2 and 8, ed. Karl Rosenkranz & Friedrich Wilhelm Schubert (Leipzig: Leopold Voss, 1838).

Kant, Immanuel. *Critique of Pure Reason, Translated from the German of Immanuel Kant*, trans. J.M.D. Meiklejohn (London: Henry G. Bohn, 1855).

Kant, Immanuel. *Kritik der reinen Vernunft*, ed. Wilhelm Weischedel (Darmstadt: Wissenschaftliche Buchgesellschaft, 1983).

Kuklick, Bruce. "The Place of Charles Hodge in the History of Ideas in America," in *Charles Hodge Revisited. A Critical Appraisal of His Life and Work*, ed. John W. Stewart and James H. Moorhead (Grand Rapids: Eerdmans, 2002), 63–76.

Kuklick, Bruce. *A History of Philosophy in America, 1720–2000* (Oxford: Clarendon, 2001).

Leibniz. G.W. *Die philosophischen Schriften von Gottfried Wilhelm Leibniz*, ed. C.J. Gerhardt, vol. 4 and 6 (Berlin: Weidmann, 1880 and 1885).

Leibniz, G.W. *Remarques sur le livre d'un Antitrinitaire Anglois,* in *Gothofredi Guillielmi Leibnitii ... opera omnia,* ed. Louis Dutens, vol. 1 (Geneva: De Tournes, 1768), 24–27.

Mansel, Henry Longeville. *The Limits of Religious Thought, Examined in Eight Lectures Delivered Before the University of Oxford in the Year MDCCCLVIII* (Boston: Gould & Lincoln, 1859).

Michelet, Carl Ludwig. *Geschichte der letzten Systeme der Philosophie in Deutschland von Kant bis Hegel*, vol. 2 (Berlin: Duncker & Humblot, 1838).

Molhuysen, P.C. *Bronnen tot de geschiedenis der Leidsche Universiteit,* vol. 3 ('s-Gravenhage: Martinus Nijhoff, 1918),

Moor, Bernhardinus de. *Commentarius perpetuus in Johannis Marckii Compendium theologiae christianae didactico-elencticum,* vol. 2 (Leiden: Johannes Hasebroek, 1763).

Muller, Richard A. *Post-Reformation Reformed Dogmatics. The Rise and Development of Reformed Orthodoxy, ca. 1520 to ca. 1725,* 4 vols. (Grand Rapids: Baker Academic, 2003).

Pannenberg, Wolfhart, *Systematische Theologie,* vol. 1 (Göttingen: Vandenhoeck & Ruprecht, 1988).

Pannenberg, Wolfhart. *Theologie und Philosophie. Ihr Verhältnis im Lichte ihrer gemeinsamen Geschichte* (Göttingen: Vandenhoeck & Ruprecht, 1996).

Revius, Jacobus. *Suarez repurgatus, sive syllabus disputationum metaphysicarum Francisci Suarez, societatis Jesu Theologi, cum notis* (Leiden: Frans Heger, 1644).

Revius, Jacobus. *Methodi cartesianae consideratio theologica* (Leiden: Hieronymus de Vogel, 1648).

Revius, Jacobus. *A Theological Examination of Cartesian Philosophy. Early Criticisms (1647),* ed. Aza Goudriaan (Leiden: Brill, 2002).

Ruler, J.A. van. *The Crisis of Causality. Descartes and Voetius on God, Nature and Change* (Leiden: Brill, 1995).

Ryan, A. "Hamilton, Sir William Stirling, baronet (1788–1856)," *Oxford Dictionary of National Biography,* https://doi.org/10.1093/ref:odnb/12144.

Schaff, Philipp and Samuel Macauley Jackson (eds.), *Encyclopedia of Living Divines and Christian Workers of All Denominations* (New York: Funk and Wagnalls, 1887).

Schütt, Hans Peter. *Die Adoption des "Vaters der modernen Philosophie." Studien zu einem Gemeinplatz der Ideengeschichte* (Frankfurt/Main: Vittorio Klostermann, 1998).

Spinoza, Benedictus de. *Benedicti de Spinoza opera quae supersunt omnia,* ed. Heinrich Eberhard Gottlob Paulus, 2 vols. (Jena: Bibliopolus academicus, 1802–1803).

Stahl, Friedrich Julius Stahl, *Philosophie des Rechts,* vol. 2.1, Rechts- und Staatslehre auf der Grundlage christlicher Weltanschauung, 4th edition (Heidelberg: J.C.B. Mohr, 1870).

Stewart, John W. "Bibliography of the Works by and about Charles Hodge," in *Charles Hodge Revisited. A Critical Appraisal of His Life and Works,* ed. John W. Stewart and James H. Moorhead (Grand Rapids: Eerdmans, 2002), 335–375

Sytsma, David. *Richard Baxter and the Mechanical Philosophers* (New York: Oxford University Press, 2017).

Turner, James. "Charles Hodge in the Intellectual Weather of the Nineteenth Century," in *Charles Hodge Revisited. A Critical Appraisal of His Life and Works*, ed. John W. Stewart and James H. Moorhead (Grand Rapids: Eerdmans, 2002), 41–61
Vander Stelt, John C. *Philosophy and Scripture. A Study in Old Princeton and Westminster Theology* (PhD dissertation, VU Amsterdam) (Marlton NJ: Mack Publishing, 1978).

Ryan M. McGraw

3. Charles Hodge on Theology as a Science: Shifting Patterns in the Nature and Genus of Theology

Theological and philosophical ideas shifted in the eighteenth and nineteenth centuries often dramatically.[1] Using terms common to the Western theological tradition, authors in this time-period often suffused such terms with new definitions and ideas. The way they treated the nature and genus of theology illustrates this point well. Charles Hodge more or less defined theology as the science of God. On the surface, this stood in contrast to earlier Reformed orthodox treatments of the question, which usually defined theology as the doctrine of living to God. The difference lay between focusing on theology as the scientific summarizing of the teaching of Scripture, and the application of that teaching to the true saving knowledge of God. While readers can detect such differences when reading Hodge alongside early-modern Reformed orthodox authors, the nuanced implications of these differences are not always easy to explain clearly. As the material below demonstrates, the subtle shift in definitions of science and scientific method, and the omission of earlier Aristotelian laden treatments of the genus of theology, illustrate how Hodge's nineteenth century context made a difference in his definition and method of theology.

The primary contention in this chapter is that Hodge's definition of theology as a science had points of continuity and discontinuity with Reformed orthodoxy.[2] To explain this assertion, this essay examines classic Reformed treatments of the nature and genus of theology flowing from medieval trajectories, Hodge's treatment of theological science with reference to some of his contemporaries, an analysis of the philosophical and scientific shifts underlying Hodge's viewpoint, and a concluding assessment of the significance of this historical shift in thinking.

---

1 I cannot express adequate thanks to John Fesko and to Andrew Wortman for their help on this chapter. John provided extensive critical feedback on the draft, clarifying many points. Andy, as the GPTS librarian, sent along a steady stream of articles and books for research.

2 As Mark Noll observed about Princeton theology generally, "The Princeton theology was a distinctly American and a distinctly nineteenth-century expression of classical Reformed faith." Mark A. Noll, "The Princeton Theology," in *Reformed Theology in America: A History of Its Modern Development*, ed. David F. Wells (Grand Rapids, MI: Baker Academic, 1997), 15.

3.1 Reformed Orthodoxy on the Nature and Genus of Theology

By the time Charles Hodge came on the scene in nineteenth century Princeton, science had new connotations, establishing a fresh trajectory for defining and explaining the nature of theology in relation to it.[3] While earlier authors treated *scientia* as a genus of a discipline, post-Enlightenment authors treated it primarily as a method of obtaining knowledge. Readers should note in advance that this terminological shift risks creating some equivocation in this essay by interchanging *scientia* and science. Although "science" was a fair translation of *scientia* in early modern theology, keeping in view the shift from a genus of a mode of knowing to a methodological process may promote some clarity through a somewhat messy narrative.

A Western tradition of theology stood behind authors like Hodge, and this tradition did not disappear wholly, even where nineteenth century authors modified it. To provide a general backdrop for Hodge's explanation of theology as a science, it is important to gain a glimpse into the broader Christian tradition on this point. This section sketches some brief samples of Medieval prolegomena, then traces Hodge's Reformed sources, and focusses on features Reformed orthodox teaching on the nature and genus of theology.

3.1.1 A Brief Medieval Trajectory

Science (*scientia*) and wisdom (*sapientia)* were terms always attached to theology in the so-called Middle Ages. John of Damascus, Thomas Aquinas, Anselm of Canterbury, Peter Lombard, and Bonaventure can help give readers a sense of the general use of these terms in relation to the nature and genus of theology. Most of the ideas presented here reappeared in post-Reformation theology, setting a backdrop for Hodge's teaching.

John of Damascus (675–749), who became the primary theologian of the Eastern church, began his *Orthodox Faith* by treating theology as the knowledge of God. Building on the premise of God's simplicity and incomprehensibility, he stated, "It is not within our capacity, therefore, to say anything about God or even to think of Him, beyond the things which have been divinely revealed to us, whether by word or by manifestation, by the divine oracles at once of the Old Testament and of the New."[4] Rather than defining theology directly, he restricted it to the true knowledge

3 For an excellent study of Hodge's relation to modern science, see John W. Stuart, *Mediating the Center: Charles Hodge on American Science, Language, Literature, and Politics*, Studies in Reformed Theology and History (Princeton, NJ: Princeton Theological Seminary, 1995).

4 John of Damascus, *Exposition of the Orthodox Faith*, trans. S. D. F. Salmond, vol. 9, Nicene and Post-Nicene Fathers: Second Series (Peabody, MA: Hendrickson Publishers, 2004), 2. Book 1, 1.2.

of the true God in light of Scripture, since Scripture revealed things about God, especially his Triunity, which nature could not offer. Exercising a powerful influence on Thomas Aquinas (1225–1274), for similar reasons Thomas noted, "We ought not to say about God anything which is not found in Holy Scripture either explicitly or implicitly."[5] Without delving into how such authors regarded church tradition, which was also, in their view, the Word of God subordinate to Scripture, the main point is that reflecting on and knowing God rested on Scripture primarily as its foundation.[6] Knowing God and the beatific vision of God in heaven also loomed large in their accounts of the end or goal of theology.

Aquinas became to Western theology what Damascus became to Eastern theology. Even to casual readers of Hodge's *Systematic Theology*, references to Thomas's *Summa* appear rhythmically. This fact makes Aquinas a particularly relevant medieval source on the nature of theology. In *prima pars, q*uestion 1, article 2, Aquinas wrote that "sacred doctrine is a science."[7] Yet theology was a superior science (*superioris scientia*) because it is "the science of God and the blessed."[8] Answering the question as to whether sacred doctrine was a matter of argument in question 8, Aquinas asserted that, like other sciences or modes of knowing, theology rested on its first principles instead of proving them. Yet unlike other sciences, theology did not rest on human reason. Reason had a subservient role in explaining articles of faith, but reason could not establish theological truths. Not only reason, but the doctors of the church, gave probable arguments for truth at best because faith rested on divine revelation given through the apostles and prophets.[9] While theology was a science because it entailed knowledge drawn from first principles, theology was unlike other sciences in that it was concerned with God, man's approach to God, and man's return to God [ref.]. Aquinas was less concerned with mere knowledge about God than with obtaining saving knowledge of the Triune God. For this reason, in

---

5 Thomas Aquinas, *Summa Theologiae*, trans. Lawrence Shapcote, Latin/English Edition of the Works of St. Thomas Aquinas (Steubenville, OH: Emaus Academic, 2012), 1:367. Prima Pars, 36.2. All references to Aquinas below will follow volume and page number, followed by part, topic, and paragraph, if applicable.

6 For sometimes competing views on the relationship between Scripture and tradition in late medieval theology, see Heiko Augustinus Oberman, *The Harvest of Medieval Theology: Gabriel Biel and Late Medieval Nominalism* (Grand Rapids (Mich.): Baker Academic, 2000).

7 Aquinas, *Summa Theologiae*, 1:5. 1.1.2, responsum. "sacra doctrina esse scientiam."

8 Aquinas, *Summa Theologia*, 1:5. 1.1.2. ad primum.

9 Aquinas, *Summa Theologiae*, 1.12; 1.1.8, *ad secundum*. "Nevertheless, sacred doctrine makes use of these authorities as extrinsic and probable arguments; but properly uses the authority of the canonical Scriptures as incontrovertible proof, and the authority of the Doctors of the Church as one that may properly be used, but merely as probable. For our faith rests upon the revelation made to the apostles and prophets who wrote the canonical books, and not on the revelations (if any such there are) made to other doctors."

the *Summa Contra Gentiles,* Thomas treated theology as the source of true wisdom, resulting in friendship with God.[10] Refuting people who opposed Christianity and rejected Scripture, Aquinas sought to refute their errors by showing them that nothing in nature contradicted Christian articles, in order to remove obstacles to bringing them into friendship with God.[11] In the *prima secundae* of the *Summa Theologiae,* Thomas related wisdom and science as intellectual virtues thus:

> Wisdom is a kind of science, insofar as it has that which is common to all the sciences; viz., to demonstrate conclusions from principles. But since it has something proper to itself above the other sciences, inasmuch as it judges of them all, not only as to their conclusions, but also to their first principles, therefore it is a more perfect virtue than science.[12]

Theology was a science because it involved knowledge, yet it was a special science because it involved saving knowledge of God, which pulled theology into spiritual wisdom. Aquinas drew this conclusion explicitly in article six of the first question of the *Summa Theologiae.*[13] For Aquinas, knowledge through revelation in Christ, wisdom through the Spirit, and the goal of theology in eternal blessedness in the knowledge of God intersected.[14] If theology fell into the genus of a science, then it was a special science intertwined with spiritual wisdom based on supernatural revelation and principles.

Backing up a bit in history, Anselm of Canterbury (1033–1109), Peter Lombard (d. 1160?), and Bonaventure (d. 1274) further highlight the nature and genus of theology in medieval thought, albeit more indirectly than Aquinas. Anselm's writings followed his general pattern of faith seeking understanding.[15] What he meant was that faith received divine revelation and the established articles of the Christian faith, and then sought prayerfully to understand the reasons behind what one already believed. Thus, in the *Proslogion*, believing that God is both just and

---

10 Thomas Aquinas, *Summa Contra Gentiles*, trans. Lawrence Shapcote (Steubenville, OH: Emaus Academic, 2018), 1:2. Book 1, introduction 2.

11 For Aquinas on friendship with God, see the relevant chapter in Matthew Levering and Gilles Emery, eds., *Aristotle in Aquinas' Theology* (Oxford: Oxford University Press, 2018).

12 Aquinas, *Summa Theologiae*, 3:504. 2a.57.2, ad primum.

13 Aquinas, *Summa Theologiae*, 1:8–10. 1.1.6. The *responsum*, Aquinas noted, "This doctrine is wisdom above all human wisdom; not merely in any one order [*genere*], but absolutely [*simpliciter*]." In his reply to objection three he explained that this was the case because the Holy Spirit was the supernatural origin of sacred doctrine.

14 Aquinas, *Summa Theologiae*, 3:26–27. 2a.2.8, where Aquinas argued that God is man's chief end and happiness to the exclusion of all creatures because God is the chief and highest good.

15 Anselm, *Anselm of Canterbury: The Major Works*, ed. Brian Davies and G. R. Evans, Oxford's World Classics (Oxford: Oxford University Press, 2008), 83 (*Proslogion*).

merciful, he posed ideas on how these two divine attributes consisted with each other, confessing in the end that while he did not know the answer fully, he believed both ideas.[16] Faith receiving divine revelation in devotion to God was essential to true theology, in his view. Making a sharp distinction between faith as content, corresponding to *scientia*, and faith as trust, he wrote, "It is, therefore, possible and suitable enough to say, while the faith that merely believes what it ought to believe is dead the faith that believes in what it ought to believe is alive."[17] Theology was more than right content because faith was more than science, resulting in personal trust in God. Accordingly, in *The Incarnation of the Word,* Anselm added that a corrupt conscience subverted faith, connecting the theologian's character with the nature of theology.[18] Anselm made one more relevant connection in the *Monologion* when treating Christ as the essential wisdom of God, proceeding from the Father eternally by generation.[19] The Son is the Father's eternal Word and Wisdom, who assumed true humanity into his person.[20] While Anselm did not explicitly draw out the connection, which Aquinas and others did, the Son as both the essential wisdom of God and the incarnate wisdom of God, provided a pattern for faith receiving theology as spiritual wisdom communicated from God to believers by the Spirit.

Peter Lombard set the tone for all subsequent medieval theology. Aquinas, Bonaventure, and many others wrote commentaries on Lombard's *Sentences* to teach Christian theology. Even Lambert Daneau (1530–1590) in the Reformed tradition wrote a commentary on the first book of the *Sentences,* illustrating the long-lasting influence of Lombard on Western theology.[21] Lombard aimed to collect the opinions of the fathers (*senetentiae*), harmonizing them in a single book, which opposed errors along the way.[22] Later Reformed authors, most notably John Daille (1594–1670),[23] mimicked this practice, showing patristic precedents for Protestant

16 Anselm, *Works, Proslogion*, 91–94.

17 Anselm, *Works, Monologion*, 78.

18 Anselm, *Incarnation of the Word*, 237.

19 Anselm, 57.

20 Anselm, 249.

21 Lambert Daneau, *In Petri Lombardi Episcopi Parisiensis (qui Magister Sententiarum Appellatur) Librum Primum Sententiarum, Qui Est De Vero Deo, Essentiâ Quidem Uno: Personis Autem Trino: Lamberti Danaei Commentarius Triplex. Unus, Ad Marginem Ipsius Libri, in Quo Singularum Distinctionum Artificium Breviter Explicatur. Alter, Ubi Locorum À Lombardo Prolatorum Accurata Collatio Facta Est. Tertius, Qui Censuram Doctrinae, Methodique Lombardi, Tum Ex Ipso Dei Verbo, Tum Ex Veris Sententiarum Scribendarum Praeceptis Habet* (Genevae: Apud Eustathium Vignon, 1580).

22 Peter Lombard, *The Sentences*, trans. Giulio Silano (Toronto: Pontifical Institute of Mediaeval Studies, 2007), 1:4. Prologue.

23 Jean Daille, *De Usu Patrum Ad Ea Definienda Religionis Capita, Quae Sunt Hodie Controversa, Libri Duo* (Geneva, 1656). For the role of such books on the church fathers in constructing the Reformed system of doctrine, see Byung Soo Han, *Symphonia Catholica: The Merger of Patristic*

doctrine. While Lombard did not address the question of whether theology was *scientia* or *sapientia,* he laid the foundation of his *Sentences* on signs and things, and use and enjoyment (*uti* and *frui*).[24] Though Lombard did not cite the work, dividing theology into signs and things likely came from the *Celestial Hierarchy* of Pseudo-Dionysius. Lombard drew use and enjoyment explicitly from Augustine, as did Aquinas.[25] The Triune God is the focal point of the "things" theology is concerned with, while the "signs" refer to how God reveals himself, with special stress on the sacraments, but not exclusively so. Things enjoyed make us blessed, while things used are means to this blessedness,[26] since we enjoy only those things that have no higher end in view. This meant that the Triune God alone was the only proper object of enjoyment, making everything else means to this end.[27] While Christians enjoyed God both now and in the future, enjoyment belonged properly to the future in the Beatific Vision in which the Trinity would be the highest and unchangeable good.[28] Without answering the question as to whether theology was science or wisdom (or something else), Lombard's primary concern lay clearly in theology as the pursuit of enjoyment of the Triune God in eternal life. Themes related to the Beatific Vision of the Triune God as the end of theology, shaping its character, would resurface in Reformed prolegomena, though it is muted in Hodge.

Bonaventure provides a clear example of the trajectory of medieval thought regarding the connection of theology to knowledge and wisdom. Beginning his *Breviloquium* with Paul's Trinitarian prayer from Ephesians 3:14–19, he introduced theology with a tone of doxology. His prologue began with Scripture as the source of the knowledge of the Triune God, originating from the Father through Christ, with the Holy Spirit flowing into our souls.[29] Scripture has breadth, length, height, and depth. These terms corresponded to the canon of Scripture, to its content (divided into seven ages of the world), to the hierarchy of subcelestial, celestial, and supercelestial things, all related to what we need to know for salvation, and finally to the interpretation of Scripture.[30] The end or fruit of Scripture is "the fullness of everlasting happiness."[31] Scripture encompassed both moral truth and

---

and Contemporary Sources in the Theological Method of Amandus Polanus (1561–1610), vol. 30, Reformed Historical Theology (Göttingen: Vandenhoeck & Ruprecht, 2015).

24 Peter Lombard, *Sentences*, 1:5–6. Bk. 1, dist. 1, cap. 1, paragraphs 1–2. Hereafter numbered citations from Lombard follow this order.

25 Aquinas, *Summa Theologiae*, 3:115–20, 153–158. 2a, questions 11 and 16, respectively.

26 Peter Lombard, *Sentences*, 1:6. 1.1.2.1.

27 Peter Lombard, *Sentences*, 1:6. 1.1.2.4–5.

28 Peter Lombard, *Sentences*, 1:7–8.1.1.2.2–3.

29 Bonaventure, *Breviloquium*, ed. Dominic Monti, vol. 9, Works of St. Bonaventure (New York: The Franciscan Institute, 2005), 2. Prologue, 2.

30 Bonaventure, *Breviloquium*, 9:2–3. Prol. 3.

31 Bonaventure, *Breviloquium*, 9:4. Prol. 4.

speculative knowledge.[32] Contrasting theology and philosophy, Bonaventure noted that theology was a science based on faith in things revealed by the Spirit. Theology was more than science or knowledge because it was concerned "with grace and glory, and even eternal Wisdom."[33] Grace is the knowledge that believers had of God in this life, while glory related to the vision of God in heaven. Theology involved three forms of knowledge: innate, imposed, and infused, which corresponded to nature, Scripture, and grace.[34] The first involved knowledge of God through nature, the second saving knowledge of God through Christ, and the third true mystical knowledge of God by the Spirit. Thus, Theology was "a science founded upon faith as revealed by the Holy Spirit" concerning grace and glory and "Eternal Wisdom."[35] Bonaventure appealed here to Pseudo-Dionysius' division of the knowledge of God into subcelestial (ecclesiastical), celestial (angelic), and supercelestial (divine) hierarchies, with the incarnate Christ as "Hierarch" of the ecclesiastical and angelic hierarchies, and the "the middle person of that supercelestial hierarchy of the Blessed Trinity." Given that his primary division was between the creaturely and the divine, with Jesus Christ being the link between the two, such ideas naturally paved way for Reformed teaching on archetypal and ectypal theology, as well as the theology of union, which we will see and explain below. In summary, Bonaventure divided the knowledge of God into the stages of grace and glory, with Jesus Christ as the central figure in supercelestial, celestial, and subcelestial knowledge of God. Theology was *scientia* based on divine revelation. Yet having eternal happiness in God as its chief end, theology was wisdom as well as knowledge, through the Spirit dwelling in the heart of the theologian.[36] For these reasons, as Dominic Monti notes, Bonaventure taught that theology could not be a science "in the same way

---

32 Bonaventure, *Breviloquium*, 9:6. Prol. Section 1.2. In footnote 11, the translator commented that Aristotle believed that theology was a practical and not merely a speculative science. This allowed room in Aristotelian categories to treat theology as a special science.

33 Bonaventure, *Breviloquium*, 9:12. Prol. Section 3.2. Bonaventure also mentions that the knowledge of God exists in the soul through "Eternal Art," which the editor explains as "the wisdom of God as it exists in the Word, containing in perfection all things that the Father wishes to bring forth in the work of creation."

34 Bonaventure, *Breviloquium*, 9:9. Prol. Section 2.2.

35 Bonaventure, *Breviloquium*, 9:12. Prol. Section 3.2.

36 In section 4 on the interpretation of Scripture, this was why Bonaventure argued that human beings needed more than the literal sense of texts. They needed to know what to believe (allegorical), what to do (tropological), and what to desire in terms of the Beatific Vision (anagogical). *Breviloquium*, 13–16. Reformed authors later shared these goals in their prolegomena, but tended to shift these categories into the uses of Scripture in lieu of the *quadriga*, or fourfold sense.

as other sciences," since it invited people to faith in God's word above rational analysis.[37]

The general picture emerging from this brief sketch of medieval thought on the nature of theology is that theology was either *scientia* (intellectual knowledge), spiritual wisdom, or both. If theology was *scientia,* then it must be in a category of its own, distinguishing it from all other sciences because it rested on supernatural principles. The end of theology was the glory of God, experienced most fully in the Beatific Vision, and the character of the theologian mattered to the study of theology. All of these ideas passed into Reformed orthodoxy, with some modification. Hodge's familiarity with such ideas made his redefinition of theology without mention of the western tradition on this point stand out. Moreover, *scientia* in Latin basically translated into "science" in English, though the meaning of the term changed from an intellectual habit to a method.

3.1.2 A Note About Hodge's Sources

Before tracing the Reformed development of the nature and genus of theology, it is important to trace what sources he was familiar with. Hodge's sources are hard to nail down definitively. For the purposes of this chapter, we do not need to detect every author he relied on, but only to highlight examples of the range of authors he knew, focusing on post-Reformation sources. Hodge cited Aquinas regularly throughout his work, with occasional references to other medieval authors like Lombard.[38] Roman Catholic references regularly included Robert Bellarmine and the Council of Trent, but ranged through John Henry Newman (1801–1890)[39] and the First Vatican Council as well.

With regard to Reformed sources, most secondary literature has noted Hodge's dependence on Francis Turretin.[40] Hodge's references to Turretin are apparent throughout, though often unstated and lying behind the text.[41] Calvin's *Institutes* is

---

37 Bonaventure, *Breviloquium,* 9:xlvi. Bonaventure later associated theological science with wisdom by stating "Thus theology is the only perfect science" because it includes both First Principle and end. It includes the summit and the abyss. 3. "Theology is also the only perfect wisdom" because it begins with the supreme cause of all things and it brings experiential knowledge of God in salvation. Page 28, Part I, Ch. 1.2–3. Citing 1 Tim. 6:3, a key text for later authors like Mastricht in defining theology, Bonaventure added that faith was the foundation of theology as the doctrine according to piety. Page 30, Part I, Ch. 2.3–4.

38 To cite only one example, Charles Hodge, *Systematic Theology* (Grand Rapids, MI: Eerdmans, 1999), 3:53. Representative samples of citations from Aquinas include 3:54, 61, 82.

39 1:106, 124, 127; 3:88, 454, 459, 461, 822.

40 See the chapter in this volume by Paul Gutjahar, for example.

41 Hodge, *Systematic Theology,* 1:138, 370, 402, 468.469, 598–599, 604; 3:3, 61, 100, 145 ("with his characteristic precision"), 853. In the rest of this paragraph, I simply provide examples of where

another obvious influence on Hodge's Reformed identity, explicit references appearing frequently.[42] Additionally, he appealed to post-Reformation Reformed authors like Franciscus Gomarus,[43] Johannes Piscator,[44] Theodore Beza,[45] Johannes Heidegger,[46] Bimius,[47] Jean Daille,[48] Ulrich Zwingli,[49] Johannes Marckius,[50] Bernardinus de Moor,[51] Campegius Vitringa,[52] Samuel Maresius (who inspired Turretin's *Elenctic Theology)*,[53] Andreas Rivetus,[54] Heinrich Bullinger,[55] Wolfgang Musculus,[56] Zacharias Ursinus,[57] John Howe,[58] John Owen,[59] Jonathan Edwards,[60] Solomon Stoddard,[61] Cotton Mather,[62] Leonard Ryssenius,[63] Johannes Alsted,[64] and others. Hodge also included sporadic references to Lutheran authors like Luther,[65] Melanchthon,[66] Quenstedt,[67] Chemnitz,[68] Hollaz,[69] Flaccius Illyricus,[70] Gerhard,[71]

---

author's names appear through volume and page references. While not exhaustive, this list is more extensive than the index included in volume 1 of Hodge's ST.

42 1:191, 194, 409, 462, 466–468, 593, 598, 648; 2:98, 209; 3:3, 23, 80, 90, 100, 131–134, 181, 233, 300, 317, 319, 321, 369, 371, 373, 501, 582, 596, 628–629, 639, 641, 642, 644, 646, 824.

43 3:564.

44 2:209, 620; 3:182, 185, 413.

45 1:556, 559; 3: 413, 608, 853.

46 1:395, 577; 3:395.

47 3:296.

48 3:739.

49 1:409, 592; 3:409, 491, 498, 626, 639.

50 2:211, 3:563.

51 1:19; 2:207, 214; 3:61, 562–563, 566.

52 2:180, 230; 3:146, 337, 562, 563, 566.

53 1:598; 2:98.

54 2:206.

55 3:114, 304, 469.

56 1:409.

57 3:642.

58 1:382; 3:61.

59 1:201, 350; 2:686; 3:3, 61, 131, 146, 147, 155.

60 1:85 (by allusion), 580; 2:207–208, 217; 3:107, 116, 146, 505, 563, 569, 571, 669, 675, 853.

61 3:563.

62 3:568, 572.

63 1:577.

64 1:577.

65 1:466,, 637, 642, 647; 2:98, 103, 324, 414; 3:79–80, 302, 484–485, 504, 661, 853.

66 1:479; 559; 2:180, 324, 720; 3:238, 375, 504.

67 1:156, 370, 373, 384, 386, 391, 402, 599, 601–602; 2:656–657; 3:480, 481, 853.

68 1:632; 3:289, 507.

69 1:370, 325, 581; 2:326, 657; 3: 321, 481, 514, 853.

70 3:6, 23.

71 1:395, 630, 632; 2:180, 624, 632, 645; 3:441, 488–489, 519, 605, 606, 608, 672, 676.

Baier,[72] George Major,[73] and Amsdorf.[74] Among such citations, Quenstedt stands out in terms of number of references. Periodically, Hodge referred Remonstrant authors like Limborch,[75] Episcopius,[76] and Curcellaeus[77] as well.

Though Calvin and Turretin stand out, citations from other Reformed authors are simultaneously sporadic and wide-ranging from early to late orthodoxy, showing Hodge's general familiarity with the post-Reformation Reformed tradition. He likely read and knew more than he cited as well. This enables us to appeal to a large cross-section of Reformed authors to explain Reformed definitions of theology in relation to Hodge's views.

3.1.3 A Sketch of Reformed Orthodoxy

Post-Reformation Reformed theology classified theology as spiritual wisdom more properly than science.[78] Due to Hodge's reliance on Calvin, Calvin is an obvious place to begin. Paul Helm notes that Calvin's *Institutes* primarily focused on theology as wisdom.[79] Beginning with "true and sound wisdom" consisting in knowing God and ourselves, Calvin jumped into his subject matter without asking explicit questions about the nature and genus of theology.[80] While Reformed prolegomena did not develop as a distinct topic until after Calvin's death, in line with Helm's assessment, Calvin's emphasis on wisdom in connection to the knowledge of God would match the tone of Reformed orthodoxy.

To grasp the meaning of Reformed definitions of theology as spiritual wisdom, it is important to situate this topic in the broader trajectory of Reformed orthodox prolegomena. Franciscus Junius (1545–1702) serves a necessary reference point because he wrote the first Reformed prolegomena and set the tone for subsequent

72 2:180; 3:481, 519, 853.

73 3:239.

74 3:239.

75 1:576; 2:97, 327 655, 676; 3:137, 189, 253, 491, 744.

76 1:382; 2:366; 3:189, 253, 594.

77 2:486; 3:191

78 See volume one of Richard A. Muller, *Post-Reformation Reformed Dogmatics: The Rise and Development of Reformed Orthodoxy, Ca. 1520 to Ca. 1725*, 2nd ed., 4 vols. (Grand Rapids, MI: Baker Academic, 2003). [pages].

79 Michael Allen and Scott R. Swain, eds., *The Oxford Handbook of Reformed Theology* (Oxford: Oxford University Press, 2020), 207.

80 John Calvin, *Institutes of the Christian Religion*, ed. John T. McNeill, trans. Ford Lewis Battles, vol. XX–XXI, Library of Christian Classics (Philadelphia: Westminster Press, 1960), 1:35. Bk. 1, cap. 1, paragraph 1.

treatments among Reformed authors.[81] The nature and definitions of theology came early in Junius' book, starting with page one. The material in this section reflects Junius' content generally, incorporating references to later authors analytically rather than chronologically.[82] Beginning with ancient definitions of the term *theologia,* which is admittedly not a biblical term, Junius defined theology as divine and saving wisdom, coming by the illumination of the Spirit, through his promises in Christ, that we might be blessed in God.[83] Following a line from Junius through Peter Ramus, to William Perkins, and William Ames, authors defined theology as *doctrina bene vivendi* and, more commonly, *doctrina Deo vivendi.*[84] The "doctrine of living to God" quickly became the dominant definition of theology. Ames, reflecting Junius, stressed that the doctrine of living to God came only through faith in Christ, produced by the Spirit's work in human hearts.[85] Peter van Mastricht, building explicitly on Ames, defined theology as *doctrina Deo vivendi, per Christum,* incorporating the Holy Spirit into his treatment.[86] Both Ames and Mastricht placed

---

81 Willem J. van Asselt, "The Fundamental Meaning of Theology: Archetypal and Ectypal Theology in Seventeentt-Century Reformed Thought," *Westminster Theological Journal* 64, no. 2 (2002); Franciscus Junius, *A Treatise on True Theology: With the Life of Franciscus Junius,* trans. David C Noe (Grand Rapids, MI: Reformation Heritage Books, 2014). While I will draw largely from the Latin text of Junius below, the translated work cited here includes important historical material together with a reliable translation.

82 Prior to Junius, Andreas Hyperius (1511–1564) laid important groundwork for prolegomena by addressing the proper study of theology and the development of theological method, distinguishing between scholastic and popular theology. See Andreas Hyperius, *De Theologo, Seu, De Ratione Studii Theologici Libri IV* (Basileae, 1559); Andreas Hyperius, *Methodus Theologiae Adj. Eft. De Ejusdem Vita Et Obita Oratis Wigandi Arthii* (Basileae, 1562); Donald Sinnema, "The Distinction Between Scholastic and Popular: Andreas Hyperius and Reformed Scholasticism," in *Protestant Scholasticism: Essays in Reassessment* (Eugene, OR: Wipf & Stock, 2006), 127–44.

83 Franciscus Junius, *De Theologia Vera; Ortu, Natura, Formis, Partibus, Et Modo* (Lugduni Batavorum, 1594), 17.

84 Petrus Ramus, *Commentariorum De Religione Christiana, Libri, Quatuor, Eivsdem Vita a Theophilo Banosio Descripta* (Francofvrti, 1576), 6; William Perkins, *Armilla Aurea, id est, Theologiae Descrpto, Miranda Series Causarum Et Salutis & Damnationis Iuxta Verbum Dei Eius Synopsin Continet Annexa* (Cambridge, 1596), 5; William Ames, *Medulla S.S. Theologiæ, in Fine Adjuncta Est Disputatio De Fidei Divinæ Veritate. Editio Tertia Priori Longe Correctior* (London, 1629), 1. On pg. 2, Ames explained that the doctrine of living to God encompassed living well or blessedly, since living to God alone brought man to his chief end (Bk. 1, Cap. 1, paragraph 8). After noting that Scripture teaches the doctrine of living well, Perkins defined theology as *scientia beati vivendi in aeternum.* This reflects medieval uses of *scientia* in theology, but it slightly out of step with the general Reformed preference for *sapientia.*

85 Ames, *Medulla Theologiae.*

86 Peter van Mastricht, *Theoretico-Practica Theologia. Qua, Per Singula Capita Theologica, Pars Exegetica, Dogmatica, Elenchtica & Practica, Perpetua Successione Conjugantur* (Trajecti ad Rhenum, & Amstelodami: Sumptibus Societatis, 1724). John Owen made a similar Trinitarian move in his treatment of theology. See John Owen, *Theologoumena Pantodapa, Sive, De Natura, Ortu, Progressu,*

saving faith prior to treating the system of doctrine proper, reinforcing the idea that saving faith was prerequisite to studying theology as the doctrine of living to God.[87] Ames argued that the faith by which one believes and faith as the content of what one believes comes first in theology because faith is the first principle and act of spiritual life.[88] Doctrine stressed the content of divine revelation in Scripture, while living to God illustrated the character and effect of sound doctrine on the theologian. For this reason, Ames noted that the perfection of theology was contained in praxis.[89]

Hovering behind this definition of theology was the question as to whether theology was theoretical, practical, or some combination of the two. This again borrowed from medieval treatments of the question. For instance, Aquinas stressed that theology was both theoretical and practical because it involved devout contemplation of God as well as resulting piety and practices.[90] Stressing the beatific vision as the goal of theology, Aquinas argued that theology was more theoretical than practical. This did not mean that theology was primarily an intellectual system, however. As we have seen above, drawing from Augustine's distinction between *uti* and *frui*, Aquinas (and Lombard) argued that God alone was the proper object of enjoyment or delight, while all other things were to be used to enjoy God. His characterization of theology as primarily theoretical did not mean that theology was merely *scientia*, or intellectual knowledge, but that theology aimed at enjoying God above all other results.[91] Among Reformed authors, Johannes Maccovius (1588–1644) appears to have followed Aquinas most closely, contending that theology was primarily theoretical because theoretical knowledge focused on God and led to praxis.[92] Most

Et Studio Veræ Theologiæ, Libri Sex Quibus Etiam Origines & Processus Veri & Falsi Cultus Religiosi, Casus & Instaurationes Ecclesiæ Illustiores Ab Ipsis Rerum Primordiis, Enarrantur (Oxoniæ, 1661), 5–6, 462–463. My description of Owen's trinitarian definition of theology is summary and conclusion primarily of books I and VI of this work. The pages cited are representative.

87 Adriaan C. Neele, *Petrus Van Mastricht (1630–1706) Reformed Orthodoxy: Method and Piety* (Leiden; Boston: Brill, 2009); Ryan M. McGraw, "Petrus van Mastricht and Reformed Orthodoxy," in *Petrus Van Mastricht (1630–1706): Text, Context, and Interpretation*, ed. Adriaan C. Neele, vol. 62, Reformed Historical Theology (Gottingen: Vandenhoeck & Ruprecht, 2020), 19–38.

88 Ames, *Medulla Theologiae*, 4. Bk. 1, Cap. 2, paragraph 4.

89 Ames, 3. "Praxis ista vitae tam perfecte in theologia continetur…" (Bk. 1, Cap. 1, paragraphs 10–12).

90 Aquinas, *Summa Theologiae*, 1:7. 1.1.4, *responsum*.

91 Aquinas, *Summa Theologiae*, 1:7. 1.1.4, *responsum*: "Still, it is more speculative than practical, because it principally leads us to divine things rather than human acts; though it does treat even of these latter things insofar as man is ordained through them to the perfect knowledge of God, in which eternal beatitude consists." Translation is my own. Generally speaking, the categories of theoretical and practical reflected whether one prioritized the intellect or the will in the knowledge of God.

92 Johannes Maccovius, *Loci Communes Theologici* (Amstelodami, 1658), 1. In his first line, Maccovius defined theology as *discplina partim theoretica, partim practica docens modum, bene beateque vivendi in aeternum*. This reflects what we have seen already from Ramus, Perkins, and Ames.

Reformed authors stated instead that theology was both theoretical and practical, though primarily practical due to its connection with living for God.[93] This presentation encompassed the enjoyment of God and true piety on the practical side of the equation, drawing from the theoretical components of theology in order to know and serve the right God in the right way. Functionally, this did not differ from Aquinas, depending on how one defines theory and praxis. Van Mastricht held both sides together tightly by writing a *Theoretico-practia theologia*. Whichever side of the equation one fell on, it is clear that the theoretical and practical components of true theology were inseparable and implied one another. Defining theology as the doctrine of living to God retained both parts by stressing doctrine and living in a single sentence.

A related question that arose was the genus of theology, or what kind of discipline it was. Reformed treatments of this question borrowed Aristotelian categories. [94] Aristotelian influences are perhaps clearest when considering the question of the genus of theology, as well as in Junius' application of fourfold causation in relation to theology.[95] The genus of theology is directly relevant here. These included intellect, scientia, sapientia, prudence/skill, and art.[96] Junius stated simply, "Our definition of theology encompasses all of these simultaneously."[97] Theology, being theoretical and practical, fit the category of spiritual wisdom better than science, partly because it included science. Theology was *sapientia* encompassing *scientia* rather than *scientia* leading to *sapientia*. Turretin, whom Hodge relied on heavily, for this reason wrote, theology *"non est scientia,"* because *scientia* was not broad enough to approximate what such Reformed authors detected in Scripture about the true knowledge of the

93 For example, Johannes Hoornbeeck, *Theologia Practica Pars 1*, 2 vols. (Francofurti & Lipsiae: Bailliar, 1698), chapter 1.

94 For some examples of Aristotelian categories in medieval and early modern Reformed theology, see Levering and Emery, *Aristotle in Aquinas*; Ulrich G. Leinsle, "Sources, Methods, and Forms of Early Modern Theology," in *The Oxford Handbook of Early Modern Theology, 1600–1800*, ed. Ulrich L. Lehner, Richard A. Muller, and A. G. Roeber (Oxford: Oxford University Press, 2016), 25–42; W. J. van Asselt et al., *Introduction to Reformed Scholasticism*, trans. Albert Gootjes (Grand Rapids, MI.: Reformation Heritage Books, 2011).

95 Junius, *Theologia Vera*, chapter 15. Though the focus here is on the efficient cause of *theologia nostra*, dividing the topic into principal and instrumental efficient causation, Junius situated this discussion in broader fourfold causation. Instrumental causation as a subcategory of efficient causation was a theological use of the term not found in Aristotle.

96 Bernardinus De Moor (1709–1780) is a good late orthodoxy example of doing so. Bernardinus de Moor, *Continuous Commentary on Johannes Marckius' Didactico-Elenctic Compendium of Christian Theology*, trans. Stephen Dilday, vol. 1, 7 vols. (Culpeper, VA: L & G Reformation Translation Center, 2014). *Intelligentia* referred to intellectual capacity, *scientia* to actual knowledge, *sapientia* to wisdom, *prudentia* to the practical application of wisdom, and *ars* to an external production. Many theologians collapsed *sapientia* and *prudientia*, while De Moor distinguished them, as did Aquinas.

97 Junius, *A Treatise on True Theology*, 101.

true God.[98] For his reason de Moor expounded theology as spiritual wisdom from John 17:3, from Proverbs, from the commonly cited 1 Corinthians 2, and many other passages in volume 1 of his work. We will see below that Hodge passed over this discussion in silence, including the exegetical process of defining theology, even though he was familiar with the standard sources. Moreover, his use of "science" had taken on a meaning differing greatly from Turretin's, since science came to mean Baconian scientific induction instead of a genus or intellectual habit.

Wedded to this discussion of the genus of theology was the issue of different kinds of theology. The two primary divisions of theology were archetypal and ectypal theology. Junius, and most Reformed authors, defined archetypal theology as God's omniscience, or knowledge of himself in all things in relation to himself.[99] Archetypal theology was uncreated, incomprehensible, and incommunicable to creatures. This point secured divine transcendence in unsurpassable ontological and epistemological divide between the Creator and the creature. Creaturely theology was labeled ectypal theology. Creatures made in God's image could receive knowledge of God through divine revelation in a way that was analogous to God in some measure, without using terms about God univocally or equivocally.[100] While creatures could not comprehend God, they could apprehend him or lay hold of him through divine revelation.[101] They could know him truly without knowing exhaustively, as he knows himself. Junius described ectypal theology as the wisdom of divine things informed by God as the archetype from the communication of grace towards glory itself.[102] It is noteworthy that some Dutch Reformed orthodox authors diverged from these definitions of archetypal and ectypal theology, resulting in an alternative strand of thought. Johannes Cloppenberg (1592–1652) redefined archetypal theology as divine revelation in Scripture, and ectypal theology as our approach to the

98 Francis Turretin, *Institutio Theologiae Elencticae*, vol. 1, 3 vols. (Geneva, 1679). In this regard, the English translation of Turretin to the effect that theology "is not knowledge," can prove misleading in a seventeenth century context. Vol.1:19; 1.6.5. The full statement is, "It is not knowledge because it is not founded upon the evidence of reason, but only upon testimony."

99 Junius, *Theologia Vera*, 29; Amandus Polanus, *Syntagma Theologiae Christianae Ab Amando Polano a Polansdorf: Juxta Leges Ordinis Methodici Conformatum, Atque in Libros Decem Digestum Jamque Demum in Unum Volumen Compactum, Novissime Emendatum* (Hanoviae, 1610), 10–11. Junius wrote that archetypal theology is *nimirum Dei ipsius sapientia*, and that, as such, it is uncreated and eternal. Polanus similarly wrote that archetypal theology is *sapientia rerum divinarum, in Deo residens, essentialis ipsi et increata.*

100 Junius, *Theologia Vera*, 31; Polanus, *Syntagma Theologiae Christianae*, 11.

101 Ames, *Medulla Theologiae*, 10. Cap. 4.2.

102 Junius, *Theologia Vera*, 38; Polanus, *Syntagma Theologiae Christianae*, 12. Polanus lifted his definition verbatim from Junius without citation, illustrating Junius' formative influence on subsequent generations.

biblical pattern of theology.[103] Later authors like Johannes Marckius (1656–1731) and Bernardinus de Moor (1709–1780) continued in this vein.[104] This redefinition shifted the question away from the distinction and relationship between the Creator and the creature to the relationship between Scripture and the theologian. While this point is worthy of further investigation, this alternative strand of Reformed thought passed down to Hodge's time, for example in the writings of James Henley Thornwell (1812–1862), with whom Hodge often clashed ideological swords.[105] Yet Hodge again bypassed this discussion entirely in his definition of theology as science.

The distinction between archetypal and ectypal theology next led to further subdivisions of ectypal theology, moving from the highest instances to the lowest. The highest kind of ectypal theology was the *theologia unionis,* which was the incarnate Christ's knowledge of God.[106] Christ's knowledge of the Father was simultaneously uncreated and created, archetypal and ectypal. As the eternal Son, he shared divine omniscience, but as the incarnate Son, he became the pattern for creaturely ectypal knowledge of God. Christ's creaturely knowledge of God came by the Holy Spirit dwelling in him.[107] Jesus was the pattern towards which the same Spirit drove believes by dwelling and working in them. Christ's knowledge of God was the goal of theology, while remaining unique due to the hypostatic union of the two natures in one person. Thus, *theologia unionis* referred to the union of natures in Christ in relation to his knowledge of God, rather than to the believer's knowledge of God through union with Christ, though the indwelling Spirit was the link between Christ's knowledge of God and theirs. Next came the beatific vision (*theologia beatorum*), which was the highest degree of the knowledge of God for Christians, and the goal of true theology.[108] This set an eschatological tone at the outset of Reformed orthodox prolegomena, even as it reflected medieval precedents

---

103 Johannes Cloppenburg, *Exercitationes Super Locos Communes Theologicos* (Franekerae, 1653). Unfortunately this work is unpaginated, but this discussion is in the first chapter.

104 Johannes Marckius, *Compendium Theologiae Christianae Didactico Elencticum: Immixtis Problematibus Plurimis & Quaestionibus Recentioribus Adauctum* (Amstelodami, 1696); de Moor, *Continuous Commentary on Marckius.*

105 James Henley Thornwell, *The Collected Writings of James Henley Thornwell: Volume One Theological,* ed. John B. Adger, vol. 1 (Birmingham, AL: Solid Ground Christian Books, 2004), 28–29.

106 Polanus, *Syntagma Theologiae Christianae*, 62–63.

107 Polanus, *Syntagma*, 63.

108 Junius, *Theologia Vera*, 42. Junius divided ectypal theology into union (the incarnate Christ), vision (beatific vision), and revelation (*theologia nostra*). Medieval precedent included the *theologia angelorum*, following Pseudo-Dionysius's division of theology into supercelestial (God), celestial (angels), and subcelestial (human beings) knowledge of God. Some Reformed authors followed suit on this point.

set by Lombard, Aquinas, and Bonaventure.[109] The lowest level of ectypal theology was *theologia viatorum*, or *theologia nostra*. This referred to the knowledge of God believers possessed in this life on the way to the beatific vision. Present knowledge of God by the Spirit in union with Christ was of the same kind of knowledge as the beatific vision, though in a lesser degree. Polanus described *theologia viatorum* as coming from Christ, through the Holy Spirit leading believers by gracious communication, incrementally illuminating them in the contemplation of God and divine things. Such theology rested on divinely inspired revelation through the Prophets and Apostles.[110] It was fundamentally Trinitarian as well. In summary, Reformed orthodoxy maintained that theology was the doctrine of living to God, which is spiritual wisdom, aiming towards the highest degree of ectypal theology in the beatific vision, with Christ as its pattern, and the Spirit as the link between believers and Christ.

The final component and capstone of classic Reformed prolegomena related to the ends of theology and the character of the theologian. The highest end of theology was the glory of God, while the subordinate end of theology was the salvation of the elect.[111] This is why the Westminster Shorter and Larger Catechisms began by stating that man's "chief and highest end was to glorify God and fully to enjoy him forever." Enjoying God was not the primary end of theology, but was related to it integrally. This meant that the character of the theologian mattered in the true study of true theology. Theology was the doctrine of living to God. It required spiritual wisdom from Spirit-filled theologians. John Owen (1616–1683) went so far to say that someone who understood the system of doctrine taught in Scripture yet was devoid of the indwelling Spirit was a philosopher rather than a theologian.[112]

Most of the points treated above show continuity with key components of medieval prolegomena. This makes Hodge's treatment of the nature and genus of theology below all the more striking, since he omitted most of these questions. This leads us to spell out Hodge's presentation of theology as a science, and then to explore some of the contextual reasons informing it.

---

109 This is evident in Polanus, who treated man's highest good in chapter 5, man's blessedness in union with God in chapter 6, the incarnate Christ's knowledge of God in chapter 7, and the *theologia beatorum* in chapter 8, concluded by *theologia viatorum seu nostra* in chapter 9.

110 Polanus, *Syntagma Theologiae Christianae*, 67–68.

111 Junius, *Theologia Vera*. Cap. 16.

112 Owen, *Theologoumena Pantodapa*, 467: "...Philosophicos Christianos censemus non Theologicos Evangelicos." For similar assertions, see de Moor, *Continuous Commentary*, 1:175.

3.2 Hodge's Prolegomena and Theological Science

When one turns to Hodge's prolegomena, the topics he covers (or does not) is striking in relation to the material above. Similarities and differences stand out even in the table of contents. This section will explain Hodge's definition of theology, and the next will give some possible reasons as to why he treated the material the way he did.

3.2.1 The Scope of Hodge's Prolegomena

Surveying the scope of Hodge's prolegomena provides readers with a reference point for his treatment of theology as a science. The six chapters comprising his prolegomena encompass method, theology, rationalism, mysticism, Roman Catholic views of the rule of faith, and the Protestant rule of faith. The first two chapters, spanning roughly thirty-three pages, correspond most nearly to Junius more than two-hundred-page treatment of prolegomena. In six sections, chapter one ("On Method") explores theology as a science, theological method, speculative, mystical, and inductive methods, and Scripture. "Inductive method" reflects key aspects of the effects of shifting views of science on Hodge's treatment of theology as a science, since he indicated that induction was tied to the theologian being "governed by [the] same rules as a man of science," and that "the Scriptures contain all the facts of the theology."[113] Note again the shift in *scientia,* translated into "science," from a genus of knowledge to am investigative method. This point will come to foreground when explaining some historical background to nineteenth century scientific method below. His second chapter ("Theology") is subdivided into the nature and definition of theology and natural theology, the revelation of God in the facts of nature, the insufficiency of natural theology for theological science, and Christian theology and its loci. The sections on rationalism and mysticism addressed pressing philosophical and theological trends in Hodge's day. Treating the Roman Catholic rule of faith paved the way to addressing the relationship between Scripture and church tradition, concluding his prolegomena with a chapter establishing Scripture as the sole rule of faith in Protestantism. Theology as a science suffuses this material, with indicators of nineteenth century views of science and scientific method and post-Enlightenment philosophical and religious concerns lying on the surface.[114]

Hodge's treatment of natural theology and supernatural theology in chapters two and six correspond roughly to Junius' tenth and eleventh topics. While Hodge

---

113 Charles Hodge, *Systematic Theology*, 3 vols. (Grand Rapids, MI: Eerdmans, 1999), 1:vii.

114 See the chapter in this volume on Hodge on philosophy.

implicitly treated Scripture as the principium cognoscendi of theology,[115] he largely bypassed God as its *principium essendi,* arguing later from theism generally to Christian theism particularly in the first five chapters on Theology proper. Like Turretin and others, Hodge addressed the use of reason in matters of faith in the fifth section of chapter three, asserting that "reason must judge the credibility of revelation," in contrast to his Reformed predecessors who argued that the nature of faith is to receive the testimony of another.[116] Archetypal and ectypal theology, including the eschatological beatific vision with its Christological and Pneumatological emphases, was missing entirely, as were questions related to the genus and causes of theology. This broad overview invites us to examine the content of his first two chapters more carefully as we seek to understand what Hodge taught about theological science and method before stepping back to explain why he likely did so.

3.2.2 Hodge's Treatment of Theology as Inductive Science

Hodge began his *Systematic Theology* treating science rather than theology itself. Every science, he argued, included "facts and ideas."[117] Facts led to more than mere knowledge, because "[science] must embrace an exhibition of the internal relation of those facts, one to another, and each to all."[118] Hodge assumed without argumentation that theology was a science and that it must follow the methods

---

115 Hodge, *Systematic Theology,* 1:152.

116 Hodge, *Systematic Theology,* 1:vii; For a standard Reformed orthodox viewpoint on the nature of faith in relation to revelation, see John Owen, *The Reason of Faith, or, an Answer Unto That Enquiry, Wherefore We Believe the Scripture to Be the Word of God with the Causes and Nature of That Faith Wherewith We Do so: Wherein the Grounds Whereon the Holy Scripture Is Believed to Be the Word of God with Faith Divine and Supernatural, Are Declared and Vindicated* (London, 1677). Yet Hodge still noted that the nature of faith was to receive testimony (1:41). While his concern was here that Christians believe things that they cannot comprehend, his assertion still follows a rational ground for believing in the authority of Scripture. Faith thus receives testimony only after reason establishes that testimony. However, Hodge maintained that rational demonstration cannot ultimately be the ground of faith (1:42). The question is whether his grounding theology in scientific induction was consistent with his Reformed views on the nature of faith. For gradual shifts in Reformed orthodoxy on this point in the early Enlightenment period see the chapter on Baxter, Bates, and Howe in Dewey D. Wallace, *Shapers of English Calvinism, 1660–1714: Variety, Persistence, and Transformation* (New York: Oxford University Press, 2011).

117 Hodge, *Systematic Theology,* 1:1. Bozeman notes that the method of scientific induction in biblical interpretation and theology "reached its ultimate expression" in Hodge's Systematic Theology where he used the term "fact" or its equivalent twenty-seven times in the first three pages. Theodore Dwight Bozeman, *Protestants in an Age of Science: The Baconian Ideal and Antebellum American Religious Thought* (Chapel Hill: University of North Carolina Press, 1977), 147.

118 Hodge, *Systematic Theology,* 1:1.

common to natural science. Science, in his view, was always a systematic endeavor, adding that the Bible is no more a system of theology "than nature is a system of chemistry or mechanics."[119] While biblical theology gathered the facts of Scripture, systematic theology, as a science, determined the relationship between biblical facts, showing the harmony and consistency of the whole. He concluded, "This is not an easy task, or one of slight importance."[120] He asserted that the reason why God gave the Bible as a collection of facts rather than as a scientific system was that the human mind by nature could not be satisfied with receiving pre-digested and pre-organized facts.[121] The bottom line was, "What is true of other sciences is true of theology."[122] As God gave scientific facts in nature for human beings to discover the laws relating them, so he did in Scripture. Hodge added that NT epistles provided partial models for systematizing biblical facts, noting that the theologian's task was to augment and complete these models in light of the whole Bible.[123]

Several assumptions lay behind Hodge's assertions. First, scientific method was paramount, and science addressed facts and the interrelationship between the ideas drawn from those facts. Second, the systematic ordering of facts was natural to the human mind, at least from nineteenth century perspective, and scientific method in theology was a given. Third, theology must be a science because genuine knowledge is largely scientific. While Aristotelian categories provided Reformed orthodox authors with several options regarding the nature and genus of theology, Hodge worked with two only. Either theology was a science, or it was a vague sense of dependence and religious experience, exemplified by Friedrich Schleiermacher (1768–1834) and other pantheistic theologies and philosophies of the day.

With these assumptions in hand, Hodge next treated theological method. He noted that since every science had its own method proper to its nature, it was vital to start with a right method.[124] He assumed, however, that like natural science, theological method followed scientific "induction." In his view, scientific induction was based on two ideas: that laws of nature exist, giving unity to the facts studied; and that "those laws are uniform."[125] Rather than starting with God and divine revelation as Turretin and other did, he built his method on the assumption of

119 Hodge, *Systematic Theology*, 1:1.

120 Hodge, *Systematic Theology*, 1:2.

121 Similarly, see A. A. Hodge, *Outlines of Theology* (Edinburgh: Banner of Truth Trust, 1999), 22. "The human mind must seek unity in all its knowledge."

122 Hodge, *Systematic Theology*, 1:2. So John Dick (1764–1833), a Scottish Presbyterian theologian, wrote that in dogmatic or didactic theology, "the theologian proceeds in the same manner as a teacher of any other science." John Dick, *Lectures on Theology* (Stoke-on-Trent: Tentmaker Publications, 2004), 1:6.

123 Hodge, *Systematic Theology*, 1:3; Dick, *Lectures on Theology*, 7.

124 Hodge, *Systematic Theology*, 1:3.

125 Hodge, *Systematic Theology*, 1:4.

the uniform order of nature.[126] Since theology involved the mind and ideas, he added the mind had permanent fixed laws as did matter. He examined three approaches to these mental laws: the speculative, the mystical, and the inductive, all of which, he noted, have "prevailed in the church."[127] Frist, speculative method began with a priori assumptions. This method could be rationalistic, dogmatic, or transcendental. Deism represented the first by beginning with moral axioms drawn from the human mind alone.[128] In Hodge's view, dogmatic assumptions reduced the teaching of Scripture to a coherent a priori philosophical system. The "schoolmen" represented this approach, beginning with Anselm's *Cur Deus Homo,* who was the "father of scholastic theology."[129] Hodge added that Christian Wolff (1679–1754) and Gottfried Leibnitz (1646–1716) followed this pattern in their own way. He likely had in mind the semi-Cartesian ideas of these philosophers, who sought to begin with basic assumptions about existence and the perfection of the universe rather than coming to conclusions through inductive scientific reasoning. He was concerned that they deduced religion from reason, sometimes overthrowing Scriptural doctrines.[130] Given that Hodge rooted his own scientific method in the assumption of natural laws, it is hard to see how his starting point differed substantially from the models he classed as rationalism. This does not mean that Hodge was a rationalist, but it reflects some of the reasons why Mark Noll questioned how consistently Hodge could wed his piety with his appropriations of Baconian scientific assumptions.[131]

Second, mystical theology made theology a matter of feeling instead of thought. He countered that our moral nature followed laws as well as reason, and that moral

126 Behind this assumption of the laws of the mind and of nature stood Hodge's appropriation of Common Sense Realism. Jennings Ligon Duncan, "Common Sense Realism and American Presbyterianism: An Evaluation of the Impact of Scottish Realism on Princeton and the South" (Covenant Theological Seminary, 1987); Owen Anderson, *Reason and Faith in the Theology of Charles Hodge: American Common Sense Realism* (New York: Palgrave Macmillan, 2014). For an explanation of this theme, see the chapter in this present volume on Hodge's philosophy.

127 Hodge, *Systematic Theology*, 1:4.

128 Hodge, *Systematic Theology*, 1:4.

129 Hodge, *Systematic Theology*, 1:5. Defining scholastic method can be difficult. For a study that roots scholasticism much earlier in church history, see the excellent study by Ulrich G. Leinsle, *Introduction to Scholastic Theology*, trans. Michael J. Miller (Washington, D.C.: Catholic University of America Press, 2010). However, in his introduction to Bonaventure's *Breviloquium*, Dominic Monti assumes that Anselm as the father of scholastic theology is an accepted idea (xxviii).

130 Hodge, *Systematic Theology*, 1:5. Hodge included Transcendentalism in this critique of the speculative method.

131 W. Andrew Hoffecker, *Charles Hodge: The Pride of Princeton.* (Phillipsburg, NJ: P & R Publishing, 2011), 10. "I am not as convinced as Hoffecker seems to be that Hodge's piety, theology, and method functioned smoothly together."

nature is "supreme in the soul."[132] Though Hodge did not mention Schleiermacher here, he consistently expressed concern throughout his work about Schleiermacher's reduction of religion to religious feeling.[133] Hodge asserted that if we relegated "mysticism" to the supernatural illumination of the Spirit, then this view would be true and admitted "by all Evangelical Christians."[134] The problem was that mysticism made revelation and inspiration "figments," denuding the Bible of its infallible authority. Christianity became a life instead of a doctrine, theologians interpreting their own consciousness' instead of Scripture.[135] Underlying Hodge's critique both of dogmatism and mysticism was the idea that both undercut the scientific method of investigating Scripture. The former because dogmatic assumptions prevented one from following the facts of Scripture wherever they led, and the latter by shifting the facts of theology away from Scripture.[136]

Hodge's third category of theological investigation, induction, revealed the heart of his scientific method. He asserted without argumentation that induction in theology "agrees in everything essential" with the inductive method as applied to natural science.[137] As we saw above, Reformed orthodoxy believed that theology was rooted in Spirit-wrought faith receiving divine testimony, with which Hodge agreed. However, his intellectual world was shaped by the scientific revolution, with inductive reasoning from facts being the primary means of obtaining knowledge[138] Adding complexity to such methodological assumptions, Hodge still maintained the idea of saving faith resting on divine testimony for the true knowledge of God.[139] The question is whether his treatment of theology strictly along the lines of modern scientific induction harmonized well with his Reformed views of saving faith and regeneration. Faith received divine revelation based on assumed axioms,

---

132 Hodge, *Systematic Theology*, 1:7.

133 E. g., Hodge, *Systematic Theology*, 1:21, 65, 173, 202.

134 Hodge, *Systematic Theology*, 1:7.

135 Hodge, *Systematic Theology*, 1:8–9.

136 This contrast between dogmatism and mysticism as two opposite extremes, with induction as the preferred method, is remarkably similar to Francis Bacon's introduction to his *Novum Organum*, in which he sought to outline a new scientific method. Francis Bacon, *Novum Organum, or, True Suggestions for the Interpretation of Nature* (London, 1844), 1. I will treat the effects of the scientific revolution on Hodge's views of theology below.

137 Hodge, *Systematic Theology*, 1:9.

138 For background on the scientific revolution beyond Europe, see Lawrence M. Principe, *The Scientific Revolution: A Very Short Introduction* (Oxford: Oxford University Press, 2011); William E. Burns, *The Scientific Revolution in Global Perspective* (New York: Oxford University Press, 2016). Scientific method will appear later in this chapter.

139 E. g., Hodge, *Systematic Theology*, 1:41.

while scientific induction aimed to develop axioms only after the patient process of inductive experimentation.[140]

The fifth section in Hodge's first chapter illustrates his understanding of scientific induction generally, and its particular application to theological science in several ways. Frist, science assumed the following: the reliability of sense perception (contra David Hume, without citing him),[141] the trustworthiness of mental operations, and the certainty of truths embedded in the constitution of our nature and not learned by experience (i. e., innate ideas). His primary example was the assumed relation of effects to causes. Rather than refuting Hume, Hodge assumed that denying that normal human beings could not live with denying the connection of causes and effects. Second, proceeding on these grounds, the student of science gathered and combined facts, without imposing preconceived interpretations on them.[142] Third, scientists deduced the laws undergirding the facts that they had collected. Such laws then became reliable assumptions that could inform further investigation.[143] Hodge argued that these laws were not human constructions imposed on the facts of nature, but that they were present in nature itself, waiting for discovery. Axioms followed rather than preceded induction, yet once discovered, they informed further induction.[144]

Hodge adapted these three principles to studying theology, stating bluntly, "The Bible is to the theologian what nature is to the man of science. It is his store-house of facts."[145] First, he assumed laws of belief "which God has impressed upon our nature." This included things like the idea that God cannot require anything contrary to virtue and that sin deserves punishment. Yet we cannot merely assume such things as "first truths" incapable of proof or testing, since "laws of belief" must stand the test of "universality and necessity."[146] This meant that "laws of belief" must be self-evident truths that force themselves on the mind of "every intelligent creature."[147] At first glance, Hodge's first plank of theological science raises questions as to whether

---

140 Bacon, *Novum Organum, or, True Suggestions for the Interpretation of Nature*, 12. Aphorism 18.

141 Hodge took Hume's denial of sense perception to task explicitly elsewhere. E.g., Hodge, *Systematic Theology*, 1:43, 60, 178, 203.

142 Hodge, *Systematic Theology*, 1:9. "He must take them as they are."

143 Hodge, *Systematic Theology*, 1:10. "It is in this way that the vast body of modern science has been built up."

144 By contrast, southern Presbyterian minister, John Girardeau (1825–1898), argued that theology rested on faith judgments rather than induction. Therefore, axioms "are not *inferred* from the data of consciousness: they are themselves the data of consciousness." John L. Girardeau, *Discussions of Theological Questions*, ed. George A. Blackburn (Harrisonburg, VA: Sprinkle Publications, 1986), 32. Hodge's assessment agreed more with that of Bacon mentioned above.

145 Hodge, *Systematic Theology*, 1:10.

146 Hodge, *Systematic Theology*, 1:10.

147 Hodge, *Systematic Theology*, 1:11.

the standard principia of Reformed orthodoxy, namely God and revelation, could still constitute the axioms from which proceeded all other things, and on which faith rested. Second, like natural scientists, Christian theologians must collect facts, though facts revealed and contained in the Bible. The Word gave a clearer revelation of God's truth in nature, making the Bible "the norm and the standard" of religious experience.[148] While Hodge believed that the Spirit's work went beyond nature, the effects of the Spirit's work in people remained subject to scientific investigation in theology.[149] The third point reinforced his opening statement: "the theologian must be guided by the same rules in the collection of facts, as govern the man of science."[150] This required diligence and care in handling facts accurately, with as comprehensive a collection of facts as possible. He illustrated the point with the doctrine of Christ's incarnation, showing that the anti-Trinitarian Faustus Socinus (1539–1604) did not take all of the facts into account, resulting in heresies on the Trinity and the atonement.[151] While Francis Bacon (1561–1626) regarded his inductive scientific method as "an entirely different course" and "new" in the early seventeenth century,[152] the scientific revolution had become so thorough in Hodge's day that he could largely assume its validity in theology.[153]

Hodge's depiction of induction in theology raises the question whether a theological scientist could understand fully and account for all of the facts in Scripture. In light of divine incomprehensibility, could a theologian obtain a "comprehensive" view of the facts in Scripture? Did this model allow a theologian to remain consistent when saying, "I don't know?" After all, Hodge stressed "complete induction" of the biblical facts.[154] His concern was that we must take facts in Scripture as they are, and take them all into account.[155] While this shared the aim of earlier authors to see the "consent of all the parts, and scope of the whole" in Scripture,[156] one wonders whether the kind of "complete" view of all of the parts of Scripture that Hodge seemed to advocate was possible for theologians on the way who have not yet reached the beatific vision. The partial character of ectypal theology, with its focus on the *theologia unionis* and the *theologia beatorum* was the Reformed orthodox

---

148 Hodge, *Systematic Theology*, 1:11.

149 Hodge, *Systematic Theology*, 1:11.

150 Hodge, *Systematic Theology*, 1:11.

151 Hodge, *Systematic Theology*, 1:12.

152 Bacon, *Novum Organum, or, True Suggestions for the Interpretation of Nature*, 5, 16.

153 Theodore Bozeman argued persuasively in chapter 1 of his work on scientific view among American Presbyterian authors that Baconian induction was mediated to American Presbyterianism through Scottish Common Sense Realism. Bozeman, *Protestants in an Age of Science*. See Aza Goudriaan's chapter in this present volume for more details on Hodge's inherited philosophical ideas.

154 Hodge, *Systematic Theology*, 1:12.

155 Hodge, *Systematic Theology*, 1:13.

156 Westminster Larger Catechism 4.

answer to this problem, yet Hodge bypassed such categories.[157] It is one thing to search Scripture harmonizing the parts into a coherent whole. It is another thing to say that the theologian must account for all of the parts in a "comprehensive" way. Hodge clearly maintained divine incomprehensibility, not requiring exhaustive knowledge of God in order to know him truly.[158] Yet such descriptions of complete or comprehensive induction at least raise questions about consistency of language that is worthy of more attention.

Hodge added a fourth point, relating induction to biblical facts, opening with an illustration. Just as principles of magnetism are deduced from natural facts, so theologians must not impose presupposed doctrines on Scripture, but they must deduce such things from Scripture.[159] They must "exhibit" God's system of truth rather than their own, deriving a philosophy from the Bible rather than imposing one onto it. The "fundamental principle" of all sciences is that "theory is to be determined by facts, and not facts by theory."[160] Echoing Bacon again, he noted that natural science was chaos and theology was speculation before the principle of induction became dominant in both.[161] *Scientia* was no longer a genus, but an assumed method of investigating facts. While this observation involves a bit of equivocation related to *scientia* and science, such equivocation reflected a genuine historical shift in terminology. Philosophy and methods had changed, and Hodge's treatment of theology began with science, instead of with the question of the genus of theology in light of its theoretical and practical nature. Without evaluating whether this shift was good or bad, it is important to take note of it. Section six of Hodge's prolegomena expanded his treatment of inductive method to the facts of Scripture in more detail, but one point bolsters the observations in this paragraph. Building on the Spirit's inward testimony, instilling unshakable confidence in Scripture, Hodge argued that some people have mistaken theologies of the head with a sound knowledge of God in their hearts.[162] This was his way of saying that people could know God across denominational lines while making

---

157 While it is possible that he assumed rather than bypassed these categories, the material below shows that most nineteenth century Reformed authors did indeed omit the older familiar paths of Reformed prolegomena.

158 For example, "By knowledge is meant, not full comprehension of its object, but a firm belief of what is true on appropriate grounds addressed to our reason." Charles Hodge, "Can God Be Known?," *Biblical Repertory and Theological Review* 36, no. 1 (1864): 144. Thanks to John Fesko for directing me to this reference.

159 Hodge, *Systematic Theology*, 1:13.

160 Hodge, *Systematic Theology*, 1:14.

161 Hodge, *Systematic Theology*, 15; Bacon, *Novum Organum, or, True Suggestions for the Interpretation of Nature*, 11. Bacon wrote in aphorism 11, "As the present sciences are useless for the discovery of effects, so the present system of logic is useless for the discovery of the sciences."

162 Hodge, *Systematic Theology*, 1:16.

intellectual mistakes in their inductive reasoning.[163] While earlier authors might have said that such people knew theology as spiritual wisdom to a greater or lesser degree, Hodge's scientific inductive method led him to posit two different kinds of theology. The theology of the heart was potentially a different kind of theology than theological science, though the two should ideally harmonize. Piety was conjoined with theological science, without being an essential part of theological induction.[164] Ideological winds had shifted indeed.[165]

In spite of the clarity of his first chapter, Hodge devoted chapter two to the definition of theology as a science more directly. Beginning by noting that his preceding chapter was enough to show what theology is, the topic was important enough to him to say more. Hodge asserted first that it was "obviously true" that the truths or facts in the Bible presented their own arrangement, just as the facts of natural science did.[166] Underscoring his "comprehensive" view of scientific facts, he added that theologians must adopt an entire system of thought, illustrating with the example that either the Augustinian system is true, or the Romanist or Remonstrant system is. On the surface, this idea stands in tension with the more eclectic approach of Reformed orthodox theologians to their sources.[167] After all, Augustine was useful to these authors on free will, divine sovereignty, and human sin, but not so much on the perseverance of the saints, ecclesiology, and baptism.

163 Hodge, *Systematic Theology*, 1:17.

164 An example of Hodge's concern for character as it affected theology is Charles Hodge, "Suggestions of Theological Students, on Some of Those Traits of Character, Which the Spirit of the Age Renders Peculiarly Important in the Ministers of the Gospel," *Biblical Repertory and Theological Review* 5 (1833): 100–113. He argued that theologians needed a sacred regard for God's truth, a sacred regard for their moral obligations, activity in doing good, and "unusual mental discipline and furniture," and "a spirit of elevated piety" (112).

165 It is admittedly difficulty to covey the historical nuances of this point. Slight discontinuity on defining theology as science does not mean no continuity. For instance, B. B. Warfield, who studied under Hodge, defended theology as a science following scientific method, but he added, "As long as we remain in the region of the pure intellect we remain out of the proper region of Theology" because theological science appealed to man's religious nature. B. B. Warfield, "Theology a Science," in *Selected Shorter Writings of Benjamin B. Warfield*, vol. 2 (Phillipsburg, NJ: P&R, 2001), 212. Hodge held a similar viewpoint. The main historical developments were that Enlightenment scientific methodology carried over into theology, and that spiritual wisdom no longer took precedence over science in systematic theology. Warfield illustrated this well in the same essay when he divided 2 Timothy 3:15–17 in half in relation to systematic and practical theology. Systematic theology could "make one wise," while practical theology was "for salvation" (209). For a similar construction, see Dick, *Lectures*, 1:8.

166 Hodge, *Systematic Theology*, 1:18.

167 John Fesko argues at length that this quest for a comprehensive self-consistent worldview was itself a nineteenth and twentieth century phenomenon. J. V. Fesko, *Reforming Apologetics: Retrieving the Classic Reformed Approach to Defending the Faith* (Grand Rapids, MI: Baker Academic, 2019).

Hodge himself was more eclectic in using historic Christian sources and systems than his "comprehensive" inductive method might appear to allow at first glance as well. Hodge added that one vital thing distinguishing theological science from other sciences was that Scripture presented facts not available through nature.[168]

Hodge's survey of alternative definitions of theology is particularly illuminating in relation to Reformed orthodox treatments of the subject. Like them, Hodge began with ancient authors like Orpheus, Homer, and Aristotle, who said that theology was "a discourse concerning God."[169] However, rather than noting the insufficiency of this definition, Hodge accepted its general validity. Notably absent is any attempt to define the term from Scripture, which theologians like de Moor did at length. This exegetical material was what led most Reformed authors to conclude that theology was *sapientia* rather than *scientia.* In spite of Hodge's appeal to the vital importance of Scripture in theology, he largely relegated his treatment of theology as a science to intuition or common sense. Option two in Hodge's list was "the science of the supernatural."[170] The defect of this definition, in his view, was that it reduced theological science to pneumatology and its psychological implications. Citing Richard Hooker's *Ecclesiological Polity,* he noted that Hooker defined theology as "the science of divine things."[171] However, Hooker's definition likely reflected a Thomistic background in which Aquinas defined theology as a special kind of science, as noted above. Hodge merely noted ambiguity in "divine things." Third, Hodge flagged theology as "the science of religion" as a more common current definition. Citing Schleiermacher among others, he concluded that this definition lacked value due to competing understandings of the meaning of religion.[172] His great fear was that studying theology as religion would result in detaching theology from the Bible in favor of mere religious experience.[173] Aristotelian categories of *intelligentia, scientia, sapientia, prudentia,* and *ars* are missing. Moreover, other than Hooker, Hodge did not cite any early modern Protestant authors on defining theology. This omission is glaring considering his extensive uses of such sources elsewhere in his *Systematic Theology.* Definitions two and three targeted nineteenth century concerns rather than the Christian tradition.

In light of the failure of these definitions, Hodge concluded that we are relegated to defining theology as, "the science of the facts of divine revelation so far as those facts concern the nature of God and our relation to him, as his creatures, as sinners,

168 Hodge, *Systematic Theology*, 1:19.

169 Hodge, *Systematic Theology*, 1:19.

170 Hodge, *Systematic Theology*, 1:19.

171 Hodge, *Systematic Theology*, 1:20.

172 So later Princeton professor Benjamin Breckinridge Warfield, "The Task and Method of Systematic Theology," in *The Works of Benjamin B. Warfield*, vol. 9 (Grand Rapids, MI: Baker Books, 2003), 96.

173 Hodge, *Systematic Theology*, 1:21.

and as the subjects of redemption."[174] Theology as *doctrina Deo vivendi*, or, *doctrina bene vivendi* did not come into the conversation, even though he believed that God's glory and living to God were the ends of theology. Hodge appeared to treat such older definitions as irrelevant to the questions he faced in his own context, bypassing the Reformed orthodox tradition without comment. Junius, whose work shaped generations of Reformed prolegomena, is conspicuously absent in all three volumes of Hodge's *Systematic Theology*. The closest Hodge came to connecting the definition of theology to spiritual wisdom was, when treating the Trinity, he noted that "truth is in order to holiness."[175] This statement echoes 1 Timothy 6:3, which Mastricht and others cited to argue that theology was the doctrine of living to God. It is possible that one reason behind this fact is that some of his main theological influences, especially Calvin, did not address such questions explicitly. Calvin did not do so partly because Reformed prolegomena developed after his death. It is hard to determine what other Reformed orthodox sources Hodge knew and read in his own ministerial training, or even what he had access to by way of libraries. He had indirect Puritan influences through his predecessor and mentor, Archibald Alexander (1772–1851), but such sources rarely came to the surface in his *Systematic Theology*.[176] Hodge assumed that theology proceeded along the lines of scientific induction, teaching that theology was the science of God and other things in relation to God, while bypassing the early church, medieval, and post-Reformation periods. This alone indicates that his treatment of theology as a science reflected a new trajectory in Christian history. It is equally striking that his contemporaries followed the same track, as we will see below.

This chapter omits Hodge's treatment of natural theology and its insufficiency. More to the point is the fourth and final part of his second chapter, on "Christian theology."[177] He here added one more piece to help readers understand the implications of assuming that theology is a science governed by inductive and comprehensive scientific method. Hodge asserted that the facts of Scripture divide naturally into several loci, or departments. These loci included theology proper,

---

174 Hodge, *Systematic Theology*, 1:21.

175 Hodge, *Systematic Theology*, 1:453. Similarly, in volume 3 when treating regeneration, Hodge distinguished "intellectual knowledge of the facts and doctrines of the Bible," from "spiritual discernment." 3:33. Yet this was consistent with his view that theology was a science collecting biblical facts about God and all things related to God. Spiritual discernment, piety, and religion grew out of theological science rather than being integral to systematic theology as a discipline.

176 While Stuart rightly makes the point that students of Hodge should study his articles and not merely his ST in order to grasp his thought, most of Hodge's direct material on theology as a science is relegated to his ST. Stuart, *Mediating the Center: Charles Hodge on American Science, Language, Literature, and Politics*.

177 Hodge, *Systematic Theology*, 1:31.

anthropology, soteriology, eschatology, and ecclesiology.[178] He admitted that this division was "far from exhaustive," omitting things like moral theology.[179] Reflecting his general view of inductive science, he treated such loci and order as "natural" to theological science. In other words, these loci were facts inherent in the system of doctrine taught in Scripture.[180] Yet the church historically aimed to teach the same truths using other methods of organization. The early church, stretching into the medieval, Reformation, and post-Reformation periods used the Apostle's Creed, the Ten Commandments, and the Lord's Prayer. Both Westminster Catechisms included these, following a generally Ramist bifurcation model, dividing the material into what man is to believe concerning God, and the duty God requires of man. The Westminster Confession of Faith approximates Hodge's loci method, though differing slightly in order and detail. Other authors, like William Bucanus (d. 1603), treated the Trinity first, followed by Christology, since Christ was fundamentally the second person in the Trinity, then moving back to creation and other standard topics.[181] While the relationship between doctrines and the harmony of Scripture as a whole was important to these authors, the order and structure of the system was more flexible than Hodge seemed to allow for. Treating theology as following the rues of scientific induction pervaded his entire approach to the methods and organization of systematic theology.

3.2.3 Conclusion: Theological Science Among Hodge's Contemporaries

Looking briefly at Hodge's contemporaries rounds out the historical picture of defining theology as a science, bringing this section to a conclusion. Doing so widens the reference point to Reformed orthodoxy. Barring Schleiermacher and other modern thinkers, it is worth considering other Reformed authors like James Henley Thornwell, John Girardeau (1825–1898), W.G.T Shedd (1820–1894), John Dick (1764–1833), and Hodge's Son, A. A. Hodge (1823–1886). Rather than treating these authors in order, this section synthesizes their teaching with reference to theology as a science, and how Hodge compared to them.

---

178 Hodge, *Systematic Theology*, 1:32.

179 Hodge, *Systematic Theology*, 1:33. Prior to Schleiermacher, who divided theology and ethics, moral theology was usually encompassed within systematic theology via the decalogue. See Donald Sinnema, "The Attempt to Establish a Chair in Practical Theology at Leiden University (1618–1626)," in *A Companion to Reformed Orthodoxy*, ed. H. J. Selderhuis, vol. 40, Brill's Companions to the Christian Tradition (Leiden: Brill, 2013), 415–42.

180 By contrast, John Girardeau asserted that both Hodge's "adopt a prevalent German method" in dividing systematic theology, and that this method had "grave, if not fatal defects" because it had no unifying principle. Girardeau, *Discussions of Theological Questions*, 52.

181 William Bucanus, *Institutiones Theolgicae, Seu, Locorum Communium Christanae Religionis* (Geneva, 1648).

All the authors listed here, like Hodge, defined theology as a science. Yet not all of them explained theological science in the same way. Dick and Shedd assumed theological science, stressing the application of logical induction to Scripture in a manner analogous to natural science.[182] Dick incidentally provided insight as to why so many assumed that theology was a science by noting that all knowledge must either relate to mind or matter, which corresponded to science and art. In other words, science was only one of two available options for the genus of theology.[183] Aristotelian categories being jettisoned, like Hodge, Dick defined theology as the "science of God," and of all things in relation to God. However, A. A. Hodge, Thornwell, and Girardeau all defined theology as "the science of religion."[184] We have seen that Hodge rejected religion from his definition of theology because he believed that this would relegate theology to Schleiermacher's study of religious experience. Yet Thornwell explained that the science of religion was a better term than the science of God because theology involved "spiritual apprehension" produced by the Spirit and leading to piety, and not merely the scientific arrangement of truth.[185] [186]Echoing Ames and Mastricht, though likely following de Moor more directly, he stressed the necessity of saving faith as prerequisite to theology, since faith "knows not for the purpose of knowing, but for the purpose of loving."[187] Theology thus included man as subject and God as object in religion.[188] Explicitly expanding on Thornwell, and interacting critically with Hodge, Girardeau defined

182 Dick, *Lectures on Theology*, 1:1; William G. T. Shedd, *Dogmatic Theology*, ed. Alan W Gomes (Phillipsburg, NJ: P & R Publishing, 2003), 43.

183 Dick, *Lectures on Theology*, 1:2.

184 Hodge, *Outlines of Theology*, 15; Thornwell, *Collected Writings Volume One*, 1:32; Girardeau, *Discussions of Theological Questions*, 1, and throughout the first essay.

185 Thornwell, *Collected Writings Volume One*, 1:36.

186 Theodore Bozeman notes that Hodge and Thornwell were the "two preeminent intellects of the Old School church during the last two decades before the Civil War" (153). He noted that "Thornwell had caught the vision of theology as inductive science," expressing his views clearly in his inaugural address at Columbia Theological Seminary (154). Concerning Hodge, he added that while Hodge did not interact with Bacon directly the "Baconian pattern" became "a basic foundation for his systematic work" and that Hodge adopted modern scientific methods more than most of his contemporaries (154–155). Bozeman, *Protestants in an Age of Science*.

187 Thornwell, *Collected Writings*, 1:37. Also contra Hodge, Girardeau argued that the role of faith in theology meant that theologians did not simply deduce axioms by examining facts. Faith brought its own axioms and commitments to the facts of divine revelation. Girardeau, *Theological Questions*, 32–34.

188 Thornwell, *Collected Writings*, 1:41. Incidentally, Thornwell's threefold division of theology into God's moral government in itself, moral government modified by the covenant of works, and moral government modified by the covenant of grace corresponds roughly to Aquinas' division of theology into God, man's approach to God, and man's return to God. Aquinas and de Moor are cited frequently in Thornwell's treatment of theology, and the influences of both are clear.

theology as "the science of true religion," distinguishing Christian religion from false religion.[189] In his view, religion was a useful term because it was both objective and subjective, focusing on God and his relations to all other things. Reflecting discussions as to whether theology was theoretical, practical, or both, Girardeau noted that theology as the science of religion encompassed both theory and its application.[190] Targeting Hodge's objection to including "religion" in the definition of theology, he added that religion included both to what one believed in terms of creed, as well as to personal character resulting from that creed.[191] Girardeau noted that Hodge's definition stressed the "connection and harmony" of the facts of divine revelation without furnishing the "nexus" between them, which is "religion." His fear was that Hodge had no unifying principle in his theology, and that he blunted the salvific purposes of biblical revelation by relegating theology to the science of God. While science remained the key term among such nineteenth century authors, some explained theological science more in line with the Reformed orthodox idea of the doctrine of living to God than other did. Hodge's definition of theology as a science was more rigidly scientific than most.

A few other observations are in order in relation to Hodge and his contemporaries in the way that they treated theology as a science in comparison to Reformed orthodoxy. Most of these authors omitted archetypal and ectypal theology, the theology of union, and the beatific vision. Thornwell did treat archetypal and ectypal theology, though he shifted archetypal theology away from the Creator/creature distinction to Scripture as the pattern of theology, as noted above.[192] On the next page, he followed de Moor's treatment of the *theologia unionis,* with somewhat muted stress on the beatific vision and the Trinitarian underpinnings of Reformed orthodox prolegomena. Girardeau mentioned the Trinity only in relation to contrasting Christian theology with Islamic monotheism.[193] Shedd was virtually alone in noting that "the Trinity was the basis" of ancient, medieval, and Reformation theology, seeking to retain this foundation.[194] What is particularly striking is that, along with Hodge, nineteenth century Reformed theologians did not bolster their definitions of theology with much biblical exegesis. Hodge, Dick, and Shedd included none at all, while Thornwell and Girardeau drew only from John 17:3, with one allusion to 1 Corinthians 2 in Thornwell.[195]

---

189 Girardeau, *Discussions of Theological Questions*, 13.

190 Girardeau, 19.

191 Girardeau, 39.

192 Thornwell, *Collected Writings Volume One*, 1:29.

193 Girardeau, *Discussions of Theological Questions*, 8–11.

194 Shedd, *Dogmatic Theology*, 43.

195 Thornwell, *Collected Writings Volume One*, 1:41, 51; Girardeau, *Discussions of Theological Questions*, 20, 69. These passages appeared in most early modern Reformed definitions of theology.

The first two major divisions of this essay provide two models for defining theology. The first model generally characterized theology as spiritual wisdom, or at least as a special science tending towards wisdom, defining theology as the doctrine of living to God or living well. Hodge and his contemporaries generally defined theology as a science, with Hodge's special stress on comprehensive inductive methodology. Continuity existed in that *scientia* regularly factored into definitions of theology, both in Reformed orthodoxy and in the nineteenth century. Faith receiving Scripture also factored into both time periods. Discontinuities included tendencies towards defining theology as science, and omitting Aristotelian categories, the *theologia unionis*and the beatific vision, biblical exegesis, and archetypal and ectypal theology. What remains is to introduce some hints as to the reasons for the differences between these times periods in light of the scientific revolution.

3.3 The Context of Hodge's Views of Theology as a Science

It is important to step back and explain why Hodge understood theology in light of modern inductive science. We can see this in light of the effects of the scientific revolution on the meaning of science, the method of science, and the primacy of science.

First, the scientific revolution affected the meaning of science. One gets the impression that the meaning of *scientia,* or its English equivalen t"science," had shifted from its earlier pre-Enlightenment uses. As Christopher Cleveland notes, Reformed theology declined after Francis Turretin at the cusp of the Enlightenment, bringing the rejection medieval influences on Reformed theology, and that this trend largely carried over into the nineteenth century.[196] Whether or not readers agree with this assertion, Cleveland highlights an intellectual shift, which shows itself most clearly in relation to terminology and categories used in the church for centuries. Aristotelian terms, while not gone entirely, were no longer the primary point of reference in post-Enlightenment conceptions of science. While similarities and differences in definitions and methodology can be hard to trace and distinguish at points, it is easy see that Turretin wrote that *theologia non est scientia,* while Hodge taught that theology was the science of God and creatures in relation to God. Writing in Latin, Francis Bacon marked this equivocal use of *scientia,* since his main argument related to shifting away from Aristotelian uses of the term to a description of inductive method, which stands behind the difficulty in evaluating continuities and discontinuities on this point. Recognizing this historical shift in ideas, Thornwell noted that earlier Reformed authors could not easily define

196 Allen and Swain, *The Oxford Handbook of Reformed Theology*, 31.

theology as a science because the Aristotelian categories they worked with reduced science to intellectual content, excluding loving God as the purpose of theology.[197] While Thornwell sought to alter modern definitions of science to fit the objective and subjective elements of theology, Hodge appears to have accepted modern assumptions about science in his working understanding of theological science. The main difference, for him, between theological and natural science was that theological science worked with the laws of the mind (governed by Scripture) instead of the laws of nature.

A vital clarification is in order here regarding the potential equivocation between *scientia* and "science." Causation was perhaps the key issue in explain the shift in the meaning of these terms following the scientific revolution. Michael Dodds describes this issue clearly in relation to the effects of modern scientific method on Aristotelian fourfold causation. Following Aristotle, Aquinas taught that science was "knowledge of a thing through its cause."[198] This definition related to Aristotelian fourfold causation, in which the form making a thing what it is was in the thing itself, which is known as hylomorphism. These causes were material, formal, efficient, and final. Material causes related to what a thing was made out of. Formal causes made the thing what it is in distinction from other things. Efficient causes respected the agent producing an effect, while final causes reflected teleology or purpose.[199] However, Dodds helpfully observers that modern scientific views, as represented by Galileo and others, effectively excluded traditional metaphysics from scientific methodology, reducing science to mathematical quantitative empirical science. This meant that unquantifiable causes were either excluded or ignored. Final causes were sidelined because "no number could be assigned to purpose." Likewise, formal causes identifying a thing to be what it is were off the table from scientific investigation. While material causes as the stuff out of which things were made might remain, the problem was that "there was no place for primary matter as the mere possibility of being."[200] In relation to the theological underpinnings of authors like Aquinas and Hodge, this brought the idea that God as first cause was no longer relevant to scientific method, which Aquinas could not have lived with and Hodge refused to live with. Dodds concluded that only efficient causes remained in modern scientific method, which in natural science reduced to "the force that moved atoms."[201]

197 Thornwell, *Collected Writings Volume One*, 1:38.

198 Michael J. Dodds, OP, "The Reception of Aquinas in the Philosophy of Nature and Science," in *The Oxford Handbook of the Reception of Aquinas*, ed. Matthew Levering and Marcus Plested (Oxford: Oxford University Press, 2021), 539.

199 Dodds, "Philosophy of Nature and Science," 541.

200 Dodds, "Philosophy of Nature and Science," 543.

201 Dodds, "Philosophy of Nature and Science," 543.

The absence or irrelevance of God as first cause, giving form and end to scientific knowledge, was precisely Hodge's target in, *What is Darwinism?,* where he labelled Darwin's scientific method effectively as atheism. Hodge faced the dilemma of seeking to apply modern scientific methods to theological science while remaining aware of the unacceptable metaphysical vacuum left by Darwinian science, at least. Such observations illustrate why, with Mark Noll, I detect a tension between Hodge's religious convictions and piety on the one side, and his identification of the methods of theology with modern scientific methodology. This tension is present in Hodge's thought, while it does not appear to mark the thought of contemporaries like Thornwell and Girardeau, who reintroduced metaphysical and religious concerns by defining theology as "the science of religion."

Second, the scientific revolution reshaped the method of science. Francis Bacon had argued for something like Hodge's "comprehensive induction" in order to account for the facts of any science. Yet William Dampier noted that Bacon's method overreached itself by its stress on obtaining certainty by accounting for "all available facts," and most scientists aimed at probability only.[202] Hodge's Baconian scientific approach to the Bible led to what is often called "proof texting," treating the Bible as a collection of facts from which one deduces axioms[203]. This approach to interpreting Scripture as a collection of facts waiting to be interpreted stands in partial contrast to earlier authors, such as Francis Turretin, as well as the authors of the Westminster Standards, which loomed large in Hodge's Reformed identity. Turretin's use of Ezekiel 37 in arguing for the resurrection of the dead is a good example. In the midst of a lengthy treatment of the gradual unfolding of the resurrection from the Old Testament to the new,[204] Turretin sought to understand Ezekiel both in context of the restoration from Babylonian captivity, and as a typological precursor to the final resurrection.[205] This showcases an example of how early modern authors methodologically sought to understand biblical texts in their contexts, relate OT texts to the teaching of the whole Bible by way of typology, and draw together theological conclusions from the big picture. Theoretically, Hodge's scientific assumptions regarding the analogy between the facts of nature and the facts of consciousness and of Scripture could mute biblical reasoning and

---

202 William Cecil Dampier Dampier, *A History of Science and Its Relations with Philosophy & Religion* (New York: Macmillan, 1944), 137–38.

203 Bozeman argues that the inductive method in nineteenth century American theology led to prioritizing biblicism over "doctrinal authority." Bozeman, *Protestants in an Age of Science*, 153. This created tensions for orthodox Presbyterians like Hodge.

204 Francis Turretin, *Institutes of Elenctic Theology*, ed. James T Dennison, trans. George Musgrave Giger (Phillipsburg, N.J.: P&R Publishing, 1992), 3:562–67.

205 Turretin, *Institutes*, 3:564.

contexts in favor of proof texting. As Ronald Numbers noted in passing, Hodge in his theology "had adopted the methods of science."[206]

However, scientific "proof texting" was not the end of the story for Hodge. It is important to remember that in addition to teaching Systematic Theology, he taught New Testament at Princeton. Moreover, he only wrote his *Systematic Theology* near the end of his life, drawing from his exegetical expertise. His fame as an author and theologian rested initially on his commentary on Romans, as well as on his later commentaries on Ephesians and both epistles to the Corinthians.[207] Reflecting on his time studying exegesis under Hodge, B. B. Warfield observed that Hodge's sense of the meaning of biblical texts was "unsurpassed," but that he also "often" quoted texts to support doctrines not treated in those texts. Warfield did not mean to slight his teacher, however, concluding, that "this affected details only, the general flow of thought in a passage he never failed to grasp, and few men could equal him in stating it."[208] Warfield believed that Hodge's true strength was as a systematic theologian rather than an exegete. None of this implies that Hodge was not sensitive to biblical contexts as he constructed his theology. If anything, it shows that he may have overreached in his theoretical insistence on applying scientific method to Scripture.

Third, the scientific revolution elevated the primacy of science. Taken broadly, science historically referred to an intellectual habit. Reflecting Aquinas, earlier theologians argued that theology was the queen of the sciences. However, the Enlightenment brought a stress on knowing truths available primarily to human reason.[209] Many, though not all, post-Enlightenment theologians began to seek to reduce systems of doctrine to truths available through nature alone.[210] Natural science became the primary academic endeavor, resting entirely on natural revelation. People viewed science as objective, since they still assumed the uniform order of the laws of nature and of universal truths available to people through induction and experimentation. Science became both optimistic and primary in the pursuit of

206 Ronald L. Numbers, "Charles Hodge and the Beauties and Deformities of Science," in *Charles Hodge Revisited: A Critical Appraisal of His Life and Work*, ed. John W. Steward and James H. Moorhead (Grand Rapids, MI: Eerdmans, 1997), 100.

207 Incidentally, John Girardeau listed Romans and the epistles to the Corinthians as some of the primary NT models, with Hebrews, of moving in the direction of systematizing biblical teaching. Girardeau, *Discussions of Theological Questions*, 25–26.

208 B. B. Warfield, "Dr. Charles Hodge as a Teacher of Exegesis," in *Selected Shorter Writings of Benjamin B. Warfield*, vol. 1 (Phillipsburg, NJ: P&R, 2001), 438–39.

209 For the context of the Enlightenment in America, see Henry F. May, *The Enlightenment in America* (New York: Oxford University Press, 1976).

210 James T. Dennison, "The Twilight of Scholasticism: Francis Turretin and the Dawn of the Enlightenment," in *Protestant Scholasticism: Essays in Reassessment* (Eugene, OR: Wipf & Stock, 2006).

knowledge. Theology was largely displaced from its throne by the natural sciences, which Hodge could not live with. Yet when Hodge assumed that theology was a science, subject essentially to the same rules and methods as natural science, he reflected his broader intellectual context. Science was primary in the world in which he lived. For theology to remain the queen of the sciences, Hodge had to show that theology was both respectable among, and superior to, other modes of modern science. Two ways in which theology was superior to other sciences, in his view, were the facts that theology rested on supernatural revelation as well as the illumination of the Holy Spirit. This last point illustrates well Hodge's simultaneous continuity with the Westminster Standards, and the effects of modern scientific views on his thinking.

This truncated sketch of the scientific revolution illustrates why Hodge worked uncritically with definitions of science largely unknown to early modern Protestants.[211] While older ideas and scholastic terms did not disappear entirely, natural science's theoretical aim to let the facts lead wherever they would without imposing preconceived ideas on them dominated the nineteenth century. In part, Hodge defined theology as a science because science was the preoccupation of the times in ways that it had not been in previous centuries.

3.4 Conclusion

Hodge's treatment of the nature and genus of theology in some ways marked a shift away from his self-identified Reformed orthodoxy. Yet was this a seismic shift? This question admits three tentative conclusions.

First, though Hodge defined theology as a science, his treatment of the subject marked substantial continuity with earlier authors, who treated theology as spiritual wisdom. He and his contemporaries held in common with Turretin and others the idea that piety and religion were vital goals of theology because theology aimed at glorifying and knowing God. However, instead of viewing regeneration by the Spirit[212] and saving faith in Christ as prerequisite to pursuing theology as spiritual

---

211 Though the tide was shifting slowly in the seventeenth century, as Bozeman illustrates through Richard Baxter's (1615–1691) endorsement of Francis Bacon's scientific methodology. Bozeman, *Protestants in an Age of Science*, 143.

212 E. g., Amandus Polanus, *Analysis Libelli Prophetae Malachiae: Aliquot Praelectionibus Genevae Proposita a Amando Polando a Polansdorf; Praemissi Sunt Duo Indices, Adiunctae Sunt Orationes Quatuor: I. De Incarnatione Immanuelis Nostri Iesv Christi, Ii. De Crucis Christi Scientia & Communione, Iii. De Vita & Obitu Oecolampadii, Cui Disputatio De Primatu Papae Inserta, Iv. De Prophetia Danielis* (Basileae, 1597), 1.

wisdom,[213] one could say that Hodge regarded theology as scientific knowledge designed to result in spiritual wisdom. Theoretically, this meant that someone could be a theologian, constructing an accurate scientific system of biblical doctrine, without pursing the end of theology in glorifying and knowing God. Though this should not be, yet it could be. By contrast, as noted above, John Owen contended that one who constructed a right system without Spirit-wrought faith in Christ was a Christian philosopher rather than a true theologian.[214] The trajectory set by Junius for Reformed orthodoxy illustrates that the character of the theologian was integral to the nature of theology. While Hodge taught the necessity of knowing God, he worked from altered definitions of science, and he virtually bypassed the Reformed tradition without comment when he defined theology. That being said, it is hard on some level to assess discontinuity between nineteenth century definitions of theology and those found in Reformed orthodoxy.[215] Both models included doctrine and practice, at least in theory.[216] Thornwell, Girardeau, and perhaps A. A. Hodge moved closer to theology as spiritual wisdom by defining it as the science of religion. Yet it helps to remember that instead of asking whether the genus of theology was intelligence, science, wisdom, prudence, or art, John Dick seemed to indicate that science and art were the only viable categories left. Hodge incorporated earlier treatments of theology into his definition less than some of his contemporaries, while retaining some of their goals.

Second, Hodge's definition of theology as a science shows discontinuity with earlier Reformed authors in its virtual lack of exegetical grounding. Detecting differences is easier at this point. In contrast to lengthy exegetical treatments of theology in Reformed orthodoxy, Hodge's definition was devoid of exegesis. Even Thornwell and Girardeau showed only traces of the earlier tradition in this regard.

---

213 Ames, *Medulla Theologiae*, 5–10; Mastricht, *Theoretico-Practica Theologia*, 2.

214 Owen, *Theologoumena Pantodapa*, 467. Owen, *Theologoumena Pantodapa*, 467: "...Philosophicos Christianos censemus non Theologicos Evangelicos." Also see de Moor, *Continuous Commentary*, 1:175 for similar ideas.

215 Part of the difficultly lies in the nineteenth century American adoption of Baconian induction itself. Induction was often set against the deductive reasoning of the scholastics, and we have seen that Bacon regarded his scientific method as entirely new. However, Dominic Monti notes that Aquinas exemplified a standard Scholastic inductive method through drawing probable arguments from accumulated evidence in the *Summa Theologica*, while authors like Bonaventure and Richard St. Victor sought demonstrations of truth through deductive reasoning. Bonaventure, *Breviloquium*, ed. Dominic Monti, vol. 9, Works of St. Bonaventure (New York: The Franciscan Institute, 2005), xxv, xxx. Methodologically, theologians before and after the Scientific Revolution mingled a combination of inductive and deductive methods of arriving at conclusions. This makes continuities and discontinuities with respect to science difficult to pinpoint. Discontinuity is easier to detect than it is to describe.

216 Bozeman rightly notes that all studies of this period must account for how "piety and dogma were interconnected." Bozeman, *Protestants in an Age of Science*, 164.

While all sides acknowledged that theology was not a biblical term, Reformed orthodox authors sought to fill it with biblical content, using Aristotelian categories as organizational tools. Hodge bypassed exegetical arguments and sidestepped well-known categories, giving the impression that his definition of theology as a science was more assumed than established.

Third, the Trinity and the Beatific Vision, so integral to medieval and Reformed prolegomena, disappeared in Hodge. Few authors in the nineteenth century treated archetypal and ectypal theology. This meant that they also bypassed discussions of the theology of union and the beatific vision prior to examining "our theology."[217] This resulted in dropping the inherently eschatological and Trinitarian foundation of the earlier Christian tradition. The virtual eclipse of the Trinity in nineteenth century prolegomena, in contrast to the first eighteen centuries of church history, is both striking and palpable.

At the very least, this chapter should give readers pause in relation to Hodge oft quoted idea that Princeton taught nothing new in relation to theology.[218] Every theologian in Christian history is affected by their contexts, Charles Hodge being no exception. Other areas in Hodge's prolegomena deserve further investigation along these lines, such as the question of the role of reason in theology, the *principia* of theology, and the epistemological foundations of faith in Scripture. This chapter is a modest attempt to show a general trajectory of persistence and change between Hodge's nineteenth century definition of theology as a science, and earlier Reformed orthodox depictions of the discipline.

Works Cited

Allen, Michael, and Scott R. Swain, eds. *The Oxford Handbook of Reformed Theology.* Oxford: Oxford University Press, 2020.

Ames, William. *Medulla S.S. Theologiæ, in Fine Adjuncta Est Disputatio De Fidei Divinæ Veritate. Editio Tertia Priori Longe Correctior.* London, 1629.

Anderson, Owen. *Reason and Faith in the Theology of Charles Hodge: American Common Sense Realism.* New York: Palgrave Macmillan, 2014.

Anselm. *Anselm of Canterbury: The Major Works.* Edited by Brian Davies and G. R. Evans. Oxford's World Classics. Oxford: Oxford University Press, 2008.

Aquinas, Thomas. *Summa Contra Gentiles.* Translated by Lawrence Shapcote. Steubenville, OH: Emaus Academic, 2018.

———. *Summa Theologiae.* Translated by Lawrence Shapcote. Latin/English Edition of the Works of St. Thomas Aquinas. Steubenville, OH: Emaus Academic, 2012.

---

217 Thornwell being a partial exception. Thornwell, *Collected Writings Volume One*, 1:30–31.

218 This idea is cited in Numbers, "Charles Hodge and the Beauties and Deformities of Science," 79.

Asselt, W. J. van, T. Theo J. Pleizier, P. L. Rouwendal, and Maarten Wisse. *Introduction to Reformed Scholasticism.* Translated by Albert Gootjes. Grand Rapids, MI: Reformation Heritage Books, 2011.

Asselt, Willem J. van. "The Fundamental Meaning of Theology: Archetypal and Ectypal Theology in Seventeentt-Century Reformed Thought." *Westminster Theological Journal* 64, no. 2 (2002).

Bacon, Francis. *Novum Organum, or, True Suggestions for the Interpretation of Nature.* London, 1844.

Bonaventure. *Breviloquium.* Edited by Dominic Monti. Vol. 9. Works of St. Bonaventure. New York: The Franciscan Institute, 2005.

Bozeman, Theodore Dwight. *Protestants in an Age of Science: The Baconian Ideal and Antebellum American Religious Thought.* Chapel Hill: University of North Carolina Press, 1977.

Bucanus, William. *Institutiones Theolgicae, Seu, Locorum Communium Christanae Religionis.* Geneva, 1648.

Burns, William E. *The Scientific Revolution in Global Perspective.* New York: Oxford University Press, 2016.

Calvin, John. *Institutes of the Christian Religion.* Edited by John T. McNeill. Translated by Ford Lewis Battles. Vol. XX–XXI. 2 vols. Library of Christian Classics. Philadelphia: Westminster Press, 1960.

Cloppenburg, Johannes. *Exercitationes Super Locos Communes Theologicos.* Franekerae, 1653.

Daille, Jean. *De Usu Patrum Ad Ea Definienda Religionis Capita, Quae Sunt Hodie Controversa, Libri Duo.* Geneva, 1656.

Dampier, William Cecil Dampier. *A History of Science and Its Relations with Philosophy & Religion.* New York: Macmillan, 1944.

Daneau, Lambert. *In Petri Lombardi Episcopi Parisiensis (qui Magister Sententiarum Appellatur) Librum Primum Sententiarum, Qui Est De Vero Deo, Essentiâ Quidem Uno: Personis Autem Trino: Lamberti Danaei Commentarius Triplex. Unus, Ad Marginem Ipsius Libri, in Quo Singularum Distinctionum Artificium Breviter Explicatur. Alter, Ubi Locorum À Lombardo Prolatorum Accurata Collatio Facta Est. Tertius, Qui Censuram Doctrinae, Methodique Lombardi, Tum Ex Ipso Dei Verbo, Tum Ex Veris Sententiarum Scribendarum Praeceptis Habet.* Genevae: Apud Eustathium Vignon, 1580.

Dennison, James T. "The Twilight of Scholasticism: Francis Turretin and the Dawn of the Enlightenment." In *Protestant Scholasticism: Essays in Reassessment.* Eugene, OR: Wipf & Stock, 2006.

Dick, John. *Lectures on Theology.* 4 vols. Stoke-on-Trent: Tentmaker Publications, 2004.

Dodds, OP, Michael J. "The Reception of Aquinas in the Philosophy of Nature and Science." In *The Oxford Handbook of the Reception of Aquinas,* edited by Matthew Levering and Marcus Plested, 539–53. Oxford: Oxford University Press, 2021.

Duncan, Jennings Ligon. "Common Sense Realism and American Presbyterianism: An Evaluation of the Impact of Scottish Realism on Princeton and the South." Covenant Theological Seminary, 1987.

Fesko, J. V. *Reforming Apologetics: Retrieving the Classic Reformed Approach to Defending the Faith.* Grand Rapids, MI: Baker Academic, 2019.

Girardeau, John L. *Discussions of Theological Questions.* Edited by George A. Blackburn. Harrisonburg, VA: Sprinkle Publications, 1986.

Han, Byung Soo. *Symphonia Catholica: The Merger of Patristic and Contemporary Sources in the Theological Method of Amandus Polanus (1561–1610).* Vol. 30. Reformed Historical Theology. Göttingen: Vandenhoeck & Ruprecht, 2015.

Hodge, A. A. *Outlines of Theology.* Edinburgh: Banner of Truth Trust, 1999.

Hodge, Charles. "Can God Be Known?" *Biblical Repertory and Theological Review* 36, no. 1 (1864): 122–52.

———. "Suggestions of Theological Students, on Some of Those Traits of Character, Which the Spirit of the Age Renders Peculiarly Important in the Ministers of the Gospel." *Biblical Repertory and Theological Review* 5 (1833): 100–113.

———. *Systematic Theology.* 3 vols. Grand Rapids, MI: Eerdmans, 1999.

Hoffecker, W. Andrew. *Charles Hodge: The Pride of Princeton.* Phillipsburg, NJ: P & R Publishing, 2011.

Hoornbeeck, Johannes. *Theologia Practica Pars 1.* 2 vols. Francofurti & Lipsiae: Bailliar, 1698.

Hyperius, Andreas. *De Theologo, Seu, De Ratione Studii Theologici Libri IV.* Basileae, 1559.

———. *Methodus Theologiae Adj. Eft. De Ejusdem Vita Et Obita Oratis Wigandi Arthii.* Basileae, 1562.

John of Damascus. *Exposition of the Orthodox Faith.* Translated by S. D. F. Salmond. Vol. 9. Nicene and Post-Nicene Fathers: Second Series. Peabody, MA: Hendrickson Publishers, 2004.

Junius, Franciscus. *A Treatise on True Theology: With the Life of Franciscus Junius.* Translated by David C Noe. Grand Rapids, MI: Reformation Heritage Books, 2014.

———. *De Theologia Vera; Ortu, Natura, Formis, Partibus, Et Modo.* Lugduni Batavorum, 1594.

Leinsle, Ulrich G. *Introduction to Scholastic Theology.* Translated by Michael J. Miller. Washington, D.C.: Catholic University of America Press, 2010.

———. "Sources, Methods, and Forms of Early Modern Theology." In *The Oxford Handbook of Early Modern Theology, 1600–1800,* edited by Ulrich L. Lehner, Richard A. Muller, and A. G. Roeber, 25–42. Oxford: Oxford University Press, 2016.

Levering, Matthew, and Gilles Emery, eds. *Aristotle in Aquinas' Theology.* Oxford: Oxford University Press, 2018.

Maccovius, Johannes. *Loci Communes Theologici.* Amstelodami, 1658.

Marckius, Johannes. *Compendium Theologiae Christianae Didactico Elencticum: Immixtis Problematibus Plurimis & Quaestionibus Recentioribus Adauctum.* Amstelodami, 1696.

Mastricht, Peter van. *Theoretico-Practica Theologia. Qua, Per Singula Capita Theologica, Pars Exegetica, Dogmatica, Elenchtica & Practica, Perpetua Successione Conjugantur.* Trajecti ad Rhenum, & Amstelodami: Sumptibus Societatis, 1724.

May, Henry F. *The Enlightenment in America.* New York: Oxford University Press, 1976.

McGraw, Ryan M. "Petrus van Mastricht and Reformed Orthodoxy." In *Petrus Van Mastricht (1630–1706): Text, Context, and Interpretation,* edited by Adriaan C. Neele, 62:19–38. Reformed Historical Theology. Gottingen: Vandenhoeck & Ruprecht, 2020.

Moor, Bernardinus de. *Continuous Commentary on Johannes Marckius' Didactico-Elenctic Compendium of Christian Theology.* Translated by Stephen Dilday. Vol. 1. 7 vols. Culpeper, VA: L & G Reformation Translation Center, 2014.

Muller, Richard A. *Post-Reformation Reformed Dogmatics: The Rise and Development of Reformed Orthodoxy, Ca. 1520 to Ca. 1725.* 2nd ed. 4 vols. Grand Rapids, MI: Baker Academic, 2003.

Neele, Adriaan C. *Petrus Van Mastricht (1630–1706) Reformed Orthodoxy: Method and Piety.* Leiden; Boston: Brill, 2009.

Noll, Mark A. "The Princeton Theology." In *Reformed Theology in America: A History of Its Modern Development,* edited by David F. Wells, 15–38. Grand Rapids, MI: Baker Academic, 1997.

Numbers, Ronald L. "Charles Hodge and the Beauties and Deformities of Science." In *Charles Hodge Revisited: A Critical Appraisal of His Life and Work,* edited by John W. Steward and James H. Moorhead, 77–102. Grand Rapids, MI: Eerdmans, 1997.

Oberman, Heiko Augustinus. *The Harvest of Medieval Theology: Gabriel Biel and Late Medieval Nominalism.* Grand Rapids (Mich.): Baker Academic, 2000.

Owen, John. *The Reason of Faith, or, an Answer Unto That Enquiry, Wherefore We Believe the Scripture to Be the Word of God with the Causes and Nature of That Faith Wherewith We Do so: Wherein the Grounds Whereon the Holy Scripture Is Believed to Be the Word of God with Faith Divine and Supernatural, Are Declared and Vindicated.* London, 1677.

———. *Theologoumena Pantodapa, Sive, De Natura, Ortu, Progressu, Et Studio Veræ Theologiæ, Libri Sex Quibus Etiam Origines & Processus Veri & Falsi Cultus Religiosi, Casus & Instaurationes Ecclesiæ Illustiores Ab Ipsis Rerum Primordiis, Enarrantur.* Oxoniæ, 1661.

Perkins, William. *Armilla Aurea, id est, Theologiae Descrpto, Miranda Series Causarum Et Salutis & Damnationis Iuxta Verbum Dei Eius Synopsin Continet Annexa.* Cambridge, 1596.

Peter Lombard. *The Sentences.* Translated by Giulio Silano. 4 vols. Toronto: Pontifical Institute of Mediaeval Studies, 2007.

Polanus, Amandus. *Analysis Libelli Prophetae Malachiae: Aliquot Praelectionibus Genevae Proposita a Amando Polando a Polansdorf; Praemissi Sunt Duo Indices, Adiunctae Sunt Orationes Quatuor: I. De Incarnatione Immanuelis Nostri Iesv Christi, Ii. De Crucis Christi Scientia & Communione, Iii. De Vita & Obitu Oecolampadii, Cui Disputatio De Primatu Papae Inserta, Iv. De Prophetia Danielis.* Basileae, 1597.

———. *Syntagma Theologiae Christianae Ab Amando Polano a Polansdorf: Juxta Leges Ordinis Methodici Conformatum, Atque in Libros Decem Digestum Jamque Demum in Unum Volumen Compactum, Novissime Emendatum.* Hanoviae, 1610.

Principe, Lawrence M. *The Scientific Revolution: A Very Short Introduction.* Oxford: Oxford University Press, 2011.

Ramus, Petrus. *Commentariorum De Religione Christiana, Libri, Quatuor, Eivsdem Vita a Theophilo Banosio Descripta.* Francofvrti, 1576.

Shedd, William G. T. *Dogmatic Theology.* Edited by Alan W Gomes. Phillipsburg, NJ: P & R Publishing, 2003.

Sinnema, Donald. "The Attempt to Establish a Chair in Practical Theology at Leiden University (1618–1626)." In *A Companion to Reformed Orthodoxy,* edited by H. J. Selderhuis, 40:415–42. Brill's Companions to the Christian Tradition. Leiden: Brill, 2013.

———. "The Distinction Between Scholastic and Popular: Andreas Hyperius and Reformed Scholasticism." In *Protestant Scholasticism: Essays in Reassessment,* 127–44. Eugene, OR: Wipf & Stock, 2006.

Stuart, John W. *Mediating the Center: Charles Hodge on American Science, Language, Literature, and Politics.* Studies in Reformed Theology and History. Princeton, NJ: Princeton Theological Seminary, 1995.

Thornwell, James Henley. *The Collected Writings of James Henley Thornwell: Volume One Theological.* Edited by John B. Adger. Vol. 1. 4 vols. Birmingham, AL: Solid Ground Christian Books, 2004.

Turretin, Francis. *Institutes of Elenctic Theology.* Edited by James T Dennison. Translated by George Musgrave Giger. 3 vols. Phillipsburg, N.J.: P&R Publishing, 1992.

———. *Institutio Theologiae Elencticae.* Vol. 1. 3 vols. Geneva, 1679.

Wallace, Dewey D. *Shapers of English Calvinism, 1660–1714: Variety, Persistence, and Transformation.* New York: Oxford University Press, 2011.

Warfield, B. B. "Dr. Charles Hodge as a Teacher of Exegesis." In *Selected Shorter Writings of Benjamin B. Warfield,* 1:437–40. Phillipsburg, NJ: P&R, 2001.

———. "Theology a Science." In *Selected Shorter Writings of Benjamin B. Warfield,* 2:207–12. Phillipsburg, NJ: P&R, 2001.

Warfield, Benjamin Breckinridge. "The Task and Method of Systematic Theology." In *The Works of Benjamin B. Warfield,* 9:91–105. Grand Rapids, MI: Baker Books, 2003.

Scott Cook

4. More Modern than Orthodox?: Charles Hodge and the Doctrine of God

4.1 Introduction

Charles Hodge saw himself as a guardian of Reformed Orthodoxy. For Hodge, theological novelty was no virtue and Reformed theological repristination was no vice. He once wrote to his friend William Cunningham (1805–1861), "I have never advanced a new idea, and have never aimed to improve on the doctrines of our fathers."[1] Hodge confidently declared in his fiftieth year as a professor at Princeton Seminary, "I am not afraid to say that a new idea never originated in this Seminary."[2] But Hodge's theology was more complicated than he recognized. While he claimed to have never improved on the theology of the Reformers, the doctrine of God is one area where he, in fact, attempted to correct the Reformed tradition.

Hodge bears the marks of a great mind: originality and complexity. He was, to be sure, a champion of Reformed theology overall. However, he was also a man of his times. Hodge was an American theologian who drank deeply from both Ancient, classically Reformed, and Modern intellectual wells. As a result, he cast his understanding of Reformed theology in distinctly modern expressions. The doctrine of God particularly illustrates the complexity of Hodge's theological identity. At some points, Hodge sounds more like a Reformed Orthodox theologian, while at others, his doctrine seems to be completely foreign to the Westminster Divines, Turretin, and Reformed Orthodoxy.

This chapter explores Charles Hodge's complex relationship with Reformed Orthodoxy and Modernism in his formulation of theology proper. The focus will be on two important areas, the first of which is philosophy. Hodge's use of a particular strand of Scottish Common Sense Realism contrasts with the eclectic Aristotelianism of Reformed Orthodoxy. Hodge's understanding of Common Sense shaped his doctrine of God. The second focal point is the attributes of God. Specific attention is given to the classification of the attributes in general and key metaphysical

1 Archibald Alexander Hodge, *The Life of Charles Hodge* (Edinburgh; Carlisle, Pennsylvania: Banner of Truth Trust, 2010), 430.

2 Hodge, *The Life of Charles Hodge*, 521; See also, C. A. Salmond, *Princetoniana, Charles & A. A. Hodge: With Class and Table Talk of Hodge the Younger* (New York, New York: Scribner and Welford, 1888), 13.

and moral attributes in particular. Hodge consistently criticized and amended the Scholastic doctrine of God in favor of a modified doctrine of God. The basic assertion of this chapter is that Hodge's doctrine of God is more Modern than Orthodox.

4.2 Some Preliminary Considerations

Before delving into the three areas singled out in this chapter, some preliminary observations about Hodge's sources, philosophical knowledge, and methodology are in order. All of these issues receive more attention below, but grouping them here will help readers better understand why Hodge's doctrine of God became more Modern than Orthodox. The continuity and discontinuity one sees in Hodge regarding the Reformed Orthodox doctrine of God results from a number of factors. As this chapter interacts with Hodge on the doctrine of God, there are several trajectories present in Hodge that will emerge. First, Hodge interacts with both Ancient and Modern sources. Hodge frequently worked with the thought of Augustine (354–430), Aquinas (1225–1274), and numerous classical authors. He also drew from a number of representatives of the Scholastic tradition, both Catholic and Protestant, Lutheran and Reformed. However, Hodge often spoke of the "schoolmen" without specifying which author(s) he had in mind. These pre-Modern sources appear alongside decidedly Modern authors. While both Continental and British authors appear in Hodge's writings, he tends to draw most consistently from German and Scottish thinkers. Friedrich Schleiermacher (1768–1834) is the most common German author to appear, while William Hamilton (1788–1856) is the most commonly cited British Scottish author. Hodge's doctrine of God contains categories and elements from these diverse sources.

Second, Hodge displayed a surprising lack of philosophical and theological precision at points. This lack of sophistication gives some portions of Hodge's doctrine of a God a messy, inconsistent quality. He occasionally misrepresented the positions of authors with whom he interacted. His understanding of the doctrine of simplicity, for instance, contains contradictory and irreconcilable tensions stemming from an apparent misunderstanding of the Scholastic resources he analyzes. Hodge also appears to have been unable to comprehend the disparity between the Reformed Orthodox doctrine of God and Pantheism due to a lack of appreciation for the complexity of the Scholastic tradition.

Third, Hodge's theological methodology contains a strong anthropocentric impulse. Apologetic concerns drove this impulse. For reasons that this chapter will elaborate, Hodge was concerned with protecting the knowability of God against many of his contemporaries, who argued that God is beyond knowledge. Hodge combated these arguments with a Scottish Common Sense Realism approach that relied on human consciousness as the lynchpin for maintaining the knowability of God. The net effect of this apologetic method was that Hodge often recast his doctrine of God in an anthropocentric mold. Hodge argued that the attributes of God must be intelligible to the consciousness of man. This move prevented any formulation of God that turned God into the unknowable absolute. However, a byproduct of this theological move was that Hodge largely rejected the Reformed Orthodox doctrine of God because the Scholastics, in Hodge's mind, overemphasized the transcendence of God.

Finally, Hodge formulated his doctrine of God with a particular concern for avoiding the dangers of theological pantheism. The nineteenth century saw a resurgence of pantheistic models of theology proper. Specifically, G. F. W. Hegel's (1770–1831) pantheistic tendencies loomed large over the century as his particular form of Idealism sought to slip the horns of the dilemma posed by Immanuel Kant's (1724–1804) Copernican Revolution, dichotomizing the noumenal and the phenomenal realms. For Hodge in particular, the fear of pantheism likely came also from his study under Friedrich Schleiermacher. Schleiermacher's appropriation of Pietism, Romanticism, and Enlightenment Rationalism produced a doctrine of God, Man's "whence," that resulted in either a pantheist or, at best, a panentheistic system. Additionally, while Hodge did not directly mention Jonathan Edwards (1703–1758), he might also have been concerned about the pantheistic impulses produced by the Edwardsians in New England.[3] Fears of pantheism caused Hodge to move away from the Reformed Orthodox doctrine of God in order to avoid the contemporary specter of pantheism.

With these ideas in mind, we can now turn directly to examining how Hodge modified the classic doctrine of God in light of his philosophical sources and in relation to God's existence and attributes.

3 Hodge expressed concerned about the theology of Edwards, particularly his view of creation. See Charles Hodge, *Systematic Theology* (New York: Scribner, 1871), vols. 1, 578–580. A number of Edwards scholars have noted his tendcy to pantheism or panenthism. However, Hodge does not directly express concern over these trajectories in his writings on theology proper. Nonetheless, the influence of Edwards was profound in American Christianity. For more on Edwards, see Oliver D Crisp, "On the Orthodoxy of Jonathan Edwards," *Scottish Journal of Theology* 67, no. 3 (2014): 304–22; Sang Hyun Lee, *The Philosophical Theology of Jonathan Edwards* (Princeton, NJ: Princeton Univ Press, 1988); John W. Cooper, *Panentheism–The Other God of the Philosophers: From Plato to the Present* (Grand Rapids, MI: Baker Academic, 2006), 77.

4.3 Philosophical Resources

Philosophical categories often shape and mold expressions of the doctrine of God. The differences between Hodge and Reformed Orthodoxy regarding the attributes of God are a case in point since many of the conceptual categories of God's existence and essence came from philosophy. The Scholastics had a variegated philosophical mindset. While all of their philosophical sources were pre-Modern, there was no single philosopher or philosophy from which all Reformed Scholastics drew. Though Aristotle was usually the philosopher most commonly used in Reformed Orthodoxy, Scholastic thinkers often reshaped or rejected parts of Aristotle as they saw fit.[4] Hodge, by contrast, drew more from Modern than pre-Modern philosophers. He shaped his thought in particular with a set of philosophical tools borrowed from Scottish Common Sense Realism (SCSR). Moreover, Hodge utilized the consciousness-based approach of Sir William Hamilton and Henry Mansel (1820–1871) in building his epistemology. SCSR recast Hodge's thinking on the doctrine of God, leading him to regard the Classical Theist model exemplified in Reformed Orthodoxy as dangerously close to pantheism.

4.3.1 Reformed Orthodoxy and Philosophy

Reformed Orthodoxy was a chronologically and philosophically diverse movement. Richard Muller and Aza Goudriaan agree that Reformed Scholastics were not committed to a single philosopher or philosophical school.[5] Rather, various philosophical influences helped shape the contours of Reformed Scholasticism. Aristotelianism stands out as the single greatest influence among the different philosophical voices in the Reformed tradition.[6] Yet the well-trained philosopher will easily detect the influences of Ramsim, Descartes, and others as he reads the Reformed Scholastics.[7] This section outlines the most common philosophical influences in Reformed Orthodoxy with their relevance to the doctrine of God,

---

4 The Reformed Orthodox followed the lead of the Medieval Scholastics in their selective use of Aristotle. For some good examples of this Medieval pattern, see Matthew Levering and Gilles Emery, eds., *Aristotle in Aquinas's Theology* (Oxford: Oxford University Press, 2018), 1–28, 48–69, 205–32.

5 Aza Goudriaan, "Theology and Philosophy," in *A Companion to Reformed Orthodoxy*, ed. Herman Selderhuis, vol. 40, Brill's Companion to the Christian Tradition (Leiden: Brill, 2013), 28.

6 Goudriaan, "Theology and Philosophy"; Richard A Muller, "Scholasticism, Reformation, Orthodoxy, and the Persistence of Christian Aristotelianism," *Trinity Journal* 19, no. 1 (1998): 81–96; Richard A Muller, "Reformation, Orthodoxy, 'Christian Aristotelianism,' and the Eclecticism of Early Modern Philosophy," *Nederlands Archief Voor Kerkgeschiedenis* 81, no. 3 (2001): 309–19.

7 See Stephen J. Reid and Emma Annette Wilson, eds., *Ramus, Pedagogy and the Liberal Arts: Ramism in Britain and the Wider World* (Farnham: Ashgate, 2011), 1–24; Frank Pierrepont Graves, *Peter Ramus and the Educational Reformation of the Sixteenth Century* (New York: The Macmillan Company, 1912);

providing a backdrop for assessing continuities and discontinuities between Hodge and Reformed Orthodoxy.

By far, Aristotle was the most common philosophical influence on Reformed Orthodoxy. However, the "Aristotelianism" of Reformed Orthodoxy did not entail a uniform set of philosophical axioms. "A caveat is needed, however, because the term 'Aristotelianism,'" Goudriaan explains, "may suggest a clearly defined set of 'Aristotelian' tenets, whereas in reality early modem so-called Aristotelianism represented a variety of viewpoints and was a rather eclectic complex which was able easily to combine elements from different traditions of philosophical thinking."[8] Muller helpfully identifies many Reformed Scholastics with the "Christian Aristotelianism" that developed during the Middle Ages.[9] No Christian theologian in the West appropriated Aristotle without significant modifications to his thought. For instance, no significant Medieval figure accepted Aristotle's notion that creation was eternal along with with "God." However, numerous theologians saw in Aristotle a system of terms, such as "substance" and "accident," and concepts, such as primary and secondary causation, which they could deploy in the service of Christian theology.[10] The rhetoric of the Reformers might give the impression that they opposed the use of Aristotle carte blanch. However, a careful study of John Calvin (1509–1564) and Peter Martyr Vermigli (1499–1562) shows that they too appropriated the eclectic Christian Aristotelianism of the Middle Ages as they searched for a "sound philosophy" to aid the work of theology.[11]

The variegated permutations of Christian Aristotelianism in Reformed Orthodoxy had at least two consequences for the doctrine of God. First, the Reformed Orthodox tradition typically argued for the existence of God based on a posteriori arguments.[12] Most Reformed Scholastics did not prefer the a priori orientation of the Augustinian tradition. While some Reformed Orthodoxy combined Platonism and Neo-Platonism with their doctrine of God—as Anselm did centuries before—most Scholastics did not use a priori ontological arguments for God's existence. Rather, they preferred a posteriori arguments, such as the teleological and cosmological arguments, as did the Medieval Aristotelians, notably Aquinas. In

---

Stephen Voss, *Essays on the Philosophy and Science of René Descartes* (New York: Oxford Univ Press, 1993).

8 Goudriaan, "Theology and Philosophy," 36.

9 Richard A Muller, *Post-Reformation Reformed Dogmatics: The Rise and Development of Reformed Orthodoxy, ca. 1520 to ca. 1725* (Grand Rapids, Mich.: Baker Academics, 2003), vol. 1:362–363.

10 Muller, "Reformation, Orthodoxy, 'Christian Aristotelianism,' and the Eclecticism of Early Modern Philosophy," 313–15.

11 Muller, *Post-Reformation Reformed Dogmatics*, vol. 1:365–367.

12 Sebastian Rehnman, "The Doctrine of God in Reformed Orthodoxy," in *A Companion to Reformed Orthodoxy* (Leiden: Brill, 2013), 368–71.

other words, Aristotelian empiricism had theological entailments. Second, eclectic Aristotelianism also entailed a commitment to Classical Theism. The Reformed Orthodox were conscious of their place within what Craig Carter calls "the Great Tradition."[13] The pre-Modern orientation of Christian Aristotelianism shielded many of the Reformed Scholastics from adopting radical or new conceptions of the doctrine of God.

The second philosophical influence in Reformed Orthodoxy was Ramism. Peter Ramus (1515–1572) was an educational reformer who self-consciously rejected the Aristotelianism of the Middle Ages, especially regarding the method of logic. He valued Aristotle but despised—and that is not too strongly worded—the way Aristotelianism developed in the Medieval university. Ramus had several significant followers in the Calvinist world of the seventeenth century. His influence was mostly confined to the British Isles as Continental Reformed thinkers were less sanguine about his approach. William Perkins (1558–1602) and William Ames (1576–1633) appropriated Ramism and transmitted it into Puritanism.[14] While Ramus offered a number of unique philosophical insights, he is perhaps best known for his emphasis on clear definitions through the method of dichotomizing subjects into related parts. This is evident, for example, in the twofold division of both Westminster Catechisms into what man is to believe concerning God and the duty God requires of man, generally following a further division into the creed, the ten commandments, the sacraments, and the Lord's Prayer. Ramist bifurcation is obvious on the surface of important theological systems as well, such as those of Amandus Polanus (1561–1610) and Johannes Wollebius (1586–1626). These systems also illustrate, however, that even Ramism was not an airtight method of organization since such authors freely explained various doctrines without bifurcating every issue into groups of two. Importantly, Ramus emphasized the practical dimension of thought where the main goal of education was to bring change in ordinary life.[15] One can see the influence of Ramism in the dichotomized structure of many questions in the Westminster Shorter Catechism, such as Westminster Shorter Catechism 3.

The final philosophical influence to note for Reformed Orthodoxy is the thought of Rene Descartes (1596–1650). Most Reformed authors viewed Descartes's epistemology of systematic doubt as radical.[16] His methodological use of doubt caused many Reformed Scholastics, such as Peter van Mastricht (1630–1706) and Gisbertus Voetius (1589–1676), to criticize any appropriation of his thought. His sense

---

13 Craig A. Carter, *Interpreting Scripture with the Great Tradition: Recovering the Genius of Premodern Exegesis* (Grand Rapids, MI: Baker Academic, 2018).

14 Goudriaan, "Theology and Philosophy," 41–42.

15 Chapter 3 of this present volume illustrates how this played out in defining theology as "the doctrine of living well," and "the doctrine of living to God."

16 Goudriaan, "Theology and Philosophy," 43–53.

of doubt was so strong that it was thought by many to be contrary to the biblical injunction to reject doubt in order to have faith. Thus most Reformed authors, with exceptions such as Christoph Wittich (1625–1687), rejected Descartes' method in favor of the more traditional "faith seeking understanding" approach exemplified in authors like Augustine, Anselm, and Aquinas. Moreover, many saw the anti-empiricist approach of Cartesianism as problematic. An a priori epistemology reconstructed metaphysics in such a way that a posteriori arguments for God's existence were no longer valid. Hence, many Reformed Scholastics rejected Descartes, even though some found Cartesianism attractive as a building block for a sound philosophy. Cartesianism tended to have consequences for the doctrine of God. For instance, some Cartesians had a strong voluntaristic impulse to the point that they would argue God could deceive if He so chose to do so.[17] In summary, Reformed Orthodox approaches to philosophy in relation to theology were ultimately eclectic, critical, and cautious. No philosophical system remained untouched where Reformed authors appropriated philosophical categories into their theologies.[18]

4.3.2 Charles Hodge and Philosophy

Philosophy is critical for much of the work of systematic theology. Charles Hodge recognized this fact himself. "To understand any theological system," Hodge writes, "we must understand the philosophy that underlies it and gives it its peculiar form."[19] Yet the contrast between Hodge and Reformed Orthodoxy regarding philosophy is striking. While the Reformed Orthodox were eclectic in their philosophical influences, Hodge was indebted to one main philosophical influence, namely Scottish Common Sense Realism. Hodge was not alone in drawing upon SCSR. SCSR was, in a real sense, a near-universal influence on American Protestant theologians of the nineteenth century.[20] The Princetonians were no exception to this trend in American religious thought.[21] Hodge drew from SCSR sources in foundational

17 Goudriaan, "Theology and Philosophy," 49–50.

18 For more information on philosophical influences on Reformed Orthodoxy, see Aza Goudriaan, *Reformed Orthodoxy and Philosophy, 1625–1750: Gisbertus Voetius, Petrus van Mastricht, and Anthonius Driessen* (Leiden: Brill, 2006).

19 Charles Hodge, "What Is Christianity?," *The Biblical Repretory and Princeton Review* 32 (n.d.): 121.

20 See E. Brooks Holifield, *Theology in America: Christian Thought from the Age of the Puritans to the Civil War* (New Haven, Conn.: Yale University Press, 2005); Sydney E Ahlstrom, "The Scottish Philosophy and American Theology," *Church History* 24, no. 03 (1955): 252–72; Theodore Dwight Bozeman, *Protestants in an Age of Science: The Baconian Ideal and Antebellum American Religious Thought* (Chapel Hill: University of North Carolina Press, 2012).

21 See J. Wayne Denny, *The Influence of Scottish Common Sense Realism on B.B. Warfield and His Formulation of the Doctrine of Inerrancy*, 2006; David Kinney Garth, *The Influence of Scottish Common Sense Philosophy on the Theology of James Henley Thornwell and Robert Lewis Dabney*,

areas of philosophy and theology.[22] His confederation with SCSR produced significant changes in his understanding of the doctrine of God. The net effect is that Hodge found Classical Theism, as expressed in the Reformed Scholastics, to be problematic at best and near Pantheistic at worst. As we will see below, this created tensions in Hodge's adherence to the Westminster Standards on the doctrine of God in ways that he was likely not fully aware of.

Before demonstrating Hodge's approval of SCSR, one should first note the particular form of SCSR he appropriated. Hodge seldom referenced Thomas Reid (1710–1796), the most significant figure in the development of SCSR. Rather, SCSR came to Hodge mediated through the thought of Sir William Hamilton. Hamilton's chief characteristic as a thinker was his attempt to fuse Immanuel Kant's Copernican Revolution in epistemology with Thomas Reid's direct realism. He attempted this philosophical emulsion by emphasizing the role of consciousness in philosophy. Hamilton highlighted man's consciousness both as a vehicle to emphasize the mind's role in the knowing process (Kant) and create a realistic structure of knowledge by removing "ideas" as a mediating concept between the mind and extra mental objects (Reid). It was Hamilton's unique model of SCSR that Hodge found attractive. Hamilton's influence on Hodge was architectonic for Hodge's doctrine of God. Hodge constantly used the tools he learned from Hamilton as he worked through the attributes of God in general and the metaphysical attributes of God in particular.

Thomas Reid sought to answer Hume's skepticism with two novel philosophical moves. First, he emphasized the importance of the sensibilities of the common man. That is, Reid argued that the mass of humanity and its basic philosophical intuitions were more significant for philosophy than the imaginations of technical thinkers. Second, he argued that the root of Hume's skepticism lay in the idealist tradition that began with John Locke (1632–1704).[23] Reid argued contrary to Locke that both perception and *judgments* are foundational to one's epistemology, not perception and simple ideas.[24] God created mankind to have these automatic judgments built into our epistemic faculties. Hence, denying the immediate, universal, and necessary

---

1982; Sung Shik Jang, "Contextualization in the Princeton Theology, 1822–1878: Scottish Common Sense Realism and the Doctrine of Providence in the Theology of Charles Hodge" (1993).

22 O Anderson, *Reason and Faith in the Theology of Charles Hodge: American Common Sense Realism.* (Place of publication not identified: Palgrave Pivot, 2015); Peter Hicks, "The Philosophy of Charles Hodge: A 19th Century Evangelical Approach to Reason, Knowledge, and Truth" (Lewiston, N.Y. : Edwin Mellen Press, 1997); Jang, "Contextualization in the Princeton Theology, 1822–1878."

23 Frederick Copleston, *A History of Philosophy Vol. V: Modern Philosophy* (New York: Image Books, Doubleday, 1994), 366.

24 Copleston, *A History of Philosophy Vol. V: Modern Philosophy*, 367.

judgments of mankind—such as the reality of cause and effect—leads immediately to absurdity.[25]

Hamilton inherited these basic philosophical commitments from Reid. However, Hamilton sought to fortify Reid's Common Sense ideas with an additional psychological dimension. Hamilton argued that one must turn to the study of the mind—the study of psychology—as the *principium* of all philosophy.[26] John Veitch identified three key questions that Hamilton answered in his philosophical investigations: what are the facts or the "phenomena" that must be studied? What are the laws or "universal facts" that govern our epistemic faculties? What may we infer from consciousness (or what may we legitimately build upon the foundational datum of consciousness)?[27] Hamilton's fusion of Reid's direct realism, emphasizing the common judgment of mankind, the absurdity of contradicting mankind's common sense, and an emphasis on consciousness, was the form of SCSR that Hodge found most attractive. One sees the influence of SCSR on Hodge from the beginning of his section on the doctrine of God.

Hodge's formal acceptance of SCSR appears markedly in the section of his systematic theology dealing with the knowledge of God. Specifically, Hodge gives his approval to SCSR as taught by William Hamilton and Henry Mansel.[28] While Hodge criticized Hamilton and Mansel for denying that man can know the infinite God, he applauded Hamilton's commitment to "the Philosophy of Common Sense."[29] Hodge reduced the essence of this philosophy to four basic principles. First, the dictates of consciousness are undoubtedly true. Second, whatever the "laws of our nature" require us to believe must also be received as true. Third, the principle of the unqualified reception of our consciousness and nature must be further extended to all parts of our person, so that the dictates of our nature, reason, senses, and consciousness must be accepted as true, adding a theological ground for this commitment. "We cannot," Hodge wrote, "rationally or consistently with our allegiance to God, deny what our senses, reason, or conscience pronounce to

25 Copleston, 367; Thomas Reid, *An Inquiry into the Human Mind, On the Principles of Common Sense.* (Edinburgh: J. Robertson, 1818), 394–95.

26 See William Hamilton, *The Metaphysics of Sir William Hamilton: Collected, Arranged, and Abridged, for the Use of Colleges and Private Students*, ed. Francis Bowen (Cambridge: Sever and Francis, 1865); William Hamilton and Robert Turnbull, *Discussions on Philosophy and Literature, Education and University Reform: Chiefly from the Edinburgh Review* (New York: Harper & Bros., 1853).

27 John Veitch, *Hamilton* (Philadelphia: Lippincott, 1882), 42.

28 For more information on Henry Mansel, see Henry Mansel, *Metaphysics or The Philosophy of Consciousness, Phenomenal and Real* (Edinburgh: Adam and Charles Black, 1883); Henry Mansel, *Philsophy of the Unconditioned* (Norderstedt, Germany: Hansebooks, 2016); Kenneth Freeman, *The Role of Reason in Religion: A Study of Henry Mansel* (The Hague: Springer, 1969).

29 Hodge, *Systematic Theology*, vol. 1:360–361.

be true."[30] Finally, Common Sense appealed not just to the sense of man, but to the *common* sense of man. That is, someone can appeal to common sense only on the basis of the universal approbation of mankind, which Hodge called "the criteria of universality and necessity."[31]

In Hodge's opinion, Hamilton did further service for the intellectual world by proving that such principles of Common Sense have "been recognized by the leading philosophic minds in all ages."[32] Hamilton demonstrated the apparent danger of contradicting any of these fundamental principles, which enable the existence of both science and religion. Questioning the testimony of consciousness leads us straight into the arms of complete skepticism. The importance of consciousness to our epistemology is so apparent that even John Stuart Mill (1806–1873), who was no proponent of SCSR, would not allow consciousness to be questioned. Hodge agreed that consciousness must not be questioned because it alone was the source for many of our fundamental categories necessary to human thought. He followed the lead of Mansel in arguing that our notions of substance, personality, causation, and morality all come from our consciousness.[33] Hodge further affirmed Mansel's conclusion that this commitment to consciousness was the true expansion of Descartes' *Cogito* ("I think") and the real *Ding an sich* ("thing in itself").[34]

While this section of Hodge's *Systematic Theology* is short, it has profound implications for his theology in general and particularly in relation to his doctrine of God. Here we find the hermeneutical key to understanding why Hodge deviates from the classical, Scholastic, and catholic doctrine of God. Three important observations must be made about Hodge's commitment to SCSR. First, Hodge's understanding of Common Sense Philosophy appears to be fairly accurate. Hodge's four pillars of Common Sense fit well within the mainstream tradition of SCSR. It is important to our argument that Hodge's reception of SCSR helps to explain some of Hodge's discontinuity with Reformed Orthodoxy in relation to the doctrine of God. If Hodge had warped or misconstrued Reid or Hamilton's thought, then the source of Hodge's doctrine of God would not be SCSR per se but his own idiosyncratic epistemological principles.

Second, Hodge insisted that the testimony of consciousness must be accepted as true without question. This insistence that consciousness is the universal and necessary source of data in the knowing process reemerges continually in Hodge's theology. His unwavering commitment to consciousness explains why Hodge never

30 Hodge, *Systematic Theology*, vol. 1:361.

31 Hodge, *Systematic Theology*, vol. 1:361.

32 Hodge, *Systematic Theology*, vol. 1:361.

33 Hodge, *Systematic Theology*, vol. 1:361. The problems arising from such assumed views of personality and personhood receive extensive attention in chapter five of this present volume.

34 Hodge, *Systematic Theology*, vol. 1:361.

considered classical notions of simplicity or immutability to be viable; entertaining doctrines that appear to be out of step with the consciousness of man was, in his view, to open the Pandora's box of skepticism.

Third, notice the particular areas of knowledge where consciousness alone provides us with information: substance, personality, causation, and morality. Each of these philosophical categories was fundamental to our conception of God. Substance relates to our understanding of the nature of God's spirituality and simplicity. Personality is a fundamental concept for Trinitarian theology. Causation is an essential part of our understanding of God's power, providence, and relationship to the world. Morality is a concept that directly interfaces with our understanding of the moral attributes of God. We shall discover in the course of our investigation that Hodge's commitment to SCSR shaped his view of all of these categories, causing him to reshape the classical doctrine of God to accommodate them. As a result of his commitment to consciousness, he undercut the Creator-creature distinction by formulating his doctrine of God inside an essentially anthropocentric cast.

Hodge's use of SCSR stands in contrast to Reformed Orthodoxy's use of Aristotle and other ancient sources. As the rest of this chapter will show, SCSR shaped the philosophical theology of Hodge in such a way that he found the Classical Theism of both Ancient and Scholastic Christianity to be problematic. The emphasis on consciousness as the regulating principles of epistemology produced an anthropocentric impulse in Hodge's theology. As a result, he often found the Orthodox doctrine of God to be too transcendent, dangerously close to pantheism.

4.4 Nature and Taxonomy of the Divine Attributes

Hodge's continuity with the Reformed orthodox doctrine of God becomes less pronounced when we turn directly to his treatment of the divine attributes. This section illustrates this point by comparing Hodge and his Reformed predecessors on the nature and taxonomy of the divine attributes.

4.4.1 Reformed Orthodoxy on the Nature and Taxonomy of the Attributes

The Reformed Orthodox inherited an inchoate formulation of the doctrine of God from first-generation reformers. The doctrine of God was not a major issue of contention between Protestants and Catholics since both operated within the received tradition of Classical Theism, mediated through Medieval Scholasticism. Calvin, for instance, did not devote a section of the *Institutes of the Christian Religion* to the attributes of God. Rather, his view of the attributes is found scattered throughout his commentaries and theological treatises. The Reformed Scholastics began to work on the doctrine of God in a manner appropriate to a formal school room in the context of training ministers. This led them to devote careful consideration to both the nature and the taxonomy of the attributes.

Richard Muller notes that the Scholastics developed a careful set of definitions for terms such as "attributes," "accidents," and "properties." Any term that humanity predicates of God is, strictly speaking, an attribute. Properties are what is true of a nature regardless of human predication. "Simply put," Muller explains, "an attribute is strictly a characteristic or quality attributed to or predicated of an object, whereas a property is a characteristic that belongs to an object."[35] Properties are accidental or essential depending on whether or not the object can be removed or abstracted from the object. Reformed Orthodox writers argued that God's attributes are properties of his nature, distinct from the personal properties which constitute the persons of the Godhead. Some properties are essential while others are relational, contingent upon God's relationship to the creation (i. e. God's eternity is an essential property, while his being Creator is a relational or relative attribute).[36]

The Scholastics also considered carefully the taxonomy of the divine attributes. They developed a variegated set of different taxonomical schemes to classify the attributes: first and second order attributes; essence, life, intellect, and will; a priori and a posteriori; essential, actuosity, and relationality; *quid, quantus,* and *quails sti Deus;* communicable and incommunicable.[37] Heinrich Heppe (1820–1879) and Louis Berkhof (1873–1957) followed Turretin in arguing that the "communicable and incommunicable" scheme was the dominant approach.[38] Muller has shown, however, that no single approach earned the title of the majority opinion of Reformed Orthodoxy. No uniform way of classifying divine attributes existed, even though distinct patterns emerged, and not two lists of divine attributes were precisely identical. These various approaches tended to fall along lines of schools and groups of scholars, so that there are recognizable trajectories in Reformed Orthodox theologians.[39] In light of divine incomprehensibility, as William Bucanus (d. 1602) represented the Reformed tradition well when he noted that one could describe God without ever being able to define God with a decisive list of perfectly classified attributes. Both divine attributes and how one organized those attributes illustrated

35 Muller, *Post-Reformation Reformed Dogmatics*, vol. 3:214.

36 Muller, *Post-Reformation Reformed Dogmatics*, vol. 3:215–216.

37 Muller, *Post-Reformation Reformed Dogmatics*, vol. 3:216–226.

38 Heinrich Heppe, *Reformed Dogmatics: Set Out and Illustrated from the Sources*, ed. Ernst Bizer, trans. G. T. Thomson (Grand Rapids, Michigan: Baker Book House, 1950), 60–61; Louis Berkhof, *Systematic Theology* (Grand Rapids, MI: W. B. Eerdmans, 2018), 55; Francis Turretin, *Institutes of Elenctic Theology*, ed. James T Dennison, trans. George Musgrave Giger (Phillipsburg N.J: P & R Publishing, 1992), vol. 1:189–191.

39 Muller, *Post-Reformation Reformed Dogmatics*, vol. 3:216–217.

that approximated human understanding was not the measure of the immeasurable God.[40]

4.4.2 Hodge on the Nature and Taxonomy of the Attributes

Hodge carefully considered the nature of and classification of the divine attributes as well, though in a slightly different trajectory than his Reformed predecessors.. He showed awareness of both Modern and Orthodox issues related to the definition of the attributes. Hodge referred to the Scholastic distinctions, but, driven by his commitment to SCSR, he opted for a more Modern formulations of the attributes. His commitment to SCSR manifests itself in the very definition of the attributes. "To the divine essence, which in itself is infinite, eternal, and unchangeable, belong certain perfections revealed to us in the constitution of our nature and in the word of God."[41] The anthropocentric quality of Hodge's definition is striking when contrasted with typical definitions in Reformed Orthodoxy. Some Reformed Orthodox highlighted the distinction between the Creator and the creature in their definition, making man analogous to God rather than God analogous to man. Francis Turretin defined attributes as, " the essential properties by which he makes himself known to us who are weak and those by which he is distinguished from creatures; or they are those which are attributed to him according to the measure of our conception in order to explain his nature."[42] Others emphasized further that the attributes were God's way of communicating truth about himself to man. Amandus Polanus defined divine attribute as, "those titles, which are attributed to God by some means, according to our capacity to declare his essence better unto us."[43] Attributes said something meaningful about the incomprehensible divine essence, while retaining the idea that we could apprehend God without comprehending him.

Hodge acknowledged that there were further elaborations on the attributes of God given by Scholastics or "older theologians." Scholastics clarified that some attributes were relational, others were essential properties, and other still were relational properties. Hodge accurately reflected some of the distinctions made by Reformed Orthodoxy in these respects. He continued displaying a knowledge of Reformed Orthodoxy when he took up the classification of the attributes. In

---

40 Gulielmus Bucanus, *Institutiones Theolgicae, Seu, Locorum Communium Christanae Religionis* (Geneva, 1648), 3.

41 Hodge, *Systematic Theology*, vol. 1:368.

42 Turretin, *Institutes of Elenctic Theology*, vol. 1:187.

43 Amandus Polanus, *The Substance of the Christian Religion*, trans. Elijahu Wilcocks (London: Felix Norton, 1600), 2–3. (This edition of Polanus was written in 1600 and so the spelling of the work is archaic. The references to this work in this chapter have updated the spelling without altering the meaning of the text.)

Hodge's opinion, much of the ink spilled over the classification was needless: "On few subjects have greater thought and labor been expended than on this. Perhaps, however, the benefit has not been commensurate with the labor." The goal of classification should be clarity of thought and presentation. So long as clarity is achieved, Hodge remained somewhat ambivalent about the method or categorization.[44] Hodge noted a number of the potential schemes, while opting himself to follow the list of attributes in the Westminster Shorter Catechism, which did not seek to classify attributes into distinct categories.

He appeared next to refer to some Modern authors, such as Mansel or Hamilton, who gave no classification because God as "the Absolute" is beyond classification,[45] passing over this method with little comment. Hodge also discussed the method in which one classifies the attributes by the in which they are revealed to man. Hodge had in mind here the Scholastic method of causation and negation that, in Hodge's estimation, leads to the communicable/incommunicable method. There was also the psychological method, where the attributes fall along the lines of essence, intellect, and will. Some authors preferred the natural and moral classification (though Hodge did not explain the connection between this category and the communicable and incommunicable distinction). Natural attributes represented incommunicable properties of God's nature without respect to creation, while moral ones found analogical reflection in God's rational creatures. Hodge also noted Schleiermacher's "peculiar" method of discussing the attributes in line with the sense of dependence upon the whence. Hodge rejected all of these methods,[46] preferring the simple method of following the fourth question of the Westminster Shorter Catechism.[47] "It is proposed," Hodge writes, "in what follows to accept the guidance of the answer given in the "Westminster Catechism," to the question, What is God? It is assumed in that answer that God is a self-existent and necessary Being; and it is affirmed of Him, I. That He is a Spirit. II. That as such He is infinite, eternal, and immutable. III. That He is infinite, eternal, and immutable, (1.) In his being. (2.) In all that belongs to his intelligence, namely, in his knowledge and wisdom. (3.) In all that belongs to his will, namely, his power, holiness, justice, goodness, and truth."[48] Without specifying the fact, this definition corresponded at points to both absolute and relative divine attributes, as well as to psychological classifications of essence, intellect, and will.

---

44 Hodge, *Systematic Theology*, vol. 1:374.

45 Salmond, *Princetoniana, Charles & A. A. Hodge: With Class and Table Talk of Hodge the Younger*, 137.

46 Hodge, *Systematic Theology*, vol. 1:374–376.

47 Which states, "God is a Spirit, infinite, eternal, and unchangeable, in his being, wisdom, power, holiness, justice, goodness, and truth."

48 Hodge, *Systematic Theology*, vol. 1:376.

In this section more than any of the other surveyed so far, Hodge shows a knowledge of the tradition of Reformed Orthodoxy. He did not cite any Reformed Orthodox authors or creeds, with the notable exception the Shorter Catechism. However, he expressed awareness of various taxonomies in the Scholastic tradition. His choice of the Shorter Catechism method was not, for Hodge, a serious methodological commitment. Rather, he appears to have been pragmatic in his choice, not seeing any one method as prima facia superior to the others, while clearly ruling out some options such as Schleiermacher's. Like his arguments for God's existence, his taxonomy of the divine attributes reflected basic continuities and underlying commitments about divine incomprehensibility with Reformed orthodoxy. Discontinuity only begins to surface clearly in his treatment of specific divine attributes.

4.5 Specific Divine Attributes

Hodge's modifications of the Reformed orthodox doctrine of God, through the lens of his SCSR, begin to emerge in his treatment of particular divine attributes. The three divisions below illustrate stronger points of discontinuity between Hodge and Reformed orthodoxy in light of his nineteenth century American context. The first two sections here address metaphysical attributes, or attributes of being, the first of which is divine simplicity. The second section continues treating attributes of being through infinitude, immutability, and eternity. The third moves from attributes of being to complete the psychological division of attributes via intellect and will.

4.5.1 Divine Simplicity

4.5.1.1 Reformed Scholasticism on Divine Simplicity

As we will see, Hodge expressed unease over classic and long-standing formulations of divine simplicity. The doctrine of divine simplicity historically maintained that God exists without any form of composition.[49] The Westminster Confession of Faith ably states the doctrine when it denies body, parts, or passions in the divine nature. Divine simplicity excludes all material and theoretical composition from the divine nature. God's divine excellence so exceeds finite reality that there are no material, metaphysical, or logical parts in the divine essence. As one theologian expresses the traditional doctrine, [t]he Doctrine of Divine Simplicity teaches that (1) God is identical with his existence and his essence and (2) that each of

49 William E. Mann, "Divine Simplicity," *Religious Studies* 18, no. 4 (1982): 451–471; Eleonore Stump and Norman Kretzmann, "Absolute Simplicity," *Faith and Philosophy* 2, no. 4 (October 1985): 353–82.

his attributes is ontologically identical with his existence and with every other one of his attributes. There is nothing in God that is not God.[50] This definition reflects the Christian tradition from authors like Augustine, John of Damascus, Anselm, Richard St. Victor, Thomas Aquinas, Bonaventure, and many others. Since the doctrine of divine simplicity asserts that everything in God is identical to God, divine simplicity is sometimes called the "identity account" of God's divine essence.[51]

The Reformed Orthodox accepted the "identity" thesis as their understanding of the simplicity of the divine essence.[52] No Scholastic theologian that we know of deviated from standard Christian expressions of divine simplicity. There were, however, debates as to how best to explain the diverse effects of the divine nature in the world while affirming the absolute simplicity of God's nature and essence. Theologians used three different models to affirm divine simplicity: Formal, Virtual, and Nominalist models.[53] The Reformed Scholastics adopted various elements of all three models. Some veered more towards the Nominalist position, arguing that the different attributes are distinguished conceptually in the human mind without

---

50 James E Dolezal, *God Without Parts: Divine Simplicity and the Metaphysics of God's Absoluteness* (Eugene, Or.: Pickwick Publications, 2011), 1; Polanus, *The Substance of the Christian Religion*, 3–4; Francis Cheynell, *The Divine Trinunity of the Father, Son, and Holy Spirit, or, The Blessed Doctrine of the Three Coessentiall Subsistents in the Eternall Godhead without Any Confusion or Division of the Distinct Subsistences or Multiplication of the Most Single and Entire Godhead Acknowledged, Beleeved, Adored by Christians, in Opposition to Pagans, Jewes, Mahumetans, Blasphemous and Antichristian Hereticks, Who Say They Are Christians, but Are Not* (London: Samuel Gellibrand, 1650), 116.

51 Dolezal, *God Without Parts*, 125.

52 Muller, *Post-Reformation Reformed Dogmatics*, vol. 3:275–279.

53 Proponents of these different models all adhere to core tenet of divine simplicity, that the attributes of God are all identical to each other and to the divine nature itself. The weakest model of simplicity is the Formal Model. Formalists argue that the attributes are genuinely distinct from each other according to form but not according to substance. Nominalism, by contrast, gives the strongest account of divine simplicity. Nominalists argue that no objective distinctions exist between the divine attributes. The distinction human beings make between the love and justice of God, for instance, are purely subjective. The human mind makes these distinctions for ease of thought. No objective foundation for these distinctions exists in God. The Virtual Model is a mediating position between the Formal and Nominalist account of the attributes. The Virtual account claims while the attributes of God are not metaphysically distinct in God, the distinctions human beings make between the attributes are grounded in the effects of the divine essence in the world of creation. Love and justice are not distinct in God. The divine essence, however, causes love and justice in the world, and these differing effects explain why human beings attribute different attributes to the one undivided essence.See Richard A Muller, *Dictionary of Latin and Greek Theological Terms: Drawn Principally from Protestant Scholastic Theology* (Grand Rapids, Mich.: Baker Book House, 1985), 93–94; Dolezal, *God Without Parts*, 128–35.

an emphasis on these distinctions being grounded in the divine nature itself.[54] Van Mastricht, for example, leaned in the Nominalist direction by placing the ground of the distinct effects of God wholly outside the divine being. In response to the objection, "[t]hat external actions differ from the agent himself," Van Mastricht argued, "that the thing produced extrinsically by an action does differ from the divine essence, though not the power and producing action. Nor does the relation with what is produced, which from the production belongs to the producer, make that producer a composite. For that relation is not a being of any sort, nor does it imply composition in God (for things are related to something, not in something)."[55] Others generally adopted the Virtual Model,[56] though some such as Francis Turretin opted to draw language from both Virtual and Formal models.[57] Whatever differences existed among Reformed expressions of divine simplicity, this attribute remained fundamental for distinguishing God's self-existent being from his creatures.

While the Reformed Orthodox expressed their view of divine simplicity with different philosophical tools, the logic behind simplicity was the independence and perfection of God. A Brakel expresses this concern well when he writes, "since we must recognize, however, that all composition implies imperfection, dependency, and divisibility, we may not think of God as being composite even in the remotest sense of the word."[58] What we shall see is that Hodge has the exact opposite reaction to divine simplicity. Where the Reformed Orthodox saw simplicity as essential for maintain the integrity of the divine nature, Hodge will see divine simplicity as a speculative notion that compromises the integrity of Christian theism by coming dangerously close to pantheism.

4.5.1.2 Charles Hodge on Divine Simplicity

Living in a vastly different intellectual context, Hodge gravitated against traditional expressions of divine simplicity. His treatment of divine simplicity illustrates

54 Muller, *Post-Reformation Reformed Dogmatics*, vol. 3:289–290; Polanus, *The Substance of the Christian Religion*, 3.

55 Petrus Van Mastricht, *Theoretico-Practical Theology: Faith in the Triune God*, ed. Joel Beeke, trans. Todd Rester, vol. 2 (Grand Rapids, Michigan: Reformation Heritage Books, 2019), 185.

56 Cheynell, *The Divine Trinunity of the Father, Son, and Holy Spirit, or, The Blessed Doctrine of the Three Coessentiall Subsistents in the Eternall Godhead without Any Confusion or Division of the Distinct Subsistences or Multiplication of the Most Single and Entire Godhead Acknowledged, Beleeved, Adored by Christians, in Opposition to Pagans, Jewes, Mahumetans, Blasphemous and Antichristian Hereticks, Who Say They Are Christians, but Are Not*, 116–18.

57 Muller, *Post-Reformation Reformed Dogmatics*, vol. 3:295.

58 Wilhelmus A Brakel, *The Christian's Reasonable Service*, ed. Joel R Beeke, trans. Bartel Elshout (Grand Rapids: Reformation Heritage Books, 2015), vol. 1: 96.

his often-complex relationship to the Reformed tradition he laid claim to, while he sought to defend and adapt Reformed ideas in nineteenth century America. Working logically through the nature of the divine attributes, Hodge discussed the relationship between the attributes and essence of God, urging readers to avoid two extremes. On the one hand, one must avoid the errors of the strong realist position, which introduces composition in the divine being by construing the attributes as differing *in res* from one another. On the other hand, one must also avoid the errors of the Medieval nominalists who confounded the attributes by, "making them all mean the same thing, which is equivalent to denying them all together."[59] "Occam, Biel, and other Nominalists taught," according to Hodge, "Attributa divina nec rei, nec rationis distinctione, inter se aut ab essentia divina distingui; sed omnem distinctionem esse solum in nominibus."[60] Hodge explains that Lutheran and Reformed theologians tended towards the excesses of the nominalists by rejecting any and all categories of material, metaphysical, and logical composition in the divine nature.[61] The basic reason that explains Hodge's rejection of Reformed Orthodoxy's notion of divine simplicity is that he conflated the Identity Thesis with the Nominalist position, as is clear in the body of Hodge's argument. That is, Hodge had a visceral reaction to the arbitrary nature of Nominalist theology, and he did not see the different models of divine simplicity embraced with Reformed Orthodox. In order to avoid a perceived disconnect between our understanding of God and God's essence, Hodge opted to reject divine simplicity at points in favor of real distinctions between the attributes, while at other places in his corpus he appears to be more favorable to simplicity.

Fearing agnosticism regarding God's essence, Hodge explained the way these theologians handled the apparent difference between the attributes: the distinctions between the attributes are only distinctions in humanity's conceptions of them and are not to be predicated of the divine nature itself. Quoting Aquinas and Quenstedt at some length to demonstrate this tendency,[62] Hodge used the classic example of sunlight to show how this position argued for a simple substance producing multiple effects in the created world. Without being composite, the sun's rays produce illumination, heat, and chemical reactions based on the substances with which it interacts.[63] A further illustration of how far these theologians were willing to take this concept of simplicity emerges by way of their use of negative examples: the attributes of God are not like the attributes of the human soul that, while simple, both reasons and wills.

---

59 Hodge, *Systematic Theology*, vol. 1:369.

60 Hodge, *Systematic Theology*, vol. 1:369.

61 Hodge, *Systematic Theology*, vol. 1:369.

62 Hodge, *Systematic Theology*, vol. 1:370.

63 Hodge, *Systematic Theology*, vol. 1:370.

In Hodge's estimation, a more plausible construal of the relationship between the attributes and the divine essence is found in the writings of Hollazius and Turretin. They proposed, in his view, no distinction in *realiter,* but in *virtualiter.* There is, on the Virtual Distinction Model, "a real foundation in the divine nature for the several attributes ascribed to Him."[64] Hodge's primary support for this model came from considering not only the relationship between attributes and essence in God, but by considering the relationship between attributes and substance in nature. Hodge based his rationale on what Reid deemed "common sense." He wrote, "[i]t is also evident that this is a subject about which one man knows just as much as another; because all that can be known about it is given immediately in consciousness."[65] Hodge's elaboration of the evidence from human consciousness in explaining attributes in relation to essence is worth quoting at length:

> This subject has already been referred to. We are conscious of ourselves as a thinking substance. That is, we are conscious that that which is ourselves has identity, continuance, and power. We are further conscious that the substance self thinks, wills, and feels. Intelligence, will, and sensibility, are its functions, or attributes, and consequently the attributes of a spirit. These are the ways in which a spirit acts. Anything which does not thus act, which has not these functions or attributes, is not a spirit. If you take from a spirit its intelligence, will, and sensibility, nothing remains, its substance is gone; at least it ceases to be a spirit. Substance and attributes are inseparable. The one is known in the other. A substance without attributes is nothing, i. e., no real existence. What is true of spiritual substances is true of matter. Matter, without the essential properties of matter, is a contradiction.[66]

Hodge concluded that no further evidence was needed, since our consciousness supplies the relationship between substance and attributes. This evidence must be carried into the theological world to correct false representation on this subject.[67] We should identify the shift away from classic conceptions of divine simplicity in Hodge's assertion that while substance and attributes are inseparable, both in man and in God, they were no longer identical in God. This gives the impression that God is analogous to man instead of man being analogous to God, human consciousness dictating his definition of divine simplicity. It is also clear that Hodge formally approves of Turretin's view but is actually out of step with it. Hodge speaks of the simplicity of God relative to the simplicity of the human soul. Turretin contrasts the

---

64 Hodge, *Systematic Theology*, vol. 1:370.
65 Hodge, *Systematic Theology*, vol. 1:371.
66 Hodge, *Systematic Theology*, vol. 1:372.
67 Hodge, *Systematic Theology*, vol. 1:371.

simplicity of the soul with the simplicity of God. God is absolutely simple while the human soul is merely relatively simple. Turretin affirms, in other words, that there is absolutely no composition in God whatsoever. Hodge, as we shall see, accepts real distinctions between the attributes.

There can be no question as to how forcefully Hodge wished to make his case here. He lumped together the views of Augustine, Aquinas, Scotus, and Mansel on this point, arguing that their views of divine simplicity destroyed any true knowledge of God.[68] When we speak of the attributes of God as being identical to one another, we are, according to Hodge, "using words without meaning when we attribute any perfection to God."[69] We must either reject this view of God, or otherwise reject God's revelation that comes to us in "the constitution of our nature," the external world, and in his Word.[70] In other words, because mankind cannot conceive of identity of essence and attributes, then divine attributes must mark real distinctions in the divine essence. This marked a substantial point of discontinuity in Hodge, not only with Reformed orthodoxy, but with the Christian tradition.

At this point, two themes emerge in Hodge's writing on divine simplicity. First, Hodge lacks a sophistication in understanding both the doctrine of divine simplicity and the various stands of Scholastic thought on simplicity. Hodge lumps together Nominalists, Realists, and Formalists all together. He confounds the Identity Thesis narrowly with the Nominalist position. It is no wonder that Hodge struggled with the concept of simplicity given his lack of precision in interpreting in the Scholastic sources he references. Second, he formally adopted the Virtualist position, more in theory than in practice. He rightly identifies Turretin as a proponent of the Virtual Distinctions Model and explicitly identifies with this tradition. However, Hodge muddied the waters by both rejecting and affirming the Virtual Model in his writings. While agreeing with Turretin that we know God through the powerful operation of his works *ad extra,* he disagreed with him by asserting that this necessitated real distinctions in God.

Ultimately, Hodge denied Virtual Model when he affirmed the Realist Model in the next section of his *Systematic Theology.* He argued that one cannot assert that the faculties and properties of God are identical in God without destroying the idea of God and subverting his personality as it would destroy any connection between divine and human personhood. He uses the knowledge and power of God as an example of the dangers of identifying the attributes to closely with one another. To accept the classical position that knowledge and power are identical in God is to make creation eternal and God the only true agent of both good and evil

68 Hodge, *Systematic Theology*, vol. 1:372.

69 Hodge, *Systematic Theology*, vol. 1:372.

70 Hodge, *Systematic Theology*, vol. 1:372.

because God must necessarily create all that he knows, including evil. Moreover, this conception would sever any distinction between the possible and actual, since both are present in the divine mind.[71] Either God would have to be finite, or the world infinite, in order to sustain this model, in his view. For if the knowledge of God is creative, a finite world must come from finite knowledge in God. Hodge also sees the identity of the attributes with God's essence as a threat to the personhood of God. Real distinctions between the attributes, Hodge argues, are essential to personhood. "It is not only a much higher idea," Hodge writes, "but one essential to personality, that there should be a real distinction between the divine attributes. That which from its nature and by necessity does all that it can do, is a force, and not a person. It can have no will."[72] Such a notion of divine simplicity would result in pantheism, according to Hodge. Hodge quotes from the Danish theologian Martensen, who aligns himself with a particular form of realism which teaches "that the attributes of God are objectively true as revealed, and therefore have their ground in the divine essence."[73] While earlier Reformed authors allowed an element of mystery in divine simplicity in light of divine incompressibility, Hodge believed that because human consciousness could not identify essence and attributes in anything else, neither could it do so in God. Unintentionally, he made human understanding the starting point of the study of God.

After affirming a form of Realism, Hodge curiously reaffirmed the Virtualist model. Certain theologians, whom he left unnamed, avoided the "blank ignorance of God" into which the "extreme view of simplicity" leads us by making a distinction between "the ratio rationantis and the ratio rationatæ. That is, the reason as determining, and the reason as determined."[74] In other words, the attributes do not differ in *res,* but in *ratione.* Hodge writes at length:

> But we are not to give up the conviction that God is really in Himself what He reveals Himself to be, to satisfy any metaphysical speculations as to the difference between essence and attribute in an infinite Being. The attributes of God, therefore, are not merely different conceptions in our minds, but different modes in which God reveals Himself to his creatures (or to Himself); just as our several faculties are different modes in which the inscrutable substance reveals itself in our consciousness and acts.[75]

71 Hodge, *Systematic Theology*, vol. 1:372.
72 Hodge, *Systematic Theology*, vol. 1:372.
73 Hodge, *Systematic Theology*, vol. 1:372.
74 Hodge, *Systematic Theology*, vol. 1:373.
75 Hodge, *Systematic Theology*, vol. 1:373.

As if Hodge had not confused his reader enough to this point, he adds further confusion by denying accidental properties in God.[76] This is a confusing move for Hodge to make because, historically, those who affirm a strong doctrine of divine simplicity deny accidental properties in God. If, however, one takes a realist approach, there is no reason why some attributes or properties cannot be accidental to God by virtue of his relationship to creation. Hodge details his views as he writes,

It follows also that God is a simple Being, not only as not composed of different elements, but also as not admitting of the distinction between substance and accidents. Nothing can either be added to, or taken from God. In this view the simplicity, as well as the other attributes of God, are of a higher order than the corresponding attributes of our spiritual nature. The soul of man is a simple substance; but it is subject to change. It can gain and lose knowledge, holiness, and power. These are in this view accidents in our substance. But in God they are attributes, essential and immutable.[77]

What should one make of Hodge's doctrine of simplicity relative to Reformed Orthodoxy? Several things stand out. First, Hodge was aware of the board tradition of Reformed Orthodoxy regarding divine simplicity. He rightly noted that the Reformed Orthodox affirmed the Identity Thesis and a strong doctrine of divine simplicity. Second, Hodge lacked sophistication and sufficient nuance, both in his reading of Reformed Orthodoxy and his handling of simplicity as a doctrine. He identified the Virtual position within Reformed Orthodoxy, but he failed to distinguish properly between it and the Nominalist and Virtualist accounts. Moreover, he pitted Aquinas and Turretin against one another when both held to the Virtual Model. Moreover, Hodge demonstrated no awareness of the relationship between the divine simplicity and the Formal, Virtual, and Nominalist models. Fourth, Hodge's position on divine simplicity is incoherent in general, but leans towards a form of Realism. Hodge, whatever the details of his view are, affirmed real distinction between the attributes within the divine essence. Hence, Hodge stands in discontinuity with Reformed orthodoxy, which uniformly advocated for a strong form of divine simplicity. This divergence appears to have been the result of his SCSR view of the testimony of human consciousness. Mankind could not believe such things about God that found no direct analogy in human beings.

76 Accidental properties are those properties which are not essential to the substance of a person or object. A horse, for instance, may have differing accidental properties of colors while still sharing the essence of "horseness."

77 Hodge, *Systematic Theology*, vol. 1:379.

4.5.2 Infinity, Immutability, and Eternity

4.5.2.1 Reformed Orthodoxy and Infinity, Immutability, and Eternity

Infinity, immutability, and eternity further highlight ways in which Hodge modified classic Reformed ideas. The doctrine of the infinity of God received much attention in the Medieval Scholastic tradition.[78] The Reformers accepted the infinity of God without much concern for philosophical speculation. Rather, they affirmed that God is infinite in his being and all his perfections as stated in the Scripture.[79] Reformed Orthodox theologians followed suit by reaffirming that God is unlimited in any respect, especially in relation to time and space.[80] Van Mastricht gives a common definition of infinity when he writes, "we call infinite that which has every perfection that anyone can conceive, or that can possibly exist."[81] One concern that the Reformed Scholastics had was the view of Aristotle. Aristotle argued that God is not infinite. He reasoned from his particular view of infinity—for Aristotle, an infinity is an unending series. As such, infinity assumed dimensionality and extension (generally) in space. Infinity, then, could not belong to the divine essence.[82]

The Reformed Scholastics argued, with Aquinas and the Reformers, that infinity is not necessarily a spatially and temporally indexed term. Instead, infinity had both positive and negative dimensions that asserted that God transcended all finite extension and dimensionality, whether in time or space. In other words, infinity excluded extension or comprehension. Omnipotence, omnipresence, and omniscience are merely the infinite nature of God with respect to power, space, and knowledge. God's infinite existence was intimately related to God's relationship to change and time, according to the Reformed Orthodox. God is eternal and unchanging because he is infinite. This point is reflected in the Shorter Catechisms' application of infinitude to every other divine attribute.

How God's infinitude related to time, however, was particularly complex. From the Medieval to Modern eras, theologians and philosophers grappled with how best to describe how God transcends time while using language that is inherently temporally indexed. However, the Reformed Orthodox agreed with the Christian tradition that God did not experience succession of moments in his being or consciousness. Behind the Reformed Orthodoxy definition of eternity (infinitude with

---

78 See Leo Sweeney, *Divine Infinity in Greek and Medieval Thought* (New York: P. Lang, 1998).

79 Van Mastricht, *Theoretico-Practical Theology: Faith in the Triune God*, 2:222–23.

80 Rehnman, "The Doctrine of God in Reformed Orthodoxy," 379–81.

81 Van Mastricht, *Theoretico-Practical Theology: Faith in the Triune God*, 2:224.

82 Muller, "Reformation, Orthodoxy, 'Christian Aristotelianism,' and the Eclecticism of Early Modern Philosophy," 85.

respect to time)—and, indeed, the whole pre-Modern world—was Aristotle's definition of time. Aristotle considered time to be the measure of change in the world. Hence, change and time were inseparably linked to each other. God's infinity with respect to time, then, must include a denial of succession or duration in the divine being. It is right to take the Scholastics as arguing that God is timeless, without regarding this idea as an obstacle to God's relationship to his creation. (Footnote Muller here). The infinite God's relation to the temporal world might have been beyond comprehension, but both sides of the coin remained true.

The relationship of God to change was thus also an important part of the Reformed Orthodox doctrine of God. The Reformed Scholastics held to a strong view of divine immutability, which argues that God experiences no change in his being or action. "Immutability is an incommunicable attribute of God," Turretin writes, "by which is denied of him not only all change, but also all possibility of change, as much with respect to existence as to will."[83] The immutability of God is required both by the clear teaching of Scripture and by good and necessary consequence from God's other attributes.[84] Van Mastricht, as an example, ties the immutability of God directly to God's aseity and simplicity.[85] Others connect immutability to eternity, as Polanus does, because God's atemporal existence implies that there can be no change in God whatsoever.[86] For the Scholastics, creation and redemption do not compromise the changelessness of God.[87] God creates the world by producing change in the created order without undergoing any change himself. "It is one thing to change the will; another to will the change of anything," Turretin writes.[88] Even the incarnation and suffering of Christ occur without any compromise to the immutability of the divine nature. "The Reformed, on the contrary, also acknowledge that the Son of God, the second person of the Trinity, can be called incarnate, but in this sense: not by being acted upon but only by acting, that is, by assuming a human nature. They also acknowledge that God suffered, though not in himself, but in the assumed human nature."[89]

A common thread running through the Reformed Orthodox view on infinity, eternity, and immutability is the transcendence of God. God's nature is unlimited in any manner. Therefore, God must transcend time and change in a wholly unique manner. As such, the Reformed Orthodox highlighted the difference between the Creator and the creature. This is expressed by the fact that infinity, eternity, and

---

83 Turretin, *Institutes of Elenctic Theology*, vol. 1:204.
84 A Brakel, *The Christian's Reasonable Service*, vol. 1:100.
85 Van Mastricht, *Theoretico-Practical Theology: Faith in the Triune God*, 2:194.
86 Polanus, *The Substance of the Christian Religion*, 7–8.
87 Muller, *Post-Reformation Reformed Dogmatics*, vol. 3:315–317.
88 Turretin, *Institutes of Elenctic Theology*, vol. 1:205.
89 Van Mastricht, *Theoretico-Practical Theology: Faith in the Triune God*, 2:199.

immutability were categorized as incommunicable attributes of God. There was no fear that the concept of infinity would blur the distinction between God and the world. Rather, these attributes were thought to be essential for distinguishing God and the world.

4.5.2.2 Charles Hodge and Infinity, Immutability, and Eternity

Charles Hodge thought quite differently from the Scholastics about God's infinite relationship to time and change, as we shall see. Hodge was concerned about the threat of Pantheism. The specter of Pantheism explains why Hodge found the Classical Theist views of eternity and immutability as expressed in Reformed Orthodoxy to be potentially problematic. He feared that too much transcendence would make God an abstract absolute being, rather than the living God of Scripture. He also feared that the Scholastic view of God's limitless being would compromise man's ability to know God. If God did not reflect the parameters of human consciousness, then man could not know God.

The infinity of God, Hodge explained, lies as the center of God's transcendence and immanence. "The ideas with which we are most familiar," Hodge wrote, "are often those of which we are the least able to give an intelligent account. Space, time, and infinity, are among the most difficult problems of human thought."[90] Hodge noted some of the failures of contemporary philosophers, such as Kant and Hamilton, to explains basic concept of "space" Problems in defining such a basic category was not unique to the nineteenth century. However, Modern philosophers set them in a new light. Hamilton followed Kant in applying the Copernican Revolution to epistemology in that, to differing degrees, time, space, and related categories became categories of the mind. Kant subjectivized the concept of space and time by making them part of the synthetic a priori concepts that the mind applies to the objects of sense perception. The complications for one's doctrine of God are seismic: God becomes the Absolute. As infinite being he is, therefore, beyond human knowledge. While human beings could understand space and time subjectively, such ideas did not correspond clearly to the knowledge of God. However, Hodge appeals to a common sense in opposition to Kant and Hamilton. One must accept the limitations of human knowledge and acknowledge that space and time might be beyond humanity's ability to fully comprehend them

Defining infinity, Hodge affirmed that "no limitation can be assigned to his essence."[91] But infinity is not merely a negative concept for Hodge. Yes, Hodge explains, the concept of infinity is a negation of finitude. However, he rejected the

90 Hodge, *Systematic Theology*, vol. 1:380.

91 Hodge, *Systematic Theology*, vol. 1:381.

idea of Hamilton that infinity was unintelligible to the human and, therefore, it implied a negation of human knowledge about God. The human mind, Hamilton argued, could not positively affirm or understand the existence of something infinite. Hodge rejected this line of reasoning, writing, "[e]very man, however, knows that the propositions 'Space is infinite,' and 'Space is finite,' express different and equally definite thoughts. When, therefore, we say that God is infinite, we mean something; we express a great and positive truth."[92] The positive assertion is that God transcends the bounds of time (eternity) and space (immensity). The infinity of God must also be affirmed as the opposite of the pantheistic tendencies of the nineteenth century. The infinite is not "the all," Hodge argued. Mansel and Spinoza contended strongly for the infinity of God as a ground for their pantheistic doctrine of God by equating God with all things.[93]

So far Hodge has not clearly indicated how his view of infinity relates to the Scholastics. His primary concern was to distance the idea of infinity from the Pantheistic notions of many of his contemporaries. The main information on the more positive aspects of the infinity of God come as Hodge applies the concepts to God's relationship to space, time, and change. We now turn our attention to God's relationship to time to see how he applies the concept of infinity to time.

Hodge argued that God's eternality is the product of an infinite God relating to time in the same way that omnipresence is the way an infinite God is related to space.[94] God transcended space and time even as he filled both space and time. As God is not limited by space, so God is not limited by time. Yet Hodge argued that God experiences the past, present, and future without any distinction between them. All events are equally present to God, and he experiences only an "eternal now."[95] He referred to a number of Scriptures including Psalm 90:2 to Psalm 102:25–27, as well as to the divine name in Exodus 3:14 to make his case.[96] Thus far Hodge stands in continuity with Reformed Orthodoxy. Hodge explained that two common threads ran through all the scriptural teaching on God's eternality: God has neither a beginning nor end, and the past and the future are equally present to him.[97] The idea that God is thus without succession of moment is absent but could be implied in the second theme. However, Hodge explicitly rejects the Reformed Orthodox notion of successionless eternity as he elaborated his views further.

Hodge cited Augustine, Aquinas, and Quenstedt on eternity with approval, yet he reserves judgment on whether one should "deny all succession in the divine

---

92 Hodge, *Systematic Theology*, vol. 1:381–382.

93 Hodge, *Systematic Theology*, vol. 1:382.

94 Hodge, *Systematic Theology*, vol. 1:385.

95 Hodge, *Systematic Theology*, vol. 1:385.

96 Hodge, *Systematic Theology*, vol. 1:386.

97 Hodge, *Systematic Theology*, vol. 1:386.

consciousness."[98] As Hodge saw it, succession appears to be fundamental to consciousness in understanding time, and consciousness is essential for personhood. The next chapter below explores historic post-Enlightenment shifts in defining personhood. In general, people in Hodge's context understood personhood as individual self-consciousness, or individual willing subject, instead of the relationship of a specific being to the substantial hypostatic existence of that being. In place of explaining the relationship of being to personhood, "person" now focused on what were previously regarded as rational faculties. "The ideas of space and duration," Hodge added, "are necessarily given in the consciousness of continuous existence....We therefore know, from consciousness or from experience, of no kind of duration which is not successive."[99] This sentiment betrays an SCSR impulse as Hodge deviates from the Scholastic view of eternity. Once again, analogies drawn from human consciousness became the standard for the knowledge of God.

Hodge builds on the arguments of contemporary pastor and philosopher George Jamieson (1815–1903) in considering whether God experiences any succession of moments in his eternal being.[100] One cannot remove succession from the concept of eternity without destroying both thought and personality, Jamieson argued.[101] Hodge noted that there are two types of succession in time: objective succession, whereby events causally follow one another, and subjective succession, where the conscious mind necessarily conceives of one event or object after another.[102] The argument against eternality without any succession follows this pattern: God is a person; to be a person is to be a self-conscious agent; succession is necessary for consciousness; therefore, either God is a person and experiences subjective succession, or God does not experience any subjective succession and, hence, is not a person. Hodge added the need for modesty in making assertions about the divine nature. "We have no right," says Hodge, "to affirm or deny, when we cannot know what our affirmations or denials may involve or imply."[103] Nevertheless, his modifications of eternity in relation to successive moments of time would have, in the view of earlier theologians, threatened divine immutability, among other things.

---

98 Hodge, *Systematic Theology*, vol. 1:386.

99 Hodge, *Systematic Theology*, vol. 1:387.

100 Jamieson was a Scottish minister who wrote on philosophical and theological subjects. For Jamieson's full thought on eternity, see George Jamieson, *The Essentials of Philosophy: Wherein Its Constituent Principles Are Traces Through the Various Departments of Science with Analytical Strictures on the Views of Some of Our Leading Philosophers* (Edinburgh: T. & . T. Clark, 1859), 199–206.

101 Hodge, *Systematic Theology*, vol. 1:387; Jamieson, *The Essentials of Philosophy*, 199–202.

102 Hodge, *Systematic Theology*, vol. 1:388.

103 Hodge, *Systematic Theology*, vol. 1:388.

Though Hodge advocated modesty in such matters, he founded his view of eternity ultimately on the divine consciousness and succession via SCSR arguments. God is a person, and all that human personhood entails must be true of God, even if certain differences remained between divine and human personhood. Yet since being a personal God is greater than being an impersonal force, any "limitations" of personhood are actually part of God's infinite perfection, including succession of moments.[104] Hodge argued that whatever was true of man as a person must be true of God as a person. Underpinning this argument about God and personhood is SCSR and the regulative power of human consciousness. There is a tentative quality in Hodge's thought because he is not sure how to interpret the data of human consciousness clearly as applied to eternity. He is clear, in principle, that whatever our consciousness teaches us about subjective succession and thought must be true of God as well, but because Hodge saw the operation of the mind in this regard as mysterious, he would not fully commit to a clear conception. "If we are unable to comprehend ourselves," Hodge concludes, "we should not pretend to be able to comprehend God. Whether we can understand how there can be succession in the thought of Him who inhabits eternity or not, we are not to deny that God is an intelligent Being, that He actually thinks and feels, in order to get over the difficulty. God is a person, and all that personality implies must be true of Him."[105]

Yet again the anthropocentric impulses of Hamilton's consciousness centered version of SCSR leads Hodge to invert the nature of analogical predication, making man the primarily analog in the Creator-creature relationship. The Reformed Orthodox theologians began with the assumption that God, being infinite, will be radically different from man in his relationship to time. The fact that the human mind cannot comprehend an successionless existence is, to the mind of a Scholastic theologian, not a great concern because eternity is an incommunicable attribute. Hodge, to the contrary, does not want to ascribe any quality to God that cannot be demonstrated through human consciousness. Consciousness becomes a limiting factor for Hodge as he addresses God's relationship to time.

Hodge manifested the same pattern when he explained God's relationship to change by voicing concern about classic Reformed expressions of immutability. At first, Hodge appears to be in line with Scholasticism as he defined immutability by discussing relevant scriptural data. His definition of immutability is remarkably close to the traditional definition found in Reformed Orthodoxy. "As an infinite and absolute Being," Hodge wrote, "self-existent and absolutely independent, God is exalted above all causes and even above the possibility of change."[106] Both God's

---

104 Hodge, *Systematic Theology*, vol. 1:388.

105 Hodge, *Systematic Theology*, vol. I:389.

106 Hodge, *Systematic Theology*, vol. 1:390.

"essence and attributes" are beyond any sort of change; his metaphysical and moral attributes are beyond any increase or decrease, and his decree can never be altered. [107] As Hodge gave explicit scriptural evidence for his model of immutability, he cited many of the same texts that Reformed Orthodox theologians used, including James 1:17, Numbers 23:19, and Malachi 3:6.[108] Hodge then discussed philosophical aspects of divine immutability, at which point his attitude towards the Scholastic tradition changed significantly.

Hodge is concerned that the Scholastics were unbalanced in their assertion of divine immutability. He explained, "[t]heologians, in their attempts to state, in philosophical language, the doctrine of the Bible on the unchangeableness of God, are apt to confound immutability with immobility. In denying that God can change, they seem to deny that He can act."[109] He criticized Augustine, Turretin, and Quenstedt for confounding immutability with immobility. Hodge took exception to Quenstedt for defining immutability as "the perpetual identity of the divine essence and all its perfections, with the absolute negation of all motion, either physical or ethical."[110] Hodge is more appreciative for Turretin because he appreciated a certain "caution" in dealing with immutability. Turretin elaborates on the relationship between immutability and the action of God, writing, "the power of varying his own acts is not the principle of mutability in itself, but only in its objects."[111] Hodge's mild deference to Turretin does not make much sense when comparing Turretin to other Reformed Scholastics. In context, Turretin is making the case that God may act differently without implying imperfection in his will so long as his various actions are necessitated by some flaw in God's divine plan. It is not obvious that this is out of accord with a strong doctrine of immutability nor that Turretin is making a concession that softens his view of immutability.

Strangely, Hodge does not give any substantial explanation as to why he understood Augustine, Quenstedt, or Turretin as arguing for an immobile God. To avoid this pitfall, Reformed authors asserted the standard scholastic idea that God is *purus actus,* meaning that God was all actuality with no potentiality. On the Scholastic view, God is always fully actuated and always acts in himself and as himself. Whether misunderstanding this point, or merely neglecting it, Hodge argued that such assertions assumed an unwarranted level of confidence about our understanding of the divine nature. One must, Hodge insisted, hold both that God

107 Hodge, *Systematic Theology*, vol. 1:390.

108 Hodge, *Systematic Theology*, vol. 1, 390–391; cf. Turretin, *Institutes of Elenctic Theology*, vol. 1:205; Bernardinus de Moor, *Didactio-Elenctic Theology*, trans. Steven Dilday (Central, SC: Reformation to Reformation Translations, 2019), vol. 4:245.

109 Hodge, *Systematic Theology*, vol. 1:391.

110 Hodge, *Systematic Theology*, vol. I:391.

111 Hodge, *Systematic Theology*, vol. I:391; Turretin, *Institutes of Elenctic Theology*, vol. 1:206.

is immutable and active. "It is in vain for us to presume to understand the Almighty to perfection," Hodge wrote. "We know that God is immutable in his being, his perfections, and his purposes; and we know that He is perpetually active. And, therefore, activity and immutability must be compatible; and no explanation of the latter inconsistent with the former ought to be admitted."[112] What is puzzling is why Hodge thought older authors also asserted that God was immobile while also affirming their view of God in other places as *actus purus*. Hodge never mentions that the Scholastic tradition holds that God is the most "active" being in the world because he is pure actuality. In this regard, Hodge's assertion of immutability was less is not in continuity with Reformed Orthodoxy. He seemed to have been unsettled by the idea of a God who experiences no development. Hodge also offers no appeals to "consciousness" here as he does with many of the other attributes of God. Whatever the reasons for the brevity of Hodge's writing on this point, he is self-consciously rejected the Reformed orthodox view of immutability, as he understood it.

The infinite nature of God with respect to time and change is a key nexus of theology proper. These three attributes often show express the larger trends of a theologian's system of thought. Here we see discontinuity between Hodge and Reformed Orthodoxy. The Reformed Scholastics had a high view of the transcendence of the infinite God and they, as a consequence, had a strong view of God's transcendence of time and change. God was without succession of moments, and so atemporal, and also was beyond the possibility of change. Hodge, by contrast, found these views problematic. He affirmed that God was infinite in that he had no limitations, but his view of infinity was quite different from Reformed Orthodoxy. His requirement that theology be processed through the grid of human consciousness caused Hodge to reject, or at best be ambivalent towards, the Scholastic views of infinity, eternity, and immutability.

4.5.3 Attributes of Knowledge and Will

4.5.3.1 Reformed Orthodox on Knowledge and Will

The Reformed Orthodox addressed the doctrines of God's knowledge and will in a number of related, but distinct ways. They generally addressed the faculty and content of divine knowledge under the broad categories of wisdom (*sapientia*), understanding (*intelligentia*), and knowledge (*scientia*).[113] Muller notes that the

---

112 Hodge, *Systematic Theology*, vol. 1:391.

113 For an example, see Van Mastricht, *Theoretico-Practical Theology: Faith in the Triune God*, 2:292.

ordering of the three had some dogmatic consequences—some approaches emphasizing the psychology of faculty of knowing where others emphasized the object or nature of the knowledge—but that there was not a great deal of divergence among the Reformed Scholastics on these points.[114] In the Middle Ages, Dominicans and Franciscans differed in emphasis on the intellect and will with consequences for whether theology was primarily theoretical or practical, and whether the Christian life was primarily contemplative or active. However, both traditions rooted theology and Christian living in God's character with the beatific vision as the goal of theology. Chapter 3 above illustrates how such questions transferred seamlessly into Reformed orthodoxy.

The doctrine of the knowledge and wisdom of God was considered a second order attribute of God.[115] That is, the knowledge and wisdom of God took a particular shape because the Scholastics formulated them in light of divine infinity and simplicity. The net effect was that the Reformed Orthodoxy emphasized the distinction between the Creator and the creature with regard to the process and content of divine knowledge. Knowledge and wisdom might be communicable to rational creatures analogically, but they still bore unique characteristics in God in light of infinitude and simplicity. Leonard Rijssen (1636–1700) summarized well the distinction between the Creator and the creature with regard to knowledge. "The knowledge of God differs," Rijssen wrote, "from that of creatures, 1) in its objects, for God knowledge all things. 2) In its manner, [since he knows] all things according to his essence. 3) In its degree, [since he knows] all things perfectly."[116] Divine knowledge is qualitatively different from human knowledge, and not merely quantitatively different. It was not simply a matter of how much God knows, but the way in which he knows that was in view.

God's knowledge thus differs from mankind's knowledge both in the manner and the object of knowledge. Human knowledge is related to object outside of man's consciousness. Man's knowledge grows through the process of learning and is, therefore, both discursive and inductive. Moreover, man knows according to the ability of his finite status, meaning that his knowledge is not perfect. The Reformed Orthodox emphasized the qualitative and quantitative difference between God and man in the knowing process.[117] For the Reformed Orthodox, God knows infinitely while man knows finitely. God's knowledge is based on his aseity and simplicity. God also knows by virtue of being the Creator for whom nothing outside Himself exists without His express consent.[118] Therefore, God knows, the Reformed

114 Muller, *Post-Reformation Reformed Dogmatics*, vol. 3:384–391.

115 Polanus, *The Substance of the Christian Religion*, 3.

116 Muller, *Post-Reformation Reformed Dogmatics*, vol. 3:397.

117 Muller, *Post-Reformation Reformed Dogmatics*, vol. 3:398–399.

118 A Brakel, *The Christian's Reasonable Service*, vol. 1:102–103.

Orthodox argued, by knowing His essence and His will. His knowledge does not have the same relationship to external objects as is the case with finite man and his knowledge of external objects.[119] Moreover, God is immutable and eternal. His knowledge has no potentiality and so God cannot grow in His knowledge.[120] His knowledge is perfect and complete just as He is. Being eternal, He does not experience change of psychological states or the succession of moments in His consciousness.[121] God cannot then have memory and recall in the way in which human being do. God, then, knows Himself in a single, indivisible, non-inductive, non-discursive, intuitive act.[122]

The Reformed Scholastics typically considered the will of God after the knowledge of God, which generally followed the pattern set by Aquinas.[123] They gave careful attention to the will of God. "Indeed," Muller explains, "[the will of God] is the most exhaustive and detailed category of the attributes in many of the systems [of theology]."[124] As Muller summarizes the Reformed Orthodox on the will of God, he notes new fewer than seventeen common distinctions made by the Scholastics regarding the will of God.[125] The Scholastics defined the will of God as an attribute or property of the divine nature. "The will of God," wrote Polanus, "is an essential property of God, by which he willeth all the things that he willeth, and that from all eternity, of himself also, and that by one constant act."[126] Again, God is all actuality and no potentiality, and he is always active. His decree is thus an eternal act of the counsel of his will. Others emphasized the will is an attribute by which God is inclined towards the Good, which is God himself. "With these points touched upon," Van Mastricht observed, "we have stated that the will in God is nothing but his most wise propensity toward himself as the highest end, and toward the creatures, on account of himself, as the means. It is called a propensity partly so that it may be distinguished from his intellect, which is only a simple intuition, and partly so that we may employ such an expression expression that is fit to connote all the acts of our own will."[127] Reflecting the nature of the divine will, the Westminster Confession of Faith outlined its chapter on the divine decree along these lines, making such ideas fall under Hodge's purview.

119 Muller, *Post-Reformation Reformed Dogmatics*, vol. 3:399–401.
120 Turretin, *Institutes of Elenctic Theology*, vol. 1:206–207.
121 de Moor, *Didactio-Elenctic Theology*, vol. 4:293–298.
122 Muller, *Post-Reformation Reformed Dogmatics*, vol. 3:401–403.
123 Turretin, *Institutes of Elenctic Theology*, vol. 1:218.
124 Muller, *Post-Reformation Reformed Dogmatics*, vol. 3:443.
125 Muller, *Post-Reformation Reformed Dogmatics*, vol. 3:453–473.
126 Polanus, *The Substance of the Christian Religion*, 11.
127 Van Mastricht, *Theoretico-Practical Theology: Faith in the Triune God*, 2:336.

The will of God is an expression of the nature of God. Since God is a necessary being with a perfect and immutable nature, does that mean that God has no freedom of will? Must God, for instance, create the world? The Reformed Orthodox answered negatively. God's will is both necessary and determined by his nature, while remaining free to his works *ad extra*.[128] God wills the good because he wills himself, but this necessary self-willing does not come from external sources of influence. God is free in willing the creation as well.[129] Wilhelmus a Brakel wrote accordingly, "[God] had the freedom of will either to create or not create, or to elect or not elect men."[130] In other words, God has the freedom to will that which is according to his nature without external influence or compulsion.[131] As Muller helpfully summarizes, "[t]he divine freedom, then, is initially defined as a freedom from coaction or coercion, including the freedom from impediment or resistance on the part of the create order. There can be nothing higher than God and nothing below God that can impede or determine his willing."[132] This model of a divine will where both the realist impulses of a will that is conditioned upon knowledge that simultaneously preserves a freedom for God more akin to Voluntarism was designed by the Scholastic to protect the freedom and sovereignty of God.[133] In other words, God necessarily acts according to his attributes, without willing or doing anything *ad extra* necessarily.

As we have seen, the Reformed Orthodox developed their view of the knowledge and will of God based upon the simplicity, eternity, and immutability of God. God's knowledge and will take on the quality of these incommunicable attributes. Hence, there is a distinct difference in the manner and object of God's knowledge and will when compared with the human beings. Hodge will find this distinction problematic. As we shall see, Hodge will find the Reformed Scholastic views to veer dangerously close to the Pantheistic system.

4.5.3.2 Charles Hodge on Knowledge and Will

If the Reformed Orthodox emphasized the distinction between the Creator and the creature in the knowing process, then Hodge emphasized the near identity between God and man in the process of knowledge. Guarding against any hint of Pantheism, Hodge emphasized that the knowledge and wisdom of God are as similar to man's knowledge and wisdom as possible. One may fairly say that while

128 Van Mastricht, *Theoretico-Practical Theology: Faith in the Triune God*, vol. 2, vols. 339–340.

129 Turretin, *Institutes of Elenctic Theology*, vol. 1:218–219.

130 A Brakel, *The Christian's Reasonable Service*, vol. 1:115.

131 Polanus, *The Substance of the Christian Religion*, 11–12.

132 Muller, *Post-Reformation Reformed Dogmatics*, vol. 3:447.

133 Muller, *Post-Reformation Reformed Dogmatics*, vol. 3:448–450.

the Scholastics emphasized the qualitative and quantitative distinction between God and man regarding knowledge, Hodge emphasized the quantitative dimension while muting the qualitative one. Hodge expressed concern that Modern theologians and philosophers who considered God to be the "Absolute" denied any real knowledge in God. But Hodge was also concerned that even many of the "theologians of the highest rank" constructed a model of divine knowledge that destroyed God's knowledge of finite reality. However, Hodge does not supply an example of any of the theologians he has in mind here. As we shall see shortly, he moves on to discuss Pantheistic theories of divine knowledge, mentioning Mansel and Hamilton along with others. Therefore, he likely has these thinkers in mind. What is their chief error according to Hodge? By stressing qualitative differences between divine and human knowledge over quantitative ones, Hodge feared that God would become unknowable since there could be no bridge between divine and human knowledge. Fears of pantheism and modern concerns once again led Hodge to alter classic Reformed views of the divine attributes.[134]

The nineteenth century saw a surge of Pantheistic thought about which Hodge was rightly concerned. He rejected the ideas of Manuel, Hamilton, and Spinoza on this score. He devoted considerable attention to the problems posed by Pantheism throughout his ST and elsewhere.[135] Yet Hodge appeared to regard the Scholastic doctrine of knowledge and divine simplicity as fraught with the same difficulties as Pantheism. Knowledge, according to Hodge, ceased to be knowledge if it was identical to divine power via simplicity. "It is deeply to be regretted," Hodge wrote,

> that not only the Fathers, but also the Lutheran and Reformed theologians, after renouncing the authority of the schoolmen, almost immediately yielded themselves to their speculations. Instead of determining the nature of the divine attributes from the representations of Scripture and from the constitution of man as the image of God, and from the necessities of our moral and religious nature, they allowed themselves to be controlled by a priori speculations as to the nature of the infinite and absolute.[136]

He quoted Augustine, Scotus, Aquinas, and Gerhard to this end, noting that the Reformed Scholastics formulated the knowledge of God in light of divine simplicity, and thereby destroyed the knowledge of God in mankind.[137] Furthermore, by

134 Hodge, *Systematic Theology*, vol. 1:393.

135 Hodge, *Systematic Theology*, vol. 1:299–335; Charles Hodge, "Can God Be Known?," *The Princeton Review* XXXVI, no. 1 (January 1864): 122–52; Salmond, *Princetoniana, Charles & A. A. Hodge: With Class and Table Talk of Hodge the Younger*, 148–50.

136 Hodge, *Systematic Theology*, vol. 1:394.

137 Johann Gerhard, *Theological Common Places: Exegesis, or A More Copius Explanation of Certain Articles of the Christian Religion, On the Natuure of God and the Most Holy Mystery of the Trinity*, ed.

consequence of classic views of divine simplicity, making the knowledge and will of God identical entailed the idea that God knows all that He wills, wills all that he knows, and, because he knows and wills from eternity, creation necessarily becomes eternal. "We are thus led, by these speculations," Hodge concluded, "into pantheistical views of the nature of God and of his relation to the world."[138] He believed that simplicity erased the distinction between God and his works by actuating the eternal will of God in time alone, making all things part of God. For this reason, he connected the Scholastic view of knowledge with the pantheism of Schleiermacher and Johann Bruch (1792–1874). His assessment to this end apparently resulted from his unwillingness to maintain qualitative differences between divine and human knowledge based on the judgment of human consciousness.

The classic Reformed position on divine knowledge, rooted in Scripture, was that the knowledge of God is a distinct faculty in God in such a manner that it does not compromise his unity and simplicity. Yet Hodge developed his own view based on a strong analogy between human and divine psychology. Knowledge, power, and will are identical in man, Hodge explained, in that they are not separate substances. They are merely different "modes in which the life or activity of the soul manifests itself."[139] Theologians must thus think of God as having knowledge in Himself in a manner where all fragility of finitude and the moral stain of sin is removed without destroying the meaning of the phrase "knowledge." "God, therefore, does and can know in the ordinary and proper sense of the word Yet again, rather than viewing man as approximately, though imperfectly, analogous to God, Hodge acted as though things could not be true of God unless they found an analogy in man. This appears to unintentionally transform analogous language about God, which Hodge affirmed, into univocal language in which the same terms meant essentially the same things for God and man.

Reformed Orthodox theologians found a more positive role at other points in Hodge's theology, however. God knows himself and all things outside himself in relation to himself—here Hodge worked with the Scholastic distinction between *scientia necessaria* and *scientia libera*. However, in his own estimation, he did not find this distinction to be significant.[140] Hodge noted in passing that he could not understand how "orthodox theologians" holding the identity of God's knowledge and will could maintain the difference between actual and possible knowledge. The key issue for Hodge was that God is "a spirit, who can do more than he does,"

Benjamine T. G. Mayes, trans. Richard Dinda (St. Louis, Missiour: Concordia Publishing House, 2007), 133–39.

138 Hodge, *Systematic Theology*, vol. 1:395.

139 Hodge, *Systematic Theology*, vol. 1:396.

140 Hodge, *Systematic Theology*, vol. 1:397.

appearing to argue that the only way to avoid necessitarianism or eternal creation is by denying God as *actus purus.*[141]

The Reformed Scholastics also found more favor with Hodge regarding the divine will. Older theologians and philosophers used the "will of God" in sometimes a very broad sense. In this broadest sense, God wills the Good and, therefore, wills Himself. He provides citations from Calovius, Quenstedt, and Turretin. "Although the word seems to be taken in different senses in the same sentence," Hodge explains, "God's willing Himself means that He takes complacency in his own infinite excellence; his willing things out of Himself, means his purpose that they should exist."[142] Hodges estimates that the general sense of the term "will" is meant in the narrower sense of "self-determination." God has a will because He is a spirit, and as a spirit He is a "voluntary agent."[143] God also had a will by virtue of his personal existence.

God's will is both personal and free in two senses. According to Hodge, God has liberty of acting and acting according to his own sense of right and wrong.[144] God does not act because of any "necessity of his nature" regarding things outside of himself. God is free to create or not create. Just as God will not violate his word, so God's nature determines the ethical actions he may take. But there is nothing in God constraining the will to act or not act in any particular manner. God wills both the decrees of what will happen and what should happen, what Hodge calls his secretive will and his perceptive will—what some theologians refer to as the *voluntas beneplaciti et signi.*[145]

Hodge also treated the Euthyphro dilemma—the relationship between the will of God and the ethical standards of mankind. It is the will of God that is the "ultimate ground of moral obligation to all rational creatures. No higher reason can be assigned why anything is right than that God commands it."[146] Hodge, however, was neither a Nominalist nor a Voluntarist. He argued that the nature of God determined the will of God so that He cannot will that which is sinful nor is that which he wills arbitrary.[147]

Hodge's treatments of God's knowledge and will thus evidence both continuities and discontinuities with Reformed orthodoxy. Continuities appear in his definitions. Discontinuities are clear in areas in which he sought to redefine divine knowledge and will in light of perceived analogies in human consciousness. This results in a picture of Hodge as having both one foot in the past and another in the present.

---

141 Hodge, *Systematic Theology*, vol. 1:398.

142 Hodge, *Systematic Theology*, vol. 1:402.

143 Hodge, *Systematic Theology*, vol. 1:402.

144 Hodge, *Systematic Theology*, vol. 1:403.

145 Turretin, *Institutes of Elenctic Theology*, vol. 1:225.

146 Hodge, *Systematic Theology*, vol. 1:406.

147 Hodge, *Systematic Theology*, vol. 1:406.

Nineteenth century philosophical ideas and culture existed alongside of Reformed orthodox ones, often resulting in unclear expressions of the divine attributes. Hodge appreciated some of the distinctions the Reformed Orthodox made when discussing the divine will. However, he feared that he could not follow the Scholastics in their connection between divine simplicity and God's knowledge and will for fear of losing the connection between God and man in the knowing process. Moreover, the Scholastic views of God's knowledge and will appeared to be too similar to Pantheism. In the final assessment, Hodge took some of the form of Reformed Orthodox thought while leaving much of the substance behind.

4.6 Conclusion

Hodge's formulation of the doctrine of God shows continuity and discontinuity with Reformed Orthodoxy. The strongest area of continuity is in how Hodge organized his taxonomy of the divine attributes, as he followed the Westminster Shorter Catechism, and in certain sections under the heading of the will of God.

However, Hodge absorbed Modern philosophical influences into his thought as well, particularly the SCSR philosophy of William Hamilton, which led him to reformulate the divine essence and attributes at key points. Hodge's deviation from Reformed Orthodox was motivated not only by his philosophical influences. His fear of the pantheism so common in his time caused him to react against the Classical Theism of Reformed orthodoxy. In this he was not alone, since other nineteenth century American authors followed suit.[148] Hodge's doctrine of God became a conservative, mediating position between Reformed Orthodoxy on the one hand and more radical revisions of the doctrine of God found in Schleiermacher or William Hamilton on the other. Hodge's use of consciousness as a regulating principle for epistemology dictated a doctrine of God that was limited by man's self-understanding. If man could not conceive of a doctrine, then it could not be true of God. Instead of viewing mankind as imperfectly analogous to God, Hodge implied that God must be analogous to man's consciousness. This move allowed less room for qualitative differences between God and man. While affirming divine incomprehensibility, Hodge's approach to the knowledge of God made God a little more comprehensible than he had been in earlier Reformed thinking.

The high view of the transcendence of God as articulated by the Church Fathers, clarified by the Medieval Scholastics, and reaffirmed in Reformed Orthodoxy found no place in Hodge's doctrine of God in many instances. The reasonable conclusion

---

148 For an example, see the parallel sections in Robert Lewis Dabney, *Systematic Theology* (Edinburgh; Carlisle, Pa.: Banner of Truth Trust, 1985).

is that Hodge was not always as theologically conservative as he thought he was. While he claimed to present no novel ideas in his theology, significant novelty lay at the core of his doctrine of God. As it always difficult for people to see in themselves the influences of the world in which they live, so Charles Hodge was moved by modern influences far more than he realized.

Works Cited

A Brakel, Wilhelmus. *The Christian's Reasonable Service.* Edited by Joel R Beeke. Translated by Bartel Elshout. 4 vols. Grand Rapids: Reformation Heritage Books, 2015.

Ahlstrom, Sydney E. "The Scottish Philosophy and American Theology." *Church History* 24, no. 03 (1955): 252–72.

Anderson, O. *Reason and Faith in the Theology of Charles Hodge: American Common Sense Realism.* Place of publication not identified: Palgrave Pivot, 2015.

Berkhof, Louis. *Systematic Theology.* Grand Rapids, MI: W. B. Eerdmans, 2018.

Bozeman, Theodore Dwight. *Protestants in an Age of Science: The Baconian Ideal and Antebellum American Religious Thought.* Chapel Hill: University of North Carolina Press, 2012.

Bucanus, Gulielmus. *Institutiones Theolgicae, Seu, Locorum Communium Christanae Religionis.* Geneva, 1648.

Carter, Craig A. *Interpreting Scripture with the Great Tradition: Recovering the Genius of Premodern Exegesis.* Grand Rapids, MI: Baker Academic, 2018.

Cheynell, Francis. *The Divine Trinunity of the Father, Son, and Holy Spirit, or, The Blessed Doctrine of the Three Coessentiall Subsistents in the Eternall Godhead without Any Confusion or Division of the Distinct Subsistences or Multiplication of the Most Single and Entire Godhead Acknowledged, Beleeved, Adored by Christians, in Opposition to Pagans, Jewes, Mahumetans, Blasphemous and Antichristian Hereticks, Who Say They Are Christians, but Are Not.* London: Samuel Gellibrand, 1650.

Cooper, John W. *Panentheism–The Other God of the Philosophers: From Plato to the Present.* Grand Rapids, MI: Baker Academic, 2006.

Copleston, Frederick. *A History of Philosophy Vol. V: Modern Philosophy.* New York: Image Books, Doubleday, 1994.

Crisp, Oliver D. "On the Orthodoxy of Jonathan Edwards." *Scottish Journal of Theology* 67, no. 3 (2014): 304–22.

Dabney, Robert Lewis. *Systematic Theology.* Edinburgh; Carlisle, Pa.: Banner of Truth Trust, 1985.

Denny, J. Wayne. *The Influence of Scottish Common Sense Realism on B.B. Warfield and His Formulation of the Doctrine of Inerrancy,* 2006.

Dolezal, James E. *God Without Parts: Divine Simplicity and the Metaphysics of God's Absoluteness.* Eugene, Or.: Pickwick Publications, 2011.

Freeman, Kenneth. *The Role of Reason in Religion: A Study of Henry Mansel.* The Hague: Springer, 1969.

Garth, David Kinney. *The Influence of Scottish Common Sense Philosophy on the Theology of James Henley Thornwell and Robert Lewis Dabney*, 1982.

Gerhard, Johann. *Theological Common Places: Exegesis, or A More Copius Explanation of Certain Articles of the Christian Religion, On the Natuure of God and the Most Holy Mystery of the Trinity.* Edited by Benjamine T. G. Mayes. Translated by Richard Dinda. St. Louis, Missiour: Concordia Publishing House, 2007.

Goudriaan, Aza. *Reformed Orthodoxy and Philosophy, 1625–1750 : Gisbertus Voetius, Petrus van Mastricht, and Anthonius Driessen.* Leiden: Brill, 2006.

———. "Theology and Philosophy." In *A Companion to Reformed Orthodoxy,* edited by Herman Selderhuis, Vol. 40. Brill's Companion to the Christian Tradition. Leiden: Brill, 2013.

Graves, Frank Pierrepont. *Peter Ramus and the Educational Reformation of the Sixteenth Century.* New York: The Macmillan Company, 1912.

Hamilton, William. *The Metaphysics of Sir William Hamilton: Collected, Arranged, and Abridged, for the Use of Colleges and Private Students.* Edited by Francis Bowen. Cambridge: Sever and Francis, 1865.

Hamilton, William, and Robert Turnbull. *Discussions on Philosophy and Literature, Education and University Reform: Chiefly from the Edinburgh Review.* New York: Harper & Bros., 1853.

Heppe, Heinrich. *Reformed Dogmatics: Set Out and Illustrated from the Sources.* Edited by Ernst Bizer. Translated by G. T. Thomson. Grand Rapids, Michigan: Baker Book House, 1950.

Hicks, Peter. "The Philosophy of Charles Hodge: A 19th Century Evangelical Approach to Reason, Knowledge, and Truth." N.Y. : Edwin Mellen Press, 1997.

Hodge, Archibald Alexander. *The Life of Charles Hodge.* Edinburgh; Carlisle, Pennsylvania: Banner of Truth Trust, 2010.

Hodge, Charles. "Can God Be Known?" *The Princeton Review* XXXVI, no. 1 (January 1864): 122–52.

———. *Systematic Theology.* New York: Scribner, 1871.

———. "What Is Christianity?" *The Biblical Repretory and Princeton Review* 32 (n.d.): 118–61.

Holifield, E. Brooks. *Theology in America: Christian Thought from the Age of the Puritans to the Civil War.* New Haven, Conn.: Yale University Press, 2005.

Jamieson, George. *The Essentials of Philosophy: Wherein Its Constituent Principles Are Traces Through the Various Departments of Science with Analytical Strictures on the Views of Some of Our Leading Philosophers.* Edinburgh: T. & . T. Clark, 1859.

Jang, Sung Shik. "Contextualization in the Princeton Theology, 1822–1878: Scottish Common Sense Realism and the Doctrine of Providence in the Theology of Charles Hodge," 1993.

Lee, Sang Hyun. *The Philosophical Theology of Jonathan Edwards.* Princeton, NJ: Princeton Univ Press, 1988.

Levering, Matthew, and Gilles Emery, eds. *Aristotle in Aquinas's Theology.* Oxford: Oxford University Press, 2018.

Mansel, Henry. *Metaphysics or The Philosophy of Consciousness, Phenomenal and Real.* Edinburgh: Adam and Charles Black, 1883.

———. *Philsophy of the Unconditioned.* Norderstedt, Germany: HANSEBOOKS, 2016.

Moor, Bernardinus de. *Didactio-Elenctic Theology.* Translated by Steven Dilday. Central, SC: Reformation to Reformation Translations, 2019.

Muller, Richard A. *Dictionary of Latin and Greek Theological Terms: Drawn Principally from Protestant Scholastic Theology.* Grand Rapids, Mich.: Baker Book House, 1985.

———. *Post-Reformation Reformed Dogmatics: The Rise and Development of Reformed Orthodoxy, ca. 1520 to ca. 1725.* Grand Rapids, Mich.: Baker Academics, 2003.

———. "Reformation, Orthodoxy, 'Christian Aristotelianism,' and the Eclecticism of Early Modern Philosophy." *Nederlands Archief Voor Kerkgeschiedenis* 81, no. 3 (2001): 306–25.

———. "Scholasticism, Reformation, Orthodoxy, and the Persistence of Christian Aristotelianism." *Trinity Journal* 19, no. 1 (1998): 81–96.

Polanus, Amandus. *The Substance of the Christian Religion.* Translated by Elijahu Wilcocks. London: Felix Norton, 1600.

Rehnman, Sebastian. "The Doctrine of God in Reformed Orthodoxy." In *A Companion to Reformed Orthodoxy,* 351–401. Leiden: Brill, 2013.

Reid, Stephen J., and Emma Annette Wilson, eds. *Ramus, Pedagogy and the Liberal Arts: Ramism in Britain and the Wider World.* Farnham: Ashgate, 2011.

Reid, Thomas. *An Inquiry into the Human Mind, On the Principles of Common Sense.* Edinburgh: J. Robertson, 1818.

Salmond, C. A. *Princetoniana, Charles & A. A. Hodge: With Class and Table Talk of Hodge the Younger.* New York, New York: Scribner and Welford, 1888.

Sweeney, Leo. *Divine Infinity in Greek and Medieval Thought.* New York: P. Lang, 1998.

Turretin, Francis. *Institutes of Elenctic Theology.* Edited by James T Dennison. Translated by George Musgrave Giger. Phillipsburg N.J: P & R Publishing, 1992.

Van Mastricht, Petrus. *Theoretico-Practical Theology: Faith in the Triune God.* Edited by Joel Beeke. Translated by Todd Rester. Vol. 2. Grand Rapids, Michigan: Reformation Heritage Books, 2019.

Veitch, John. *Hamilton.* Philadelphia: Lippincott, 1882.

Voss, Stephen. *Essays on the Philosophy and Science of René Descartes.* New York: Oxford Univ Press, 1993.

Ryan M. McGraw, Scott Cook

5. Charles Hodge on the Trinity: Personhood and Subordination Language

This book is about persistence and change, continuity and discontinuity, between Charles Hodge and Reformed orthodoxy. Hodge identified himself with Reformed orthodoxy, both through the Westminster Standards, as well as in his copious use of early modern Protestant authors. Yet he was a post-Enlightenment American Reformed theologian. Like the foundation of a house after a major earthquake, philosophical and theological terms often shifted in meaning during his time-period. This makes assessing his relationship to earlier Reformed thought both challenging and rewarding. Challenging, because once-stable ideas in classic Christian theology took on fresh nuances, often without comment, yet sometimes self-consciously, in the nineteenth century. Rewarding, because studying Hodge in relation to Reformed orthodoxy can help provide big picture historical trajectories in this history of ideas.

Personhood language in relation to the Trinity is an ideal case in point. While early church, medieval, and early modern theologians regarded personhood as the individuation of essence, post-Enlightenment authors tended to define personhood in terms of the individual willing subject, or rational consciousness. This subtle shift created an implicit tension for the nineteenth century church in retaining classic Trinitarian formulations, particularly with respect to the relationship between person and essence in God. The contention of this essay is that Hodge's defense of the doctrine of the Trinity retained essential elements of the doctrine, while being vague at points with respect to personhood. We can see this trajectory in Trinitarian theology, with its continuities and discontinuities, in light of personhood in the Christian tradition up to Reformed orthodoxy, shifts in post-Enlightenment treatments of personhood, personhood in Hodge's defense of the Trinity in his *Systematic Theology*, and a comparison between Hodge and the earlier Reformed tradition. Among other things, the pervasive use of "subordination" language in nineteenth century Reformed Trinitarian theology makes the task of understanding Hodge's teaching challenging, both in relation to earlier precedents and to his post-Enlightenment American context.

5.1 Trinitarian Personhood up to Reformed Orthodoxy

Defining personhood was always a tricky affair in classic Christian theology.[1] Hodge himself recounted the painful process the church underwent in distinguishing *hypostasis* and *ousia*, substance and subsistence, suppositum and mode of subsistence, *prosopon*, *homoousios*, and other terms.[2] Without rehashing a well-established narrative, this section focusses on samples of early church and medieval struggles to define personhood in the Trinity, leading up to and focusing on Reformation and post-Reformation models as a backdrop to Hodge's place in the Reformed tradition.[3]

5.1.1 Trinitarian Personhood in the Early Church and Middle Ages

Boethius (d. 524) famously, and sometimes infamously, defined person as "an individual substance of a rational nature."[4] This definition simultaneously sought to encapsulate the teaching of the early church on Trinitarian personhood, and it served as a bridge to medieval discussions on the Trinity. Earlier definitions were often vaguer, while later ones were often clearer. What Boethius fundamentally achieved was to reduce personhood to individuated essence. Thus, human persons became instances of generic human nature as the relation of species to genus. However, since there is only one instance of God, personhood referred to personal distinction inherent to and within the single and simple divine essence. Personhood and essence were thus distinguishable, but not separable in God. God had genus, but not species. This gives us a vantage point from which to look backwards into early church Trinitarian theology, and forwards into medieval Trinitarian theology.

---

1 For examples, see chapters 5–8 in Stephen T. Davis, Daniel Kendall, and Gerald O'Collins, eds., *The Trinity: An Interdisciplinary Symposium on the Trinity* (Oxford: Ohio University Press, 2003).

2 Charles Hodge, *Systematic Theology* (Grand Rapids, MI: Eerdmans, 1999), 1:453–54.

3 For books relevant to this study, see Gilles Emery and Matthew Levering, eds., *The Oxford Handbook of the Trinity* (Oxford; New York: Oxford University Press, 2011); Peter C Phan, *The Cambridge Companion to the Trinity* (Cambridge; New York: Cambridge University Press, 2011); Lewis Ayres, *Nicaea and Its Legacy: An Approach to Fourth-Century Trinitarian Theology* (Oxford: Oxford University Press, 2009); Mark S. Smith, *The Idea of Nicaea in the Early Church Councils, Ad 431–451*, Oxford Early Christian Studies, 2018; Rik Van Nieuwenhove, *An Introduction to Medieval Theology* (Cambridge: Cambridge University Press, 2012); Richard A. Muller, *Post-Reformation Reformed Dogmatics: The Rise and Development of Reformed Orthodoxy, Ca. 1520 to Ca. 1725*, 2nd ed., 4 vols. (Grand Rapids, MI: Baker Academic, 2003), volume 4. The first book in this list, and part of the second, sketch the general trajectory of Trinitarian theology well. Ayres and Smith focus on the reception of Nicaean Trinitarian theology in the fourth through sixth centuries. Nieuwenhove tells the story of medieval theology with special focus on the Trinity. Lastly, Muller introduces post-Reformation Trinitarian theology on the backdrop of medieval and Reformation thought.

4 *Patrologia Latina*, ed. J. P. Migne, 271 v., indexes 4 v. [Paris 1878–90] 64:1345.

In the early church, person was at once a vital and problematic term. Vital, because the term expressed the greatest mystery in Christian theology, who is God? Problematic, because the term "person" was not developed in any serious way before the advent of Christ. Christian theologians created what became the modern term "person" in order to explain the Trinity and the doctrine of Christ.[5] *Prosopon,* and its Latin equivalent *persona,* were ancient terms signifying literary devices of "prosographic exegesis" where actors would use masks to create dialogue between characters in a play.[6] Tertullian (155–220) and others drew words from this literary device to underscore the dialogical nature of the members of the Godhead.[7] Christian theology further developed the term "person" in the first four centuries by highlighting the concept of relationship. The persons of the Godhead, defined in tandem with a strong commitment to divine simplicity, were nothing less than real relationships existing within the Godhead. Augustine (354–430) appropriated this relationship model of Trinitarian personhood, arguing that one may make substance or relationship predications concerning God. Relative predication was always with reference to the persons.[8] The details regarding the Cappadocian fathers' Trinitarian theology is, as recent scholarship shows, far more complicated than some theology textbooks explain.[9] However, they too defined the persons of the Godhead in relational terms, while emphasizing the properties constituting the relations.[10] While Hodge read Augustine and the Cappadocian fathers, he was aware of significant departures from the Patristic relational model of the Trinity. The Cappadocians and Augustine at least illustrate the point of the struggle to define personhood, having the advantage of being authors that Hodge read and identified with in relation to Nicene theology.[11]

---

5 Hans Urs von Balthasar, "On the Concept of Person," *Communio* 13, no. 1 Spring (1986): 18–19.

6 Joseph Ratzinger, "Concerning the Notion of Person in Theology," *Communio* 17, no. 3 Spring (1990): 439–41.

7 Edmund J. Fortman, *The Triune God: A Historical Study of the Doctrine of the Trinity* (Grand Rapids, MI: Baker Book House, 1972), 107–13.

8 Augustine, *The Trinity*, trans. Stephen McKenna (Washington, D.C.: Catholic University of America Press, 2002), Book V, Chapter 5.

9 For a recent discussion, see Joseph T. Lienhard, "Ousia and Hypostasis: The Cappadocian Settlement and the Theology of One Hypostasis," in *The Trinity: An Interdisciplinary Symposium on the Trinity*, ed. Stephen T. Davis, Daniel Kendall SJ, and Gerald O'Collins SJ (Oxford: Oxford University Press, 2002), 99–122. The Cappadocian fathers were Gregory of Nazianzen, Gregory of Nyssa, and Basil the Great.

10 Fortman, *The Triune God: A Historical Study of the Doctrine of the Trinity*, 79–85; Gerald O. O'Collins, *The Tripersonal God: Understanding and Interpreting the Trinity* (New York: Paulist Press, 1999), 131–34.

11 Lewis Ayres, *Augustine and the Trinity* (Cambridge: Cambridge University Press, 2014); Lucian Turcescu, *Gregory of Nyssa and the Concept of Divine Persons* (Oxford: Oxford University Press, 2005).

Some medieval authors clarified personhood, expanding on, and sometimes correcting, Boethius's definition. Richard St. Victor (1110–1173) and Thomas Aquinas (1225–1274) are most relevant here due to the ways that their treatments of personhood resurfaced in authors like Calvin and Turretin, on whom Hodge relied heavily.

Richard Saint Victor was known for his mystical Trinitarian theology. Richard's contributions to Western Trinitarian theology come by his definition of Trinitarian personhood, his rational argumentation for the Trinity focusing on divine love, and his mystical explanation of the psychological dynamics of the trinity.[12] He primarily defined personhood in God as "an incommunicable existence of the divine nature,"[13] which more or less became standard language among some Reformation and post-Reformation authors. The Westminster Larger Catechism Question 9, for instance, states that the three persons of the Godhead are the same in substance, though they are "distinguished by their personal properties."

Book four of Richard's *De Trinitate* builds on plurality in God, pulling towards the Trinity by defining personhood. In chapters 4–5, Richard explains why the Holy Spirit directed the church to use the term "person," which he preferred over "subsistence." For example, while "animal" applied to all sensible substances, "person" applied only to rational substances, which is one sole and singular substance.[14] This approximately echoed Boethius' famous definition of person as an individual substance of a rational nature, with some terminological differences. Under the *intelligenitia* of substance is the *subintelligentia* of properties common to all animals, the further *subintenlligentia* of man encompassed properties common to all human beings, and under the name person "*subintelligetur*" certain properties fitting to one only and designated by a proper name. His categories of intelligence and subintelligence thus led from one general category of substance, to animal, to man, to person, each subintelligent category being more precise and narrower than the last. The question of personhood, then, was to how designate specific categories in relation to general ones. Translating intelligence and subintelligence is admittedly difficult here, and the translator opted for "substance" and "property."[15] While losing the tight logical connections of the Latin text, this conveys the general meaning well enough. Perhaps chapter 16 was the source of John Calvin's later restriction of eternal generation to the Son's personhood to the exclusion of communication of essence, since Richard argued that it is proper for divine substance to have its

12 Rik Van Nieuwenhove, *An Introduction to Medieval Theology* (Cambridge, UK: Cambridge University Press, 2014), 137–47.

13 Richard St. Victor, *On the Trinity*, trans. Ruben Angelici (Eugene, OR: Cascade Books, 2011), 164.

14 Richard St. Victor, *Richard Saint-Victor, On the Trinity*, ed. Jean Riballier, trans. Aage Rydstro-Poulsen, vol. 4, Brepolis Library of Christian Sources (Turnhout, Belgium: Brepolis, 2021), 166.

15 St. Victor, *Trinity*, 167.

being from itself, but proper for divine persons to originate from another person (178). If so, then this diverged from the standard medieval (and Reformed) model of viewing eternal generation as communication of the divine essence through personal subsistence. However, Richard later assigned self-existence to the Father alone as an incommunicable property of his personal existence, which would make Calvin uneasy.[16] Richard ultimately defined person in God as incommunicable existence, or incommunicable property, reflecting the origin of the person (Ch. 18). Chapters 20 and following modified Boethius' definition by shifting towards person as individual existence of a rational substance, marked by a singular incommunicable property. Richard's concern was to define personhood in a way that could apply to all persons, whether divine, angelic, or human (ch. 25). In his mind, "existence" indicated a relationship to a broader category of being (*sistere*). As we will see below, Calvin approximated Richard's definition of person in some respects, while Hodge differed from both to an extent (more from Richard than from Calvin).

Aquinas is particularly important on divine personhood, both due to his subsequent influence on the Western church, and due to his clarity. Like Richard, he commented on Boethius' definition explicitly, seeking both to incorporate and modify it into his own clear teaching on divine personhood.[17] For Aquinas, personhood referred primarily to relation of origin, reflecting Richard's concern to stress "existence" as meaning having one's being out of another.[18] This meant that the Son originated eternally from the Father by communication of the divine essence, and that the Spirit did so from the Father and the Son. Personhood thus described the sense in which each divine person was God. The Father was God of none, the Son was God of the Father, and the Spirit was God of the Father and Son together. Regarding the *filioque*, Aquinas argued among other things that if the Spirit did not proceed from the Father and the Son together, then he would have no distinct relationship of origin from the Son, resulting in two Sons instead of one.[19] Much more can be said about Aquinas' Trinitarian theology.[20] Relevant here is that he distinguished, but did not separate, essence and personhood in God. The eternal processions in the Trinity resulted in relations of opposition within the one God, thus avoiding quaternity, which treated the divine essence as a fourth thing in the Trinity in addition to persons. One vital aspect of Aquinas' Trinitarian theology was

16 St. Victor, *Trinity*, 208. Bk. 4, ch. 4.

17 Thomas Aquinas, *Summa Theologiae*, trans. Lawrence Shapcote, Latin/English Edition of the Works of St. Thomas Aquinas (Steubenville, OH: Emaus Academic, 2012), 308. Part 1, Q. 29.

18 Questions 27–28.

19 Question 36.

20 For two outstanding studies on Aquinas' Trinitarian theology, see Gilles Emery, *The Trinitarian Theology of Saint Thomas Aquinas* (Oxford: Oxford University Press, 2010); Dominic Legge, *The Trinitarian Christology of St Thomas Aquinas* (Oxford: Oxford University Press, 2018).

that he asserted that creatures were analogous to God and not God analogous to creatures. This meant that we must understand personhood in relation to God first and then in humanity.[21] We must avoid projecting ideas of human personhood onto God because God is the original and his creatures are always the imperfect copy. This point is easily missed in Hodge's context, since Hodge commonly redefined human speech about God because there was no human analogy to understanding terms like eternity as no succession of moments.[22] For Aquinas the analogy was always God downward, while in Hodge's practice at least the analogy was often man upward. Both Richard and Aquinas reminded readers persistently that as God's image, man was both like God and unlike him, though the unlikeness remained greater than the likeness.[23] This is important to remember below as we see how Hodge waded through historical definitions of personhood in his nineteenth century American context.

5.1.2 Trinitarian Personhood in Reformation and Post-Reformation Theology

Reformation theology rejected Roman Catholic views of infallible church tradition. Yet they maintained an apostolic succession of sorts in a succession of true doctrine. The Puritan William Perkins (1858–1602) famously wrote his *Reformed Catholic* to show how far Protestants agreed with Roman Catholic teaching and where they must differ.[24] The general idea embedded in Reformation and post-Reformation theology was that Reformed doctrine retained catholic doctrine of the Christian church insofar as it faithfully interpreted Scripture. Retaining and interacting with early church and medieval notions of Trinitarian personhood was no exception. Due to Hodge's heavy dependence on John Calvin (1509–1565), this brief sketch of Reformation and post-Reformation teaching on divine personhood begins with Calvin, and traces personhood through representative samples of Reformed orthodox authors.

Calvin's conception of Trinitarian personhood was controversial, and his views influenced even nineteenth century authors like Hodge and B. B. Warfield. In his

21 For example, concerning the Father he noted that "paternity" applied first and properly to God the Father and to only secondarily to human beings (*prius dicuntur de Deo quam de creaturis*). 1.22.2, reply to objection 4. Pg. 345.

22 Hodge, *Systematic Theology*, 1:388, 578.

23 St. Victor, *Trinity*, 248. Bk. 6, ch. 1.

24 William Perkins, *Catholicus Reformatus, Hoc Est, Expositio et Declaratio Praecipiuarum Aliquot Religionis Controversiarum: Quae Ostendit, Quatenus Ecclesiae Ex Dei Verbo Reformatae in Iis Cum Ecclesia Rom. Qualis Est Hodie Est, Consentiunt, et Quatenus Ab Edadem Dissentiunt, Adeoque in Quibus Numquam Ei Consentire Debent* (Hanoviae, 1601).

Institutes, Calvin followed Philip Melanchthon's (1497–1560) model of treating the Trinity while devoting little direct attention to the divine attributes. Setting a high importance on the Trinity, Calvin referred to Triunity as God "distinctive mark" distinguishing the true God from idols.[25] Generally, he echoed Richard St. Victor's definition of person in God as an "incommunicable quality," meaning that the Son and the Spirit were all that the Father was except Father, and so on.[26] However, while affirming the Nicene Creed, Calvin objected to how early church theologians understood "very God of very God." Believing that communication of essence from Father to Son, and from Father and Son to Spirit, would result in inequality or subordination with respect to the divine essence, Calvin argued that eternal generation (and procession) referred to the Son's person, but not to his essence. He thought that understanding eternal generation as communication of the divine essence threatened the Son's aseity, or self-existence, making him a different kind of God from the Father.[27] Instead of the Father being *fons deitatis*, he was only *fons trinitatis*.[28] The distinction between person and essence became a separation between person and essence by relegating eternal generation to personhood to the exclusion of communicated essence. Calvin still maintained that there was one God, that all three persons were God, that all three persons were distinct, and that the order of Father, Son, and Spirit was irreversible. Yet his rejection of the idea of person as relation of origin passed tacitly into Hodge's conception of personhood, and explicitly into Warfield's, as we will see below. Coupling this fact with nineteenth century ideas of personhood complicates any evaluation of Hodge's ideas on this point.

Calvin's shift in understanding Trinitarian personhood gained long-standing attention, both within the Reformed world and without. Pierre Caroli (1480–1550)

---

25 See throughout Richard A. Muller, *The Unaccommodated Calvin: Studies in the Foundation of a Theological Tradition*, Oxford Studies in Historical Theology (Oxford: Oxford University Press, 2002).

26 John Calvin, *Institutes of the Christian Religion*, ed. John T. McNeill, trans. Ford Lewis Battles, vol. XX–XXI, Library of Christian Classics (Philadelphia: Westminster Press, 1960), 1:128. Bk. 1.13.6

27 Calvin, *Institutes*, 1:154. 1.13.25. "Therefore we say that deity in an absolute sense exists of itself; whence likewise we confess that the Son since he is God, exists of himself, but not in respect of his Person; indeed, since he is the Son, we say that he exists from the Father. Thus his essence is without beginning; while the beginning of his Person is God himself." By contrast, Richard, and especially Anselm, believed that Christ possessed aseity by eternal communication of the divine essence from the Father. Calvin divided essence and person while these other authors merely distinguished them, leaving them inseparable.

28 The standard treatment of this issue is Brannon Ellis, *Calvin, Classical Trinitarianism, and the Aseity of the Son* (Oxford: Oxford University Press, 2012). This is a robust and careful historical study on a difficult and nuanced historical question. In his conclusion, Ellis expresses sympathy for Calvin's construction of aseity.

accused Calvin (and his friend William Farel) of Arianism and Sabellianism.[29] Anti-Trinitarian humanist Valentine Gentile (1520–1566) accused Calvin of teaching quaternity, which Calvin's more orthodox opponents echoed.[30] Both Roman Catholics and Lutherans opposed Calvin's view of eternal generation, while Reformed authors ran to his defense. This debate spilled over into Calvin's exegetical works somewhat tangentially, when the Lutheran Aegidius Hunnius (1550–1603) accused Calvin of being a "Judaizer" by failing to find the deity of Christ and the Trinity sufficiently in his biblical commentaries. Thus, two strands of controversy emerged surrounding Calvin's Trinitarian theology, which carried over into the seventeenth century.[31] The relevant issue here is that both Roman Catholics and Lutherans detected something different from the Christian tradition in Calvin's defense and uses (or lack thereof) of the doctrine of the Trinity.

Keeping Hodge's dependence on Calvin in view, a few examples of post-Reformation treatments of the Trinity, including at least one substantial defense of Calvin, can help show the general trajectory of Reformed thought that Hodge inherited. William Perkins, Francis Cheynell (1608–1665), and Francis Turretin (1623–1687) serve as useful focal points, Perkins due to his influence on English speaking Reformed theology, Cheynell for his defense and interpretation of Calvin, and Turretin due to his immediate influence on Hodge. In his *Golden Chain*, Perkins began by defining personhood in God via Richard St. Victor and Calvin's preference, at least implicitly, for incommunicable property.[32] Such properties marked the modes of subsistence of the divine persons. Holding together person and essence in the eternal processions, Perkins argued that the Son and the Spirit had the whole divine essence by eternal communication from the Father.[33] The remainder of his short chapter on the Trinity treated the fact that the missions of the Son and the Spirit reflected their eternal order and subsistence in terms of the Son's eternal generation of the Father and the Spirit's eternal procession from the

29 Emery and Levering, *The Oxford Handbook of the Trinity*, 228.

30 Ellis, *Calvin, Classical Trinitarianism, and the Aseity of the Son*, 53.

31 For the narrative of these debates over Calvin between post-Reformation Reformed and Lutheran authors, stressing the exegetical work of Jerome Zanchius (1560–1590), see Benjamin R Merkle, *Defending the Trinity in the Reformed Palatinate: The Elohistae*, Oxford Theology and Religion Monographs (Oxford, 2016).

32 William Perkins, *Armilla Aurea, id est, Theologiae Descrpto, Miranda Series Causarum Et Salutis & Damnationis Iuxta Verbum Dei Eius Synopsin Continet Annexa* (Cambridge, 1596), 12.

33 Perkins, *Armilla Aurea*, 14. Readers should note that Reformed authors in this period referred to eternal generation and procession to describe the personal properties of the Son and the Spirit. "Processions," as I use it here, includes both categories into a broader one, primarily reflecting Aquinas. The meaning, however, remains the same in describing modes of subsistence in God for Aquinas and Perkins. The Son's eternal generation and the Spirit's eternal procession reflect specific kinds of processions within the Godhead.

Father and the Son. Reflections of Aquinas on moving from the external temporal missions to the internal eternal processions are obvious here. While Perkins echoed Calvin on defining person as incommunicable property, he explained personhood as relation of origin, without using the term explicitly, entailing eternal communication of the divine essence.

Francis Cheynell addressed Calvin's Trinitarian concept of personhood in relation to aseity directly. A member of the Westminster Assembly, the Assembly commissioned Cheynell to publish two books on the Trinity, one a positive treatment and the other a refutation of Socinianism.[34] Cheynell illustrates a frequent occurrence in post-Reformation Reformed treatments of Trinitarian personhood. While defending Calvin's orthodoxy, he reinterpreted Cavin's teaching on aseity in light of his own views. In his fourth chapter, Cheynell echoed Aquinas by treating God in absolute and relative terms.[35] An elaborate description follows in which he argued from Scripture that the absolute divine nature subsisted in three persons.[36] While we can distinguish essence and personhood, we cannot divide them.[37] It was not until chapter six that he defined person as,

> A divine person is a spiritual and infinite *subsistent*, related indeed to those other *uncreated* persons, which subsist in the same divine nature with it, but distinguished from those *coessential* persons by its peculiar manner of subsistence, order of subsisting, singular relation, and incommunicable property. In these few lines there is matter enough to fill many sheets, and I am to treat of the distinction of person at large in the next chapter.[38]

"Incommunicable property" agreed with Calvin and Richard St. Victor, but Cheynell's explanation of the manner of subsistence and singular relation better

34 Sarah Mortimer provides previously the previously bypassed origin of English Socinianism during this time period. Paul Lim expands this narrative with a special stress on the responses of John Owen and Francis Cheynell. Sarah Mortimer, *Reason and Religion in the English Revolution: The Challenge of Socinianism* (Cambridge: Cambridge University Press, 2010); Sarah Mortimer, "Early Modern Socinianism and Unitarianism," in *The Oxford Handbook of Early Modern Theology, 1600–1800*, ed. Ulrich L. Lehner, Richard A. Muller, and A. G. Roeber (Oxford: Oxford University Press, 2016), 361–72; Paul Chang-Ha Lim, *Mystery Unveiled: The Crisis of the Trinity in Early Modern England* (New York: Oxford University Press, 2012).

35 Francis Cheynell, *The Divine Triunity of the Father, Son, and Holy Spirit, or, the Blessed Doctrine of the Three Coessentiall Subsistents in the Eternall Godhead Without Any Confusion or Division of the Distinct Subsistences or Multiplication of the Most Single and Entire Godhead Acknowledged, Beleeved, Adored by Christians, in Opposition to Pagans, Jewes, Mahumetans, Blasphemous and Antichristian Hereticks, Who Say They Are Christians, but Are Not* (London, 1650), 18.

36 Cheynell, *Divine Triunity*, 21–40.

37 Cheynell, *Divine Triunity*, 42.

38 Cheynell, *Divine Triunity*, 96.

matched Aquinas' idea of person as relation of origin. In his view, the Son's eternal generation involved eternal communication of Godhead from the Father, as did the Spirit's double procession from Father and Son.[39] Cheynell's construction both harmonized with the early and medieval church, and it did not allow room for distinguishing the Father as *fons trinitatis* from *fons deitatis*. Personhood in God was an incommunicable property, but Godhead was communicable from Father to Son and from Father and Son together to Spirit. Simultaneously, this was not Calvin's view, and neither was it the view Hodge would later adopt.

Cheynell explicitly sought to defend Calvin's orthodoxy in chapter six.[40] Modern readers should not understand this appeal to Calvin as indicating that Calvin was to Reformed theology what Luther was to Lutheran theology. Calvin was not the founder of a theological tradition, but one luminary among others.[41] Cheynell flagged Calvin because of the controversies surrounding his Trinitarian theology. He argued that Calvin maintained that the divine persons subsisted within the one divine essence, and that "*The single Godhead, the whole Godhead is in every single person, and it is common to all three in a singular and glorious way*."[42] He spelled out that this meant that "every single person is God in himself."[43] However, on the same page, he asked, "How can you describe a divine person, if you abstract his personality from his divinity?" Yet abstracting personhood from divinity was precisely what sparked the controversy over Calvin's teaching on the Trinity. Cheynell taught that personhood was an incommunicable quality describing a relation of origin, so that the Son and the Spirit were divine persons by communication of the divine essence. Cheynell subtly gave the impression that this was precisely what Calvin meant by treating persons as subsistences in the divine essence. Just prior to Cheynell's second defense of Calvin, he argued that the Son must have aseity in order to be God, but that the Father communicates the divine essence to the Son through begetting his personal subsistence.[44] Generation does not come through essence considered abstractly, but from the Father as a divine person. Again, this reflected classical Trinitarian doctrine, but this was not Calvin's view. Whether this was a theological slight of hand, manipulating Calvin's views to match his own, or that Cheynell

39 Cheynell, *Divine Triunity*, e. g., 159, 224.

40 And Calvin and Beza again on pages 232–235, referring readers to Daniel Chamier (1564–1621), Franciscus Gomarus (1563–1641), and Gisbertus Voetius (1589–1676) for fuller defenses.

41 For extensive refutation of the idea that Calvin was the benchmark of Reformed thought, see Richard A. Muller, *Christ and the Decree: Christology and Predestination in Reformed Theology from Calvin to Perkins* (Grand Rapids, MI: Baker Academic, 2008); Richard A. Muller, *After Calvin: Studies in the Development of a Theological Tradition* (Oxford; New York: Oxford University Press, 2003), among his many other books and essays on Reformed orthodoxy.

42 Cheynell, *Divine Triunity*, 78.

43 Cheynell, *Divine Triunity*, 79.

44 Cheynell, *Divine Triunity*, 231.

could only read such Trinitarian language in light of his historical theology, or some other cause, we cannot know certainly. Yet this is a good example of how post-Reformation authors defended Calvin's orthodoxy while teaching more classic catholic Christian ideas on personhood.[45]

Francis Turretin was an important source for Hodge's thought in general. As the first chapter in this volume notes, Hodge required his students to read Turretin in Latin prior to the publication of his own *Systematic Theology* in English, and Turretin's influences are clear throughout Hodge's work. Turretin's treatment is an ideal inroad to Hodge's exposition of Trinitarian personhood, both for his exceptional clarity and his clear dependence on authors like Boethius and Aquinas. His treatment of the Trinity comprises questions 23–31 of topic three of his *Institutes*. Questions twenty-three, twenty-five, and twenty-nine are most relevant to this essay, since these sections define personhood, show the relationship between person and essence in God, applying these ideas to eternal generation. The ideas of person as incommunicable property and relation of origin, entailing the communication of the divine essence, stand out clearly throughout.

Question twenty-three largely defines Trinitarian language, leading with the idea of person as relation in God. Person, or mode of subsistence, was the key idea in his treatment of the Trinity, since everything else was common to the divine essence, treated in earlier sections. Paragraphs three and four defined essence, or the quiddity of a thing, and substance, as opposed to subsistence rather than to accidents.[46] This mirrored Aquinas' teaching that person involved relations of opposition, in which personal properties were restricted to each divine person. Personhood language became his main focus in paragraphs five through eight. Echoing Boethius, subsistence, or mode of subsistence, denoted the mode of existence of a proper substance, or the mode in which a substance existed, and this term was functionally equivalent to *persona*.[47] After noting the initial confusion between East and West over *hypostasis* and *persona*, he concluded that both terms referred to an intellectual *suppositum*, again reminiscent of Boethius and especially Aquinas.[48] Turretin next took the opportunity to defend "our Calvin's" orthodoxy by observing that *persona* could be either concrete or abstract, referring either to a single divine person, or

45 I trace this question through many more early modern Reformed authors in chapter two of Ryan M. McGraw, *"A Heavenly Directory:" Trinitarian Piety, Public Worship, and a Reassessment of John Owen's Theology*, Reformed Historical Theology (Göttingen: Vandenhoeck & Ruprecht, 2014).

46 Francis Turretin, *Institutio Theologiae Elencticae*, vol. 1 (Geneva, 1679), 269. 3.23.3–4.

47 Turretin, *Instititio*, 1:269–270. 3.23.5. He added using Thomistic language that Christ's human nature had no suppositum, since his humanity was in hypostatic union with the person of the eternal Son.

48 Turretin, *Instititio*, 1:270. 3.23.6–7. Turretin expounded Heb. 1:3, which was a key text in understanding *hypostasis*

primarily with respect to the divine essence, Calvin opting for the latter definition.[49] Later, in question twenty-four, noting the Roman Catholic and Lutheran opposition to Calvin, he merely repeated Calvin's assertion that he rejected the language of ancient authors on eternal generation without rejecting the thing that they taught.[50] When addressing whether there are three distinct persons in question twenty-five, Turretin rejected the idea of quaternity on the grounds that the three persons are not really distinct from the divine essence, but they differ only by their mode of subsistence.[51] In paragraph twenty he added that this essence was inseparable from person (*essentia est inseprabilis a personis*). Paragraph twenty-six clarified that the divine essence was communicated in eternal generation and spiration.[52] All of this shows that he defined *persona* as an incommunicable property that supposed communication of the divine essence in relations of origin with respect to the Son and the Spirit.

Question twenty-seven focuses on the distinction between essence and person, noting both that person is an incommunicable property, and that each person has the whole divine essence.[53] A few points stand out with respect to personhood as relation of origin. In paragraph five, he noted that whatever is essential and absolute is God himself, yet that which is personal and relative is not equivalent to God's essence.[54] Likewise, essence is predicated of persons in the concrete, but the persons are not the essence in the abstract.[55] Paragraph twelve added the important qualification that we cannot restrict our understanding of divine personhood to human personhood, since human beings are analogous to God and not vice versa.[56] This is important because it simultaneously hearkened back to Aquinas's idea that God is the original and human beings are the imperfect copies, making analogies always run God downward rather than man upward, and because we have already seen that Hodge could sometimes redefine divine attributes because he thought that the human analogy was unintelligible.[57] Finally, paragraphs 16–20 treat person as incommunicable property, asserting that the Father is *fons Deitatis* by eternal communication of the divine essence to the Son, and, with the Son, to the Spirit. Generation by the Father did not refer to the divine essence absolutely, but to the Father as a divine person, essence and personhood remaining conjoined. Instead of

49 Turretin, *Institito*, 1:270. 3.23.8.
50 Turretin, *Institito*, 1:274. 3.24.17.
51 Turretin, *Institito*, 1:286. 3.25.17.
52 Turretin, *Institito*, 1:287. 3.25.26.
53 Turretin, *Institito*, 1:294. 3.27.1.
54 Turretin, *Institito*, 1:295. 3.27.5.
55 Turretin, *Institito*, 1:295. 3.27.7.
56 Turretin, *Institito*, 1:296. 3.27.12.
57 See chapter 4 of this volume.

arguing, like Calvin, that eternal generation referred to the Son's personhood but not to communication of divinity, Turretin's treatment of this question refused to separate essence and personhood in God. The fundamental ideas surround *persona*, for Turretin, were relation of origin and incommunicable property, which also secured the irreversible order in God's being and works of Father, Son, and Spirit. Defining person as relation of origin was precisely what determined the eternal order in the Godhead without subordination or inequality. As we will see below, the absence of this idea would resurface in relation to subordination language and in Warfield's rather extreme appropriation of Calvin's modification of personhood and eternal generation.

Lastly, Question twenty-nine, on the eternal generation of the Son clarifies the above principles through their application. Turretin argued that the Son was the same essence as the Father, though distinct by ineffable generation. He argued strongly that all generation, whether divine or human, entailed communication of essence, though unlike human generation, divine generation involved the perfect communication of the entire divine essence.[58] In other words, God was a genus without species, since all three divine persons were not instances of the nature of God, but they were inherent to God's being, making the connection between person and essence tight and inseparable. Guarding against quaternity again, he added that generation is from person to person in God, and not by an abstracted divine essence, which he believed would result in Tritheism.[59] In the same vein, the first three paragraphs of question thirty-one on the procession of the Spirit, argued that the procession of the Spirit from Father and Son (*filioque*) is alone what differentiated the Spirit's personhood from the Son's, since he had a distinct relation of origin.[60] The same arguments had appeared in Anselm of Canterbury, Richard St. Victor, and Thomas Aquinas, but they largely disappeared in Hodge and his orthodox nineteenth century contemporaries. As we will see below, this fact illustrated that definitions of personhood had substantially changed trajectories.

5.1.3 Conclusion to Section 1

The early church and medieval development of the idea of personhood in the Trinity revolved around Boethius in many respects. If personhood taken generically was individuated essence, then divine persons could not result in distinct individuals, since there is only one God. This is why divine simplicity was always integral to classic Trinitarian theology, since God is three persons and he cannot consist of

58 Turretin, *Instititio*, 1:310. 3.29.4. Think of Richard's assertion that man is more unlike God than like him.

59 Turretin, *Instititio*, 1:310. 3.29.6. This reminds us of Gentile's accusations against Calvin.

60 Turretin, *Instititio*, 1:327. 3.31.1–3.

three persons as parts of a larger whole. Personhood as subsistence in the Godhead, reflecting incommunicable properties, and describing relation of origin, passed into post-Reformation theology under language of communicated essence and the Father as *fons deitiatis*. Calvin stood out as a notable exception in his division of essence and personhood, relegating eternal generation to personhood alone to the exclusion of essence. Interestingly, ascribing aseity to the Son was not as new as Warfield later assumed, since Anselm of Canterbury (d. 1109) asserted it. Only, Anselm explained that the Son was self-existent by eternal communication from the Father.[61] Reformed orthodoxy generally fit this explanation of aseity as well. Calvin's restriction of eternal generation and procession to personhood passed into Princeton theology and joined itself with modern conceptions of personhood, while the better-established view of personhood as relation of origin, involving communicated essence, largely did not.

5.2 Post-Enlightenment Shifts in Personhood

To understand the intellectual context in which Hodge wrote on the Trinity, it is important to show shifts in Trinitarian theology generally and in definitions of personhood particularly. The Trinity was generally in decline during this time while Unitarianism was on the rise.[62] John Locke (1632–1704) and other Enlightenment thinkers had redefined key theological terms and they sought to replace Aristotelian logic and categories with their own alternatives.[63] This section introduces the effects of such trends on definitions of personhood, with the aim of adding then current ideas to the background of Hodge's reception of the Reformed tradition, especially

61 Anselm, *Anselm of Canterbury: The Major Works*, ed. Brian Davies and G. R. Evans, Oxford's World Classics (Oxford: Oxford University Press, 2008), 57. *Monologion*. He explained, "The Father is wholly the supreme essence, and the Son is wholly the supreme essence. So the Father and Son, each exists as a whole through himself, just as each is wise through essence and wisdom. But this does not mean he is any less wholly wisdom…The Son exists through himself and has existence from the Father. This is not a contradiction. [citing Jn. 5:26]….If this were not the case, the being of the Father and Son would not be the same, and the Son would not be equal to the Father…So then, it is not contradictory for the Son to exist both through himself and from the Father. This is because the Son has, necessarily, his very ability to exist through himself from the Father."

62 For the general trajectory of this trend and some suggested reasons, largely in relation to failures to find essential uses for the Trinity, see Philip Dixon, *Nice and Hot Disputes : The Doctrine of the Trinity in the Seventeenth Century* (London ;New York: T & T Clark, 2003).

63 For example, Isaac Watts (1674–1748), famous for his evangelical hymnody, wrote a book on logic seeking to defends the Christian faith using Lockean rather than Aristotelian logic. Isaac Watts, *Logick: Or, the Right Use of Reason in the Enquiry After Truth. with a Variety of Rules to Guard Against Error* (London, 1768).

Calvin, in order to better evaluate elements of persistence and change in Hodge's teaching.

Generally, post Enlightenment philosophy redefined person as an individual willing subject. The only significant Enlightenment thinker who defended the classic view of trinitarian personhood was G. W. Leibniz (1646–1716).[64] Leibniz wrestled with the rationality of Trinitarian theology, devoting several treatises to the subject, arguing in favor of the Augustinian notion that "persons" are relations.[65] The trajectory for Enlightenment influenced Trinitarian thought was set by two key philosophers, Rene Descartes (1596–1650) and Immanuel Kant (1726–1804). Descartes famously reconstructed his epistemic system around his ability to doubt his own existence, which is expressed in his saying "Cogito, ergo sum" ("I think, therefore I am"). Descartes' focus on consciousness in generally, and self-consciousness particularly, paved the way for a radical shift regarding personhood.[66] Descartes reimagined personhood in terms of a self-conscious being who thinks and wills.[67] The influence of Descartes explains, at least in part, why more radical authors like Thomas Hobbes (1688–1679) reverted to an old Roman, pre-Christian idea of person as an actor or agent.[68]

Kant rejected the doctrine of the Trinity itself as it did not fit into his conception of religion within the bounds of reason.[69] Yet he indirectly influenced the development of Trinitarian theology with his general definition of personhood. He emphasized that a person is a center of moral freedom and autonomy.[70] The most basic definition of a person was, for Kant, a thing which is "conscious of the numerical identity of itself at different times."[71] Kant would add that the concept of "psychological personhood" required both a rationality and accountability that entailed personal autonomy.[72] With these various philosophical influences afoot, it is not surprising

---

64 Fortman, *The Triune God: A Historical Study of the Doctrine of the Trinity*, 248.

65 Maria Rosa Antognazza, "Leibniz de Deo Trino: Philosophical Aspects of Leibniz's Conception of the Trinity," *Religious Studies* 37, no. 1 (March 2001): 1–13.

66 O'Collins, *The Tripersonal God: Understanding and Interpreting the Trinity*, 155.

67 Andrea Christofidou, "Self and Self-Consciousness: Aristotelian Ontology and Cartesian Duality.," *Philosophical Investigations* 32, no. 2 (April 2009): 134–62.

68 Thomas Hobbes, *Leviathan* (Oxford: Clarendon Press, 1929), 16.1; Ulrich L. Lehner, "The Trinity in the Early Modern Era (c.1550–1770)," in *The Oxford Handbook of the Trinity*, ed. Gilles Emery and Matthew Levering (Oxford: Oxford University Press, 2011), 245–46.

69 Cyril O'Regan, "The Trinity in Kant, Hegel, and Schelling," in *The Oxford Handbook of the Trinity*, ed. Gilles Emery and Matthew Levering (Oxford: Oxford University Press, 2011), 254–55.

70 O'Collins, *The Tripersonal God: Understanding and Interpreting the Trinity*, 155.

71 Immanuel Kant, *Anthropology From a Pragmatic Point of View* (Cambridge: Cambridge University Press, 2006), 361.

72 Howard Caygill, *A Kant Dictionary*, The Blackwell Philosopher Dictionaries (Mauldin, MA: Blackwell Publishers, 1995), 315–16.

that Locke would define a person as a "thinking, intelligent being, the has reason and reflection, and can consider it self as it self, the same thinking thing in different times and places; which it does only by that consciousness, which is inseparable from thinking."[73] Locke's emphasis on the person as a distinct center of self-consciousness, knowledge, and will profoundly influenced later philosophical and theological ideas.

G. F. W. Hegel (1770–1831) stands out among the eminent Enlightenment philosophers as one who used the Trinity to shape the contours of his thought. However, his "Trinitarian" patterns are not the least related to confessional Nicene Trinitarianism. Hegel developed his system whereby God, the World Spirit (Geist), manifested reconciliation with the world through a three-fold pattern.[74] However, Hegel rejected any notion of a tri-personal God.[75] Hegel's primary influence on the theological world was through his injection of a strong current of pantheism into nineteenth century theology, which gripped Hodge's attention persistently. Hegel rejected pantheism explicitly in his writings. However, nearly all scholars of Hegel agree that he rejected the name while embracing the substance of pantheism in his philosophical system.[76] Hodge would feel the effects of Hegel's Trinitarian pantheism as he was writing and teaching, repeatedly addressing the pantheistic tendencies prevalent in his time. It is likely that Hodge nevertheless drew from a concept of personhood similar to the tradition of Locke as an antidote to the Hegel-influenced philosophical speculation that God, as the Absolute, could not be personal, let alone tripersonal.

Scottish Common Sense Realism was another form of Enlightenment thought that influenced Hodge's view of Trinitarian personhood. Scottish Common Sense was a philosophical response to Hume's skepticism, which sought to establish essential categories of thought, such as cause and effect, on the basis of an appeal to the immediate judgment of universal human reason and consciousness. The best known advocate of Scottish Common Sense was Thomas Reid (1710–1796). However, the figure who was most significant in mediating Reid's influence to Hodge was Sir William Hamilton (1730–1803). Hamilton's emphasis on the consciousness as the regulative principle for epistemology had a profound effect on theology. Specifically, Hamilton's influence led Hodge to reflect on theological doctrines, including the Trinity, on the basis of the constraints of human consciousness.[77]

---

73 John Locke, *An Essay Concerning Human Understanding*, ed. Peter Nidditch (Oxford, England: Oxford University Press, 1975), 2.27.9.

74 See Dale M. Schlitt, *Hegel's Trinitarian Claim: A Critical Reflection* (Albany, NY: SUNY Press, 2012).

75 O'Regan, "The Trinity in Kant, Hegel, and Schelling," 257–62.

76 C. E. Plumptre, *General Sketch of the History of Pantheism.*, vol. 2 (London: W. W. Gibbings, 1878), 187–96.

77 For more details on Common Sense Realism, see chapters 1 and 4 above.

Matthew Kadane's interesting essay on anti-Trinitarianism and Republicanism provides some useful material on the British context of changing ideas of personhood with the rise of the Enlightenment and Unitarianism.[78] He notes that Isaac Newton and John Locke's agreement with Unitarian authors like Stephen Nye (1648–1719), who argued that the Trinity could not develop via Scripture alone, resulted in most eighteenth and nineteenth century Presbyterian ministers followed suit in England.[79] Kadane exemplified the prevalent post-Enlightenment definition of personhood by adding that Samuel Bourn (1689–1754), who wrote a popular anti-Trinitarian catechism, defined personhood as "an individual, intelligent, free, active Being or Substance."[80] While the terms individual and intelligent are reminiscent of Boethius to an extent, this definition marked a shift to defining personhood as an individual willing subject, which left no room for divine persons with a single divine will who were not distinct individuals. Interestingly, Archibald Alexander (1772–1851), Hodge's mentor and surrogate father, acknowledged that many Unitarians rejected the Trinity as self-contradictory because a person was "a distinct, intelligent, and voluntary agent."[81] He argued that the primary error in such thinking was defining divine personhood in light of human personhood, adding that the term person always suffered from ambiguities. However, rather than criticizing this modern assumed definition of person, he went on to use person to refer merely to distinction in God without further explanation or redefinition. Instead of recovering classic Christian views of personhood, orthodox nineteenth

---

78 Sarah Mortimer traces the rise of Socinianism in the 1640's in England, which is much earlier than other scholars recognized previously. Mortimer, *Reason and Religion in the English Revolution*; Mortimer, "Early Modern Socinianism and Unitarianism."

79 Matthew Kadane, "Anti-Trinitarianism and the Republican Tradition in Enlightenment Britain," *Republic of Letters* 2, no. 1 (2010): 44. Francis Cheynell and others addressed this objection to Trinitarian doctrine, though targeting Roman Catholic objections against the sufficiency of Scripture on this point. Cheynell, *Divine Triunity*, 296–305. Lim's *Mystery Unveiled* provides a fuller narrative of this point, often noting that Socinians accused Reformed authors of Romanism in their Trinitarian doctrine. Ryan Fields argues persuasively that Locke's view of Scripture set him apart from Enlightenment rationalism to a large extent. However, this does not mean that Locke's views were evangelical rather than Socinian in tendency, since Socinians claimed to follow the plain reading of Scripture. Archibald Alexander, Hodge's mentor and surrogate father, noted that the Socinian plane reading of Scripture assumed that the Bible could not teach the Trinity because it appeared to be "repugnant to reason." Ryan C. Fields, "A Generous Reading of John Locke: Reevaluating His Philosophical Legacy in Light of His Christian Confession," *Themelios* 45, no. 3 (December 2020): 602; Archibald Alexander, *A Brief Compendium of Bible Truth* (Grand Rapids, MI: Reformation Heritage Books, 2005), 33–34. Locke's confession that Jesus was the Savior revealed in Scripture did not obviate this point. Dick made similar comments to this effect in *Lectures*, 2:83.

80 Kadane, "Republican Tradition," 49.

81 Alexander, *Brief Compendium*, 35.

century theologians like Alexander often continued to use the term person while ignoring its modern use, leaving personhood somewhat vague and undefined beyond the idea of some kind of undefined and undefinable incommunicable property.

Enlightenment assumptions about personhood as an individual willing subject instead of an individual subsistence of a rational nature flourished and carried over into eighteenth and nineteenth century America. It is perhaps unsurprising that Unitarian ideas rose in tandem with such modern assumptions of personhood. Persons as individual willing subjects resulted either in viewing the Trinity as a contradiction in terms, or it entailed Tritheism by importing three wills into God.[82] Arguably, distinct willing subjects in God also opened the door to subordinationism, since three wills related to each other in the place of one will finding expression through three divine persons.

Given such shifts in personhood language and the growing prevalence of Unitarian ideas, it is surprising that neither Hodge nor the *Biblical Repertory and Theology Review*, which he edited for decades, devoted much attention to either issue.[83] J. W. Alexander (1804–1859) wrote an essay on Michael Servetus, whom Calvin participated in burning at the stake for Trinitarian heresy, but with a focus on the context of this event more than on the doctrine itself.[84] Searches for terms like Trinity, Trinitarian, Unitarian in the journal pull up little. Nothing in the voluminous articles Hodge contributed directly related to Trinitarian theology in the topics he covered. His essay, "Can God be Known?" focused on God's knowability and incomprehensibility, but not overtly on the divine persons.[85] More common were indirect arguments for the Trinity in relation to the divinity of Christ, such as "Christianity Without Christ."[86] Christ's divinity came to bear on Hodge's treatments of the atonement as well.[87] The Trinity came tangentially into view in Hodge's relatively long critical review of a book by Samuel Baird, but largely on the grounds

---

82 Adonis Vidu illustrates the later trajectory of redefining personhood as individual willing subject, thus attaching personhood to will rather than nature, in relation to recent trends in social Trinitarian theology. Adonis Vidu, *The Same God Who Works All Things: Inseparable Operations in Trinitarian Theology* (Grand Rapids: Eerdmans, 2021).

83 W. Andrew Hoffecker, *Charles Hodge: The Pride of Princeton.* (Phillipsburg, NJ: P & R Publishing, 2011), 300. Hoffecker argues that Hodge's preoccupation with transcendentalism and pantheism, exemplified by Ralph Waldo Emerson, likely eclipsed Hodge's concerns over Unitarianism.

84 James Waddel Alexander, "The Life of Michael Servetus," *Biblical Repertory and Theological Review* 8, no. 1 (1836): 73–96.

85 Charles Hodge, "Can God Be Known?," *Biblical Repertory and Theological Review* 36, no. 1 (1864): 122–52.

86 Charles Hodge, "Christianity Without Christ," *The Presbyterian Quarterly and Princeton Review* 5, no. 18 (1876): 352–62.

87 For example, Charles Hodge, "Christ, The Only Sacrifice: Or the Atonement in Its Relations to God and Man," *Biblical Repertory and Theological Review* 17, no. 1 (1845): 84–138.

that Baird made God too comprehensible.[88] "God in Christ" was more direct, stressing the vital importance of the Trinity, the incarnation, and the atonement, with Horace Bushnell as Hodge's target.[89] Some material from this article will resurface below in relation to Hodge's definition of personhood. However, his primary aim was to counter Bushnell's perceived rationalism and mysticism. Even in Hodge's monograph length tract, *The Way of Life*, the Trinity was not a major or explicit topic of his gospel presentation beyond his inclusion of the person and work of Christ.[90] Hodge and other authors in the BRTR did address the Trinity, but usually in conjunction with Christology and Pneumatology rather than in its own right. Considering the dominance of Trinitarian thought for most of church history, and the increasing prevalence of Unitarianism in the eighteenth and nineteenth centuries, this is somewhat surprising, particularly since the third stated purpose of the BRTR was to show the dangers of the errors of the time.[91] The shift in definitions of personhood passed into common use largely without comment by Reformed authors like Hodge.

5.3 Hodge on Trinitarian Personhood and Subordination

Taking classic and post-Enlightenment definitions of personhood in hand, we can now examine Hodge's treatment of personhood in the Trinity directly. In order to grasp his teaching, this section examines Hodge's defense of the Trinity in his *Systematic Theology* with supplements form "God in Christ," followed by devoting special attention to his use of subordination language, and concluded by a survey of a some of Hodge's prominent British and American orthodox contemporaries. While adding Hodge's friends among German theologians and Schleiermacher's views of the Trinity would add further depth, these three sections will suffice here to illustrate Hodge's continuities with Reformed orthodoxy as well as changes in vaguer definitions of personhood in the nineteenth century Reformed thinking.[92]

---

88 Charles Hodge, "The First and Second Adam: The Elohim Revealed in the Creation and Redemption of Man," *Biblical Repertory and Theological Review* 32, no. 2 (1860): 335–75.

89 Charles Hodge, "God in Christ; Three Discourses Delivered at New Haven, Cambridge, and Andover; with a Preliminary Dissertation on Language," *Biblical Repertory and Theological Review*, 1849, 259–97.

90 Charles Hodge, *The Way of Life* (Philadelphia: American Sunday School Union, 1841). See Hoffecker, *Hodge*, 224 for an analysis of the contents of this work. Even here, Hodge focused more prominently on justification than he did on Christ's person and finished work.

91 As cited in Hoffecker, *Charles Hodge: The Pride of Princeton.*, 129. Later Hoffecker added that "no major issue was exempt" from the journal (132).

92 For further details on this point, see the insightful work, Annette G Aubert, *The German Roots of Nineteenth-Century American Theology* (New York: Oxford University Press, 2013).

5.3.1 Hodge on Personhood

While this section addresses primarily Hodge's conception of personhood as it bore on the doctrine of the Trinity, a brief sketch of his Trinitarian theology is in order. In his *Systematic Theology* (chapter six of theology proper), he set forth the Trinity in seven sections. The first two dealt largely with terminology and biblical arguments for the Trinity, while the last six sketched the teaching of councils and theologians, with Hodge's evaluations of them interspersed. His treatment of personhood did not appear until section four, after the biblical material. For the most part, he noted the vagueness of the term and went no further than describing it as mode of subsistence and manner of subsistence.[93]

Hodge first reflected on the nature of personhood in his discussion of the spirituality of God. After giving some exegetical reflections of the meaning of the Greek and Hebrew words for "spirit," Hodge considered what we learn about spiritual existence from our consciousness. "In saying, therefore, that God is a Spirit," Hodge wrote, "our Lord authorizes us to believe that whatever is essential to the idea of a spirit, as learned from our own consciousness, is to be referred to God as determining his nature."[94] What does consciousness teach us regarding personhood? First, Hodge argued that consciousness teaches us that as we are conscious of our individual subsistence, we are conscious of our personality.[95] Hodge qualified that not every subsistence is a person. However, every subsistence that thinks, feels, and wills is a person. Hence, consciousness informs us of our own personhood because our subsistence has these qualities. Second, consciousness teaches us that every spirit possesses self-consciousness. Hodge did not elaborate on this insight at length, but he went go so far as saying that self-consciousness is what separates spirit from a mere force of nature.[96] Hodge concluded, "If God be a spirit, it follows of necessity that He is a person—a self-conscious, intelligent, voluntary agent."[97]

These statements appear to give a clear-cut definition of personhood. A person, according to Hodge, appears to be a self-conscious agent who thinks, wills, and feels. However, as we shall see, Hodge rejected this definition of personhood when speaking of the persons of the Godhead. Yet what he said above would appear to require that each person of the Godhead have self-consciousness and volition in order to qualify as a person according to the dictates of human consciousness. This tension would be resolved if Hodge were speaking of the divine nature in these terms of self-consciousness, thought, will, and feeling, while reserving the term

93 Hodge, *Systematic Theology*, 1:454–56.

94 Hodge, *Systematic Theology*, 1:377.

95 Hodge, *Systematic Theology*, 1:378.

96 Hodge, *Systematic Theology*, 1:378.

97 Hodge, *Systematic Theology*, 1:379.

"person" to a more technical and limited sense for divine persons. If so, then Hodge might be making a similar move to his contemporary, W. G. T. Shedd (1820–1894). Shedd argued that God is a person, and so is self-conscious through the individual consciousnesses of the three persons.[98] Hodge never directly harmonized the above ideas, calling God "a person," with his definition of Trinitarian personhood in his reflection on the Trinity.

In his opening statements on the doctrine of the Trinity proper, Hodge stressed the idea that the Trinity was peculiar to biblical revelation, that it was a practical rather than a speculative truth, and that all Christian ideas united in the Trinity.[99] Section two then provided five necessary components for the doctrine: that there is only one God, that Scripture referred to all three persons as God, that "the one divine Being subsists in three persons, that the persons had an eternal and irreversible order, and that all three persons acted in every divine work.[100] Under the fourth point, he asserted, "In the Holy Trinity there is a subordination of the Persons as to mode of subsistence and operation," to which we will return below. Hodge included appropriations under the fifth point, along with eternal processions, without using either term overtly. The rest of the section examines "the facts" of Scripture in a unified whole, using a method analogous to natural science, presenting three lines of evidence from the OT and five from the NT.[101] Hodge used the term person in these sections without defining it beyond describing it in terms of subsistence in the Godhead.

Without going into depth regarding his treatment of the teaching of the church, a few relevant points stand out from the remaining sections in relation to the material treated above. First, in the transitional period leading up to the Nicene Council, Hodge maintained that the average believer had a better intuitive sense of the truth of the Trinity than alternatives offered by heretics.[102] Perhaps this allowed for his vagueness over personhood language to stand to large extent, since precise terminology was less important than experimental knowledge of God. Second, he concluded that Nicaea taught that as persons, the Father, Son, and Spirit were not self-existent, infinite, and eternal, "but the Godhead, or divine essence" was. He explained that the Nicene fathers taught this because of their conception of eternal generation entailing eternal communication of the divine essence.[103]

---

98 William G. T. Shedd, *Dogmatic Theology*, ed. Alan W Gomes (Phillipsburg, NJ: P & R Publishing, 2003), 235–40.

99 Hodge, *Systematic Theology*, 1:442–43.

100 Hodge, *Systematic Theology*, 1:444–45.

101 Hodge, *Systematic Theology*, 1:445–48.

102 Hodge, *Systematic Theology*, 1:453.

103 Hodge, *Systematic Theology*, 1:460.

Hodge's historical accuracy is questionable here,[104] since he seemed to understand communication of essence as involving quaternity, in which the divine essence was separable from and superseded the persons. Third, in his examination of the Nicene doctrine, he distinguished the content of the Creed from its explanation by the Fathers. Particularly, he had in mind the alleged subordination of the divine persons by virtue of communication of essence.[105] Though he did not cite Calvin here, Hodge's evaluation mimicked Calvin's assessment of Nicaea almost exactly. What emerges is a tacit assumption of Calvin's rejection of communication of essence in eternal generation (and the Spirit's procession) without a clear substitute for understanding person as relation of origin in God. Boethius is missing altogether from Hodge's forty-page discussion of the Trinity as well.

Hodge's earlier essay, "God in Christ," actually says a little more about the reasons behind his vagueness in defining personhood. The article presents the Trinity in response to Horace Bushnell's (1802–1876) rejection of the doctrine.[106] Like the *Systematic Theology*, Hodge noted that church had always collected "the facts" of Scripture in formulating the doctrine of the Trinity, seeking to avoid contradictions. In a less developed form, Hodge argued for the Trinity in four points instead of five here: from one God, the Fact that all three persons are God (alluding to WLC 11),[107] that all three are personally distinct, and that that all three divine persons "cooperate" in man's redemption, with a distinct work terminating on each person.[108] This last argument approximated divine missions and appropriations, without distinguishing the two as earlier authors like Aquinas did more clearly. It differed from the fourth and fifth arguments present in the *Systematic Theology* as well by omitting irreversible order, and by narrowing the inseparable works of the Godhead to the works of redemption. Hodge added that faith in the divine persons makes Christianity a "practical religion" that is "founded" on the Trinity.[109]

After citing the WSC definition of the Trinity as a sum of the Nicene and Athanasian creeds, which are "the common faith of the Christian world," Hodge explained his use of the term person.[110] He noted that "person" was merely an attempt to account for the third set of facts in his list, showing some kind of distinction in God. Yet person did not explain the nature of such distinctions and

---

104 For a better account of Nicene theology, see Ayres, *Nicaea and Its Legacy.*

105 Hodge, *Systematic Theology*, 1:462.

106 Hodge, "God in Christ; Three Discourses Delivered at New Haven, Cambridge, and Andover; with a Preliminary Dissertation on Language," 277.

107 "The Scriptures manifest that the Son and the Holy Ghost are God equal with the Father, ascribing unto them such names, attributes, works, and worship, as are proper to God only."

108 Hodge, "God in Christ," 277–278.

109 Hodge, "God in Christ," 278.

110 Hodge, "God in Christ," 278.

relationships in God.[111] However, readers should remember that both Aquinas and Turretin used their understanding of personhood to explain more than Hodge did.[112] Person as relation of origin, involving communication of the divine essence in the cases of the Son and the Spirit, explained the reasons for the irreversible order in the Trinity. The Father was God of none, the Son was God of the Father, and the Spirit was God of the Father and the Son together. Here again Hodge did not define personhood, asserting simply that the persons were distinct from each other and that "each is the agent and object of action and can say I, and be properly addressed as Thou."[113] In spite of this studied vagueness, Hodge added that the church has always denied three consciousnesses, intelligences, and wills in God, which clearly reflected post-Enlightenment assumptions rather than early modern definitions of personhood. Hodge thus overstated his case when he asserted, "[the church] has humbly refused to press its definition of person beyond the limits just indicated, and has preferred to leave the nature of these distinctions in that obscurity, which must every overhang the infinite God in the view of his finite creatures."[114] His assertion about the church's attempt to explain personhood, and his claim that the church never defined personhood in a way that tried to explain the relations between the divine persons, at least partially, is not accurate in light of what we have seen above. Calvin recognized the church's explanations in terms of relation of origin and communication of essence and he rejected them. In this essay, Hodge simply ignored the historical record, appealing to the words of the creeds, bypassing both the theological arguments behind them and later historical developments.

In both of the above cited works, Hodge failed to define person beyond mode of subsistence. He fell short even of Calvin's preference for incommunicable property, though Calvin's reading of Nicene Trinitarian theology seemed to be in his purview. Hodge sometimes appeared to assume the definition of person in relation to an individual willing subject, though he preferred to leave the definition of the term vague, describing only undefined distinctions within God.

---

111 Hodge, "God in Christ," 278. "It is not intended to explain them."

112 John Witherspoon (1723–1794), an early president of Princeton College and signer of the Declaration of Independence, noted similarly, "The whole economy of our salvation teaches us the necessity of attending to and believing this doctrine; but I see neither necessity nor propriety in endeavoring to dip into the mode of it, and attempting to explain it. If it is a mystery and above our comprehension every attempt to explain it must be, if not criminal, yet unsuccessful." John Witherspoon, *The Works of John Witherspoon* (Harrisonburg, VA: Sprinkle Publications, 2006), 7:78.

113 Hodge, "God in Christ," 278.

114 Hodge, "God in Christ," 278.

5.3.2 Hodge's Use of Subordination Language

Hodge's use of subordination language deserves special attention in relation to his concept of personhood in the Trinity. He used subordination language explicitly in at least six places in his presentation of the Trinity in the chapter bearing that title in the *Systematic Theology*.[115] His treatment of the idea is somewhat confused, sometimes affirming it and sometimes denying it, but it relates to personhood because he used subordination to describe the order of subsistence among the divine persons.

His use of such language is both carefully explained and, from a historical standpoint, problematic. As we have seen, he said explicitly that there was "subordination" in the Trinity both "as to mode of subsistence and operation."[116] Yet he added the qualification that "subordination" did not mean that Christ was subordinate to the Father in his essence.[117] By contrast, Arianism subordinated the Son to the Father, not only in mode of subsistence, but in substance.[118] Putting the pieces together, it begins to look again as though Hodge separated, rather than merely distinguished, personhood and substance in the Trinity along the lines that Calvin did. Instead of eternal generation meaning communication of essence from Father to Son, marking the order of subsistences and the sense in which the Son was God, Hodge implied that the Son was subordinate to the Father personally, but not essentially. This was why he could assert that Nicaea included "the principle of the subordination of the Son to the Father, and of the Spirit to the Father and the Son."[119] In Hodge's conception, subordination meant "mode of subsistence and operation." Subordination thus did not mean inequality among the divine persons, but functionally it meant eternal order. This did not seem to entail for him any idea of authority and submission in the eternal Trinity.[120] Yet, Hodge added later, Scripture only ascribed subordination to the Son on account of his humanity.[121] This last assertion appears to introduce a bit of equivocation into Hodge's uses of subordination, since previously subordination meant order of subsistence, while now it meant subjection to the Father's will. Hodge held both that the Son was subordinate to the Father in the eternal Trinity, and that the Son was subordinate to the Father on account of incarnation alone, with different meanings of the term.

---

115 Hodge, *Systematic Theology*, 1:445, 451, 456, 461, 462, 477.

116 Hodge, *Systematic Theology*, 1:443.

117 Hodge, *Systematic Theology*, 1:451.

118 Hodge, *Systematic Theology*, 1:456.

119 Hodge, *Systematic Theology*, 1:460.

120 For arguments along similar lines, see Kevin Giles, "The Doctrine of the Trinity and Subordinationism," *Themelios* 28, no. 3 (July 2004): 270–84.

121 Hodge, *Systematic Theology*, 1:477.

The former marked subordination of subsistence, and the latter subordination of will, Hodge not distinguishing his two uses of subordination clearly. Subjection to the Father's will in the eternal Trinity only works if one defines person as an individual willing subject, denying a single divine will at least by implication. In summary, Hodge more or less asserted that the Son was subordinate to the Father eternally in the sense of order of subsistence, but that also the Son could only be subordinate to the Father as man because he was a divine and not a human person. His first use of subordination does not require that person meant individual willing subject, while his second use moves in that direction.

While in Catholic Christian theology, person as relation or origin secured order through communication of the divine essence, Hodge replaced this idea with subordination language largely unknown to the early church, medieval, and Reformed orthodox traditions. The origins of subordination language to describe order in the Trinity in nineteenth century Reformed theology is a bit of a puzzle, which requires further research than is possible here. However, what emerges in Hodge's thought contains simultaneously a classic idea of irreversible order among the divine persons, and a vague definition of personhood.

5.3.4 Conclusion to Section 3

Hodge's views on personhood in the Trinity largely assumed individual self-consciousness, or willing subject, while recognizing the inadequacies of such definitions for describing incommunicable properties in God. Coupled with his contemporaries, Shedd excepted, the picture emerges that person marked distinction within God without offering any explanation of the reasons for those distinctions or the relationships among the divine persons. Reformed orthodoxy, by contrast, followed the broader Christian tradition in explaining divine personhood in terms of relations of origin to explain the sense and the order in which each person was equally God. Calvin's influence is obvious among all of these authors, especially in Warfield, though Warfield was willing to ask a question that other nineteenth century authors were not: If person described distinction while explaining nothing, then why must we conclude that any reason for the order of Father, Son, and Spirit exists? Though Shedd rooted his views of the Trinity clearly in the catholic Christian tradition, he seems to have been the rare exception among nineteenth century American Reformed authors.

5.3.3 Hodge's Contemporaries on Personhood and Subordination

Many of the same trends in Hodge's treatment of personhood in the Trinity marked his Reformed contemporaries. Generally speaking, in light of the prevalence of understanding personhood as an individual willing subject in the nineteenth century, orthodox uses of personhood in defense of the Trinity took on a similarly vague quality. Recognizing the inadequacy of individual willing subject to describe divine persons, Hodge's Presbyterian Reformed orthodox contemporaries often left person largely undefined, and many of them used subordination language to describe order in the Godhead as well. This section examines two Scottish authors and four American ones to illustrate these trends.[122]

Bypassing Archibald Alexander, whose views on personhood are noted briefly above, two Scottish authors illustrate British examples of then current views of personhood. John Brown of Haddington (1722–1787) began his chapter on the Trinity in his *Systematic Theology* by defining personhood carefully as "a thinking substance, which can act by itself," and as "an intelligent agent" not sustained by another.[123] Taken generically, persons must have rational understanding and will, must admit personal pronouns, must engage in personal acts, and must "be capable of personal offices or stations, as prophet, priest, king, teacher, advocate, captain, etc." Applied to the Trinity, divine persons were not separate individuals, they had "the same individual" substance, and the divine persons are one being. Thus, "a divine person infinitely differs from a created one."[124] The order of Father, Son, and Spirit was inherent to God and God's external works followed "their natural order of subsistence."[125] Brown took a strong stance against subordination language in relation to the Trinity, asserting that "Subordinate Godhead is no Godhead at all, nor anything but a mere chimera in men's brains."[126] Yet he added immediately that calling the Father *fons Deitatis* and teaching communication of the divine essence "inadvertently hurt" the doctrine, concluding with an argument as to why the Trinity promoted piety. While it is tempting to assume that this hesitancy regarding communication of essence language resulted from Protestant views of staying close to Scripture, post-Reformation authors like Turretin, who shared this view of Scripture, had no hesitancy in adopting classic Christian ideas of personhood as relation of origin at this point. Brown's reaction against such language more likely reflects the broader shift at the time towards simplifying systems of doctrine and excising much of their scholastic form. His definition of personhood also marked a shift away from person as an instance or subsistence of the genus of

---

122 An appendix to volume 1 of Thornwell's *Collected Writings* contains some interesting material on defining personhood as well, but I omit it here for the sake of space. James Henley Thornwell, *The Collected Writings of James Henley Thornwell: Volume One Theological*, ed. John B. Adger, vol. 1, 4 vols. (Birmingham, AL: Solid Ground Christian Books, 2004).

123 John Brown, *The Systematic Theology of John Brown of Haddington* (Fearn: Christian Focus, 2002), 130.

124 Brown, *Systematic Theology*, 131.

125 Brown, *Systematic Theology*, 144.

126 Brown, *Systematic Theology*, 145.

essence towards individual self-consciousness. Writing a century earlier, he was more willing than Hodge was to try to define personhood, but he stood emphatically against subordination language with respect to divine persons.

The other relevant Scottish author for this essay is John Dick (1764–1833), who published his *Lectures on Theology* in four volumes. These lectures appeared in other nineteenth century theological works, especially in Dabney, who is treated below. Dick's treatment of the Trinity is divided into two chapters on the Trinity proper, three on the deity of Christ, and one on the Holy Spirit. His material on personhood and subordination in the first and second lectures, with scattered references to the rest of the lectures, are most relevant to building a broader context for Hodge's ideas. With regard to defining person, Dick rested on a distinction between specific and numerical nature.[127] This approximated the concern of earlier authors, who followed or modified Boethius' definition of personhood in that it retained the idea of relating particulars to a general category. "The same specific nature" meant, for example, that human beings were more than one of the same kind of being. However, "the same numerical nature" meant that God was in fact one undivided being. Dick immediately defined person as "a separate and independent being, whose existence and actions have no necessary connection with the existence and actions of any other being."[128] This definition retained the idea of the unity of the divine essence, and it reflected other nineteenth century depictions of personhood as involving independence. However, older Trinitarian theology had stressed interdependence rather than independence at this point. Person as relation of origin explained why eternal order and relations were necessary in God. In applying "person" to the Trinity, Dick approvingly cited Moses Stuart (1780–1852), of Andover seminary, which was founded partly to counter Unitarian thought, as saying, "I confess myself unable to advance a single step here in explaining what the distinction is."[129] He approached the idea of person as incommunicable property by saying that person marked "something peculiar to each," and he affirmed internal and necessary relations in God in an irreversible "order of subsistence."[130] Such ideas illuminate Hodge's intellectual context, with Dick and Hodge approximating the same kind of vagueness respecting personhood.

Regarding subordination, Dick virtually conflated subordination language with the idea of communication of the divine essence in generation and procession.[131]

127 John Dick, *Lectures on Theology* (Stoke-on-Trent: Tentmaker Publications, 2004), 2:62, 64, 141, 147.

128 Dick, *Lectures*, 2:64.

129 Dick, *Lectures*, 2:65. He expressed similar ideas in relation to the procession of the Spirit on page 75.

130 Dick, *Lectures*, 2:67, 69.

131 Dick, *Lectures*, 2:70. He cited *fons Deitatis* language here as well, and admitted that this was the teaching of the Nicene Creed.

In agreement with Brown and taking a different track from Hodge, Dick rejected both communication of essence and subordination language.[132] Hodge rejected the former while accepting the latter. In a later lecture, Dick argued that subordination language was proper only in describing Christ's incarnate state in the economy of redemption.[133] Yet communication of essence and relation of origin remained confessedly unintelligible to him, though he added the somewhat curious comment that "many modern divines" had adopted this language from the church fathers.[134] This point requires further research to understand who Dick had in mind, since Hodge and the nineteenth century authors surveyed here either rejected communication of essence language as unintelligible, or they argued that it was unprovable, even if it did not contradict Scripture. What stands out is that the trend among nineteenth century Reformed authors was towards a non-speculative biblically-directed doctrine of the Trinity that was more content than earlier authors in the Christian tradition had been to leave personhood undefined.[135] Additionally, in contrast to American theologians like Hodge, Brown and Dick emphatically rejected subordination language in relation to the eternal Trinity. Lastly, Dick's explicit and pervasive preoccupation with Unitarianism was markedly different from Hodge's practice of not confronting this issue directly in his *Systematic Theology*. Hodge believed that rationalism, mysticism, and especially pantheism were the more pressing concerns of the hour.

Archibald Alexander Hodge (1823–1886), Charles Hodge's son, became a prominent teacher at Princeton following his father. His primary systematic work was *Outlines of Theology*, which was much smaller and less ambitious than his father's work, presenting the system of doctrine in a question an answer format. Establishing himself as an independent thinker, he did not follow his father's conclusions at every point.[136] He began his treatment of the Trinity by noting that person generally distinguished individual things from each other.[137] So far this echoed the Christian tradition, following Boethius, who used personhood language to relate the particular to the general. He added, however, that we cannot adequately define

---

132 Dick, *Lectures*, 2:71.

133 Dick, *Lectures*, 2:143.

134 Dick, *Lectures*, 2:159.

135 This trend towards non-speculative Trinitarian theology stands out in Dick's treatment of the *filioque* as well. Defending the doctrine from Scripture, he concluded that the Spirit's procession from the Son as well as from the Father was a good consequence from Scripture, but not a necessary one, and that the church should largely diminish its emphasis on this debate. Dick, *Lectures*, 2:162–163. By contrast, Anselm, Richard, Aquinas, and Turretin had argued that the *filioque* was the only means of distinguishing the Son and the Spirit personally.

136 As illustrated in the preceding chapter of this book in relation to his treatment of theology as the "science of religion," which his father had rejected emphatically.

137 A. A. Hodge, *Outlines of Theology* (Edinburgh: Banner of Truth Trust, 1999), 165.

the distinct modes of subsistence in God.[138] Citing Johannes Gerhard (1582–1637), a Lutheran theologian who likely retains of the honor of writing the largest system of doctrine in Christian history, A. A. Hodge rejected Gerhard's definition of person as an incommunicable, individual, intelligent, independent substance, pressing instead Calvin's view of person as subsistence marked by "incommunicable properties."[139] This point illustrates both Calvin's continuing influence on nineteenth century Reformed Trinitarian thinking, and the shift away from modified Boethian definitions of personhood and communication of essence in authors like Turretin.

A. A. Hodge then presented six necessary points to establish Trinitarian doctrine, which was a bit more complete than his father's four or five. These were, first, that there is one God; second, that his God exists eternally as Father, Son, and Spirit; third, that personal distinctions showed themselves through personal pronouns, concurrent counsel and mutual love, and "a distinct order of operation;" fourth, that all divine attributes are "identically common" to all three persons; fifth, that there is an order of subsistence and operation; and sixth that there are "*ad intra*" works exclusive to each divine person as well as *ad extra* appropriations in divine works.[140] A five part argument from Scripture then followed.[141] The fifth category of arguments included "eternal and necessary relations which these three divine persons sustain to each other." This fleshed out necessary order in the Trinity more fully than Charles Hodge's arguments, stopping short of appealing to communication of essence to explain the sense in which each divine person was God. Under his third argument, A. A. Hodge implied an expanded definition of personhood in relation to the Spirit by ascribing to him "intelligence, volition, and rational agency."[142] This definition could fit either with modern views of person as individual self-consciousness or willing subject, or with Boethian attempts to relate the specific category of personhood to the general category of essence. He encroached on importing subordination language into the eternal Trinity by teaching that both the Son and the Spirit are "subordinate" to the Father in their official work.[143] While Brown and Dick carefully restricted subordination language to Christ's incarnate state, it is difficult to see how this applied to A. A. Hodge's inclusion of the Spirit, who did not take human flesh. Subordination appears to refer for him to function in the economy of redemption particularly, with a heavy implication that subordination and order were synonymous terms. This is less explicit than Charles Hodge's

138 A. A. Hodge, *Outlines of Theology*, 166.
139 A. A. Hodge, *Outlines of Theology*, 166.
140 A. A. Hodge, *Outlines of Theology*, 167–8.
141 A. A. Hodge, *Outlines of Theology*, 168–180.
142 A. A. Hodge, *Outlines of Theology*, 175.
143 A. A. Hodge, *Outlines of Theology*, 176.

application of subordination language to order in the eternal Trinity, but the idea is still present.

One last feature of A. A. Hodge's treatment of personhood in the Trinity is worth mentioning. This relates to his appeal to Calvin's division of personhood and essence in God and how this came to bear on personhood as relation of origin and communication of essence. Surprisingly, in light of his knowledge of authors like Turretin. Hodge asserted that the "orthodox doctrine" is that eternal generation refers to the person and not to the essence of the Son.[144] Turretin attached generation and spiration to persons rather than to an abstract divine essence to avoid the idea of quaternity. Yet A. A. Hodge appeared instead to refer eternal generation, like Calvin, to the Son's personhood to the exclusion of communication of the divine essence. He here cited Turretin on communication of essence and *fons Deitatis* language, noting that while not contradicting Scripture, this was more of a rational explanation than "a revealed fact" of Scripture.[145] He believed that the historic communication of essence view involved "derivation of essence," resulting in the "relative subordination" of the second and third persons.[146] Communication of essence as explaining the personal order of subsistence in God without subordination virtually disappeared. A. A. Hodge concluded his chapter on the Trinity by providing five reasons why the Trinity was a fundamental doctrine of the gospel, the most important of which was that when the Trinity was lost, every other fundamental doctrine went with it.[147] Similarly, he opened his lecture on the Trinity in *Evangelical Theology* by stating that the Trinity is "immeasurably important as the foundation of all knowledge and faith."[148] Like his father, A. A. Hodge was unwilling to go beyond defining person as an "incommunicable property," strengthening the picture of the nineteenth century reticence to give personhood explanatory power in Trinitarian theology.

R. L. Dabney (1820–1898) was a southern Presbyterian theologian, who often found himself at odds with Charles Hodge, especially on ecclesiological issues. Dabney's *Systematic Theology* represented his course lectures as transcribed by students. As such, it has an incomplete quality, often referring to reading assignments to explain details. However, his four chapters on the Trinity fundamentally present

144 A. A. Hodge, *Outlines of Theology*, 180.

145 A. A. Hodge, *Outlines of Theology*, 182–3. Concluding, "On such a subject, therefore, it should be held in suspense." However, he later argued that the Spirit was God of the Father and the Son by eternal communication of essence (190).

146 A. A. Hodge, *Outlines of Theology*, 193. Readers might be interested to know that A. A. Hodge also cited W. G. T. Shedd, who is treated below, numerous times in his chapter on the Trinity.

147 A. A. Hodge, *Outlines of Theology*, 198–9.

148 A. A. Hodge, *Evangelical Theology* (Edinburgh: Banner of Truth, 1990), 97.

personhood in God in terms of distinction and incommunicable quality, meaning more than mere roles but less than the "modern" use of individual.[149] Francis Turretin and John Dick appear regularly in Dabney's treatment of the Trinity as well. While not outright rejecting third and fourth century teaching on communication of essence in generation and spiration, he believed that there were not enough facts in Scripture to determine the issue.[150] He treated Aquinas' teaching on intellect and will corresponding to the processions of the Son and the Spirit as "worthless, though ingenious."[151] Affirming eternal order in the Trinity, Dabney argued for agnosticism regarding the reasons for this order in light of divine incomprehensibility, adding that the personal properties were not "constitutive" of the divine persons.[152] This mirrored Hodge's assertion that person described distinction in God while explaining nothing. Dabney defended eternal generation while refusing to define it, though he explicitly rejected the term "subordination" to describe the eternal order of persons.[153] Opposing authors like Thomas Ridgeley, Nathaniel Emmons, Moses Stuart, and "the notorious" Alexander Campbell, who taught eternal unnamed distinctions in God, Dabney still believed that the order of Father, Son, and Spirit was vital, though without clear reasons for it in terms of relations of origin.[154] He bypassed Calvin's treatment of aseity in relation to eternal generation and personhood, only citing Calvin against arguing for Triunity from the plural name *Elohim* and on the manifestation of Christ's Sonship through his resurrection.[155] Calling the *filioque* clause a doctrine "on which we should not dogmatize," Dabney's main concern was that one should retain both a common essence to all three persons as well as their incommunicable relations.[156] All of this reinforces the vague undefined quality of personhood among Reformed authors at the time.

W. G. T. Shedd stands out as a special case in relation to nineteenth century Reformed treatments of the Trinity. He held more closely to classic conceptions of divine personhood than most nineteenth century authors. This may have resulted from his patristic scholarship, especially in relation to Augustine. Shedd also treated triunity prior to the divine attributes. Though one should not make too much of the

149 Robert L. Dabney, *Systematic Theology* (Edinburgh: Banner of Truth, 2002), 175.

150 Dabney, *Systematic Theology*, 203–4.

151 Dabney, *Systematic Theology*, 180.

152 Dabney, *Systematic Theology*, 202. See pg. 178. On page 198, he added that the basis of the arguments for an "eternal and necessary relation of procession" were scarcely "solid."

153 Dabney, *Systematic Theology*, 204. However, on page 197, he used the term "subordination" to describe the economic works of the divine persons *ad extra* with respect to Christ's work of redemption. This "subordination" resulted from Christ's incarnation only.

154 Dabney, *Systematic Theology*, 206–7.

155 Dabney, *Systematic Theology*, 182, 207.

156 Dabney, *Systematic Theology*, 199.

order of topics in a systematic text, in Shedd's case, his placement of the Trinity was a self-conscious statement of its importance. Even God's oneness was unique in that it was "trinal," so that one could never talk about unity without Trinity.[157] Shedd clearly defined personhood in terms both of subsistence and relation of origin. In fact, he believed that the communication of the divine essence was the primary idea in Trinitarian personhood as it respected the relationship between the Father and the Son. He affirmed that in eternal generation, the Son received aseity, or self-existence, along with the whole and entire undivided essence. Similarly, the Spirit received eternal communication of essence by emanation from the Father and the Son. While Shedd bypassed Calvin's connection of aseity to personhood rather than to communication of essence, he shared Calvin's preference for calling the Father *fons trinitatis* rather than *fons deitatis*, albeit for opposite reasons. Shedd's concern was that *fons deitatis* ran the risk of abstracting the divine essence from the divine persons, implicitly pushing in the direction of quaternity.[158] Moreover, Shedd affirmed one divine consciousness and will, though both subsisted in the three self-consciousness of the persons, which was in reality one self-consciousness.[159] In contrast to Hodge, Shedd sought to define person by citing a host of early church, medieval, and "older Protestant" divines. He also asserted periodically that all "Catholic trinitarians" held to personhood as communication of essence in eternal subsistences and incommunicable relations in God. While not mentioning Boethius, and citing Aquinas rarely, he presented Trinitarian personhood in a way that mirrored historic treatments of personhood and eternal generation and spiration more clearly than most of his contemporaries. He also relied heavily and evidently upon Turretin throughout his treatment of the Trinity.

However, like Hodge, Shedd used subordination language to describe the eternal order in the Godhead, though with greater nuance than Hodge. Affirming the equality of the persons, he wrote, "there is at the same time a kind of subordination among them."[160] Yet this was merely "subordination in respect to order and relationship," rather than subordination of authority and submission, which applied to Christ's incarnate state only. Despite this fact, he added ambiguously that Sonship is relationally subordinate to Fatherhood. In spite of his patristic scholarship, he added the initially puzzling assertion that "filial subordination" and "trinitarian subordination" were "common [terms] in trinitarian writers," citing George Bull's (1634–1710) *Defensio Fidei Nicaeanae* and the Lutheran August Detlev Chris-

157 Shedd, *Dogmatic Theology*, 221.
158 Shedd, *Dogmatic Theology*, 256.
159 Shedd, *Dogmatic Theology*, 239.
160 Shedd, 251.

tian Twesten's (1789–1876) dogmatic lectures.[161] Shedd quotations all came from Twesten, where subordination language was clear, but his dependence on Bull's work is less clear. Shed clarified that he advocated only "subordination of person, not of essence," making subordination largely equivalent to order.[162] His concern was to distance himself from any semblance of Arian views of subordination. This form of subordination meant no inequality of being, but only "inequality" in modes of being.[163] Again, the rise of subordination language to describe order in the Trinity was relatively novel in terms of church history. Tracing both Shedd's and Hodge's German sources and influences might provide clues to its origins through further research. In Shedd's case at least, subordination language had less of an effect on his use of person language than it did for Hodge.

Hodge's younger contemporary, student, and later professor at Princeton, B. B. Warfield, stands out as a special case as well, for reasons widely different than Shedd. Warfield simultaneously rejected subordination language with vigor, and he praised and developed Calvin's modifications of eternal generation in ways that threatened ideas of any inherent order in the Trinity. However, as Scott Swain has argued, Warfield moved in a more radical direction than his contemporaries and predecessors. He largely and self-consciously omitted eternal generation and spiration from his treatments of the Trinity, not believing that the names of the divine persons indicated anything about their eternal procession or even order.[164] He adds that in doing so, Warfield was attempting to perfect Calvin's view of the aseity of the Son by erasing any inherent eternal order among the divine persons.[165] The following material sketches some of Warfield's reasoning in this direction.

Warfield's writings consisted predominantly of articles, rather than anything approaching the large-scale of Hodge's *Systematic Theology*. His primary treatments of the Trinity appear in essays including the biblical doctrine of the Trinity, Calvin on the Trinity, and on Tertullian's contributions to Trinitarian doctrine. Showing sensitivity to the progressive nature of divine revelation, the "Biblical Doctrine of the Trinity" shows how the Trinity developed from OT to NT, and why the doctrine

---

161 George Bull, *Defensio Fidei Nicaenae: A Defense of the Nicene Creed, out of the Extant Writings of the Catholick Doctors, Who Flourished During the First Three Centuries of the Christian Churchl in Which Also Is Incidentally Vindicated the Creed of Contstantinople*, 2 vols. (Oxford, 1688); August Dietlev Christian Twesten, *Vorlesungen Über Die Dogmatik Der Evangelisch-Lutherischen Kirche*, 2 vols. (Hamburg: 1826–37, n.d.).

162 Shedd, *Dogmatic Theology*, 251.

163 Shedd, *Dogmatic Theology*, 252.

164 Scott R. Swain, *The Trinity and the Bible: On Theological Interpretation* (Bellingham, WA: Lexham Academic, 2021), 34.

165 Swain, *Trinity and the Bible*, 41.

is "overheard" rather than heard as the backdrop of NT revelation.[166] Reducing the steps for establishing the Trinity found in both Hodges to three, Warfield described divine persons as "the same in substance but distinct in subsistence."[167] All three essays mentioned above are hostile to the idea of communication of essence as allegedly entailing subordination of the persons.[168] Tackling Calvin's view, Warfield believed that Calvin's doctrine of restricting eternal generation to the Son's personhood excluding his deity marked Calvin's distinctive and best contribution to Trinitarian theology, though he admitted that, "despite the influence of Calvin, the great body of the Reformed teachers remained good Nicenists."[169] In fact, Warfield demonstrated a firm grasp of Reformed orthodox theology on this point, noting that such authors tended to assert the Son's aseity through eternal communication of the divine essence from the Father in eternal generation. For Warfield, person in the Trinity meant no more than the fact that the divine persons were "the same in substance but distinct in subsistence."[170]

Most of Warfield's material on the Trinity more or less reflected the same themes found in Hodge and the other authors treated below. However, he illustrates how shifting definitions of personhood and losing the idea of relation or origin or communication of essence could lead to more drastic conclusions. Viewing "subordination" as synonymous with inherent order among the divine persons, he questioned whether the order of Father, Son, and Spirit was in fact eternal in God.[171] Contra the early church, medieval, and Reformed orthodox traditions, Warfield denied that the names "Son" and "Holy Spirit" told us anything about personal modes of subsistence.[172] Nevertheless, he confessed that "the principle of subordination," or order, was clear in the persons "modes of operation" in history.[173] Yet there was no clear or necessary connection between this order of operations and the eternal relationships between the persons, creating a potential disjunct between who God is and what he does in history. He went so far as suggesting that the order of operation or modes of operation may themselves merely have been a "convention" by way of

166 Benjamin Breckinridge Warfield, "Biblical Doctrine of the Trinity," in *The Works of Benjamin B. Warfield*, vol. 2 (Grand Rapids, MI: Baker Books, 2003), 143.

167 Warfield, 132.

168 For example, the connections he drew between Tertullian "subordination" views in their development and refinement in Nicene theology. Benjamin Breckinridge Warfield, "Tertullian and the Beginnings of the Doctrine of the Trinity," in *The Works of Benjamin B. Warfield*, vol. 4 (Grand Rapids, MI: Baker Books, 2003), 97–100.

169 Benjamin Breckinridge Warfield, "Calvin on the Trinity," in *The Works of Benjamin B. Warfield*, vol. 5 (Grand Rapids, MI: Baker Books, 2003), 275.

170 Warfield, "Biblical Doctrine of the Trinity," 133.

171 Warfield, *Bibliical Doctrine of the Trinity*, 163.

172 Warfield, *Bibliical Doctrine of the Trinity*, 165.

173 Warfield, *Bibliical Doctrine of the Trinity*, 165.

the eternal covenant of redemption.[174] The only thing he conceded certainly was that eternal distinctions existed within the unity of the divine substance, adding that Christ's incarnation throws doubt on whether we should import "subordination" into the Trinity itself. This was a fairly radical move, even in Warfield's time. Certainly going beyond Hodge, Warfield illustrates what could happen by reducing divine personhood to incommunicable properties that did not explain what kinds of relationships (of origin) existed between Father, Son, and Spirit. At least potentially, the Trinity was reduced to three undefinable distinctions without inherent order in God.

5.4 Conclusions

The premise of this book is that Charles Hodge was an American Reformed orthodox theologian. Applied to his Trinitarian theology, elements of Reformed orthodoxy persisted while Hodge's post-Enlightenment American context illustrates a historic shift in the meaning of personhood. While features like his use of subordination language admit further research in terms of their origins and causes, this chapter leads to at least four conclusions.

First, Hodge maintained some core ideas of classic Christian Trinitarianism. Reducing the case for the Trinity to three points, he argued for the unity of the Godhead, the deity of each person, and the distinction between the divine persons. In this sense, Hodge's statement concerning the BRTR that the journal contained no "original idea in theology" applied to his Trinitarian theology on the whole.[175] What was relatively new from a historical standpoint was not so much what Hodge said about the Trinity, as what he omitted. Additionally, his use of subordination language to describe eternal order in the Trinity was relatively new in relation to historical theology. Nevertheless, Hodge's first three points in defense of the Trinity reflected standard points of Trinitarian doctrine current at the time, and his fourth point pressed the need to show eternal order among the persons in their relations to one another.

Second, Hodge any many others operated under modern assumptions of personhood that differed from Reformed orthodox precedents. Instead of following the medieval trajectory of person as an individual substance of a rational nature, with necessary modifications to this definition, personhood had become individual self-consciousness or an individual willing subject. Older definitions focused on general and particular categories corresponding to essence and person. Person

174 Warfield, *Bibliical Doctrine of the Trinity*, 166.

175 As cited from Hodge's "Retrospect" in Hoffecker, *Charles Hodge: The Pride of Princeton.*, 131.

described how individual instances related to the general common essence. Since God is simple, not being composed of parts, unlike human persons, three divine persons had to be the same God. Put differently, personhood answered the question of the relationship between the general (essence) and the particular (person). For human beings, this was the relation of genus to species. Yet since God had genus, but no species, personhood became subsistence within the divine essence. Post-Enlightenment definitions of personhood appeared, by contrast, to entail the idea of distinct individuals, which was inhospitable to sound Trinitarian theology. Rather than challenging such assumptions, nineteenth century Reformed authors like Hodge tended to leave person undefined with reference to God, noting that God was different from his creatures. This resulted in treating personhood as a vague idea of distinction that categorized biblical "facts" rather than explaining anything about relations in God. These facts can make it difficult to assess nineteenth century Trinitarian theology with reference to early modern Reformed thinking on the subject.

Third, Hodge and his nineteenth century Reformed contemporaries, Shedd excepted, struggled to maintain the relationship between the divine persons. Instead of treating personhood in the Trinity as relation of origin, rooted in the Son's eternal generation and the Spirit's eternal procession, Hodge maintained eternal order in the Trinity, but he could not provide reasons for this order inherent in God. Without the idea of communication of essence from the Father to the Son, and from Father and Son to the Holy Spirit, it was easier for Hodge to maintain that the divine persons followed an order in Scripture than it was to give a reason why this was the case. Dick responded that we can simply believe that a thing is without understanding why it is.[176] Yet relations in classic Christian theology actually explained something. Because the Son had being and personhood by communication from the Father, then he was Son because he was God of the Father. Likewise, since the Spirit proceeded from both Father and Son, he had the divine essence subsisting in his personhood by distinct relation of origin, making him differ from both Father and Son personally. By rejecting such distinctions and asserting that person explained nothing about the manner in which each person was God, Hodge and his contemporaries risked losing reasons for maintaining the order of Father, Son, and Spirit, which Warfield recognized. Moreover, for those wanting to retain classical ordering of the persons, using "subordination" language to describe that order was novel, confusing, and unfortunate in light of the Christian tradition.

Fourth, the Trinity did not have the same place in Hodge's system of doctrine that it did in Reformed orthodox dogmatic texts. While this point goes beyond

---

176 Dick, *Lectures on Theology*, 2:79.

the research topic of this chapter, it is worth noting where the Trinity was missing in Hodge's thought. John of Damascus (675–749) arguably devoted most of his summary of doctrine to the Trinity and the incarnation. Most of Anselm's works were about the Trinity in some way, and both Lombard and Bonaventure grounded their theologies in the Trinity. Chapter three in this volume shows that Reformed orthodox authors integrated the Trinity into their treatments of the knowledge of God, revolving around Christ's incarnation and the beatific vision as well. Additionally, authors like Wollebius, Polanus, and van Mastricht often began chapters in their theologies by situating the doctrine at hand in the appropriate works and missions of the divine persons. Such features largely disappeared or were muted in nineteenth century Reformed theology. In spite of Hodge's strong assertion that all Christian ideas unite in the Trinity,[177] the whole Trinity did not appear explicitly very often in his *Systematic Theology*. Though he appealed to the Son and the Spirit pervasively, it is rare to find the interrelationship between all three divine persons stand out explicitly in relation to most doctrines he treated. Thus, when Fred Sanders questions to some extent how much the Trinity has actually been revived in recent theology, given that conservative Christian authors like Charles Hodge always retained it,[178] those versed in classic Trinitarian ideas still walk away with the impression that something significant is missing.

Works Cited

Alexander, Archibald. *A Brief Compendium of Bible Truth*. Grand Rapids, MI: Reformation Heritage Books, 2005.

Alexander, James Waddel. "The Life of Michael Servetus." *Biblical Repertory and Theological Review* 8, no. 1 (1836): 73–96.

Anselm. *Anselm of Canterbury: The Major Works*. Edited by Brian Davies and G. R. Evans. Oxford's World Classics. Oxford: Oxford University Press, 2008.

Antognazza, Maria Rosa. "Leibniz de Deo Trino: Philosophical Aspects of Leibniz's Conception of the Trinity." *Religious Studies* 37, no. 1 (March 2001): 1–13.

Aquinas, Thomas. *Summa Theologiae*. Translated by Lawrence Shapcote. Latin/English Edition of the Works of St. Thomas Aquinas. Steubenville, OH: Emaus Academic, 2012.

Aubert, Annette G. *The German Roots of Nineteenth-Century American Theology*. New York: Oxford University Press, 2013.

Augustine. *The Trinity*. Translated by Stephen McKenna. Washington, D.C.: Catholic University of America Press, 2002.

Ayres, Lewis. *Augustine and the Trinity*. Cambridge: Cambridge University Press, 2014.

---

177 Charles Hodge, *Systematic Theology* (Grand Rapids, MI: Eerdmans, 1999), 1:443.

178 Fred Sanders, *Fountain of Salvation: Trinity and Soteriology* (Grand Rapids, MI: Eerdmans, 2021), 178–79.

———. *Nicaea and Its Legacy: An Approach to Fourth-Century Trinitarian Theology*. Oxford: Oxford University Press, 2009.

Balthasar, Hans Urs von. "On the Concept of Person." *Communio* 13, no. 1 Spring (1986): 19–26.

Brown, John. *The Systematic Theology of John Brown of Haddington*. Fearn: Christian Focus, 2002.

Bull, George. *Defensio Fidei Nicaenae: A Defense of the Nicene Creed, out of the Extant Writings of the Catholick Doctors, Who Flourished During the First Three Centuries of the Christian Churchl in Which Also Is Incidentally Vindicated the Creed of Contstantinople*. 2 vols. Oxford, 1688.

Calvin, John. *Institutes of the Christian Religion*. Edited by John T. McNeill. Translated by Ford Lewis Battles. Vol. XX–XXI. 2 vols. Library of Christian Classics. Philadelphia: Westminster Press, 1960.

Caygill, Howard. *A Kant Dictionary*. The Blackwell Philosopher Dictionaries. Mauldin, MA: Blackwell Publishers, 1995.

Cheynell, Francis. *The Divine Triunity of the Father, Son, and Holy Spirit, or, the Blessed Doctrine of the Three Coessentiall Subsistents in the Eternall Godhead Without Any Confusion or Division of the Distinct Subsistences or Multiplication of the Most Single and Entire Godhead Acknowledged, Beleeved, Adored by Christians, in Opposition to Pagans, Jewes, Mahumetans, Blasphemous and Antichristian Hereticks, Who Say They Are Christians, but Are Not*. London, 1650.

Christofidou, Andrea. "Self and Self-Consciousness: Aristotelian Ontology and Cartesian Duality." *Philosophical Investigations* 32, no. 2 (April 2009): 134–62.

Dabney, Robert L. *Systematic Theology*. Edinburgh: Banner of Truth, 2002.

Dale M. Schlitt. *Hegel's Trinitarian Claim: A Critical Reflection*. Albany, NY: SUNY Press, 2012.

Davis, Stephen T., Daniel Kendall, and Gerald O'Collins, eds. *The Trinity: An Interdisciplinary Symposium on the Trinity*. Oxford: Ohio University Press, 2003.

Dick, John. *Lectures on Theology*. 4 vols. Stoke-on-Trent: Tentmaker Publications, 2004.

Dixon, Philip. *Nice and Hot Disputes : The Doctrine of the Trinity in the Seventeenth Century*. London ;New York: T & T Clark, 2003.

Ellis, Brannon. *Calvin, Classical Trinitarianism, and the Aseity of the Son*. Oxford: Oxford University Press, 2012.

Emery, Gilles. *The Trinitarian Theology of Saint Thomas Aquinas*. Oxford: Oxford University Press, 2010.

Emery, Gilles, and Matthew Levering, eds. *The Oxford Handbook of the Trinity*. Oxford; New York: Oxford University Press, 2011.

Fields, Ryan C. "A Generous Reading of John Locke: Reevaluating His Philosophical Legacy in LIght of His Christian Confession." *Themelios* 45, no. 3 (December 2020): 592–609.

Fortman, Edmund J. *The Triune God: A Historical Study of the Doctrine of the Trinity*. Grand Rapids, MI: Baker Book House, 1972.

Giles, Kevin. "The Doctrine of the Trinity and Subordinationism." *Themelios* 28, no. 3 (July 2004): 270–84.

Hobbes, Thomas. *Leviathan*. Oxford: Clarendon Press, 1929.

Hodge, A. A. *Evangelical Theology*. Edinburgh: Banner of Truth, 1990.

———. *Outlines of Theology*. Edinburgh: Banner of Truth Trust, 1999.

Hodge, Charles. "Can God Be Known?" *Biblical Repertory and Theological Review* 36, no. 1 (1864): 122–52.

———. "Christ, The Only Sacrifice: Or the Atonement in Its Relations to God and Man." *Biblical Repertory and Theological Review* 17, no. 1 (1845): 84–138.

———. "Christianity Without Christ." *The Presbyterian Quarterly and Princeton Review* 5, no. 18 (1876): 352–62.

———. "God in Christ; Three Discourses Delivered at New Haven, Cambridge, and Andover; with a Preliminary Dissertation on Language." *Biblical Repertory and Theological Review*, 1849, 259–97.

———. *Systematic Theology*. New York: Scribner, 1871.

———. *Systematic Theology*. 3 vols. Grand Rapids, MI: Eerdmans, 1999.

———. "The First and Second Adam: The Elohim Revealed in the Creation and Redemption of Man." *Biblical Repertory and Theological Review* 32, no. 2 (1860): 335–75.

———. *The Way of Life*. Philadelphia: American Sunday School Union, 1841.

Hoffecker, W. Andrew. *Charles Hodge: The Pride of Princeton*. Phillipsburg, NJ: P & R Publishing, 2011.

Kadane, Matthew. "Anti-Trinitarianism and the Republican Tradition in Enlightenment Britain." *Republic of Letters* 2, no. 1 (2010): 38–54.

Kant, Immanuel. *Anthropology From a Pragmatic Point of View*. Cambridge: Cambridge University Press, 2006.

Legge, Dominic. *The Trinitarian Christology of St Thomas Aquinas*. Oxford: Oxford University Press, 2018.

Lehner, Ulrich L. "The Trinity in the Early Modern Era (c.1550–1770)." In *The Oxford Handbook of the Trinity*, edited by Gilles Emery and Matthew Levering, 240–53. Oxford: Oxford University Press, 2011.

Lienhard, Joseph T. "Ousia and Hypostasis: The Cappadocian Settlement and the Theology of One Hypostasis." In *The Trinity: An Interdisciplinary Symposium on the Trinity*, edited by Stephen T. Davis, Daniel Kendall SJ, and Gerald O'Collins SJ, 99–122. Oxford: Oxford University Press, 2002.

Lim, Paul Chang-Ha. *Mystery Unveiled: The Crisis of the Trinity in Early Modern England*. New York: Oxford University Press, 2012.

Locke, John. *An Essay Concerning Human Understanding*. Edited by Peter Nidditch. Oxford, England: Oxford University Press, 1975.

McGraw, Ryan M. *"A Heavenly Directory:" Trinitarian Piety, Public Worship, and a Reassessment of John Owen's Theology*. Reformed Historical Theology. Göttingen: Vandenhoeck & Ruprecht, 2014.

Merkle, Benjamin R. *Defending the Trinity in the Reformed Palatinate: The Elohistae*. Oxford Theology and Religion Mongraphs. Oxford, 2016.

Mortimer, Sarah. "Early Modern Socinianism and Unitarianism." In *The Oxford Handbook of Early Modern Theology, 1600–1800*, edited by Ulrich L. Lehner, Richard A. Muller, and A. G. Roeber, 361–72. Oxford: Oxford University Press, 2016.

———. *Reason and Religion in the English Revolution: The Challenge of Socinianism*. Cambridge: Cambridge University Press, 2010.

Muller, Richard A. *After Calvin: Studies in the Development of a Theological Tradition*. Oxford; New York: Oxford University Press, 2003.

———. *Christ and the Decree: Christology and Predestination in Reformed Theology from Calvin to Perkins*. Grand Rapids, MI: Baker Academic, 2008.

———. *Post-Reformation Reformed Dogmatics: The Rise and Development of Reformed Orthodoxy, Ca. 1520 to Ca. 1725*. 2nd ed. 4 vols. Grand Rapids, MI: Baker Academic, 2003.

———. *The Unaccommodated Calvin: Studies in the Foundation of a Theological Tradition*. Oxford Studies in Historical Theology. Oxford: Oxford University Press, 2002.

O'Collins, Gerald O. *The Tripersonal God: Understanding and Interpreting the Trinity*. New York: Paulist Press, 1999.

O'Regan, Cyril. "The Trinity in Kant, Hegel, and Schelling." In *The Oxford Handbook of the Trinity*, edited by Gilles Emery and Matthew Levering, 254–66. Oxford: Oxford University Press, 2011.

Perkins, William. *Armilla Aurea, id est, Theologiae Descrpto, Miranda Series Causarum Et Salutis & Damnationis Iuxta Verbum Dei Eius Synopsin Continet Annexa*. Cambridge, 1596.

———. *Catholicus Reformatus, Hoc Est, Expositio et Declaratio Praecipiuarum Aliquot Religionis Controversiarum: Quae Ostendit, Quatenus Ecclesiae Ex Dei Verbo Reformatae in Iis Cum Ecclesia Rom. Qualis Est Hodie Est, Consentiunt, et Quatenus Ab Edadem Dissentiunt, Adeoque in Quibus Numquam Ei Consentire Debent*. Hanoviae, 1601.

Phan, Peter C. *The Cambridge Companion to the Trinity*. Cambridge; New York: Cambridge University Press, 2011.

Plumptre, C. E. *General Sketch of the History of Pantheism*. Vol. 2. London: W. W. Gibbings, 1878.

Ratzinger, Joseph. "Concerning the Notion of Person in Theology." *Communio* 17, no. 3 Spring (1990): 439–54.

Sanders, Fred. *Fountain of Salvation: Trinity and Soteriology*. Grand Rapids, MI: Eerdmans, 2021.

Shedd, William G. T. *Dogmatic Theology*. Edited by Alan W Gomes. Phillipsburg, NJ: P & R Publishing, 2003.

Smith, Mark S. *The Idea of Nicaea in the Early Church Councils, Ad 431–451*. Oxford Early Christian Studies, 2018.

St. Victor, Richard. *On the Trinity*. Translated by Ruben Angelici. Eugene, OR: Cascade Books, 2011.

———. *Richard Saint-Victor, On the Trinity*. Edited by Jean Riballier. Translated by Aage Rydstro-Poulsen. Vol. 4. Brepolis Library of Christian Sources. Turnhout, Belgium: Brepolis, 2021.

Swain, Scott R. *The Trinity and the Bible: On Theological Interpretation*. Bellingham, WA: Lexham Academic, 2021.

Thornwell, James Henley. *The Collected Writings of James Henley Thornwell: Volume One Theological*. Edited by John B. Adger. Vol. 1. 4 vols. Birmingham, AL: Solid Ground Christian Books, 2004.

Turcescu, Lucian. *Gregory of Nyssa and the Concept of Divine Persons*. Oxford: Oxford University Press, 2005.

Turretin, Francis. *Institutio Theologiae Elencticae*. Vol. 1. 3 vols. Geneva, 1679.

Twesten, August Dietlev Christian. *Vorlesungen Über Die Dogmatik Der Evangelisch-Lutherischen Kirche*. 2 vols. Hamburg: 1826–37, n.d.

Van Nieuwenhove, Rik. *An Introduction to Medieval Theology*. Cambridge: Cambridge University Press, 2012.

———. *An Introduction to Medieval Theology*. Cambridge, UK: Cambridge University Press, 2014.

Vidu, Adonis. *The Same God Who Works All Things: Inseparable Operations in Trinitarian Theology*. Grand Rapids: Eerdmans, 2021.

Warfield, Benjamin Breckinridge. "Biblical Doctrine of the Trinity." In *The Works of Benjamin B. Warfield*, 2:133–74. Grand Rapids, MI: Baker Books, 2003.

———. "Calvin on the Trinity." In *The Works of Benjamin B. Warfield*, 5:189–286. Grand Rapids, MI: Baker Books, 2003.

———. "Tertullian and the Beginnings of the Doctrine of the Trinity." In *The Works of Benjamin B. Warfield*, 4:3–112. Grand Rapids, MI: Baker Books, 2003.

Watts, Isaac. *Logick: Or, the Right Use of Reason in the Enquiry After Truth. with a Variety of Rules to Guard Against Error*. London, 1768.

Witherspoon, John. *The Works of John Witherspoon*. Harrisonburg, VA: Sprinkle Publications, 2006.

C. N. Willborn

6. Charles Hodge, the Sin Problem, and History

6.1 Introduction

Perhaps it is an understatement, but it must be said: "The greatest problem in theology is that of the origin of sin."[1] If this statement is applicable to theology in general, it can certainly be applied to theology in America in the nineteenth century. When one speaks of theology in the United States of America, the name that remains nearly synonymous with the science of theology is Charles Hodge.[2] This paper addresses Hodge's handling of the issue of original sin, particularly the manner of the impartation of original sin from Adam to his progeny. We shall also set Hodge in the broader context of Reformed Orthodoxy, that is, in relation to his theological heritage. Finally, we shall set out the immediate context in which Hodge worked, that which precipitated his writings, and finally a major contrast with one of his venerated contemporaries. All of this material will seek to outline Hodge's views on the imputation and transmission of sin with an eye to Reformed orthodoxy as well as to the influences of his American context.

So what of the doctrine of sin and particularly its transmission to Adam's seed? It is helpful to note that several views on the transmission of Adam's sin existed in Christian theology, perhaps as many as five. They all focus on the *mode* by which Adam's sin affects his progeny.[3] First, there is the Wesleyan view that eliminates the accusation through the second Adam's repair of the first Adam's condition. Second, is the solution offered by Jonathan Edwards the elder and his peculiar doctrine of arbitrary identity. Third, is the realist view as taught by several, including Hodge's contemporary in New York, W.G.T. Shedd (1820–94), which proposes a generic or common unity between Adam and his posterity. Fourth, is the mediate imputation view of Placæus and some of the New England school, which conflated the imputation of sin with the transmission of inherent corruption, effectively

---

1 Morton H. Smith, *Systematic Theology*, 2 vols. (Greenville, SC: Greenville Seminary Press, 1994), 1:291.

2 See chapter 3 of this present volume.

3 John Murray, *The Imputation of Adam's Sin* (Phillipsburg, NJ: Presbyterian and Reformed Publishing Co., 1959), 42. "If the union existing between Adam and his posterity is analogous to that which exists between Christ and his people and may thus be called representative union, the next question that arises is that of *the mode* by which the sin of Adam comes to be reckoned to the account of posterity" [italics added].

denying imputation. Finally, the position argued by Francis Turretin (1623–87) and most Reformed orthodox authors, in opposition to Placæus and the Saumur school, which included the federal imputation of Adam's sin and the realistic transmission of corruption by natural generation, known as immediate imputation. This last view was the paradigm adopted, or perhaps adapted, by our subject, Charles Hodge.[4] Having this in mind will work to clarify labeling latter in this chapter.

As part of this introduction, we should also define other terms that shall be used in this paper. Hodge is fond of using "Calvinists," "old Calvinists," and "Reformed." These terms, in Hodge's mind seem to reference everyone from John Owen (1616–83) to Francis Turretin to André Rivet (1573–1651), Franciscus Junius (1545–1602), Herman Witsius (1636–1708), and Bernardinus De Moor (1709–80). In amassing citations from such authors he utilizes the scholarly product of orthodoxy as defined by Willem J. Van Asselt when he uses "the term orthodoxy as the description of a period in the history of theology that stretches from the sixteenth century into the eighteenth century." Yet Hodge could also be said to be referencing "Reformed Orthodoxy," since he drew from authors whose "work actually conformed to the Reformed Confessions."[5] It is not within the purview of this paper to consider Hodge's working methodology, but it is enough to understand that he considered the work of "Reformed orthodox" men worthy of his trust and theological dependence.

Having placed Hodge within the lineage of "Reformed Orthodoxy," it may also be helpful to further identify the Princetonian within that school. Richard Muller has provided clarification regarding the epochs of scholarship within Reformed theology since the time of Calvin and the Protestant Reformation. The "early orthodox" period runs from national confessions of the second-generation Reformers (1559–66) to the period surrounding the Synod of Dort (1618–19). This first period of orthodoxy includes men such as Zacharias Ursinus (1534–83), Jerome Zanchi (1516–90), Theodore Beza (1519–1605), Francis Junius, William Perkins

4 See George P. Hutchinson, *The Problem of Original Sin in American Presbyterian Theology* (Phillipsburg, NJ: Presbyterian and Reformed Publishing Co., 1972), 75. Also of note is Warfield's list of "diverse types of theology" among Presbyterian scholars—"Federalistic," "New School," "Realistic," and "Agnostic." The question arises as to where Warfield would place Edwards; in the Princeton, "Federalistic" line or the "New School" line? Gerstner hints that Warfield may have seen Edwards as belonging to the immediate imputation school. See John Gerstner, *The Rational Biblical Theology of Jonathan Edwards* (Powhattan, VA: Berea Publications, 1992,93), 2:329. Samuel Baird, on the other hand, directly aligns him with Hopkins in the lineage of Placæus. For his discussion see "Edwards and the Theology of New England," in *The Southern Presbyterian Review* 10 (January 1858): 587. Hodge, Warfield's professor, places Edwards with Johann Friedrich Stapfer as opposed to the federal view, holding rather to mediate imputation view.

5 Willem J. Van Asselt, *Introduction to Reformed Scholasticism* (Grand Rapids: Reformation Heritage Books, 2011), 6.

(1558–1602) and Amandus Polanus (1561–1610). These men were followed by a second wave such as Franciscus Gomarus (1563–1641), John Davenant (1572–1641) and others at Dort, including William Ames (1576–1633). Scholars include even Moises Amyraut's (1596–1664) name in the early orthodox period, in spite of his notorious and controversial hypothetical universalism.

Next, Muller moves to discuss the period of "high orthodoxy," which he marks as 1640–1685–1725. This is a period of "still broader theological synthesis than early orthodoxy." He elaborates by saying of this period that "it rests upon a confessional summation of the faith, has a somewhat sharper and more codified polemic against its doctrinal adversaries, and possesses a broader and more explicit grasp of the tradition, particularly of the contribution of the Middle Ages." Names include Johann Cocceius (1603–69), Gisbertus Voetius (1589–1676), Francis Turretin, John Owen, Petrus van Mastricht (1630–1706), Herman Witsius, and Campegius Vitringa (1659–1722).

Finally, Muller summarizes "late orthodoxy" as the period after 1725.[6] This period was "less secure in its philosophical foundations, indeed, searching for different philosophical models, less certain of its grasp of the biblical standard, and often (though hardly always) less willing to draw out its polemic against other "orthodox" forms of Christianity, less bound by the confessional norms of the Reformation, and given to internecine polemics." And still, Muller concludes, "a more or less traditional Reformed theology continued to be produced" by the likes of Johann Stapfer (1718–75), John Gill (1697–1771), Alexander Comrie (1706–74), John Brown of Haddington (1722–87), and Bernardinus de Moor.[7]

Hodge drew heavily on Turretin from the "high orthodox" period as well as from John Owen. As we shall see, he believed these men excelled where even Calvin failed. But as we shall show, he also leaned heavily upon others. For example, Hodge used the work of de Moor on the doctrine of sin from the late orthodox period, while critiquing the views of Stapfer. But the Princetonian also built his views on earlier authors like Andreas Rivetus (1572–1651), the French Huguenot who labored at Leiden and who contributed to the famous *Synopsis Purioris*, which sought to displace Arminian influences at the University.[8] In making use of Reformed orthodoxy from each of the periods, we find Hodge remaining in the Reformed tradition. Muller suggests, "With little formal and virtually no substantial dogmatic

6 Richard Muller, *Post-Reformation Reformed Dogmatics*, second edition (Grand Rapids: Baker Academic, 2003), 1:32. Muller leaves the date open as to when the period ended. However, of the men representing this period in Muller's list, the latest date was that of John Brown of Haddington who died in 1787.

7 Muller, *PRRD*, 1:31, 32.

8 Andre Rivet, Dolf te Velde, et al, eds., *Synopsis Purioris Theologiae,Latin Text and English Translation* (Leiden: Brill, 2014).

alteration, orthodox or scholastic Reformed theology appears in the works of Charles Hodge, Archibald Alexander Hodge, and Louis Berkhof."[9] The work of these three men spans a century, approximately from 1830 (with the issuance of Hodge's first article on original sin) to the work of Berkhof (1873–1957), with the publication of his *Systematic Theology* in 1939.[10]

As we enter a consideration of Hodge's explication of the transmission of original sin, the question before us revolves around Muller's claim of "little formal and virtually no substantial dogmatic alteration" of what Muller calls "orthodox or scholastic Reformed theology." Hodge simply calls its "old Calvinists" theology or Reformed theology. Regardless of labels, we will raise questions that may lead to a nuancing of Muller's supposition, at least in relation to Hodge. While this may disappoint some, we believe it still of value to consider and understand Hodge's thought on its own terms and in his historical setting. This is true, if for no other reason, than to know better one of the primarily nineteenth century influencers of American Reformed thought.

6.2 Hodge and Moral Accounts of Sin's Transmission

Before expanding the context of Hodge's teaching on the transmission of sin, it is helpful to first outline his teaching on the subject. His views of the transmission of sin appeared first in the context of theological journals. We have noted Muller's statement that late orthodoxy "was given to internecine polemics." It will help the reader to know that Charles Hodge began the *Biblical Repertory* (BR) in 1825, which followed closely on the heels of the close of the late orthodox period.[11] The design of the journal was to provide articles which were "usually responses to published treatises, sermons, or even articles in other periodicals."[12] The BR was purposefully suited to engage in "internecine polemics" within the American Reformed world. Hodge wasted little time entering his first squabble early in the journal's history, which was a foray into the doctrine of sin with a New England opponent, Moses Stuart (1780–1852). It was in the form of rebuttal to an article that appeared in the *Spectator*, a journal promoting the special interests of the New Haven theology.[13]

---

9 Muller, *PRRD*, 1:29.

10 Louis Berkhof, *Systematic Theology* (1939; rprt. Grand Rapids: Eerdmans Publishing Co.), 1949.

11 The *Biblical Repertory* was designed initially to present translations of European biblical scholarship. However, Hodge recast the journal in 1829 as *Biblical Repertory and Theological Review* (BR hereafter), broadening its scope.

12 Mark Noll, *The Princeton Theology, 1812–1921* (Phillipsburg, NJ: P&R, 1983), 23.

13 Moses Stuart, "Inquiries Respecting the Doctrine of Imputation," in *The Quarterly Christian Spectator*, Vol. 2, no. 2 (1830): 339–44.

These special interests, largely theological peculiarities, were lodged in the writings of men like Nathaniel Taylor (1786–1858) of Yale, Edward Amasa Park (1808–1900) at Andover and his senior colleague, Moses Stuart. The *Spectator* article was itself a response to an earlier article which appeared in the BR entitled "The Early History of Pelagianism," which is attributed to Archibald Alexander (1772–1851).[14]

While Hodge wrote his initial article in polemical format, it largely set forth the highlights of a position he would continue to promote over the following decades. The second statement of these views came in his exegetical defense of his views or original sin in his Romans commentary, which was first published five years later in 1835 and revised in 1864.[15] The final statement of his views is found in his *Systematic Theology* (1872–73).

In the main, the New Haven theologians rejected the immediate imputation of Adam's sin to his progeny. Hodge began his discourse voicing his opinion that the New England men simply misapprehended the doctrine.

> We have long been convinced that the leading objections to this doctrine arose from an entire, and to us, unaccountable misapprehension of its nature as held among Calvinists. We therefore thought it proper, and adapted to remove prejudices, to state the common views on this subject, that our brethren might see that they did not involve the absurdities which they imagined.[16]

This statement provides us several key ideas marking this debate. First, he purports to offer the accurate view on this topic. In Hodge's estimation, his challenger displayed an "unaccountable misapprehension of its nature as held by Calvinists," illustrating Hodge's identification with historic Reformed thinking on the subject. He rebutted these authors with the proper view as held by "Calvinists" as he understood them. Second, notice the generalization he makes about his view of truth more broadly. Speaking of the doctrine at hand, imputation of sin, he speaks of "its nature as held among Calvinists." Hodge believed that historic Reformed orthodoxy represented the best expression of the teachings of Scripture. Even though his opponents considered themselves to be among Calvinists, Hodge believed that they fell short of the mark. His object was to correct them as to the view they should hold in order to be counted Calvinists in reality.

Establishing his purpose, Hodge wrote, "we, at the same time, believe that much respect is due to uniform opinions of the people of God; that there is a strong

---

14 Archibald Alexander, "The Early History of Pelagianism," in BR, vol. 2:1 (1830): 77–113.

15 Charles Hodge, *Romans* (1835; rprt. Edinburgh: The Banner of Truth Trust, 1983).

16 Charles Hodge, "Inquiries Respecting the Doctrine of Imputation," in *The Biblical Repertory and Theological Review*, vol. 2:3 (1830): 425.

presumption in favour of any doctrine being taught in the Bible, if the great body of the pious readers of the Bible have from the beginning believed and loved it." This came as a reply to *Spectator's* seeming indifference to the many citations of church fathers used by Alexander. Notice again his reference to "uniform opinions of the people of God." Hodge believed it to be unwise to stand against "the great body of the good and pious before him, [as though they] were utterly mistaken, and that he alone is right."[17] In other words, Hodge supposed a stability of divine truth in its catholic expression in the church throughout the ages. The *Spectator*, however, took this as a broad and unhelpful generalization when they knew of men from the recent past who did not agree with Hodge, especially Jonathan Edwards and Johann Stapfer.

Yet what was the common Reformed view to which Hodge referred? First, he says that imputation is "an ascription of something to those concerned" and "a determination to deal with them accordingly." To support this idea he cited Scripture and immediately follows it with the weight of "high orthodoxy" by appealing to John Owen: "To impute sin, therefore, 'is to lay it to the charge of any, and to deal with them according to its desert.—Owen."[18] Hodge concluded: "There could of course be no propriety in imputing the sin of one man to another unless there were some connection between them to explain and justify such imputation."[19] Without explaining yet the nature of imputed sin, Hodge maintained that it entailed liability to punishment on account of Adam's sin.

Not only did Hodge draw on Owen's support for the idea of imputed sin, but also upon "its general acceptance in the Christian Church."[20] In this context, he drank from the well of his theological counselor, Francis Turretin, particularly to address the connection that is sealed in imputation, stating:

> This union, however, according to Turretin, is nothing mysterious, nothing which involves a confusion of identity. The union which is to serve as the ground of imputation, he says, may be threefold, "1. Natural, as between a father and his children; 2. Moral and political, as between a king and his subjects; 3. Voluntary, as among friends, and between the guilty and his substitute." The bond between Adam and his posterity is two-fold: "1. Natural, as he is the father, and we are his children. 2. Political and forensic, as he was the prince, and representative head of the whole human race. The foundation, therefore, of imputation is not only the natural connexion [sic] which exists between us and Adam, since, in that

17 Hodge, "Inquiries," 426.

18 Hodge, "Inquiries," 435.

19 Charles Hodge, *Systematic Theology*, 3 vols. (1873; reprinted, Grand Rapids: Eerdmans Publishing Co., 1986), 2:196. Hereafter *Systematic Theology* is ST.

20 Hodge, *ST*, 2:196.

case, all his sins might be imputed to us, but mainly the moral and federal, in virtue of which God entered into covenant with him as our head."[21]

Hodge went on to explain that his theological mentor drew upon Romans 5:12–21 and that "the scope of the passage he takes to be, the illustration of the method of justification." In saying this, Turretin was "comparing [redemption] to the manner in which men were brought under condemnation." "As Adam was made the head of the whole race," explains Hodge, "so that the guilt of his sin comes on all to condemnation, so Christ is made the head of his people, and his obedience comes on all of them to justification."[22] In other words, the imputation of Christ's righteousness to believers and the imputation of Adam's sin to his posterity were parallel and inseparable.

To this point, Hodge provided the following summary of his position:

1. To impute is to reckon to, or to lay to one's account.
2. To impute sin, in Scriptural and theological language, is to impute the guilt of sin
3. A third remark in elucidation of what is meant by the imputation of Adam's sin is, that by all theologians, Reformed and Lutheran, it is admitted, that in the imputation of Adam's sin to us, of our sins to Christ, and of Christ's righteousness to believers, the nature of imputation is the same, so that the one case illustrates the others.[23]

However, how sin was transmitted and what imputed guilt entailed admitted varied answers. Upon this subject, George Hutchinson (1938–2013) expressed the sentiment of many when he wrote, "Now no one should deny that this doctrine is fraught with many difficulties which no mortal man can explain."[24] Oliver Crisp cites John Murray in the same vein as saying that Hodge realized that difficulties existed and that Hodge in fact "modified" the federal view somewhat.[25] In doing so, Murray believed that Hodge erred by transforming the nature of imputation from reckoned guilt to liability to punishment alone.[26] With that said, no one can

21 Hodge, BR (1830), 443.

22 Hodge, BR (1830), 443.

23 Hodge, ST, 2:194.

24 George Hutchinson, *The Problem of Original Sin in American Presbyterian Theology* (Phillipsburg, NJ: P & R Publishing, 1972), 27. Hutchinson studied under John Murray at Westminster Theological Seminary. This volume originated as a ThM thesis under Murray's guidance to address what Murray considered a *lacuna* in theological studies at that time.

25 Oliver Crisp, "Federalism vs Realism: Charles Hodge, Augustus Strong and William Shedd on the Imputation of Sin," in *International Journal of Systematic Theology*, vol. 8, number 1 (January 2006): 68, 69.

26 John Murray, *The Imputation of Adam's Sin* (Grand Rapids: Eerdmans, 1959), 77.

deny that Hodge thought the remedy for these difficulties were found in the Bible, and as attested by the "general acceptance in the Christian Church."

Hodge immediately qualified his teaching by expressing denials concerning imputation. Before outlining these, it is important to keep in mind the backdrop of his reaction to New England theology. Hodge identified the men in question throughout his paper with passing references to authors like Nathaniel Taylor and Samuel Hopkins. Additionally, he mentioned Timothy Dwight (1752–1817) of Yale. For our purposes, it is important to grasp what they imputed to Hodge that caused him to go to such lengths in his reply. According to Hodge, "What we deny, therefore, is, first, that this doctrine involves any mysterious union with Adam, any confusion of our identity with his, so that his act was personally and properly our act." In other words, while believers have federal and mystical union with Christ, sinners have federal though not mystical union with Adam. Second, Hodge issues another denial when he says, "that the moral turpitude of that sin was transferred from him to us; we deny the possibility of any such transfer."[27] Hodge denied the original sin involved mystical union with Adam as well as the imputed guilt of Adam's sin. On the surface, this appears to deny the federal imputation of Adam's guilt to his posterity, which we saw above that Turretin and other Reformed orthodox authors affirmed. In fact, the federal imputation of Adam's sin to his posterity was distinctive of Reformed orthodox covenant theology, which advanced historic Christian teaching beyond the transmission of inherent corruption and liability to punishment.[28]

According to Hodge, these two elements, which he excluded from his doctrine of imputation, were assigned to him by his New England opponents. "These are the two ideas," argued Hodge, "which the Spectator and others consider as necessarily involved in the doctrine of imputation, and for rejecting which, they represent us as having abandoned the old doctrine on the subject. We proceed now to show that they are mistaken on this point." On the first point—confusion of Adam's identity with us—he was notably excited, writing,

> Is there any one who has the hardihood to charge the whole Calvinistic world (who taught or teach the doctrine of imputation) with believing, that Christ personally and properly committed the sins which are said to be imputed to him or that the moral turpitude of these sins was transferred to him? Now, we ask, why is this? Why, if the imputation of Adam's sin to his posterity, supposes that they were the personal actors of his transgression, the imputation of our sins to Christ does not make him the agent of our acts? Why, since

27 BR, 436.

28 See J. V. Fesko, *The Covenant of Works: The Origins, Development, and Reception of the Doctrine* (Oxford: Oxford University Press, 2020).

> at every turn we are asked if we have ever repented of Adam's sin, is it not demanded of us, if Christ ever repented of our sins? We have never been so unhappy, as to have our hearts torn by being told that we believe and teach, that the blessed Saviour was morally a sinner that our "moral character" was transferred to him. If this is imputation, if this "transfer of moral character" is included in it, we have not words to express our deep abhorrence of the doctrine. We would hold no communion with the man who taught it.[29]

Apparently, the authors in the *Spectator* (i. e., the New England opponent) attributed to Hodge something of a personal identity between Adam and his progeny and sinners to Christ through his doctrine of imputation. This sounds as though they understood his view of imputation as involving some kind of hypostatic and mystical union with Adam and Christ in place of a federal union. As is clear from this question-filled quotation, he strenuously denied such a claim. Secondly, he once again stressed his agreement with "the whole Calvinistic world" at this point. In so aligning himself with such an august body, he distanced the doctrine of imputation from any hint of moral linkage. "[Hodge's] doctrine [of imputation]," as Hutchinson explains, "involves neither the idea of personal identification nor that of the transfer of moral character."[30] For Hodge judicial or forensic categories were the proper way to express the doctrine, without the moral sense. Yet his relation to the nature of the imputation of Adam's guilt remained ambiguous at this stage.

In Hodge's own words, "A union of representation is not a union of identity. If Adam and his race were one and the same, he was not their representative, for a thing cannot represent itself." These two ideas, representation and personal identity, are incompatible, according to Hodge. The two cannot stand together, or as he said: "Where the one is asserted, the other is denied." To maintain a representative position or that of federal union is to deny that any of Adam's progeny "sinned in him personally."[31] Hodge reflected here the idea that mankind was only coveanantally rather than realistically present in Adam, in opposition to contemporaries like Shedd and some others throughout church history.

Moving beyond this early article, in his *Systematic Theology* Hodge insisted that the doctrine common to Calvinists is that of a representational union and that union "is both natural and federal. [Adam] was their natural head." How was Adam our natural head? "Such," he says, "is the relation between parent and child, not only in the case of Adam and his descendants, but in all other cases, that the character and conduct of one, of necessity to a greater or lesser degree affect the other....But there is something peculiar in the case of Adam. Over and beyond this natural

29 Ibid., 436–37.

30 Hutchinson, 29.

31 BR, 437–38.

relation which exists between a man and his posterity, there was a special divine constitution by which he was appointed the head and representative of the whole race." As may be easily seen, while Hodge acknowledged the "natural" relation we have with our native father, he always brings us to the "special divine constitution" or forensic relationship between Adam and his posterity, which relationship is true also between Christ and his spiritual posterity.

As noted above, Hodge was concerned that the *Spectator* defined imputation as including the transfer of the moral turpitude of Adam's sin to his seed. How did Hodge respond? The imputation of Adam's sin and our inherent moral depravity must not be confused or conflated. To so confuse the two—imputation and moral depravity—is to create a major problem in relation to Christ Jesus. As Adam's sin is imputed to us, so our sin is imputed to Christ and his righteousness to us, which is Paul's argument in Romans 5:12–21. If the imputation of Adam's sin communicated moral improbity to us, then the imputation of our sin would have communicated that same wickedness to Christ Jesus. To address this and to distance himself and his common Calvinistic tradition from such a viewpoint, he cited Turretin. Following lengthy citations from Turretin's *Elenctic Theology*, Hodge concluded, "Is it possible to assert in clearer language, that the act of Adam was personally his own and only his, and that it is only on the principle of representation that it can be said to be ours?" Once again, he wrote, "These quotations from Turretin we think abundantly sufficient to establish our assertion, that the doctrine under consideration neither involves any confusion of personal identity, nor any transfer of the moral turpitude of Adam's sin to his posterity."[32] Yet Reformed Orthodox theologians did teach the imputation of Adam's sinful act to his posterity, excluding all of Adam's subsequent sins. This can be seen in Turretin who wrote: "Now the word *hemarton*...properly denotes some actual sin and that, also, past (which can be no other than the sin of Adam itself). For it is one thing to be or to be born a sinner; another, however, actually to sin."[33]

But Turretin was not enough on this topic. Because Hodge not only defended his position and that of the whole Calvinistic tradition, he believed that he was also defending the doctrine of his church. Hodge was after all a churchman as seen in his influential *The Constitutional History of the Presbyterian Church in the United States of America* (1840) and his many journal articles on church polity.[34] In defending his church's theological tradition, he referred his readers to Anthony

32 BR, 444.

33 Francis Turretin, *Institutes of Elenctic Theology*, George M. Giger, trans. and James T. Dennison, ed. 3 vols. (Phillipsburg, NJ: P & R Publishing, 1:618.

34 The various articles on church polity were posthumously published by his son A. A. Hodge under the title of *Church Polity* (1878). More recently this volume was published as Charles Hodge, *Church Polity* (repr., Seoul, NY: Westminster Publishing House, nd).

Tuckney (1599–1670) as an example, who was an English Puritan and member of the Westminster Assembly. Notably he was chairman of the Assembly in 1643 and responsible for much of the Larger Catechism, particularly the Q&A on the Ten Commandments.[35]

Moving beyond Turretin, Hodge said, "We refer in the next place to the testimony of Tuckney, not only because he was a man of great accuracy and learning, but also because he stands in an intimate relation to our church. He was a member of the Westminster assembly of divines, and of the committee which drafted our confession of faith." Lecturing at Cambridge, Tuckney produced a learned compendium of theology, which included his expositions on union with Christ and original sin. From this series of lectures, Hodge mounted a further proof against personal identity and moral transference.[36]

First, the Princetonian acknowledged the historical context and methodology on his Puritan father when he wrote that Tuckney employed "minute scholastic distinctions of the day." These he readily dismissed as unnecessary for his purposes, which reflected the generally nineteenth century tendency to diminish or mute the scholastic form of earlier theologians. Next, he drew on Tuckney's exposition of two germane passages, used already by Turretin, namely, Romans 5:18 and 2 Corinthians 5:21. Concerning these two Pauline passages, he observed,

> We have a most beautiful twofold analogy. We are made the righteousness of God in Christ in the same way that he was made sin for us. That is, by imputation. But the other, we are ac- counted righteous through Christ, in the same manner that we are accounted guilty through Adam. The latter is by imputation, therefore also the former.—P. 234[37]

Tuckney in his day targeted the Roman Catholic Cardinal Robert Bellarmine, whom Hodge believed to have been supposing the same ideas about imputation as his own nineteenth century opponents. To the complaint "that if Christ's righteousness is imputed to us, then are we really inherently righteous in the sight of God"....Tuckney replied, "Who of us has ever been so much beside himself, as to pretend that he was inherently righteous, in the sense of Bellarmin, so that he should think himself pure and immaculate —P. 226." The imputation of righteousness amounted to crediting

35 BR, 445. Hodge provided a footnote with this citation: "[James Reid], *Memoirs of the Lives and Writings of the Divines of the Westminster Assembly*, vol. ii. p. 187."

36 Tuckney's lectures were published posthumously, after being used for years in the Cambridge lecture hall, under the title of *Praelectiones Theologicae,* which is accessible online in Latin. See also Youngchun Cho, *Anthony Tuckney (1599–1670): Theologian of the Westminster Assembly* (Grand Rapids: Reformation Heritage Books, 2017).

37 BR, 445.

believers as righteous on account of union with Christ, which paralleled counting people as sinners in Adam.

To advance the argument used against Bellarmine, and by proxy the misunderstandings of the *Spectator*, Hodge quoted the Westminster divine as saying, "We are not so foolish or blasphemous as to say, or even think, that the imputed righteousness of Christ renders us formally and subjectively righteous….The righteousness of Christ belongs properly to himself, and is as inseparable and incommunicable as any other attribute of a thing, or its essence itself." Hodge imputed to Tuckney, therefore, the conclusion: "we might as well be made wise and just with the wisdom and integrity of another."[38] Likewise, Adam's sin is not infused to us, but imputed, just as our sins are not morally transferred to Christ nor his attributive righteousness to us. Rather, sin is counted to us from Adam as our federal representative and Christ's righteousness is counted to our account as He is our federal representative.

Tuckney continued, however, further distancing imputation from moral transference. First, however, Hodge established Tuckney's context by explaining that Bellarmine had another objection "which proceeds upon the same erroneous supposition, that imputation conveys the moral character of the thing imputed." His protest was that Christ must be regarded as a sinner morally, if indeed our sins were imputed to him. To this Tuckney replied, "Although we truly say that our sins are imputed to Christ, yet who of us was ever so blasphemous as to say, that they were so imputed as if he had actually committed them, or that he was inherently and properly a sinner, as to the stain and pollution of sin."[39] In other words, imputation affected one's status before God rather than one's character.

It is important to remember that Hodge's plaintiff, *Spectator* (as he called him), and Bellarmine, the Roman Cardinal, both attributed to Hodge and Tuckney, respectively, ideas that they did not teach. Furthermore, they attributed these to others in the Reformed tradition past and present. Like Hodge in the nineteenth century, Tuckney (two hundred years earlier) argued his case with reference to the Scripture, but also from history. This, in Hodge's mind, was a strength as we have already seen and so he wrote, "The testimony of Tuckney is the more valuable, as he not only clearly expresses his own opinion, but utterly denies that any of his fellow Calvinists ever understood or taught the doctrine in this manner."[40]

---

38 BR, 446.

39 Ibid.

40 Ibid., 447.

Immediately after saying this, "the Pride of Princeton"[41] called once again on Owen, an English contemporary of Tuckney, to bolster his claim. "The same views are presented by Owen," Hodge wrote, "who carried matters as far as most Calvinists are wont to do."[42] He then cites examples from Owen:

> Things that are not our own originally, personally, inherently, may yet be imputed unto us, *ex justitia,* by the rule of righteousness. And this may be done upon a double relation unto those whose they are, 1, federal; 2, natural. Things done by one may be imputed unto others, proper *relationem faederalem*, because of a covenant relation between them. So the sin of Adam was, and is imputed unto all his posterity, as we shall afterwards more fully declare. And the ground hereof is, that we stood in the same covenant with him, who was our head and representative.[43]

This is one of Hodge's kinder moments.[44] While Hodge displays a kinder, gentler tone here, his purpose is clearly to maintain his continuity with previous Reformed theologians and to prove their agreement with his federal representation view. Furthermore, he is attempting to show that Adam's sin is not communicated to us. This in Hodge's mind defended his view that only the liability of punishment for Adam's sin is communicated to the first man's progeny.

While speaking of "federal representation" it is important to mention Hodge's reliance on federal or covenant theology. Here he purports to follow Turretin particularly, but also Owen and other seventeenth century theologians. Brooks Holifield affirms this when he says,

> At the center of the evangelical principle for Hodge was the concept of "representation," which he saw pervading "the whole Scriptures" and defining "the dispensations of God from the beginning of the world." The concept had a prominent place in his thinking by 1830, and by the time he published his Systematic Theology he described it as one of the pillars of the covenant theology. It meant simply that one person–whether Adam or Christ—could properly represent others in a legal relationship. His defense of the

---

41 This appellation is attributed to Hodge by Andrew Hoffecker. For extremely helpful biographical treatments of Hodge's life see W. Andrew Hoffecker, *Charles Hodge: The Pride of Princeton* (Phillipsburg, NJ: P & R Publishing, 2011 and Paul Gutjahr, *Charles Hodge: Guardian of American Orthodoxy* (Oxford: Oxford University Press, 2011.

42 BR, 447.

43 BR, 447.

44 Gutjahr, *Charles Hodge,* 138. Hodge is described by Paul Gutjahr as providing "a long and damning review" of Stuart. On the same topic, Gutjahr points out Hodge's vitriolic posture toward Stuart's likeminded contemporary, Albert Barnes, when he said, "Hodge savaged Barnes' commentary in a fifty-five-page *Repertory* review" (139).

> idea drew him into a multi-sided debate over sin and depravity, freedom, regeneration, atonement, and theodicy.[45]

As we have already seen, we shall continue to see that the federal representative idea will guide Hodge's reading of Scripture, his alignment with Reformed orthodox, and his criticism of all who differ with his understanding of sin and salvation.

With this much said about denials, what was Hodge's positive position on the imputation and transmission of sin? Put differently, what was imputed to Adam's natural and federal offspring? Here we turn to the more direct statements we find in his *Systematic Theology.* "To impute sin, in Scriptural and theological language," Hodge said, "is to impute the *guilt* of sin. And by guilt is meant not criminality or moral ill-desert, or demerit, much less moral pollution, but the judicial obligation to satisfy justice."[46] This brings us back to where we started before addressing Hodge's qualifying denials, which played a major part in his initial essay of 1830. In his later work, he explained the positive side of of the meaning of imputation more clearly, in explaining ideas such as inherent corruption, for instance. Corruption resulted from that which was imputed to us, namely, guilt. The man born from/in Adam as guilty originally, then sins actually as a result. To put it as one has, "In the terminology of classical Reformed theology, imputation has to do, not with *reatus culpae*...but rather with *reatus poenae*."[47] This means that the cause of punishment was in view rather than the cause of guilt.

By virtue of our having been represented by Adam, God imputes to us the guilt his first sin, the liability to punishment not liability to blame. *Reatus culpae* is what Turretin called "potential guilt" and, according to Berkhof, "it attaches only to those who have themselves committed sinful deeds....Guilt in this sense cannot be transferred from one person to another."[48] *Reatus poenae* is that which is imputed to Adam's people, which is the desert of punishment, both because God established a moral standard in the Garden, and because that moral standard obligated Adam and his posterity. The result was that the breaking of that standard deserved punishment for both. Liability to punishment rather than the imputation of guilt is what Hodge claimed was imputed, since only punishment could be imputed or transferred from one person to another. Imputation of liability to punishment is what Hodge believed his doctrinal standards to mean when they said that all mankind sinned *in Adam.* Yet, the same Westminster Confession declared: "Our first parents....being the root of all mankind, the guilt of this sin was imputed, and the same death in sin and

45 E. Brooks Holifield, "Hodge, the Seminary, and the American Theological Context," in *Charles Hodge Revisited* (Grand Rapids: Wm B Eerdmans Publishing Co., 2002), 111.

46 ST, 2:194.

47 Hutchinson, *The Problem of Original Sin*, 30.

48 Louis Berkhof, *Systematic Theology*, 4th rev. (Grand Rapids: Eerdmans Publishing Co., 1941), 245–46.

corrupted nature conveyed, to all their posterity descending from them by ordinary generation."[49]

It is at this point that some have objected to Hodge's teaching on the imputation and transmission of original sin. Does imputation include liability to punishment only, or is liability to blame also involved? Hodge "maintains it is merely the liability for punishment on the basis of" the first sin committed by Adam, according to Crisp, which led Hodge "to revise the concept of original guilt used by federal theologians." Crisp maintains that the federal theology from which Hodge was veering, that of Turretin and others, promoted the imputation of Adam's sin involved Adam's guilt, and note merely liability to his punishment. For instance, Turretin said: "Adam stood in that [first] sin not as a private person, but as a public and representative person—representing all his posterity in that action and whose demerit equally pertains to all."[50] Yet with attention paid to Turretin including "whose demerit equally pertains to all," consider what we read from Hodge earlier when he said, "To impute sin, in Scriptural and theological language, is to impute the *guilt* of sin. And *by guilt is meant not criminality or moral ill-desert, or demerit,* much less moral pollution, but the judicial obligation to satisfy justice."[51] Guilt for Hodge does not include the demerit of Adam's first sin, which Turretin seem to have taught. So, Crisp piggy backs on John Murray by suggesting that Hodge "dropped the *culpa* aspect of original guilt, retaining only the *reatus,* derived solely from possession of original sin itself."[52] This made the cause of liability to punishment resulting from original sin more ambiguous and undefined in Hodge's writings than in earlier Reformed orthodox theology, constituting an element of discontinuity.

With the recognition that some have observed in Hodge a divergence from his mentor and Reformed Orthodox giant, Turretin, let us return to Hodge's debate with his contemporary nemesis, *Spectator*. *Spectator*, representing the New Haven theology, was not convinced that Hodge proved his point to be simply saying what the Calvinists before him had said. He called upon Jonathan Edwards and Johann Stapfer, men from that late orthodox period of which we wrote earlier, as witnesses. *Spectator* offered his own stack of evidences, much like Hodge had done with his men of orthodoxy. Rather than considering their arguments, which I have shown Hodge to have answered, let it suffice to summarize their main problem with his views: "The main reason why the New Haven theologians cannot accept the truth" explains Hutchinson, "is that they assume that legal obligations cannot be transferred, and consequently deny that one man can, under any circumstances,

49 Westminster Confession of Faith, 6.3.

50 Francis Turretin, *Institutes of Elenctic Theology,* 3 vols., trans. by George Musgrave Giger and ed. by James T. Dennison, Jr. (Phillipsburg, NJ: P & R Publishing, 1992), 1:616.

51 ST, 2:194. Emphasis added.

52 Crisp, 69.

suffer the penalty of the sins of another."[53] They reduced Hodge's view, along with his witnesses, to an impossible theory. Hodge shuddered at this accusation for a simple reason: to deny his view was tantamount to "either the rejection or serious modification of those [doctrines] of atonement and justification."[54] In other words, if we were not liable to the guilt of Adam's sin, then Christ could not bear this guilt in our place.

In Hodge's exegetical work, which appeared a mere five years later in 1835, he argued his case from Romans 5:12–21. In his customary "Doctrine" summary, after the exegetical work is set forth, he wrote,

> It is said that this doctrine is nothing but a theory, an attempt to explain what the apostle does not explain, a philosophical speculation, etc. This again is a mistake. It is neither a theory nor a philosophical speculation, but the statement of a scriptural fact in scriptural language. Paul says, For the offense of one man all men all men are condemned; and for the righteousness of one all are regarded and treated as righteous. This is the whole doctrine.[55]

But Hodge had more to add, explaining why his opponents reduced his view to mere theory. Quoting Albert Barnes (1798–1870) and Moses Stuart, both men influenced by the Edwardian Identity Theory, he concluded, "It will be at once perceived that these and similar objections are all founded on a misapprehension of the doctrine in question." What was the misapprehension? "They are all directed against the ideas of identity of person, and transfer of moral character," he wrote, "neither of which is, as we have seen, included in it; they are, moreover, not only inconsistent with the true nature of the doctrine, but with the statements and arguments of these writers themselves." The fact was that, as Hodge explained his point, "imputation is never represented as affecting the moral character, but merely the relation of men to God and law."[56] Yet without adding traditional Reformed views of the imputation of guilt as the ground of liability to punishment, Hodge failed to explain fully why men's relation to God and the law needed mending in terms of federal representation.

In concluding this exchange between Hodge and "Spectator," a few comments are appropriate. First, A. A. Hodge writing on his father's life, identified "Spectator," Hodge's foil for the inaugural article we have widely cited, as Moses Stuart (1780–1852) of Andover (MA) Seminary. Second, the debate between the two men—Hodge and Stuart—extended over several years and several publications, but

53 Hutchinson, *The Problem with Original Sin*, 32.

54 BR, 472.

55 Hodge, *Romans*, 181.

56 Hodge, *Romans*, 181.

with little if any addition to the arguments found in the seminal articles of 1830.[57] Third, Stuart's position has been succinctly summarized this way: "The offense of the first man…creates a universal condition preparatory to guilt. This triumph of depravity means that all men 'will all sin as soon as they are capable of sinning, and never do anything holy until they are regenerated.'"[58] In other words, mankind bore no guilt for original sin, but for actual sins only, which inevitably followed inherent corruption. Fourth, Stuart made Adam's sin and every other living man's sin to be related "but in an indistinct fashion."[59] Exegetical evidence supported man's problem residing in "actual, not putative" sin.[60] Hodge believed the Bible was clear and that the debate hinged ultimately on belief in the Bible's plain statements, especially Romans 5:12–21, which taught the immediate imputation of Adam's sin to man and Christ's righteousness to the elect. Yet as we have seen, Hodge redefined immediate imputation as liability to punishment, excluding the actual imputation of Adam's first sin. Fifth, Hodge's position opposed New England theology, which included that of Jonathan Edwards, Sr. This view of transmission of Adam's sin is denominated as the personal identity view. Edwards view is summarized in the following citation from his treatise on original sin:

If the existence of created substance in each successive moment, be wholly the effect of God's immediate power in that moment, without any dependence on prior existence, as much as the first creation out of nothing, then what exists at this moment, by this power, is a new effect; and simply and absolutely considered, not the same with any past existence, though it be like it, and follows it according to a certain established method. And there is no identity or oneness in the case, what

---

57 Moses Stuart, "Inquiries Respecting the Doctrine of Imputation," in *The Quarterly Christian Spectator*, II (1830): 339–45; Charles Hodge, "Inquiries Respecting the Doctrine of Imputation," in *The Biblical Repertory and Theological Review*, Vol. 2:3 (1830): 425–72; Moses Stuart, "Remarks of Protestant on the Biblical Repertory," in *The Quarterly Christian Spectator*, III (1831): 156–62; Charles Hodge, "The Christian Spectator on the Doctrine of Imputation," *The Biblical Repertory and Theological Review* Vol. 3:3 (1831): 407–43; Moses Stuart, *A Commentary on the Epistle to the Romans* (NY: J. Leavitt, 1832); Charles Hodge, "Stuart on Romans," in *The Biblical Repertory and Theological Review* Vol. 5:3 (1833): 381–416; Charles Hodge, *A Commentary on the Epistles to the Romans* (Philadelphia: Grigg & Elliot, 1835); Moses Stuart, "Have the Sacred Writers anywhere Asserted that the Sin or Righteousness of One is Imputed to Another?," in *The Biblical Repository and Quarterly Observer*, vol. 7, no. 22 (1836); and the final barrage, a translation of Andre Rivet, Charles Hodge, "*Decretum Synodi Nationalis Ecclesiarum Reformatarum Galliae initio Anni 1645. De imputation primi peccati; omnibus Adami posteris, cum Ecclesiarum et Doctorum Protestantium consensus, ex scriptis eorum, ab Andrea Riveto eollecto*," in *The Princeton Review* Vol. XV (1839): 553–579.

58 Stephen J. Stein, "Stuart and Hodge on Romans 5:12–21: An Exegetical Controversy about Original Sin," in *Journal of Presbyterian History*, 47 (Dec 1969): 341.

59 Stein, "Stuart and Hodge," 342.

60 Stein, "Stuart and Hodge," 355.

depends on the arbitrary constitution of the Creator; who by his wise and sovereign establishment so unites successive effects, that he treats them as one.[61]

Of significance for our purpose here is Hodge's disagreement with this view as it affected sin and imputation. He said, "This doctrine…destroys the Scriptural and common sense distinction between creation and preservation." Furthermore, Edwards "denies the existence of substance." Substance, Hodge argued, is "that which stands; which remains unchanged." Therefore, the Princetonian concludes "resolving all identity into an 'arbitrary constitution of God,' it denies that there is any real identity in any created things.…This being the case, there seems to be no foundation even for guilt and pollution in the individual soul as flowing from its own acts, because there is nothing but an apparent, not a real connection between the present and the past in the life of the soul."[62]

In taking his position against this view, he established his immediate imputation of Adam's sin based upon a federal representational view. For Hodge the contrast was one of moral (New England) versus forensic/juridical (Hodge/Princeton) imputation. Sixth, while little has been said to connect Edwards to this debate, we would be remiss if we failed to make his influences clear through Hodge's interaction with his ideas. In the seminal article to which we have referred (since the subsequent article in 1831 added no new substance), he tackled the much revered "President Edwards" with at least twenty mentions and numerous citations. His conclusion in conjoining Edwards with his New England opponents could not be clearer than when he observed,

> It is on the ground of this theory that Edwards says, as Stapfer had done, that "the sin of the apostacy is not theirs, (mankind's) merely because God imputes it to them; but it is truly and properly theirs, and on that ground God imputes it to them."—P. 559. That is, imputation, instead of being antecedent, is consequent, and founded on the view of inherent depravity.

The fact was, in his view, that Edward's whole discourse on this subject was intended more to vindicate the doctrine of native depravity than that of imputation. It is for this purpose that he entered into his long and ingenious, though unsatisfactory,

61 Cited in Hodge, ST, 1:217.

62 Hodge, ST, 1:220, 221. See John Gerstner, *The Rational Biblical Theology of Jonathan Edwards* (Orlando, FL: Ligonier Ministries, 1992) where Gerstner concludes: "[Adam's] posterity's sin is the same as his because their personal identity is the same, but it the second, third, fourth, etc.—a difference not in the thing itself but in the number of the thing. All members of the posterity repeat the very same sin as Adam. It is not truly imputed to them but repeated by them. It is a true continuous repetition—a continuous creation in so far as a creature is capable of such a thing" (326, 327).

argument on the nature of the unity and divinely constituted oneness of Adam and the human race.[63] Hodge feared that Edward's realistic participation in Adam's first sin threatened to swallow up imputation as liability to punishment.

Hodge seemed to have later understood better, or perhaps represented more clearly, Edwards' views on original sin in his *Systematic Theology*. Edwards, he argued, claimed Placaeus (mediate imputation), but this was "merely as an excrescence. It was not adopted into his system so as to qualify his theological views on other doctrines."[64] It is likely that the writers like Parks, Hopkins, and others, whom Hodge was critically addressing in his early work, were not so cautious as Edwards and applied this "excrescence" into mediate imputation to their broader system. Thus, in Hodge's estimation, Edwards was the source of their error, but indirectly, perhaps. In other words, Hodge did not believe that this unusual view of Adam's posterity and their identity affected Edwards' robust doctrine of salvation in the way that it did some of his theological successors.

With that excursus closed, Hodge partially vindicated Edwards after a series of quotations from the New England preacher-scholar by writing, "As guilt precedes punishment, if, as Edwards says, depravity or spiritual death is a punishment, then the imputation of the guilt of Adam's first sin precedes depravity, and is not consequent upon it." This is what we find throughout Edwards' works, Hodge continued. He is only guilty of drifting into a mediate position in polemical engagement when he "enters on an abstruse metaphysical discussion on the nature of oneness or identity and tries to prove that Adam and his posterity are one, and not distinct agents." Hodge added, "It is, therefore, after all, realism, rather than mediate imputation, that Edwards for the time adopted."[65] While mediate imputation denied both imputed guilt and liability to punishment for that guilt, realism retained liability to punishment for Adam's first sin. Again, it is important to remember that Hodge still replaced imputed guilt with liability to punishment, however, which was likely why he still found affinities with Edwards' realism.

While labeling Edwards' scheme "realism," Hodge admits that Edwards' theory was "not exactly the old realistic theory, it is rather a theory of his own, and depends on his peculiar views of oneness or identity."[66] Hodge's conclusion from this 1830 article to his mature statements in *Systematic Theology* remained largely consistent; his protagonists erred by understanding sin's transmission in merely in a moral sense, excluding a legal or forensic one.

63 BR, 454.

64 ST, 2:207.

65 ST 2:207, 208.

66 Ibid., 2:217.

6.3 Hodge and Calvin's Inherent Corruption Interpretation

We have noted Hodge's widespread reference to men throughout Reformed Orthodoxy in all of its periods. However, we must not ignore as a predecessor to the Reformed orthodox scholars, John Calvin. In Hodge's seminal article, which we have referenced widely above, he makes no mention of Calvin. In his second reply article to Stuart he does refer to Calvin, but almost always in response to the way Stuart used the reformer. After arguing that Stuart misread Calvin, the Princetonian said, "We have stated, that the imputation spoken of in all these cases is, in nature, the same, and therefore, that what is said of the imputation of our sins to Christ, and of his righteousness to us, is properly appealed to in illustration of the nature of imputation, when spoken of in reference to Adam's sin."[67] This is of course his recurring theme: the imputation of Adam's sin to his posterity and Christ's righteousness to his elect are analogous. While he suggests that old Calvinists held this, which seems to include Calvin, he quoted Stuart: "I cannot but notice one thing more, the reviewer [i. e., Hodge] every where in his piece, appeals to the imputation of Christ's righteousness, as decisive of the manner in which Adam's sin is imputed to us. Now this is the very point which Calvin in so many words denies." [68] Stuart's argument was that Calvin did not see Christ's imputation to sinners as parallel to that of Adam's sin transferred to mankind, at least not as precisely as Hodge did.

A few pages later Hodge said in response to this point:

> we are exposed to condemnation not on account of Adam's sin only but also on account of our own inherent hereditary depravity; whereas the righteousness of Christ is the sole ground of our justification, our inherent righteousness, or personal holiness being entirely excluded. And this is the precise point of difference referred to by Calvin, in the passage quoted by the Protestant, which he not only misunderstands, but mistranslates.[69]

Stuart read Calvin from a moral or mediate position, Hodge suggests. In opposition to Stuart and his purported support from Calvin, Hodge responded:

> does it hence follow that our justification can in no respect differ from our condemnation? or, in other words, must our relation to Christ and its consequences be, in all respects, analogous to our relation to Adam and its consequences? Paul tells us, and all the old Calvinists tell us, 'As by the offence of one, judgment came upon all men to condemnation;

---

67 Hodge, "The Christian Spectator on the Doctrine of Imputation," in *The Biblical Repertory and Theological Review* Vol. 3, no. 3 (1831): 415.

68 Hodge, "The Christian Spectator on the Doctrine of Imputation," 415.

69 Hodge, "The Christian Spectator on the Doctrine of Imputation," 417.

even so by the righteousness of one, the free gift came upon all men to justification of life,' and yet, that these cases differ."[70]

Hodge replied to Stuart's claim with a reference to "old Calvinists" once more, seemingly including Calvin. He next went to some length to show that Stuart has misunderstood Calvin. Stuart regarded Calvin's emphasis on original sin as inherent so as to nullify imputation. "Calvin," Hodge stated, "admitted both doctrines, the imputation of Adam's sin and inherent depravity."[71] "He meant to say in opposition to Pighuis and other Catholics," the Pride of Princeton continued, "that men were not condemned on the ground of the act of another, solely, without having a depraved moral character; but being inherently corrupt, were in themselves deserving of death." One finds the same argument repeated in the Princeton classroom by A. A. Hodge.[72]

The senior Hodge advanced his case by saying that, in the end, it matters not if one agrees with Calvin. It is more germane that one is a Calvinist. One sentence of Calvin does not prove or disprove a theological point, he argued. "We have not been accustomed," he said, "to suppose that they [i. e., old Calvinists] squared their faith by such a rule, or considered either his *Institutes* or *Commentaries* the ultimate and sole standard of orthodoxy. Tried by this rule, the Synod of Dort, the Westminster Divines, the old Puritans, and even Beza and Turretin were no Calvinists."[73] So what is the measuring rule for Hodge, and "old Calvinists" supposedly? "The only proper standard by which to decide what Calvinism is," he claimed, "is the confessions of the Reformed Churches and the current writings of standard Calvinistic authors."[74] While Hodge laid claim to Calvin's teaching an imputation, it is clear from his above qualifications concerning Calvin and his commentary on *Romans* that he parted company with Calvin on the issue of Adam's sin as it is transmitted to Adam's progeny.

Nowhere did he state his differences with Calvin more clearly and systematically than in his commentary on *Romans*. Before we summarize his disagreements, however, it is helpful to remember that Hodge defined that which is imputed as liability to punishment for sin, which did not include imputation of the guilt of Adam's first sin. The Princeton theologian built much on the word sin, ἀμαρτια, as meaning "regarded as theirs." Thus, when Paul says "all sinned" in Romans 5:12, he said in effect, "They sinned in Adam. His sin was regarded as theirs."[75]

70 Hodge, "The Christian Spectator on the Doctrine of Imputation," 418.

71 Hodge, "The Christian Spectator on the Doctrine of Imputation," 420.

72 Hodge, *Outlines of Theology*, 357.

73 Hodge, "The Christian Spectator on the Doctrine of Imputation," 421.

74 Hodge, "The Christian Spectator on the Doctrine of Imputation," 421.

75 Hodge, *Romans*, 152.

From here we can summarize his complaint against Calvin in the following way. First, Calvin's definition of ἁμαρτια as "all became corrupt," Hodge stated, "is contrary to the simple meaning of the words." Second, Calvin assumes from this that Paul's words—"sin entered into the world"—means "men became depraved." Hodge, of course, strenuously maintains this "is not true or adequate." Third, he avers that Calvin's view is inconsistent with Paul's argument in Romans 5:13, 14, which is "designed to prove, and do prove, that *all men* sinned in Adam; but do not prove, and cannot be made to prove that all men are inherently corrupt." Fourth, Hodge returned to his argument concerning the correspondence between Christ and Adam when he said, "It vitiates the whole analogy between Christ and Adam, and therefore saps the very foundation of the gospel." Finally, Calvin's definition of "all sinned" is inconsistent with "the true meaning of verses 15–19." Hodge believed Calvin's view, if unchecked, made our corrupt natures the ground for our condemnation rather than Adam's sin imputed. He returned to the analogy once more to make his point against Calvin: "our nature was corrupted in Adam, and has been transmitted to us in a depraved state, yet that hereditary corruption is not here represented as the ground of our condemnation, any more than the holiness which believers derive from Christ is the ground of their justification."[76]

Mixed in with his assessment of Calvin is his warning that Calvin, because of his polemical *milieu*, was not as trustworthy as authors in successive generations. Indeed, he said, "the theology of the Reformation appears in a purer form in the writers of the seventeenth, than in those of the sixteenth century."[77] Why was this true? "The whole tendency of the Reformers, therefore," he wrote, "was to go to the opposite extreme [from the Romish Church]." Because the Romish Church taught the imputation of Adam's sin, Hodge argued, the Reformer's pendulum swung to the extreme of inherent depravity.[78]

While Hodge and old Princeton in general tried to pry Calvin out of the hands of the New England theologians, they were not shy to criticize his understanding of Romans 5 and particular what exactly mankind inherited through imputation from Adam.

6.4 Hodge and Realist Theologians in Relation to Sin's Transmission

So far we have dealt with the New England personal identity theology, which made much of the moral and little of the forensic in relation to the transmission of original

76 Hodge, *Romans,* 150, 151.

77 Hodge, *Romans,* 150.

78 Hodge, *Romans,* 150. Whether Roman Catholicism taught the imputation of Adam's sin is questionable as well.

sin. We have also seen Hodge's relation to Calvin. In answering these men, Hodge opened himself to another school of thought from his own theological tradition and retained an immediate imputation position, namely, the realists. We shall consider this internecine conflict within nineteenth century American Reformed theology more briefly since it was a less vitriolic skirmish than Hodge's clash with New England theology.

Perhaps the leading proponent of the Realistic view in the United States in the nineteenth century was William G. T. Shedd (1820–94). While Shedd was some twenty years Hodge's junior, he was a respected academic with an international reputation. He was also a fellow minister with Hodge in the Presbyterian Church in the United States of America. In addition to his many volumes of church history, theological essays, historical theology, pastoral theology, homiletics, and a significant *Dogmatic Theology* in three volumes, he edited the U.S. edition of Samuel Taylor Coleridge's complete works in seven volumes. His last fifteen years were spent teaching systematic theology at Union Seminary in New York.

While Shedd had studied with Leonard Wood (1774–1854) at Andover Seminary, the school where Amasa Parks taught, he was a decided antagonist to the New England brand of theology discussed above. Shedd was ever and always convinced that a return to Augustinian thought, and older Calvinistic theology was the need of the day for the church. As such, his theology is marked by copious references to the church fathers and a more thoroughgoing use of the scholastic categories of earlier Reformed orthodoxy. Shedd believed that the Realistic view of man's existence and of Adam's sin best represented the "older Calvinistic" teaching. Shedd believed, "The great difference between this system and the several schools of Modern Calvinism, and also the Arminian theology, consists in the doctrine a self-determined and responsible fall of mankind as a species in Adam. This makes original sin to be really and literally guilty instead of only nominally and fictitiously so.[79] In other words, by being seminally present in Adam, mankind was liable to Adam's punishment by participation in his first sin instead of suffering an ungrounded liability to his punishment. Yet one might well argue that Hodge is guilty of Shedd's contention. If guilt is not imputed, but only liability to punishment only, then there is no actual federal union with Adam in his first sin. Conversely, in justification, if God declares us righteous without respect to union with Christ the righteous one, then justification becomes a legal fiction.

From this brief statement, one sees that he sets his viewpoint up as the older view of Christian theology, drawing especially from Augustine, contrasting it to "modern Calvinism" as well as to Arminianism. He also argued that other Calvinistic teachers

79 William G. T. Shedd, *Dogmatic Theology*, 3 vols., 2nd ed. (repr., Nashville, TN: Thomas Nelson Publishers, 1980), 3:iii. Hereafter *Dogmatic Theology* is DT.

believed Adam's sin to be transmitted to the first man's progeny only in name. In other words, Adam's sin did not really belong to those individuals who followed him, though many still spoke as though it did. To this nominalism he attached the accusation of legal fiction. The legal fiction accusation was and is often leveled against the representative or legal imputation viewpoint as set forth by Hodge.

Furthermore, Shedd distanced himself and the realistic view from the individual or personal identity view (i. e., Edwards), which stressed the necessity of each man sinning in order to make God just in punishing sin. "The destiny of man was wholly decided in Adam," argued Shedd, "and not at all in the subsequent generations of individuals propagated from him. Individual life and individual transgression, which in modern theological systems are largely employed to explain problem of original sin, become of no consequence." Echoing Augustine, Shedd maintained that the sin of the individual person in time is "only the necessary effect of the real cause—the voluntary determination of the race in the primitive apostacy, of which St. Paul in the fifth chapter of Romans gives a full account."[80] We see here that Shedd thus sought to avoid a problem Hodge faced in defending his views against his New England opponents.

Indeed Hodge recognized a distinction between Edwards' personal identity view, a peculiar theory according to Hodge, and the realism of Shedd. Realism "essentially differs…in that Edwards denies numerical sameness in any case. Identity, according to him, does not in any creature include the continued existence of one and the same substance. The realistic doctrine, on the contrary, makes the numerical sameness of substance the essence of identity." Edward's so-called Occasionalism stands behind this statement, in which Edwards believed that providence was a continual act of creation. Individual identity thus rested not so much on the preservation of being as on the continual creation of being, constituting individual identity moment by moment. Hodge continued in his summary of men like Shedd when he said: "The sin of Adam was, therefore, the sin of all mankind, because committed by numerally the same rational voluntary substance which constitutes us men."[81] Hodge concluded that realists were mistaken on origin of the human soul, on Adam's representative role, and, therefore, on the transmission of sin. Shedd's traducian views enabled him to maintain a seminal presence of generic human nature in Adam, individuated through actual human beings. This assertion bypassed the need for federal representation to facilitate the imputation of Adam's sin and guilt by transferring these ideas to mankind's participation in generic human nature in Adam.

80 Ibid.

81 Hodge, ST, 2:221.

Shedd admitted he was laboring upon "the much vexed and much vexing doctrine of Original Sin." With Hodge, Shedd agreed that the problem with much of their contemporaries was a rather new dependency upon psychological ideas rather than on classic metaphysical ones. Persons in the post-Enlightenment world became individual willing subjects or self-consciousnesses, rather than specific instances of the genus of humanity.[82] So it was Shedd's intent at every stage of human life "to investigate the doctrine from a metaphysical, and not merely psychological, position." He lamented the fact that little progress had been made in diligently investigating the topic from the metaphysical aspects of sin, while the "psychology of sin" carried the day.[83]

While the psychological approach was on the ascent in the nineteenth century, this had not always been the case in Christian theology. "If we turn to this subject of Augustine or Calvin," Shedd wrote, "or Turretine, or Owen, or the elder Edwards—we find the reverse to be the fact." In those men and others like them, "the essence of sin is regarded as a nature, or state of the soul, which manifests itself in a conscious and actual transgression that derives all its malignity and guilt from this, its deeper source." This approach was the only profitable one and yet, Shedd avowed, theologians had neglected it subsequent to the seventeenth century and the Westminster Confession and Catechisms. For, he writes, "we know of no distinct and strict wording of the doctrine made since then, that contains a fuller and clearer and less contradictory statement than that of the Catechism." Such neglect, and the adopting of psychological approaches to the doctrine, "is greatly injurious to the interests of practical religion," argued Shedd.[84] Current psychological ideas relegated the doctrine of sin to individual actions, precluding any notion of liability to Adam's guilt and punishment. Shedd believed that the only viable option for explaining sin was realistic participation in Adam's first sin, since he regarded imputation as a legal figure, at least as Hodge expressed it.

These few citations from his *Dogmatics* and *Essays* help the reader to understand that both Shedd and Charles Hodge agreed in disagreeing with the "modern" New England theology, which stressed the moral and psychological reading of sin. Both men believed that the psychological view of sin was injurious to the spiritual welfare of the church by removing the parallel between Adam and Christ in the imputation of Christ's righteousness. Now let us consider Shedd's perspective on this vexing doctrine of original sin and its transmission to Adam's progeny in more detail.

Shedd summarized his exegetical work from his commentary on Romans, arguing that Romans 5:12–19 teaches that death to man came "because of *one* sin, and

82 See chapter 5 of this present volume on the concept of personhood in relation to the Trinity.

83 William G. T. Shedd, *Theological Essays* (1867; repr. Minneapolis, MN: Klock & Klock, 1981), 211, 212.

84 Shedd, *Theological Essays*, 213.

only one." Furthermore, this sin "was one committed by Adam and his posterity as a *unity*." He then explained how this "posterity as a *unity*" should be understood. First, this *one* sin of Adam and his posterity "as a *unity*" is understood as being passive in its meaning. Thus, "signifying, either, 'to be sinful,' or, 'to be reckoned as having sinned.'" Second, Shedd wrote that sins can be explained as "the first sin of each individual after he is born," which was less that what Paul had in view in the passage. Finally, he concluded that sin is "active in its meaning, and denotes the first sin of Adam and his posterity as a unity." Here he calls upon Turretin who "denies that ημαρτον signifies 'to be sinful.'" This unity of mankind with Adam may be by natural union, by representation, or by both together.[85]

What was Shedd's conclusion in relation to these options? His approving quote of Owen is perhaps the best summary of his position. Quoting the Puritan divine, Shedd concurred, "we say that Adam, being the root and head of all human kind, and we all branches from that root, all parts of that body whereof he was the head his will may be said to be ours; we were then all that one man." Subsequently Shedd returned to Owen who wrote, "By Adam sin entered into the world, so that all sinned in him, and are made sinners thereby — so that also his sin is called the 'sin of the world;' in him all sinned, and his sin is imputed to them."[86] So, Shedd affirmed a natural union and a form of representational union, whereby Adam was head of the race.

Before considering Hodge's grounds for rejecting the realist position, one last matter must be inserted here. We have shown that Hodge went to great lengths, often to the exclusion of exegetical considerations, to mount evidence from the Patristics and Reformed fathers to bolster his viewpoint. It should not surprise a reader familiar with Shedd that he too cited a pantheon of theologians past and present to support his position. For instance, in his essay entitled "The Doctrine of Original Sin," he approvingly cited St Augustine (354–430), Anthony Burgess (NA-1664), Edmund Calamy (1600–66), John Calvin (1509–64), Jonathan Edwards (1703–58), John Howe (1630–1705), John Owen, and John Robinson (1576–1625).[87] It is obvious that both Shedd the Realist and Hodge the Federalist lay claim to "old Calvinists" or Reformed Orthodoxy.

---

85 Shedd, DT, II:182. Shedd cites Turretin, 1:618 where the Reformed Orthodox stalwart says, "Now the word *hemarton* cannot properly be drawn to a habit of sin or to habitual and inherent corruption, but properly denotes some actual sin and that, also, past (which can be no other than the sin of Adam itself). For it is one thing to be or to be born a sinner; another, however, actually to sin. Therefore since they did not yet exist in the nature of things, they are said to have sinned in another and must undoubtedly be considered (he committing sin) to have also themselves committed it."

86 Shedd, *Essays*, 257.

87 Shedd, *Essays*, 211–64.

With this fact in view, we return our focus to Hodge's evaluation of realism. After considering views inconsistent with his in all respects, he noted that there was a class of interpreters who taught an alternative view to his own "including commentators of every grade of orthodoxy, [who] agree in saying that what is meant is, that all sinned in Adam as their head and representative."[88] While acknowledging this group of theologians, which included authors like Shedd, how did Hodge evaluate their views of realistic participation in Adam's sin?[89] Hodge's problem with realism was their claim that Adam and his progeny were a "unity." According to Hodge, this was mere hypothesis without any Biblical support. Ironically, this was the same charge that Hodge's opponents had leveled against him. In his ST, Hodge listed seven reasons why realism was untenable. All his reasons hovered around the "unity" ideas as it related to mankind and to Christ and His union with His elect. Additionally, he denied that realists satisfactorily provided "a solution to the problems of original sin."[90] As can be seen in this citation, the Princetonian did realize the difficulty of the sin question, namely, how and why God views mankind as sinners. For the realist, it was because they all, being Adam's seed, were really in him when he sinned, thus participating in his act. For Hodge, Adam's descendants are related to Adam only through covenantal representation. He felt the tension of his position and the "legal fiction" accusation, but he could see that Shedd, *et alia,* in some sense relieved this pressure. Perhaps if Hodge had maintained the idea of the imputation of the guilt of Adam's first sin rather than mere liability to punishment, then his concerns over the accusation of legal fiction would have lessened.

Hodge thus concluded that Realism ought to be rejected because it "is a purely philosophical theory." To this he added,

> The Bible says, that Adam's sin was the cause of the condemnation of his race. It tells us that it is not the mere occasional cause, but the judicial ground of that condemnation; that it was for, or on account of, his sin, that the sentence of condemnation was pronounced upon all men. This is the whole doctrine of immediate imputation. It is all that doctrine includes. Nothing is added to the simple Scriptural statement. Realism, however, is a philosophical theory outside of the Scriptures, intended to account for the fact that Adam's sin is the ground of the condemnation of our race.

---

88 Hodge, *Romans,* 151.

89 We are aware that Oliver Crisp, no light-weight scholar, has suggested that Hodge's response to Realism was "not a response to…Shedd." This he says is because Shedd's systematic theology post-dated Hodge's. However, Hodge did interact with Shedd's *Essays* and *History of Christian Doctrine* as it pertains to his realism. And Crisp does acknowledge that Hodge, while not interacting with Shedd's *DT,* "takes seriously the problems often expressed by realists" ("Federalism vs Realism," 66).

90 Hodge, ST, 2:222.

The oft considered gentle Hodge closed his summary objection to the realist view of transmission of Adam's sin with this jab: "The Bible says we are condemned for Adam's sin. Realism denies this, and says no man is or can be condemned except for his own sin."[91] Though Hodge omitted part of earlier Reformed orthodox federal explanation of the imputation of Adam's guilt, he maintained the idea federal idea that liability to punishment could result from more than participation in actual sin.

In responding to realists and their effort to explain the transmission of Adam's sin to his progeny, as set forth in the Bible, Hodge largely dismissed their efforts with a Bible vs. Philosophy argument. While doing so, he seemed acutely aware that there remained a potential problem regarding injustice in what he perceived to be the orthodox federal view as he understood it. In seeking to avoid the problem, it appears that Oliver Crisp's observation is accurate: "Hodge's defense of immediate imputation of Adam's sin to his posterity led him to revise the concept of original guilt used by federal theologians."[92] In the end, Hodge redefined imputed guilt simply in terms of liability to punishment.

Hodge, as seen above, claims liability for Adam's first sin alone is transmitted to his seed. However, he divorced the liability or *reatus* from Adam's *culpa* or guilt. It should be noted that his view was also taken up by his son, A. A. Hodge (1823–86), and it became a more general Princeton point of view.[93] The elder Hodge acknowledged some sort of connection between guilt and punishment while simultaneously distancing them, leaving the cause of mankind's liability to punishment unclear. The singular element of Adam's first sin transmitted to all mankind is the liability to punishment, in his view. It cannot include liability to guilt for the first sin, for that was Adam's alone. This would appear to set Hodge out in some degree from the Reformed orthodox school of federalism which he sought overtly to defend. In this light, Richard Muller's conclusion that Hodge made "little formal and virtually no substantial dogmatic alteration" to the federal school among reformed orthodoxy, may need some qualification. Hodge retained the results of the federal imputation of Adam's sin common in Reformed covenant theology while removing its grounds

6.5 Hodge Under the Scrutiny of a Contemporary

In addition to the Old School Presbyterian realists' positions of Shedd and Samuel Baird (1817–1893) and the federal position of Hodge, there was another nineteenth

91 Ibid., 226, 227.

92 Crisp, "Federalism vs Realism," 68.

93 For an example of the trend Hodge introduced to Princeton see A. A. Hodge, *Outlines of Theology* (1879; rprt. Edinburgh: The Banner of Truth Trust, 1972), 357–58.

century Old School posture taken to the question before us. The latter position was first espoused in seed form by Robert J. Breckinridge (1800–1871) at Danville Seminary in Kentucky. He was a familiar name to many due to the political nature of his family and through his publications in the *Southern Presbyterian Review* and subsequently in his own, *Danville Review*. In his systematic treatment of Scripture published in 1858, he summarily offered this position:

> It is infinitely certain, that God would never make a legal fiction a pretext to punish as sinners, dependent and helpless creatures who were actually innocent. The imputation of our sins to Christ, affords no pretext for such a statement; because that was done by the express consent of Christ, and was in every respect, the most stupendous proof of divine grace. Nor is the righteousness of Christ ever imputed for justification, except to the elect: nor ever received except by faith, which is the grace of the Spirit peculiar to the renewed soul. In like manner the sin of Adam is imputed to us, but never irrespective of our nature and its inherent sin. That is, we must not attempt to separate Adam's federal from his natural headship—by the union of which he is the Root of the human race: since we have not a particle of reason to believe that the former would ever have existed without the latter. Nay Christ to become our federal head, had to take our nature.[94]

It was Breckinridge's contention that there is a distinguishable though inseparable relationship of sin imputed and the sinful corruption of human nature. To put it another way, inherent sin and imputed sin are not to be confused, but also not to be dealt with one without the other. There is a communication of the two without priority.

Here is where Breckinridge left the matter, but he urged his theological successor in the seminary, Robert W. Landis (1809–83), to expound the doctrine as he perceived it. Landis produced a sizeable volume on the topic, which was published posthumously.[95] For several reasons, however, we shall depend on the more well-known adherent of the Breckinridge position, Robert Dabney. This position has been called the "Agnostic" view since that term was first stamped upon it by B. B. Warfield in 1909. To explain, Warfield said it is "characterized by an attempt to accept the fact of the transmission of both guilt and depravity from Adam without

---

94 Robert J. Breckinridge, *The Knowledge of God, Objectively Considered* (New York: Robert Carter & Brothers, 1858), 1:498–99.

95 Robert W. Landis, *The Doctrine of Original Sin* (Richmond, VA: Whittet & Shepperson, 1884), 541 pages. George Hutchinson has described the book accurately when he said "the book is bulky and maddeningly repetive" (61, footnote 2).

framing a theory of the mode of their transmission or of their relation one to the other."[96]

According to Dabney, a serious question surrounds the teaching on imputation of Adam's sin.

> ow can it be justice, for me, who gave no consent to the federal arrangement, for me, who was not present when Adam sinned, and took no share in it, save in a sense purely fictitious and imaginary, to be so terribly punished for another man's deed.[97]

This question provided the impetus for many scholars to seek philosophical, rational, and biblical solutions to this dilemma over the course of many centuries. It takes a serious concern about any possible accusation of injustice in God and attempts to relieve the tension. In so doing, as one of Dabney's reviewers wrote, "He arrays himself against Turrettin [*sic*] and Dr. Hodge no less than against Placæus and the Arminians."[98]

The primary difficulty, as Dabney saw it, was that the immediate, precedaneous imputation doctrine—both of Turretin and Hodge—was built upon the presupposition of an exact parallelism with the imputation of Christ's righteousness. A critic of Dabney acknowledged this presupposition in Turretin and the Princeton school. At the same time, he denied that Dabney proved any "want of parallelism between the two federal transactions."[99]

This supposed exact parallelism, Dabney explained, is "an analogy... not a perfect parallel."[100] On this ground, he disputed Charles Hodge's "doctrinal use" of Romans 5:12–21.[101] From Hodge's assertions, Dabney offered what he believed to be the consequence of the Princetonian's logic:

If this is the order of thought in immediate imputation: that we, conceived as otherwise personally sinless and guiltless initially, receive Adam's guilt by imputation, and then inherent depravity as the penalty, at first, of that alone, then the

---

96 Benjamin B. Warfield, *Studies in Theology* (1932; rprt. Edinburgh: The Banner of Truth Trust, 1988), 308. This article was first published in the *New Schaff-Herzog Encyclopedia of Religious Knowledge*, 1909.

97 Robert L. Dabney, *Systematic Theology* (Edinburgh: The Banner of Truth Trust, 1985), 338.

98 Anonymous, "Dr. Dabney on Imputation" in *The Southern Presbyterian Review* 24 (January 1873): 32. The unidentified author hereafter shall be referred to as "Anonymous."

99 Anonymous, "Dr. Dabney on Immediate Imputation," 52.

100 Robert Lewis Dabney, *Discussions of Robert Lewis Dabney*, 3 vols., (Edinburgh: The Banner of Truth Trust, 1982), 1:263. Dabney also believes that Hodge is aware that "all Calvinistic doctors" teach this truth!

101 Ibid., 1:262. Dabney is simply concerned for the consequences of Turretin and Hodge's strict "immediate" doctrine. "But we shall show that the doctrinal use which is attempted to be made of the passage is not only unnecessary to the analogy of faith, but untenable and self-contradictory."

theory of justification which must result from a rigid parallelism must be this: That we are personally depraved and dead in trespasses and sins at the epoch of our justification, and afterwards, in the order of causation, we receive quickening grace, as the first fruit and effect of justifying righteousness imputed. But as justification is instrumentally by faith, faith must be in order to justification, and of course *in order to quickening.* That is, the sinner has true faith first, and is regenerated afterwards! Every one who has a *modicum* of theological knowledge knows that this is precisely Arminianism.[102]

The first issue Dabney wanted to exploit was the condition of Adam's posterity. Hodge insisted, as we have seen, that Adam's posterity, considered in their individuality, are not personally sinful and therefore guilty of personal sin. They are, Hodge averred, liable to punishment alone. With the Realists, Dabney viewed this position as opening the door to charge of injustice in God. Somehow, Dabney reasoned, we are not only liable because of Adam's sin, but really personally sinful in our first state of existence, since punishment cannot exist without prior guilt.

From this point he addressed Hodge's "rigid parallelism" between Adam and Christ. In fairness to Hodge, it should be noted that Hodge does refer to his parallelism as an analogy and he does admit points of difference.[103] Dabney, however, was not satisfied with this qualification and pressed Hodge for a greater consistency in his explanations of the Adam/Christ parallel.

The primary point Dabney wished to make was that an exact parallelism leads to untenable consequences for the Reformed scholar. An *ordo salutis* derived from an exact or rigid parallelism is one best characterized as synergistic and thus Arminian. A twentieth century student and scholar of this debate has observed:

> There is good reason to charge Hodge with ultimately falling back upon the Wesleyan doctrine of universal redemption. For in his attempt to escape the charge of Nominalism he maintains, following Calvin, that no man is finally condemned for Adam's sin alone (that is for a *peccatum alienum*) as the Nominalists taught, but also for his own inherent hereditary depravity. But Hodge further maintains, in order to defend his doctrine of universal infant salvation, that hereditary depravity is insufficient grounds for the final perdition an individual. No one will ever be finally condemned who has no actual sins to atone for, that is, for original sin alone. On what basis, then, is such a person saved? By the gracious redemption of Christ of course; there is no other way of salvation. But if every naturally born son of Adam is under condemnation, and if all these, except who live to commit actual sin, are saved by the redemption of Christ, how can one escape the

102 Ibid., 1:267.
103 Hodge, ST, 2:203.

> inference that Christ redeemed all except those who voluntarily reject that redemption by means of actual sin?[104]

Hutchinson concludes, this was effectively the doctrine of Wesley and the New School theologian, Henry B. Smith. "At least," he says, "it appears to be, in effect, the doctrine that all are in principle condemned in Adam while all are in principle redeemed in Christ."[105] Readers should note that in his ST, Hodge argued from Romans 5:12–21 that the "all" in Christ must have been absolute, leaving infants dying in infancy as the only class of people to which it could apply. His Romans commentary on these verses, however, takes a more traditional approach to the text by arguing that all who are in Christ shall be saved through union with Christ.

Neither Dabney, nor Hutchinson, imputed universal salvation to Hodge, but both foresaw a great threat to the Reformed church if Hodge's exegetical approach were accepted. Extremes, Dabney believed, always led to ecclesiastical problems. He thus often took moderate positions on issues like lapsarianism and imputation. Rather than seeing the various elements or consequences of the fall unfolding sequentially, he saw them as a whole. Hodge held with others in the tradition that "the consequences of the fall, namely guilt and depravity, must come upon the race in the same order in which they occurred him Adam." Dabney responded: "Now common sense tells us, that when a holy creature [i. e., Adam] committed his first sin, the depravation of his heart the falling under guilt were, temporally speaking, synchronous: but that, causatively speaking, the depravation, or subjective corruption, must precede, and the guilt follow."[106] Hutchinson provides helpful commentary on Dabney when he said, "Now if this was the case with Adam, who was not corrupted of God but of himself, how could it be any different with his posterity? Temporally, they are guilty when corrupted and corrupted when guilty; but causatively, put first things first, they are guilty because corrupted rather than corrupted because guilty."[107] In other words, corruption logically precedes guilt as its cause, raising the question as to whether Adam's first sin is imputed in any sense of the word.

As noted, Dabney considered the most common and difficult objection to imputation as the question of justice—"How can it be just for God to impute the penalty of a sin, except in a purely fictitious sense, which does not rightfully belong to a person." Hodge, he believed, could not answer the objection as long as he insisted on emphasizing federal union with Adam while relegating natural union to a place

104 Hutchinson, 105.

105 Hutchinson, 105.

106 Dabney, *Discussions*, 1:269.

107 Hutchinson, 78.

of near silence. Granted, Hodge did acquiesce to the truth of natural union as it is presented in the Standards of the Reformed churches and in the Holy Scripture as it related to the corruption of human nature. Indeed, he admitted that Adam was not only the federal head of mankind, but the natural spring of humanity. Union with Adam was thus both federal and natural in differing respects.[108] However, as we have seen above, Hodge retained federal liability to punishment without grounding it in the imputation of Adam's guilt, which Dabney rightly identified as an inconsistency.

Dabney penetrates this concession on Hodge's part with characteristic incisiveness. Hodge agreed that the ground for imputation is *natural* as well as federal union. He is forced to do so because his own church's doctrine states "Our first parents…being the root of all mankind, the guilt of this sin was imputed, and the same death in sin and corrupted nature conveyed, to all their posterity descending from them by ordinary generation."[109] This natural union results in a depraved and corrupted human nature. Therefore, at such a time "as their existence doth actually unite them to Adam" they are condemned[110] due to union with corrupted Adam.

It is true that Dabney found a good deal of agreement with Hodge's doctrine of sin. For instance, he found Hodge's exegetical work in relation to Romans 5:12–21, overall, as extremely helpful. On this he said, "we have no theoretic motive to reject Dr. Hodge's exposition; for his exegetical conclusions contain nothing inconsistent with our doctrine."[111] However, he remained convinced that Hodge drew harmful conclusions that might provide a "slippery-slope" for many into Arminianism, especially as they applied his principles to Christ's redemptive work. It is clear that neither Dabney nor Hodge denied the imputation of Adam's sin. The argument arises over "the grounds of that imputation and its consequences," as Hodge admits.[112] What was imputed and was there a priority of corrupted nature or imputed guilt in the transmission of sin? Hodge said liability to guilt was imputed. Dabney said both liability to guilt and culpability for Adam's sin are transmitted, but in what sense or how we do not and cannot say. Reformed orthodoxy taught that God imputed the guilt of Adam's sin to his posterity as their federal head, that this imputed sin warranted condemnation, and that original sin entailed the corruption of human nature through natural generation. The above observations illustrate that new options arose in nineteenth century American Reformed thought in ways that perhaps even proponents did not fully recognize as modified ideas.

---

108 Hodge, 2:196.

109 Westminster Confession of Faith, 6.1, 3.

110 Dabney, Discussions, 1:271. Dabney calls this simultaneous existence of corruption and guilt "one coëtaneous complex."

111 Dabney, 1:262.

112 Hodge, 2:204.

6.6 Conclusion

Charles Hodge was counted a leading defender of orthodoxy among nineteenth century Old School Presbyterians. So too were W.G.T Shedd and Robert L. Dabney. Each of these men were keenly aware of their roots in Calvin, and especially in post-Reformation scholastic orthodoxy in relation to its major proponents and confessional documents. Old Schoolers were committed to their confessional tradition and Old School theology was moored ultimately in the infallible inspiration and authority of the Bible.

Hodge is found in the center of all discussion when one comes to the topic of original sin and its transmission to Adam's posterity. On the one hand this is because of his influential setting at Princeton, which trained ministers throughout America and missionaries throughout the world. On the other hand, it is due to the influence of his early writings against the moral mediate imputation view that emanated from the New England School of Moses Stuart and Amasa Park. These men had greatly influenced the New School sector of Hodge's beloved Presbyterian Church in the USA and he felt an urgent responsibility to answer the perceived error.

Due to his place at the most influential seminary in the nation, and because of his variations of federal theology in relation to original sin, he became the target for those teaching alternative views of sin. Hodge's place between the cross hairs continued well into the twentieth century, though he died in 1878. Not only did men like Samuel Baird and W.G.T. Shedd defend their Realist answers with Hodge in mind, but so did Hodge's one-time prospective colleague at Princeton, R. L. Dabney, in his own treatment of the topic. Additionally, the Princeton product and long-time Westminster theologian and Federalist, John Murray, interacted with the esteemed Princetonian.[113]

In each case, Realist, Agnostic, and Federal, Hodge found some agreement, while being ultimately in disagreement. For the first group, the Realist, there is the maintenance of the primacy of the natural or against the federal as concerns our moral unity with Adam. In the second group, Landis and Dabney, there is agreement that neither the natural nor the legal relationship holds primacy. Both are of equal importance and are part of our union with Adam in the fall. So the transmission is both of guilt and inherent corruption without priority to order. In the case of Murray, he was in agreement with Hodge that the forensic relation between Adam and his posterity is of preeminence. "Depravity of nature," explains one, "devolves upon men by virtue of their special legal solidarity, however one designate it, with Adam." Thus, the priority of the legal. However, as Hutchinson continues, "It is inherent in the very nature of the sin imputed to them on the basis

113 John Murray, *The Imputation of Adam's Sin* (Phillipsburg, NJ: P & R, 1959).

of this legal solidarity so that, contrary to Hodge, we are really culpable for Adam's sin. The legal relationship is prior to the natural: the natural is under the aegis of the legal."[114]

So, what do we conclude about Charles Hodge's view of the imputation, but particularly transmission, of sin in relation both to Reformed orthodoxy and his American context? Michael Paget describes Hodge's position this way: "Interestingly, Hodge argues that while the sin of Adam is the ground of our condemnation, there is no sense in which his moral guilt is attracted to us."[115] Paget's use of "Interestingly" is built upon Hodge's insistence that Adam's relation to his posterity is a "union, representative and natural" and yet Hodge equally insists that there is no sense in which the descendants of the first man have any reason for remorse.[116] To Paget as well as Shedd and Dabney, Hodge's version of imputation strikes an indistinct note in relation to his Reformed orthodox predecessors. Or, we might say, Hodge's version sounds a note of discontinuity with Reformed Orthodox theologians.

The emphasis in Paget's comment is obviously on "Interestingly." Similarly, Oliver Crisp describes Hodge's position as "idiosyncratic federalism." Hodge "develops a version of federalism that is not entirely in accord with the Reformed Orthodox consensus on this subject." Here Crisp recognizes what John Murray diagnosed earlier in the twentieth century as Hodge diverging from his paragon, Francis Turretin. Dabney, as we chronicled above, found Hodge equally frustrating.[117]

It may perplex readers that all the positions observed in relation to and including Hodge—from Edwards' own peculiar twist, to Shedd, and Dabney—call upon the same authors' names listed above as falling within the Reformed Orthodox category and find support for their nuanced positions. Hutchinson may well touch on an evocative reason behind this fact when he said there is evidence that "the controversy over imputation...was never definitively settled—unless one considers the *Formula Consensus Helvetica* (1675) a definitive statement." But then he expressed his doubts when he said: "But even so one finds its great defender Turretin sufficiently ambiguous."[118] Whether Hutchinson is correct on the whole, it remains true that men from the same confessional tradition disagreed over the issue of imputation to some extent, though not all were ambiguous as was Hodge on the ground of one's culpability.

---

114 Hutchinson, 107–08.

115 Michael Paget, "Christology and Original Sin: Charles Hodge and Edward Irving" in *Churchman,* 121:3 (Autumn 2007): 231. See also Charles Hodge, *A Commentary on the Epistle to the Ephesians* (1856; Grand Rapids: Baker Book House, 1980), 108.

116 Hodge, *Romans,* 178.

117 This could be applied to Princeton in general as a school. See for example John Murray's interaction with his theological predecessors in

118 Hutchinson, 102.

Was Hodge aware of his differences from his Reformed Orthodox or "old Calvinist," as he often put it, heritage? We have shown that he was well aware of the main sources. Was Hodge accurate when he averred that he had introduced no new ideas nor attempted to improve upon the tradition?[119] In charity we think he honestly thought so. Is there reason to doubt that he maintained a position consistent with "old Calvinists" on the issue of federalism and transmission of Adam's sin? There is, we think, good reason to doubt his consistency. Did he overreach in claiming a number of post-Reformation representatives in support of his views? We have shown good reason to say so.

And, finally, was Muller's supposition accurate that Hodge made no formal or virtually no dogmatic alterations to Reformed Orthodoxy? That little word "virtually" may be the saving virtue in the statement. Yet, Hodge did alter Reformed ideas at points.

Works Cited

Alexander, Archibald. "The Early History of Pelagianism." *The Biblical Repertory* 2, no.1 (1830): 77–113.

Anonymous. "Dr. Dabney on Imputation." *The Southern Presbyterian Review* 24 (January 1873): 32.

Baird, Samuel. "Edwards and the Theology of New England." *The Southern Presbyterian Review* 10 (January 1858): 574–92.

Berkhof, Louis. *Systematic Theology*. 1939. Reprint. Grand Rapids: Eerdmans Publishing Co., 1949.

Breckinridge, Robert J. *The Knowledge of God Objectively Considered.* New York: Robert Carter and Brothers, 1858.

Cho, Youngchun. *Anthony Tuckney (1599–1670): Theologian of the Westminster Assembly.* Grand Rapids: Reformation Heritage Books, 2017.

Crisp, Oliver. "Federalism vs Realism: Charles Hodge, Augustus Strong and William Shedd on the Imputation of Sin." *International Journal of Systematic Theology* 8, no. 1 (January 2006): 55–71.

Dabney, Robert L. *Discussions.* 5 vols. 1891. Reprint. Harrisonburg, VA: Sprinkle Publications, 1992.

Dabney, Robert L. *Systematic Theology.* 1878. Reprint. Edinburgh: The Banner of Truth Trust, 1985.

Fesko, J. V. *The Covenant of Works: The Origins, Development, and Reception of the Doctrine.* Oxford: Oxford University Press, 2020.

119 Hodge's claim was made in a letter to William Cunningham in 1857; see A. A. Hodge, *The Life of Charles Hodge* (London: T Nelson and Sons, Paternoster Row, 1881), 430.

Gerstner, John. *The Rational Biblical Theology of Jonathan Edwards* (Orlando, FL: Ligonier Ministries, 1992.

Gutjahr, Paul C. *Charles Hodge: Guardian of American Orthodoxy.* Oxford: Oxford University Press, 2011.

Hodge, A. A. *Outlines of Theology.* 1879. Reprint. Edinburgh: The Banner of Truth Trust, 1972.

Hodge, A. A. *The Life of Charles Hodge.* London: T Nelson and Sons, Paternoster Row, 1881.

Hodge, Charles. *A Commentary on the Epistle to the Ephesians.*1856. Reprint. Grand Rapids: Baker Book House, 1980.

Hodge, Charles. "Inquiries Respecting the Doctrine of Imputation." *The Biblical Repertory and Theological Review* 2, no. 3 (1830): 425–72.

Hodge, Charles. "The Christian Spectator on the Doctrine of Imputation." *The Biblical Repertory and Theological Review* 3, no. 3 (1831): 407–43.

Hodge, Charles. *Romans.* Revised edition. 1864. Reprint. Edinburgh: The Banner of Truth Trust, 1983.

Hodge, Charles. "Stuart on Romans." *The Biblical Repertory and Theological Review* 5, no. 3 (1833): 381–416

Hodge, Charles. *Systematic Theology.* 3 vols. 1872. Reprint. Grand Rapids: Eerdmans Publishing Co., 1986.

Hoffecker, W. Andrew. *Charles Hodge: The Pride of Princeton.* Phillipsburg, NJ: P & R Publishing, 2011.

Hutchinson, George P. *The Problem of Original Sin in American Presbyterian Theology* Phillipsburg, NJ: Presbyterian and Reformed Publishing Co.,1972.

Landis, Robert W. *The Doctrine of Original Sin.* Richmond, VA: Whittet & Shepperson, 1884.

Muller, Richard. *Post-Reformation Reformed Dogmatics.* 3 vols. Second edition. Grand Rapids: Baker Academic, 2003.

Murray, John. *The Imputation of Adam's Sin.* Phillipsburg, NJ: P & R, 1959. Noll, Mark. *The Princeton Theology, 1812–1921.* Phillipsburg, NJ: P&R, 1983.

Paget, Michael. "Christology and Original Sin: Charles Hodge and Edward Irving." *Churchman* 121, no. 3 (Autumn 2007): 229–48.

Rivet, Andre. Charles Hodge, "*Decretum Synodi Nationalis Ecclesiarum Reformatarum Galliae initio Anni 1645. De imputation primi peccati; omnibus Adami posteris, cum Ecclesiaru et Doctorum Protestantium consensus, ex scriptis eorum, ab Andrea Riveto eollecto.*" *The Princeton Review* XV (1839): 553–579.

Rivet, Andre. Dolf te Velde, et al, eds. *Synopsis Purioris Theologiae, Latin Text and English Translation* Leiden: Brill, 2014.

Shedd, William G. T. *Dogmatic Theology.* 3 vols. 2nd edition. 1888. Reprint. Nashville, TN: Thomas Nelson Publishers, 1980.

Shedd, William G. T. *Theological Essays.* Minneapolis, MN: Klock & Klock, 1981.

Smith, Morton H. *Systematic Theology*, 2 vols. Greenville, SC: Greenville Seminary Press. 1994.

Stein, Stephen J. "Stuart and Hodge on Romans 5:12–21: An Exegetical Controversy about Original Sin." *Journal of Presbyterian History* 47 (December 1969): 340–58.
Stewart, James W. and James H. Moorhead, eds. *Charles Hodge Revisited: A Critical Appraisal of His Life and Work.* Grand Rapids: Wm B Eerdmans Publishing Co., 2002.
Stuart, Moses. "Inquiries Respecting the Doctrine of Imputation." *The Quarterly Christian Spectator* 2, no. 2 (1830): 339–44.
Stuart, Moses. "Remarks of Protestant on the Biblical Repertory." *The Quarterly Christian Spectator* 3, no. 1 (1831): 156–62.
Stuart, Moses. *A Commentary on the Epistle to the Romans.* NY: J. Leavitt, 1832.
Stuart, Moses. "Have the Sacred Writers anywhere Asserted that the Sin or Righteousness of One is Imputed to Another?" *The Biblical Repository and Quarterly Observer* 7, no. 22 (April 1836): 241–326.
Trueman, Carl and R. S. Clark, eds. *Protestant Scholasticism: Essays in Reassessment.* Carlisle: Paternoster, 1999.
Turretin, Francis. *Institutes of Elenctic Theology.* George M. Giger, trans. and James T. Dennison, ed. 3 vols. Phillipsburg, NJ: P & R Publishing, 1992.
Van Asselt, Willem J. *Introduction to Reformed Scholasticism.* Grand Rapids: Reformation Heritage Books, 2011.
Warfield, Benjamin B. *Studies in Theology.* 1932. Reprint. Edinburgh: The Banner of Truth Trust, 1988.

Alan D. Strange

7. Charles Hodge on Office and the Nature of Presbyterianism

Charles Hodge (1797–1878), stalwart of Northern Old School Presbyterianism, crossed swords on occasions with various partisans of Southern Old School Presbyterianism, especially James Henley Thornwell (1812–1862).[1] They clashed in several areas of ecclesiology and polity: this essay will focus, at least in part, on their battles over the nature of church office and of Presbyterianism itself. Their disputes will serve as a gauge of Hodge's view of office and the nature of Presbyterianism, with an eye to historic Reformed precedents and Hodge's American context. Some assessors of these disputes have deemed Thornwell to hold the better position in them and have come to regard Hodge, though they see his general theological work as helpful, as deficient in his doctrine and polity of the church.[2] Hodge was no ecclesiological incompetent, however; rather, he based his views on the church and its polity, as he did with all his theology, squarely on the Bible, seeking to understand the principles and best applications of biblical church polity.[3] Whether he or Thornwell had the better read of Scripture on these matters still divides confessional Presbyterianism.

---

1 Paul C. Gutjahr, *Charles Hodge: Guardian of American Orthodoxy* (New York: Oxford University Press, 2011), 288–292; W. Andrew Hoffecker, *Charles Hodge: The Pride of Princeton* (Phillipsburg, NJ: P&R Publishing, 2011), 268–278.

2 Sherman Isbell, Ordained Servant vol. 4, no. 4 (October 1995), 93–95—in his review of Mark R. Brown, *Order in the Offices: Essays Defining the Roles of Church Officers* (Duncansville, PA: Classic Presbyterian Government Resources, 1993)—regards Hodge, together with those who agree with him that the ruling elder is not properly a presbyter, as departing from historic Presbyterianism and providing no proper warrant for the office of ruling elder. Craig Troxel, in his "Divine Right Presbyterianism and Church Power" (Westminster Theological Seminary, Ph.D. Dissertation, 1998), 186–239 is critical throughout of Hodge's ecclesiology and polity. A number more could be cited who have a low view of Hodge's ecclesiology and polity, not the least, being his great Old School combatant, James Henley Thornwell himself: "Dr. Hodge…has never touched the questions connected with the nature and organization of the church without being singularly unhappy" in *The Collected Writings of James Henley Thornwell, vol. IV: Ecclesiastical* (1875; reprint, Edinburgh: Banner of Truth Trust, 1974), 243–244.

3 While it is true that Hodge did not address ecclesiology in his *Systematic Theology*, it was the contention of his son A. A. Hodge that he had intended to do so but death caught up with him, Charles Hodge, *The Church and its Polity* (London: Thomas Nelson Sons, 1879), iii. His son also treats the topics of this essay, A. A. Hodge, *Life of Charles Hodge*, (London: T. Nelson and Sons, 1881), 401–403, 418–423, and 446–448. Hodge wrote over the decades of his service at Princeton Theological Seminary regular articles in the *Biblical Repertory and Princeton Review* on the church, especially his annual lengthy

To begin, it might prove helpful to briefly summarize Hodge's polity views before examining what he regarded as their antecedents. Hodge's view on church office was not novel. He believed that the ruling elder[4] was not properly a presbyter; rather, the presbyter, along with the bishop, was a preacher/pastor, with the ruling elder serving as a lay church governor.[5] Hodge affirmed, to be sure, that both minister and ruling elder were divinely authorized and empowered offices, answerable ultimately to God, in keeping with *iure divino* Presbyterianism.[6] He also argued that the ruling elder, holding a different order of office than the minister, was a representative of the people, with the minister representing the clerical order.[7] For Hodge, the genius of Presbyterianism resided, at least in part, with a rule that was neither clerical, as in episcopacy, nor lay, as in congregationalism. Presbyterianism, Hodge insisted, accounted both for clerical rule, in the ministerial office, and representative lay rule, in the office of ruling elder.[8] Hodge also, with respect to the other main concern of

---

assessments of the General Assembly of the Presbyterian Church (U.S.A.), gathered and published after his death by his son A.A. in the aforementioned *Church and its Polity*.

4 While the Greek *presbuteros* (presbyter) may properly be translated as "elder," presbyter (in its Greek or English form) will herein be reserved for the usage that Hodge believed that it had as one of the titles for a preacher and pastor, with *episkopos*, "bishop," being another such title. Hodge never used "presbyter" to refer to the office of ruling elder. See Charles Hodge, *Polity* , 242–300.

5 Charles Hodge, *Polity*, 242–243; specifically, Hodge regarded the terms *episkopos* (overseer or bishop) and *presbuteros* (presbyter or elder) as synonymous, though he saw both as describing those who held the office of minister before the terms were appropriated and used in prelacy to designate higher and lower clergy, respectively. It is the case that the *Book of Church Order* (BCO) under which Hodge labored did cite I Tim. 5:17 (at FG 5) as pertaining both to ministers and elders, a position disputed by Hodge, who saw Romans 12:7–8 and I Corinthians 12:28 as the primary scriptural warrant for the office of ruling elder (also cited by Hodge's church order, along with Acts 15:25), in *The Constitution of the Presbyterian Church in the United States of America,* 1821 ed, rev. 1833 (Philadelphia: Presbyterian Board of Publication, 1839), 413–414.

6 *Iure divino* Presbyterianism embodied the conviction, especially stemming from the polity debates at the Westminster Assembly of Divines (1643–1649), that ecclesiastical government was properly in the hands of the church, not the state, and that Scripture taught such government to be Presbyterian, not episcopal or congregational. See John Richard De Witt, *Jus Divinum: The Westminster Assembly and the Divine Right of Church Government* (Kampen: J.H. Kok, 1969), especially 209–246. For Hodge's affirmation of *iure divino* Presbyterianism, see *Polity*, 122–126. Hodge conceived such differently, chiefly less restrictively, than did James Henley Thornwell, as seen below and in John Lloyd Vance, "The Ecclesiology of James Henley Thornwell: An Old Southern Presbyterian Theologian," Ph.D. Dissertation, Drew University, 1990, 183–194.

7 Hodge, *Polity*, 262–287.

8 Hodge, *Polity*, 118–133. In his treatment of Presbyterianism, Hodge argues that there is a parity among the clergy (bishops and presbyters) that eludes episcopacy and also a right of the people, through their representatives (contra congregationalism), to a "substantive part in the government of the Church," p. 119. Some see Hodge as temporizing, if not foundering, in the debates with Thornwell, especially in 1860 at the GA and its aftermath. Hodge's doctrine of Presbyterianism, however, was unchanged

this essay, had a view of what constituted divine right Presbyterianism that differed from Thornwell's. More will be said about this below.

The contention of this essay is that Hodge was not an innovator in his views of church office or government, though he may appear to be so to some, in differing from certain other Reformed theologians before, during and after his own times.[9] The well-known claim that Hodge and others made for Princeton Theological Seminary (no "new idea") remains secure when it comes to Hodge and his church polity.[10] Indeed, Hodge adhered to a view of church office and divine right Presbyterianism that earlier Presbyterians and/or Reformed had held,[11] or continued to hold, both in the European context of an established church and in the American context of a disestablished church.[12]

Though Hodge's views were distinctly American in some respects,[13] a similar office position, it should here be noted, was held not only by his European predecessors,[14] but also by his contemporary in Scotland, Peter Colin Campbell (1810–1876).

---

from what he had always held, seen in his address before the Presbyterian Historical Society, *What is Presbyterianism?* (Philadelphia: Presbyterian Board of Publication, 1855).

9 Hodge's identity of bishop and presbyter as different names for the ministerial office, while looking elsewhere for warrant for the office of the ruling elder, may appear to many Presbyterians today as odd, or perhaps weak, in defining and defending the office of ruling elder. However, it was historically rooted and has enjoyed more support than many moderns may realize, as we shall attempt to show herein, especially at the Westminster Assembly and in the convictions of theologians that preceded and followed Hodge.

10 A. A. Hodge, *Life of Charles Hodge*, 521: Charles Hodge, at his Semi-Centennial as a Princeton professor (in 1872) said, of his distinguished predecessors and colleagues Archibald Alexander and Samuel Miller, "a new idea never originated in this seminary."

11 It is unsurprising that Hodge agreed on the bishop/presbyter synonymy with Francis Turretin (1623–1687) of Geneva, whose main work Hodge employed as text in his teaching of systematic theology; Turretin was quite clear in his view that bishop and presbyter both refer to the same office, that of the minister, *Institutes of Elenctic Theology*, v. 3, translated by George Musgrave Giger, edited by James T. Dennison, Jr (Phillipsburg, NJ: P&R Publishing, 1997), 199–210.

12 Whatever political overtones attached to church office in Christendom, whether before or after the Reformation, they tended to diminish in the American context, which was a true novelty, involving the legal separation of church and state.

13 Alan D. Strange, *The Doctrine of the Spirituality of the Church in the Ecclesiology of Charles Hodge* (Phillipsburg, NJ: P&R Publishing, 2017),336–338. What most marked Hodge and his fellow Americans, including his disputants and supporters in debates, was a conviction that the American church was a providential gift to the world, needed to bring about the anticipated great revival. One of the reasons that neither Northern nor Southern theologians wanted disunion, especially in the PCUSA, when the U.S. Civil War came in 1861, was this conviction that American religious, and political, exceptionalism/superiority was what the world needed and the war imperiled.

14 Hodge claimed his views on office to be those of his own BCO and of Presbyterianism more broadly, writing, with respect to his view of the various distinctions of the ruling elder from the minister: "This is Presbyterianism; the Presbyterianism of Geneva, France, Germany, Holland, Scotland, and

Campbell's explanation of the chief reasons adopted by those who, historically, saw a clear distinction between minister and ruling elder, especially in seeing the ruling elder as a leader among, or representative of, the people (the laity), coincided with Hodge's views.[15] Ultimately Hodge's convictions, while colored by his American republicanism in some measure, are in harmony with views on church office (especially the question of the identity of bishops and presbyters) that precede, accompany, and follow him.[16]

Having noted Hodge's views on church office and Presbyterianism in summary fashion, a historical view of these debates is helpful because it allows us to see, as we shall do in this essay, the development that obtained from John Calvin (1509–1564) through to Hodge and his contemporaries, both in America and Europe, and even down to the present day. Along the way, such an approach will allow us to see how Calvin's view of office influenced the Marian exile John Knox (c. 1514–1572), including the maturation of the view in the seventeenth-century Scottish context, reaching to the conclusions of the Westminster Assembly of Divines (1643–1649) on the nature of office and divine right Presbyterianism. Key also to considering the nature of the offices of minister and elder is the particular representative nature of the office of ruling elder and the genius of that office as part of Presbyterianism. Hodge's disputes about office and Presbyterianism in the American context will receive due treatment in all of this.

7.1 John Calvin's Contribution to the Ruling Elder Question

Hodge, near the beginning of one of his most important pamphlets on the ruling elder, cites John Calvin as a Reformation proponent of the same idea of church office

---

of our fathers in America; and if we are now to have a different kind…we must get a new book," *Polity*, 275.

15 Peter Colin Campbell, *The Theory of Ruling Eldership or The Position of the Lay Ruler in the Reformed Churches Examined* (Edinburgh and London: William Blackwood and Sons, 1866), 1–2: Campbell, after noting that rule in the church is not simply clerical but also lay (represented by the ruling elders) listed as the reasons for such joint rule: "It may be viewed by one class of minds mainly as a barrier to sacerdotal domination, by another as a security for the equity and acceptableness of ecclesiastical regulations, by a third as a link between the parochial clergy and the people…" Hodge resonated, as will be seen herein, with all of these reasons for joint lay and clerical rule, consonant with a deeper and broader polity commitment than a simply national one to "republican" government.

16 Hodge's predecessor at Princeton, Samuel Miller, also spoke in republican terms about the nature of the ruling elder as a representative of the people, as did Hodge's allies on the ruling elder question, like Thomas Smyth; his opponents, like R.J. Breckinridge, James Henley Thornwell, and Robert Lewis Dabney, did as well: this was not the point of disagreement among them in terms of office or the nature of Presbyterianism. All of these will be cited at appropriate points hereinafter.

to which Hodge subscribed: specifically Hodge believed that he and Calvin saw the offices of minister and ruling elder as distinct and employing different nomenclature for those two offices.[17]Thus when Hodge defended the doctrine and polity of Calvinism as he understood it in his own time, including Calvin's doctrine of church office, Hodge saw himself as remaining faithful to Calvin's distinctions.. Calvin, to turn more directly to him, began working with Guillaume Farel (1485–1565) and others in 1536 on the Reformation that was underway in Geneva, a task that included not only doctrinal but polity reform.[18] Calvin was responding, in other words, not only to the doctrinal errors of Roman Catholicism, but also to its rigidly hierarchical clerical-dominated church polity.[19] Hodge's contemporary and co-belligerent in the church office disputes, Thomas Smyth (1808–1873) of Charleston, argued, seeing himself in agreement with Calvin as well, and ranging back from him, as Calvin did in his study of the ancient and medieval church, that we have good evidence from the earliest years of church history of a vigorous role of the laity in the life of the church. Such lay involvement had waned considerably over time, especially in the Middle Ages, after the papacy of Gregory the Great (590–604), Smyth argued that not only did ruling elder as an office held by laity, as suggested in Polycarp (c.69–155), Ignatius (c. 35–115) , and others, disappear, but the office of deacon was also subsumed within that of clergy. Deacon (or sub-deacon) became the entry level office, and presbyter (now identified with the parish priesthood) and bishop (not parochial now but diocesan) were seen as higher gradations of clerical office. In other words, bishops, presbyters, deacons, and all associated offices were clerical offices, and all rule in the church became clerical rule. This happened over a period from Irenaeus (130-c. 202), increasing in Cyprian's time (c. 210–258),

---

17 Hodge, "Warrant and Theory of the Ruling Eldership," in his *Church Polity,* 264–265 (this is a republication of an undated pamphlet of Hodge entitled, "The Elder Question). Hodge cites Calvin's Institutes, as cited herein below, noting that Calvin argues that "Scriptures...give the title bishop to all who are invested with the ministry of the word." Hodge notes that Calvin proves this from Titus 1:5, Phil. 1:1, and Acts 20:17, and then Calvin adds that "we have hitherto spoken only of those offices which are concerned in the ministry of the word," noting further, Hodge still citing Calvin, that Paul mentions no other permanent offices but two, "government and care of the poor," Calvin continuing on the office of government to say, "Governors I suppose to have been elders (seniores) chosen from among the people, who presided with the bishops over the correction of manners and the exercise of discipline." Hodge continue on pp. 264–265 to show that Calvin's views on this were Hodge's as well.

18 John Calvin, *The Necessity of Reforming the Church* (1536; rpt., Audubon, NJ: Old Path Publications, 1994).

19 Calvin sets forth his view on the corruption of church office and order that occurred under the dominance of the Roman see in the ancient and medieval church in his *Institutes of the Christian Religion* (ICR), IV.4–11, especially.

coming to be regnant especially with the development of the Roman papacy in the time of Leo (440–461) and Gregory.[20]

If clericalism, the conviction that the regular and secular clergy constitute the church, dominated the church in the Middle Ages, an anti-clerical backlash, opposed to any clerical (and, for some, any special officer) class altogether, emerged in the Renaissance and its aftermath. Calvin was concerned about not only the Roman Catholic claim to be over the state, but with Protestant anti-clericalism that went in the opposite direction, seeing the church as under the state. This was something against which Calvin and his fellow churchmen in Geneva strove mightily: restoring proper church discipline, making sure that it was placed in the hands of a church controlled by clergy and laity, on the one hand, and, on the other, not allowing church discipline to fall into the hands of the magistrate, for which Erastianism advocated.[21] Instead, Calvin sought a church and a state with distinct powers of government, which were both under God.

Calvin, came to adopt a four-fold model of church office: pastor, doctor, elder, and deacon. The pastor and doctor were clerical offices, corresponding to the meaning of the Greek terms *episkopos* (bishop) and *presbuteros* (presbyter) in the New Testament. Calvin, in contradistinction to the Lutherans rejected the distinction between a higher and lower clergy, seeing all clerics as enjoying parity, with the terms bishop and presbyter being synonymous.[22]

Where did involvement of men not ordained as ministers, but serving as officers in the church, come in for Calvin? He subsumed this idea under the third and fourth offices, namely, those of ruling elder and deacon. Calvin, took the justification for the lay office of ruling elder as coming from Romans 12:8 and I Corinthians 12:28.

---

20 Thomas Smyth examined and affirmed this history in *The Name, Nature, and Functions of Ruling Elders* (New York: Wiley and Putnam, 1845), 60–77. Some have demurred at his reading of the ancient church fathers, but Hodge and others of his day saw Smyth, along with Peter Colin Campbell, as properly supportive of the position that the ruling elder as a lay elder in the ancient church was distinct from the minister, before the time in the later 2nd century in which lay participation begin to disappear in favor of the clericalization and hierarchical organization of the church. For more on this, see Alan D. Strange, "Do the Minister and Elder Hold the Same Office?" *Ordained Servant* (Dec. 2013), at https://www.opc.org/os.html?article_id=393.

21 Erastianism was a movement that feared and eschewed clerical dominance in the Protestant context, similar to the Caesoro-papism in earlier years of the Greek Orthodox Church, named after the Swiss doctor Thomas Erastus (1524–1583), who pioneered an approach that tended to mark the Zwinglian church as well as the church in places like the Netherlands and Britain. In the latter, the king, and then the British parliament in the time of the English Civil War and Interregnum (1642–1660), claimed civil headship over the church, a matter that especially bedeviled the Westminster Assembly of Divines, as amply noted in DeWitt, *Ius Divinum*, 169–246.

22 James Tunstead Burtchaell, *From Synagogue to Church: Public Services and Offices in the Earliest Christian Communities* (Cambridge: Cambridge University Press, 1992), 23–26. This is a most useful work in tracing the view of office throughout the history of the church.

In the former passage, Paul exhorts "the one who leads" to do so "with zeal," and in the latter passage, Paul speaks of the gift of "administrating" or governing.[23] In his commentaries, Calvin treated additional passages in support of the office of ruling elder:[24] his treatment of I Timothy 5:17 seemed to admit of two orders of elders (something like ruling and teaching elders), an exegetical move that was lamented even by a present-day supporter of Hodge's position, since church polity continues to matter.[25]

Calvin saw what they came to call in Geneva the "senior," as the non-ministerial governing office that was to join with the minister(s) in the joint rule of the church, not only locally, but also at the broader (or higher) levels of church administration (in the classical, synodical, and national assemblies). Though, as noted in the previous paragraph, Calvin did not in his *Institutes* cite biblical passages that referred to this lay assistant as a *presbuteros* (presbyter), he did elsewhere, as noted, in the commentaries. Later editions of the *Institutes*, as well as the Genevan church order, never reflected any such shift, however, continuing to refer to the ruling elder as a "senior," an assistant to the minister, governing with him, and serving a one-year term.[26] Thus Hodge, as he himself claims, is largely on the same page as Calvin when it comes to distinguishing minister from ruling elder, though Calvin is at points willing to employ "presbyter" both for the minister and the ruling elder. Hodge insists throughout the corpus of his polity writings that bishop and presbyter both refer to the minister, the only the one who holds the teaching office in the

23 John Calvin, *ICR*, IV.3.8.

24 In his commentary on I Timothy 5:17, Titus 1:5–9, I Timothy 3:1–7, Calvin makes application not only to ministers but also, derivatively or suggestively, to ruling elders. The perpetual exegetical question for church polity is whether passages that clearly describe the minister (as these do), apply also to the ruling elder, either directly (for those who believe that minister and ruling elder hold the same office) or indirectly, for those who are three-office and think it fitting for the general character qualities to apply to both, since otherwise no direct catalog of qualifications exists for the office of ruling elder as it does for ministers and deacons (esp., I Timothy 3:1–13).

25 T. F. Torrance, "The Eldership in the Reformed Church," *Scottish Journal of Theology* 37.4 (1984), 503–518, throughout his article laments that Calvin, and others (like George Gillespie or Samuel Miller), employ I Tim. 5:17 (and like passages) in a way that he thinks confuses what he believes to be a clear distinction between the clerical ministerial office and the lay offices of ruling elder and deacon.

26 The *Institutes* enjoyed revisions by Calvin until 1559 in Latin and 1560 in French and the Ecclesiastical Ordinances of Geneva (1541) were revised in 1561. These revisions reflect no change in Calvin's view of the ruling elder. *The Genevan Ecclesiastical Ordinances* in P.E. Hughes (ed.), *The Register of the Company of Pastors of Geneva in the Time of Calvin* (Grand Rapids: Eerdmans, 1966) 35–42, 47–48 sets forth the Genevan order relevant to this study of office.

church. He genuinely does not believe that biblically or historically the ruling elder is a presbyter.[27]

7.2 The Reformation in 16th Century Scotland on Office and Presbyterianism

This view of the elder as an assistant to the minister(s),[28] not a presbyter in any proper sense, serving a limited term, is what John Knox brought to Scotland when he returned there in 1560 to reform the church. Hodge, as noted earlier, saw a connection between his view of office and Calvin's; he also saw a connection between his view and the Scottish view, warranting some examination of Scotland in the 16th and 17th centuries.[29] Knox regarded Calvin's Geneva (including the newly formed Academy there) as the "most perfect school of Christ on earth since the days of the Apostles," and so it is unsurprising that he brought what had prevailed there to Scotland during its time of Reformation. Not only did the church there enjoy the new Scots Confession of Faith, but in that same year (1560) a new *Book of Discipline* that outlined the order for the Scottish church. Hodge later made it

27 Hodge, *Polity*, 265–266: Hodge here notes that ministers' qualifications and duties are "given minutely in Scriptures." The duties and powers given to ministers are not given to the people themselves. The Scriptures also teach that the people have a "right to judge the qualifications of their own officers, to determine who they shall be, and to take part with them in the government of the Church. And this right they exercise partly in person, as in the election of their Church rulers, and partly by representatives, who appear in their name in all Church courts, to deliberate and vote on all questions which may come before them."

28 A survey of current Reformed and Presbyterian church orders reveals that language continues to vary in this regard. The writer's denomination (the OPC) does continue even now to describe the ruling elder as an officer who, while having a "particular concern for the doctrine and conduct of the minister of the Word," is to "help him in his labors," *Form of Government*, 10.3 in *The Book of Church Order of the Orthodox Presbyterian Church* (Willow Grove, PA: Committee on Christian Education of the OPC, 2020), 13. Thus, the OPC BCO describes the ruling elder as an auxiliary to the minister; other church orders (PCA BOCO 8, for example) speak of them holding the same office but simply having different functions.

29 Hodge, *Polity*, 263 and 275. To be frank, Hodge makes few historical connections between his view of office and that of others, connecting it chiefly to Calvin, to Scotland (though he differs from Rutherford and Gillespie) and, especially, to the definition that the Westminster Assembly (1643–49) gave to the eldership in its article, discussed below, on "other church governors" (in the *Form of Presbyterial Church Government*). Hodge did say, however, in *Polity*, 275, that his Presbyterianism was "the Presbyterianism of Geneva, France, Germany, Holland, Scotland, and of our fathers in America." The claim seems overbroad on its face, since there was too much polity diversity in those lands for them all to agree with Hodge. They often, in fact, disagreed among themselves in terms of polity details.

clear that he broadly agreed with the polity of the Scottish church, seeing American Presbyterianism as a proper continuation and development.[30]

That the *First Book of Discipline* (FBD), as it came later to be called, did not adopt what some have called Calvin's own later, more mature view of the elder, might call into question whether Calvin's view ever changed or, when it came to commenting on Scripture, he simply noted in the appropriate places that the language of "presbyter" might include both the minister and the lay assistant. That the church order at Geneva was not changed during Calvin's lifetime and the one in Edinburgh reflected what the unchanged Genevan order held might suggest that Calvin did not change his view, but merely noted wider warrant biblically for lay leadership.[31]

Whatever the case was for Calvin, Knox's leadership did not lead to a more developed view of the ruling eldership. This awaited Andrew Melville (1545–1622) and others who developed the *Second Book of Discipline* (1578) roughly a dozen and a half years later. This new church order had a clearly developed view of the office of ruling elder, referring to him as a presbyter, and arguing for life-term service instead of terms of one year. The overall tone of the *Second Book of Discipline* (SBD) suggests that living, as did the Scottish church, in a religious establishment that tended toward Erastian, in which the king and parliament had a good deal of say with respect to church government and discipline, taught the Scottish church the value of the spiritual independency of the church. Later, in the American context, this idea came to be known as the "spirituality of the church," something that Hodge ultimately defended and embraced.[32] All of this is to say that the SBD came to be appreciated in the American context, especially in its view of the church's spiritual independency, which Hodge embraced, though Hodge did not adopt its teaching on the ruling elder as a presbyter, a matter further explored below.[33]

The SBD, in its first mention of the ruling elder , unashamedly refers to it as "the eldership," noting that its purpose is for "good order and the administration of

---

30 Hodge, *Polity*, 172.

31 *The First and Second Books of Discipline* (rpt., Dallas: Presbyterian Heritage Publications, 1993), 86–91: the FBD treats the election of elders and deacons in a fashion similar to Geneva.

32 Alan D. Strange, *The Doctrine of the Spirituality of the Church in the Ecclesiology of Charles Hodge* (Phillipsburg, NJ: P&R Publishing, 2017). This book establishes that Hodge, though earlier opposing the spirituality of the church as embraced by some of his fellow Presbyterians, came to hold his own more moderate form of such.

33 Stuart Robinson, *The Church of God as an Essential Element of the Gospel* (1858; rpt., Willow Grove, PA: Committee on Christian Education of the Orthodox Presbyterian Church, 2009), champions throughout this book the SBD and sees American Presbyterianism, operating as it did in a strict disestablishmentarian context, as the genius of SBD Scottish Presbyterianism, with its notion of the spiritual independency of the church and abhorrence of Erastianism, as true Presbyterianism come into its own.

discipline." This stands over against that of the "ministry of the apostles, prophets, evangelists, pastors and doctors," whose offices, both the extraordinary, which had no successors and had ceased, and the ordinary continuing ones (like pastor and doctor), were chiefly for "the administration of the word."[34] However, whatever changes existed between the FBD and SBD, the functions marking the ministry (in its different expressions) of the ruling eldership do not markedly differ between the two books. Importantly, they do not differ from Hodge's conception of the ministry and the ruling eldership, viz., the actual roles played by the minister, as pastor and preacher, and of the ruling elder, as governor, together with the minister. The point is that those in the Scottish National Church who labored under either book cannot in any sense be said to be two-office (affirming only the offices of elder and deacon, with the former having two functions: teaching and ruling)as some later Irishmen or Scots like Thomas Witherow and Douglas Bannerman did. In practice, even Hodge's opponents in the Old School PCUSA on the nature and number of offices in the church tended to see the elder who teaches in addition to ruling and the elder who only rules as distinct offices.[35] No one, ether in Europe or America, had a two-office position before the nineteenth century. Certainly no one in the seventeenth century had the two-office views of Hodge's Scottish contemporaries, Douglas Bannerman and Thomas Witherow.[36]

---

34 *The First and Second Books of Discipline*, 135–6: the SBD addresses the elder question rather differently than earlier (in the FBD), in the aftermath of the short-lived Convention of Leith (1572), which compromised Presbyterianism and re-introduced bishops; the SBD sought to recover, and strengthen, vigorous Presbyterianism.

35 We will see below that R. J. Breckinridge, James Henley Thornwell, and Robert Lewis Dabney, though differing with Hodge on whether the ruling elder was properly a presbyter, did not adopt a two-office view that eviscerated the distinctives of the two offices and rendered them the same (or interchangeable as circumstances may allow or dictate).

36 Douglas Bannerman, in *The Scripture Doctrine of the Church* (Edinburgh: T&T Clark, 1887), 545–553, believed that ancient church order was based on the synagogue in a way that he saw any distinction between minister and ruling elder in the church as being purely functional, with both holding the same office of presbyter. Similarly, Thomas Witherow saw the office of elder and minister as interchangeable, with either able to preach the word and administer the sacraments, having the same ordination, in *The Apostolic Church* in *I Will Build My Church*, ed. by Jonathan Gibson (1869 ed., rpb., Glenside, PA: Westminster Seminary Press, 2021),132–33. In the PCA, teaching and ruling elders have distinct ordinations, and the latter cannot regularly preach (there is a special provision for licensure for quailed ruling elders) and cannot administer the sacraments,

7.3 *Ius Divinum* Church Government, Church Office, and the Westminster Assembly

The Scottish church situation (the support, or lack thereof, for Presbyterianism particularly) waxed and waned under Mary Queen of Scots (1542–1567) and James VI (1567–1603, exclusive Scotland reign).Things did not become better when James VI became James I of England (1603–1625), uniting the two crowns. A number of Puritans in England favored Presbyterianism and certainly thought that things would be better under the Scottish Stuarts than they had been under the English Tudors, but the hopes expressed in the Millenary Petition (1603) were dashed at the Hampton Court Conference of 1604 and in events that followed.[37]

Furthermore, Puritan fortunes worsened under James I's successor, his son Charles I (1625–1649), whose choice of William Laud (1573–1645) as Archbishop of Canterbury in 1633 spelled disaster for the Puritans in England and Presbyterian Scotland. Laud's imposition of the *Book of Common Prayer*, vigorously promoting episcopacy, championing Erastianism, and advocating Arminianism, wreaked havoc on those wanting further Reformation among the four Puritan parties in Anglican England. The Puritans there greatly resented all of Laud's anti-Puritan strictures. Things were worse north of the border, though. Laud's innovations created a revolt in 1638 among the Covenanters in Presbyterian Scotland.[38]

As part of the Covenanters' revolt, Samuel Rutherford (1600–1661)[39], and even more pointedly, George Gillespie (1613–1648),[40] demanded biblical warrant for not only doctrine and worship, but also ecclesiastical government, including the concept and number of church offices.[41] They argued maximally from Scripture for

---

37 David L. Edwards, *Christian England*, v. 2., *From the Reformation to the 18th century* (Grand Rapids: Eerdmans, 1983), 181–299.

38 Edwards, 255–99. Thomas F. Torrance, *Scottish Theology: From John Knox to John McLeod* Campbell (Edinburgh: T&T Clark, 1996), 1–47.

39 Samuel Rutherford set forth his view of biblical Presbyterianism in a number of his works, especially *A Peaceable and Temperate Plea for Paul's Presbytery in Scotland* (London, 1642); *The Due Right of Presbyteries, or a Peaceable Plea for the Government of the Church of Scotland* (London, 1644); and *The Divine Right of Church Government and Excommunication* (London, 1646). See also John Coffey, *Politics, Religion, and the British Revolutions: The Mind of Samuel Rutherford* (Cambridge: Cambridge University Press, 1997), 188–224.

40 George Gillespie set forth his views of biblical Presbyterianism in several works, especially *A Dispute Against the English Popish Ceremonies Obtruded on the Church of Scotland* (1637); *An Assertion of the Government of the Church of Scotland, in the Points of Ruling Elders, and of the Authority of Presbyteries and Synods* (Edinburgh, 1641); and *Aaron's Rod Blossoming, or the Divine Ordinance of Church Government Vindicated* (London, 1646). See also W.D.J. McKay, *An Ecclesiastical Republic, Church Government in the Writings of George Gillespie* (Edinburgh: Rutherford House, 1997).

41 These arguments may be found in C. Van Dixhoorn, ed., *The Minutes and Papers of the Westminster Assembly, 1643–1652* (Oxford: Oxford University Press, 2012), v. 2, 354–422.

all the particulars of an established and covenanted Presbyterianism.. Even apart from the question of covenanting, Gillespie tended to argue his case as strong as he could for *iure divino* Presbyterianism because he abhorred the episcopacy that the crown sought to impose on the church and the Erastianism that the crown and the English parliament sought to impose.[42]

The majority of the Westminster Assembly favored *iure divino* Presbyterianism. This meant at least two things: first, they thought that the Bible prescribed a pattern of church government and; second, they thought that the pattern of government it prescribed was Presbyterian (not episcopal, as the Anglican church had been, or Congregational, as the Five Dissenting, or Independent, Brethren at Westminster wanted). Differences arose most particularly in how detailed such a description was, with the many of the divines, over against the Scots, arguing that the form of church government set forth in God's Word was more broadly principled than particular in details, giving the general pattern of government but not all the particulars of how such government worked.,[43] For instance, in the debates of 22 November-7 December on questions about the ruling eldership, while the Scots were quite adamant that "presbyter" encompassed both minister and ruling elder, many others were not so sanguine and found the warrant for elders (or "other church governors") ultimately not in references to presbyters but in references to government and administration in Romans 12:8 and I Corinthians 12:28.[44]

As to the question of the nature and number of church offices, Rutherford and Gillespie (along with all Scottish Commissioners to the Assembly) argued like Calvin and Knox for four offices (pastor, doctor, elder, and deacon), though they saw the ruling elder as a presbyterin keeping with the SBD.[45] It is the case that these brethren distinguished the office of the minister and the ruling elder quite distinctly, as did Hodge. Gillespie, for instance, thought that ruling elders should not pray publicly or join ministers in the laying on of hands in ordaining officers,[46]

42 John Macleod, *Scottish Theology in Relation to Church History Since the Reformation*, 3rd ed. (Edinburgh: Knox Press, 1973), 66–102; Robert S. Paul, *The Assembly of the Lord: Politics and Religion in the Westminster Assembly and the Grand Debate* (Edinburgh: T&T Clark, 1985), 163–174, and De Witt, *Jus Divinum*, 78–86, testify to the diversity of Assembly debate on the question of the ruling elder that occurred from November 22-Dec. 7, 1643 without reaching consensus and referring it back to committee for further work; the full record of this, as noted above is in Van Dixhoorn, *Assembly Minutes*, v. 354–422.

43 De Witt, *Jus Divinum*, 81. The Scots could tend towards a biblicism in their *iure divino* convictions that corresponded with the Independents' iure divino convictions, except that the Scots thought that the Bible mandated Presbyterianism instead of congregationalism.

44 Van Dixhoorn, *Minutes*, v. 2, 411–422.

45 De Witt, *Jus Divinum*, 78–86.

46 McKay, *An Ecclesiastical Republic*, 200–201.

sounding like Hodge in his disputes against other Old School Presbyterians in the ordination debates in America in the 1840's.

The Scottish commissioners to the Westminster Assembly were not, on the point of ruling elders being presbyters, able to carry the day. Though Independents tended to agree with the conception that the Scots had of the elder (and also with *iure divino* church government, but not the connectionalism of Presbyterianism),[47] the Assembly as a whole did not, including many of the English Presbyterians (and obviously the Anglicans and Erastians). The Assembly, in its *Form of Presbyterial Church-Government* (FPCG), after much back and forth of debate on the office of ruling elder, stated:

> Other church-governors: As there were in the Jewish church elders of the people joined with the priests and Levites in the government of the church; so Christ, who hath instituted government, and governors ecclesiastical in the church, hath furnished some in his church, beside the ministers of the word, with gifts for government, and with commission to execute the same when called thereunto, who are to join with the ministers in the government of the church. Which officers reformed churches commonly call Elders.[48]

Several things are worth noting here. Elders are called, in the first place, "other-church governors," in the title that heads the section, reflecting the fact that the Assembly hesitated to call those who assisted ministers in the government of the church Elders without any qualification[49] The Assembly did not begin the definition by referring to those officers that it concedes, at the end, reformed churches "commonly call Elders," by employing any of the New Testament office-bearing language.[50] As McKay notes, "The Scottish commissioners had a high view of ruling

47 Gillespie may earlier have actually had more concord than he came later to have with the congregationalists (Independents), more so, at any rate, than Rutherford, who was divine right for connectionalism and higher judicatories all along. So argues Hunter Powell, *The Crisis of British Protestantism: Church Power in the Puritan Revolution, 1638–44* (Manchester: Manchester University Press, 2015), 35–57.

48 *The Form of Presbyterial Church Government* in *The Westminster Confession of Faith* (1645; republished, Glasgow: Free Presbyterian Publications, 1994), 402.

49 It was widely agreed that "elder" was a fair English translation of *presbuteros*, though a majority of the Assembly believed, as did Hodge, that, historically, the English words "bishop" and "presbyter" both referred to ministers (not ruling elders as well). Thus, some confusion could arise by simply referring to ruling elders as presbyters, while understanding that in the English language they were often, indeed, "commonly called Elders."

50 Chad van Dixhoorn points out that "the assembly's Presbyterians...were united [that]...the New Testament held out only two offices in the church: varieties of elders and deacons," in "Presbyterian Ecclesiologies at the Westminster Assembly," in *Church Polity and Politics in the British Atlantic World, c. 1635-66* (Manchester, GB: Manchester University Press, 2020), 117. This may well be true,

elders which is but dimly reflected in this vague statement [in the *FPCG*] addressing "other church governors."[51]

The proof texts offered by the Assembly here are particularly instructive. After the first phrase, referring to the Old Testament practice, the divines cite II Chronicles 19–8-10; after explicating the New Testament equivalent the Assembly cited Romans 12:7–8 and I Corinthians 12:28, The first citation arguably, links the service of the Levites and priests with the heads of families of Israel, otherwise identified with the elders of the people. The second citation refers to the two New Testament texts that Calvin and Hodge leaned on when seeing the ruling eldership as a distinct class from and adjunct to the minister. Conspicuously absent from Westminster's proof texts are the typical passages cited by those who would regard "other church governors" to be of the same order as ministers, especially I Timothy 5:17. The citation of only the Romans and I Corinthians texts are key indicators that the Westminster Assembly did not at this point affirm Gillespie's view of presbyter, since it did not adopt his interpretation of I Timothy 5:17 as being clearly in view in the Assembly's conception of "other church governors."[52]

Furthermore, the Assembly saw the roots of the office of elder to be both in the Jewish church and in the laity of that church ("elders of the people" being a term referring to those deemed leaders among the people, recognized and chosen by them). Even as ministers, then, are conceptualized as being New Testament equivalents of the Old Testament priesthood, so ruling elders are conceptualized as the New Testament expression of the Old Testament lay office of elder as a ruler among the people. As elders joined priests in the governance of the church in the Old Testament, so now ruling elders join ministers in the governance of the church

but such unity is not what is expressed in the FPCG's articles on the offices (pastor, doctor, other church governors, deacons). This may simply be because what the FPCG actually says reflects a compromise between presbyterian and other parties. One can hardly regard the article on "other church governors" as a ringing endorsement of Gillespie's view of the ruling elder as presbyter. Importantly, Hodge takes the statement of "other church governors" as supportive of his approach that ruling elders are not presbyters properly but those non-ministerial officers that join with ministers in the joint rule and government of the church, see Hodge, *Polity,* 263. Hodge, in this same article (p.265), further concedes that, in terms of nomenclature, "Much confusion has arisen form the use of the word elder and presbyter as synonymous; and many false conclusions have been drawn from the assumption that because both words mean an old man, therefore, every elder is a presbyter, and may do whatever a presbyter may do. The same argument would prove true that every alderman is a senator, and every senator an alderman."

51 McKay, 199.

52 *FPCG,* 402.

in the New Testament.[53] This conception of the elder would track with Hodge's view of the ruling elder.[54]

7.4 The Minister and his Distinct Call to Office

Perhaps it would be helpful to pause here and reflect that one of the problems for those that simply wish to identify the ruling elder with the biblical presbyter, which is to say, to regard the minister and ruling elder as holding the same office, is the notion of vocation or call. In short, virtually no one thinks that the ruling elder customarily has anything like, in his experience, the same sense of call to his office that the minister does to his. Certainly, those who differed from Hodge, like Dabney and Thornwell, did not conceptualize the ruling elder as enjoying the same sort of call as did the minister.[55]

To be sure, the minister was differently gifted and trained than the ruling elder: only he usually went to seminary and, as all the Old School disputants agreed, only he held the teaching office. He was also differently called, with no one expecting a ruling elder to have the kind of marked outward and inward called that the minister did. For the minister, this call meant that his life was to be dedicated to the preaching of the gospel and the pastoring of the flock. This was his full-time work and, even in the case of bi-vocational ministry, it was still believed that the minister had a call that was unique to his office and not one shared by the ruling elder or the deacon.[56]

---

53 Lee Irons, "Theories of Eldership: A Study in Presbyterian Polity," (unpublished paper), 8–17, does an excellent job in dealing with the exegesis of the Old Testament passages that support the view that the NT ruling elder is a continuation of the OT elder, who was a ruler among the people, serving together with the Levites, in the joint rule of the church.

54 Note also in Strange, "Do the Minister and Elder hold the same office?" the schematization comparing the Old Testament Levites (priests) and elders of the people with the Acts 15 apostles and elders and finally the NT ministers and elders. This diagram illumines Hodge's conception.

55 Robert Lewis Dabney, "What is a Call to the Ministry?" in *Discussions: Evangelical and Theological*, v. 2 (1891; republished, London; The Banner of Truth Trust, 1967), 26–46, makes it clear that such a call is not a murky mysterious matter but involves a practical lifelong commitment on the part of one duly gifted, the usefulness to the church not exceeded by any other calls or professions. This is key to Hodge's distinction as well of lay and clergy, a layman, even when an ordained officer (a ruling elder, e. g.), "is a man who is not a clergyman, not a minister of the gospel," and his gifting and calling are quite distinct from a minister, even though overlapping in the area of governance (i. e., they are both church governors), *Polity*, p. 294. That James Henley Thornwell also sees the call to the ministry as distinct is evident in his "The Call of a Minister," in *The Collected Writings of James Henley Thornwell, v. IV—Ecclesiastical* (1875, republished, Edinburgh: The Banner of Truth Trust, 1974), 15–42.

56 Robert Rayburn, "Ministers, Elders, Deacons," in *Order in the Offices*, ed. by Mark Brown (Duncansville, PA: Classic Presbyterian Government Resources, 1993), hits the nail on the head here: "The

Presbyterians came to see all Christians as having a call to the general office of believer, out of which God called some men to special office (of minister, ruling elder, and deacon). Part of the this "everyone has a call" or a "vocation" conviction, though, involved not only a distinctly religious call that all had in the offices of general and special believer, but also a call that extended to all of life, meaning that God had gifted everyone for service (butcher, baker, carpenter, banker, doctor, lawyer, etc.), service that even in the "secular" sphere was to be pursued to the glory of God.[57] Thus, the word "vocation" ("calling") in the post-Reformational West came to be identified with one's secular "job," especially in the post-Enlightenment development of secularism.

In all of this, it was understood that there was a distinction of a particular sort in special office. Ruling elders and deacons, though being brought into special office out of general office, enjoyed a call of a sort to such office, both an internal sense and an external confirmation that they should serve Christ and his church in special office. They continued, nonetheless, to have a general vocation, a job, and to work, as did the rest of the congregation (the rest of those who held the general office of believer). They continued, in other words, to be a part of the people, of the laity, in contradistinction to those who were their fellow special office holders: those who held the office of minister of Word and Sacrament.

Those who held the office of minister had a call not only to special office, as did the ruling elders and deacons, but a call that involved their vocation, or job, as well. Whether coming to a young man in training, who had never entered upon a profession or vocation, or coming to a man who may already be a salesman, doctor, engineer, etc., the call to the ministry is a call to give one's life to the preaching and teaching of the Word, the administration of the sacraments, prayer, and to all that accompanies pastoral office particularly, and/or ministerial office more broadly. Hodge argued that this complete dedication to the ministerial office was so important that ministers in parishes unable fully to support them should be aided

---

greatest weakness of the two-office view, in my judgment, lies in its unwitting diminishing of the special calling of the minister" (232), which amounts to, as Rayburn and others note, a downgrade of the preaching office and, concomitantly, of the preaching of the Word as that which is central to worship and thus to the life of the church.

57 William Perkins, *The Works of William Perkins*, edited by J. Stephen Yuille, v.10, "Treatise on Vocations" (Grand Rapids, Michigan: Reformation Heritage Books, 2014-),31–107. See also the recent work by Dee Aleasha Grimes, "God's Imposition: The Centrality of Vocation in the Spirituality of William Perkins," Ph.D. diss., The Southern Baptist Theological Seminary, 2021. Grimes nicely summarizes Perkin's conception of vocation: "Vocation, or the personal calling, according to Perkins, is 'a certain kind of life, ordained and imposed on man by God for the common good.' In other words, a vocation is designed by God, unique to each Christian, and for the good of the family, church, and commonwealth" (p. 188).

by the broader church.[58] Hodge's view here, on providing full support for those engaged in ministry, even by the broader church when the local church could not, became a passion of his life, reflected not only in what he wrote late in his life (as noted in the previous footnote), but what he preached to the General Assembly in delivering the moderator's sermon in 1847.[59]

Thus, "call" as applied to ruling elders and deacons had a different connotation than it did for ministers. The former involved a call to specific service in Christ's church beyond that of the general office of believer. It does not entail, however, that one should leave one's secular vocation for such service. This stood in contrast to the ministerial call, which was a call not only to special service in the church while remaining a layman with a secular job; rather the call to the ministry is a call to give up all such pursuits, to be, in fact, "free from worldly care," so that one might give oneself wholly to the life that belongs to those who receive a ministerial call, in which the whole of one's vocation is service to Christ and his church.[60] To pretend as if the ruling elder held the same office and thus has the same call as the minister would, in Hodge's view, logically follow if they were the same office, is to denigrate the office of minister and not to lift the office of ruling elder.

7.5 Hodge's Conception of Office

Disputes among Presbyterians about the nature of church office and Presbyterianism did not go away in nineteenth century America. They inevitably reemerge when circumstances warrant revisiting polity fundamentals or further developing the fuller implications of Presbyterian church government. Having looked at the polity situation on the European continent and in Britain, we turn our attention to America, focusing on Hodge in his own time. Robert J. Breckinridge (1800–1871), who played a key role in the split of American Presbyterianism that obtained until 1869, the Old School/New School division of 1837, and thus no retiring figure in disputes, argued for the right of ruling elders to join ministers in the imposition of

58 Hodge, *Polity*, 247–262.

59 The Minutes of the Assembly, but perhaps more poignantly, Hodge's customary report on the GA in the pages of the *Biblical Repertory and Princeton Review*, record that Hodge, as moderator of the previous assembly, opened the 1847 GA in the First Presbyterian Church in Richmond, VA with a sermon on I Corinthian 9:14, highlighting the church's obligation to financially support all her ministers, *BRPR* 19.3 (July 1847), 396.

60 "Free from worldly care and employment" is part of the historic language used in a call extended to a man for ministerial/pastoral service, *Form of Government* 22.9 in the *Book of Church Order of the Orthodox Presbyterian Church* (Willow Grove, PA: Issued by Stated Clerk of the GA, 2020), 39.

hands at the ordination of ministers.[61] This matter received considerable attention from the PCUSA General Assemblies of 1841–1844, resulting in the final decision to retain the historic American Presbyterian practice that only ministers should lay on hands at the ordination of a minister thus excluding the ruling elders from such.[62]

Hodge, given his understanding of the nature of the offices of minister and ruling elder, strongly supported the decision of the Assembly, over against Breckinridge and his supporters. Hodge wrote an article in the Princeton Review defending the General Assembly's determination as well as in his customary review of the General Assembly.[63] It was widely admitted that certain acts, like the blessing accompanying the apostolic salutation/benediction and the regular preaching of the Word with the accompanying administration of the sacraments, were acts of the session.. While the session (ruling elders and ministers acting in concert) properly determined in when the Lord's Supper would be observed, only the minister presides at the Table.[64] Theologians often distinguish between the power of order (that which takes place in worship, for instance) and the power of jurisdiction (that which takes place in the government of the church). The offices of minister and elder share equal governing tasks in the power of jurisdiction as exercised in the graded judicatories of the church, but only the minister, in the understanding of Hodge and others, properly ministers Word and Sacrament in the worship of the church. Hodge agrees with Gillespie, who also teaches that only the minister can lay on

61 Peter J. Wallace, "The Bond of Union": The Old School Presbyterian Church and the American Nation" (Ph. Dissertation, University of Notre Dame, 2004), 146–188, contains an excellent treatment and analysis of Breckinridge and the Elder Question.

62 Breckinridge sets forth his views in two pamphlets published at the time of the imposition of hands controversy (early 1840s) and later published in the *Southern Presbyterian Review*, "Presbyterian Government Not a Hierarchy, But a Commonwealth," 33.2 (April 1882) 258–290, and "Presbyterian Ordination Not a Charm, But an Act of Government," 33.3 (July 1882) 463–518. These two articles also reflect Breckinridge's broader concern that due, among other things, to the 1803 Act of Union with the Congregationalists, the Presbyterians had marginalized the office of ruling elder, allowing congregational "committeemen" to enjoy the same status. One of the ways he sought to rescue the office of ruling elder from such desuetude was to make sure that the ruling elder was more fully involved in the courts of the church and was not excluded in the act of laying on of hands, even in the ordination of a minister. For reflections on these events, see D.G. Hart and John R. Muether, *Seeking a Better Country: 300 Years of American Presbyterianism* (Phillipsburg, NJ: P&R Publishing, 2007), 91–108.and Lefferts A. Loetscher, *A Brief History of the Presbyterians*, 4th ed. (Philadelphia: The Westminster Press, 1978), 82–91

63 Hodge, *Polity*,288–294.

64 Edmund P. Clowney, "Answer to the Complaint in re: Laying-on of hands in the Presbytery of New Jersey (OPC)," in *Minutes of the PNJ*, v. 3 (Feb. 23, 1963), pp. 148–153. Clowney answers the question in terms of American Presbyterian history (the 1843–44 General Assemblies) and biblical theology.

hands (or pronounce excommunication).[65] Gillespie says further, "The power of order alone shall make the difference betwixt the pastor and the ruling elder,"[66] another point of agreement with Hodge. Perhaps Gillespie's and Hodge's differences are more nomenclature than were Hodge's differences with his fellow American Presbyterians like Breckinridge.

Likewise, ruling elders and ministers of the regional church joined together in examining ministerial candidates for ordination. However, at the service of ordination, only ministers, as a ministerial act carried out on behalf of the whole presbytery (both ministers and elders), lay hands on the ordinand. This was the practice of the PCUSA that Breckinridge called into question. The Assembly defended the practice of inviting only ministers to join in the imposition of hands, which practice Hodge defended as a proper understanding of biblical Presbyterianism.[67] Hodge's view on the laying-on-of-hands carried the day as the church, for the time being at least, retained the practice of only ministers imposing hands at the ordination of ministers. In general, Hodge's view of there being a clear distinction between minister and ruling elder prevailed in the PCUSA in the North.[68]

The laying-on-of-hands question resulted in reviving older debates over Presbyterian polity in relation to church offices. So had the publication of *The Ruling Elder* by Hodge's elder Princeton colleague Samuel Miller (1769–1850) in 1832. Miller was the second professor at Princeton (Hodge was the third) and served as professor of ecclesiastical history and polity. Miller's book was the first American work, after the great Scottish works, especially of Rutherford and Gillespie, to treat the office of ruling elder systematically. Miller regarded the minister and the ruling elder as distinct offices, with the latter representing the people in church councils, in numbers that served to check any improper encroachments of clergy, preserving the rights of the people and securing for ministers counsel and support of the "best possible kind."[69] Further, Presbyterianism thus conceived, allowed discipline to be carried out with "dispatch and energy," since such was in the hands not of one but many, in providing for proper tribunals of appeal, and was actually most conducive for the spread of the gospel and for promoting proper ecumenicity by exercising joint government with other churches.[70]

---

65 Mackay, 200.

66 Gillespie, *Assertion,* 13.

67 Hodge, *Polity*, 290.

68 A standard work on polity reflects such: J. Aspinwall Hodge, *What is Presbyterian Law as Defined by the Church Courts?* (Philadelphia: Presbyterian Board of Education, 1882), see 52–60, "Of Ruling Elders," especially.

69 Samuel Miller, *The Ruling Elder* (1832; republished, Dallas, TX: Presbyterian Heritage Publications, 1987), 311.

70 Miller, *Ruling Elder*, 312–318.

Hodge agreed with Miller's construction of the office of ruling elder generally, noting, "We do not differ from Dr. Miller as to the nature of the office of ruling elder. The only point of difference between him and us relates to the method of establishing the divine warrant for the office."[71] It is clear from Miller's treatment of the "Testimony of the New Testament Church" as it relates to the ruling elder that Miller viewed the presbyter as a ruling elder (as well as a pastor) in some places, particularly evident in his extensive treatment of I Tim. 5:17.[72] Hodge, as seen herein, limited the warrant for the ruling elder to Romans 12:8 and I Corinthians 12:28. In doing so, he differed from Miller in establishing the divine warrant for the office of ruling elder. On the nature of Presbyterianism, Miller, like Hodge, declined to argue for the sort of *iure divino* Presbyterianism that found the details of church government in the Bible., recognizing that divine right Presbyterianism may be general only in its details.[73]

The able Southern Old School Presbyterian Theologian James Henley Thornwell entered the office dispute on the side of Breckinridge.[74] In 1843, he wrote "The Ruling Elder a Presbyter" in support of Breckinridge's viewpoint. In that essay he argued from Scripture and church history that the ruling elder was a presbyter and, as such, was as fully authorized to lay on hands at the ordination of a minister as were the fellow ministers of the ordinand.[75] Thornwell argued further along these lines in 1848 in "The Ruling Elder," contending again that the ruling elder, over against Hodge, is in every sense a presbyter.[76] Hodge wrote, though the precise time cannot be established, more about the elder question, later published in his book on church polity, continuing to cross swords with Thornwell and others throughout his life.[77]

As noted, Hodge was quick to point out the widespread consensus of his day on the synonymous use of *presbuteros* and *episkopos*, an agreement cutting across various views of church polity (with both some episcopal and congregational approbation), many seeing both as referring to the office of minister in the early church before a hierarchical distinction between bishops and presbyters developed.[78] Many Presbyterians in the United States, with Gillespie and Rutherford

---

71 Hodge, *Polity*, 129.

72 Miller, 49–72.

73 Miller, 18–19.

74 James Henley Thornwell, *Collected Writings*, v. IV—*Ecclesiastical*, 15–42. Here Thornwell reviews several of Breckinridge's seminal works, showing himself to be decisively on Breckinridge's side.

75 Thornwell, *Writings*, IV, 115–131.

76 Thornwell, *Writings*, IV, 43–114.

77 Hodge, *Polity*, 262–287.

78 Most notably, the Anglican J.B. Lightfoot argued, in *St. Paul's Epistle to the Philippians* (1868; republished, Lynn, MA: Hendrickson Publishers Inc., 1981), 95–99, that bishop and presbyter were synonyms in the early Christian centuries for the office of minister.

before them, wanted more warrant for the ruling elder than the approach of Hodge and others afforded, arguing that *presbuteros* and *episkopos* included ministers and ruling elders equally. Others pushed back against such arguments. Though the views of many, if not most, Presbyterians reflected in the church orders regarded the ruling elder as properly a presbyter, some still favored Hodge's position in some measure, as did the modern Scottish theologian, T. F. Torrance,[79] and the Banner of Truth Trust trustee and author, Iain Murray (associated with D. Martyn Lloyd-Jones)[80].

In terms of wider scholarship, as noted, the broad consensus of the synonymous use of the two Greek terms in question that prevailed in Hodge's day dissolved. Subsequently, many liberal historians and theologians, under higher critical influence, argued that the Apostolic church was charismatically focused, concerned not with offices but with gifts, and the later focus on office was a post-Apostolic phenomenon; so too was the later focus on office found in what was alleged to be Paul's writings in the pastoral epistles.[81] These scholars found the pastorals to be of second century origins and the development of office a triumph of the "Catholic" church over her heretical opponents. Even among scholars perhaps less critically motivated, the consensus of an identity between bishop and presbyter came under fire, and a sizeable debate has ensued in the latter part of the twentieth century to the present about whether there was not, in fact, a primitive episcopacy, the main issue being that of when parochial episcopacy developed into its diocesan form.[82] This has also received pushback from some Presbyterians, like Benjamin Merkle,

79 Torrance, "Eldership in the Reformed Church," 509: though Torrance wants to see the elder-deacon as together, a view with which I disagree, I do believe that many of his observations in this piece are trenchant. He refers to the argument that ministers and ruling elders were both "presbyters" as a theory "demolished by Smyth…and by Hodge of Princeton with immense learning, "and more succinctly by Campbell of Aberdeen (508).

80 Iain H. Murray, "The Problem of the 'Eldership' and Its Wider Implications," in *The Banner of Truth* (magazine), issue 395–396 (August/September 1996), 36–56, rightly observing, "It is the *office* of the preacher which is discounted today, sometimes even condemned as 'clericalism', and this attitude is frequently defended by what are claimed to be more scriptural assertions about the 'eldership'" (37).

81 R. Alastair Campbell, *The Elders: Seniority within Earliest Christianity* (Edinburgh: T&T Clark, 1994), 182–193. A fair part of Burchtaell, *Synagogue to Church*, 61–179, is spent looking at the fate of *episkopos* and *presbuteros* in a wide range of scholarship, especially the treatment of such by theological liberalism of varying stripes.

82 Alistair C. Stewart, *The Original Bishops: Office and Order in the First Christian Communities* (Grand Rapids: Baker Academic, 2014), supporting an episcopal position, argues (pp. 11–54, especially) that the two terms are not synonymous and that there was always a distinction between bishop and presbyter, though the bishops early-on, like the presbyters, were originally identified with a single congregation.

arguing, once again, the synonymy of *presbuteros* and *episkopos*, though Merkle sees both terms as referring to ministers and ruling elders.[83]

7.6 Hodge, the Boards, and *Iure Divino* Presbyterianism

While the earlier debates of Hodge and fellow Old School Presbyterians focused on office (who may lay on hands at the ordination of a minister and the warrant for the office of ruling elder), the later debates (in the 1850s and beyond) came to focus more on the nature of Presbyterianism itself. Thus, we turn in this essay from the "office" question to that of how Old School Presbyterians affirming divine right Presbyterianism differed over how their conceptsions of church government should be constructed and understood. The debate over church boards provides a good entry point into the differing ways then current of construing divine right Presbyterianism. One might regard the kerfuffle over the question of church boards that occurred in Old School Presbyterianism, particularly at the 1860 General Assembly, as something of a tempest within a teapot. The controversy, however, concealed different conceptions of Presbyterianism, a difference that played out especially in the debate in that the 1860 Assembly, and in the aftermath, between Charles Hodge and James Henley Thornwell. Hodge argued that "to make out any plausible argument in support of the doctrine that the Boards are anti-scriptural, required, of course a peculiar theory of Presbyterianism; a theory which should exclude all discretionary power in the Church, and tie her down to modes of action prescribed as of divine authority in the word of God."[84]

One might say that Thornwell's position was simply divine right Presbyterianism, if such is taken to mean that Scripture established the specific rather than the general details of church government.[85] It would be more accurate to say that Thornwell

83 Benjamin L. Merkle, *The Elder and Overseer: One Office in the Early Church* (New York: Peter Lang, 2003).

84 Hodge, *Church Polity*, 118.

85 This is the contention of A. Craig Troxel in his "Divine Right Presbyterianism and Church Power," (PhD. Dissertation, Westminster Theological Seminary, 1998), 198–239. Hodge, Troxel noted, "dissented from the jus divinum Presbyterianism of Thornwell" (5). Brian Wingard also finds Hodge deficient in this respect, in his "As the Lord Puts Words in Her Mouth: The Supremacy of Scripture in the Ecclesiology of James Henley Thornwell and its Influence upon the Presbyterian Church of the South," Ph.D. Dissertation, Westminster Theological Seminary, 1992, 95, 128. Troxel also notes that Hodge seems excessively to stress the invisible nature of the church, 198–201, 232–239, taking up John Jay Deifell's concerns. I deal with this in my work on *The Doctrine of the Spirituality of the Church in the Ecclesiology of Charles Hodge* (pp. 162–174), granting some validity to the concern, while noting Deifell's determination as a neo-Barthian to discover all the wrong that he can in Hodge's ecclesiology.

understood what divine right meant differently than Hodge did. Hodge affirmed with Thornwell that his view of Presbyterianism was established by divine right.[86] The question had to do with what kind of detail the Bible established with respect to church offices. Did the Bible contain a detailed blueprint for church government, or did it lay down Presbyterian principles that the church had freedom in detailing in practice? Hodge leaned to the latter position while Thornwell did to the former.

The Board controversy emerged in 1859–60, in which Hodge and Thornwell were the key highly public players, particularly in their famous debate at the 1860 General Assembly.[87] All the particulars of that debate need not concern us here. What is key in their disagreement for our purposes is the definition of Presbyterianism that emerged from each author as the context of the battle over the Church Boards. Another preeminent Southern Old School Presbyterian, R. L. Dabney (1820–1898), essentially agreed with Thornwell on the identity of presbyter and ruling elder, framing the issue with his customary trenchancy: "It strikes many Presbyterians with surprise, that the General Assembly and our leading periodicals in this year 1860, one hundred and fifty [plus] years after the beginning of our church in America, should be largely occupied in discussing the question 'What is Presbyterianism?'"[88]

Dabney proceeded to answer the aggrieved hypothetical reader who asks, "Is the church never to be relieved of these debates, which thus agitate the settled foundations of our theory?" Dabney rightly answered "no," reminding his petulant interlocutors that "each generation must do its own thinking and learn for itself its own lessons in first truths and general principles. If we insist that this generation of Presbyterians shall hold our fathers' principles on trust, and by mere prescription, the result will be that they will not hold them sincerely at all."[89] Dabney is quite clearly right () in his assertion that every generation must work through these issues, even as we seek to do herein. A vital Presbyterianism is one in which we continue to contend for the faith, not only as it pertains to the being of the church in its doctrines, but also as it pertains to its well-being, which includes the polity of the church.

---

86 Hodge, *Church Polity*, 125: Having argued over the course of several pages that his own view is properly that of divine right Presbyterianism, though of a different sort than Thornwell's, Hodge writes, "We hold, therefore, to a *iure divino* Presbyterianism…"

87 For secondary sources on this, already cited herein, see the citations of Hoffecker and Gutjahr in ftn. 1 (above), and A.A. Hodge in ftn. 3. For another especially helpful secondary source, see Wallace, "Bond of Union," 657–675.

88 This article of Dabney's ("Theories of the Eldership") appeared in the *North Carolina Presbyterian*, September 1860 and is cited here from Robert L. Dabney, *Discussions: Evangelical and Theological, v. 2* (1891; rpt., London: Banner of Truth Trust, 1967), 119.

89 Dabney, 119.

Hodge, in his article in the Princeton Review (1860) that extended his discussion from the Assembly of that year, set forth Thornwell's position, seen by Hodge as consisting of five basic points. Firstly, the Presbyterian form of government is set down in Scripture as completely and clearly as the system of faith. Secondly, thus the church has no more right to create an organization (like a Board) as part of carrying out her work any more than she did to "add a new command to the Decalogue." Thirdly, the church cannot delegate her powers, but she can act only through her judicatories. Fourthly, all church power is in the hands of presbyters, "who have the same ordination and office, although differing in functions." And, finally, all church power is joint and not several: "that is, it can be exercised only by the Church courts, and not in any case by individual officers."[90] To Hodge, these five points reached beyond the data of Scripture regarding the proper definition of Presbyterianism; consequently, these five points were not something that Thornwell could impose on the whole church as necessary to Presbyterianism established by divine right and thus binding on all.

Thornwell interacted with Hodge's characterization of his theory of Presbyterianism, taking issue with Hodge at length, particularly defending his definition of Presbyterianism as true and indeed binding[91] Hodge, critical of Thornwell's use of "logic" at one point in the argumentation in which Thornwell had claimed that his view of Presbyterianism was logical and irrefutable, made an observation giving some flavor of their interchange: "Dr. Thornwell ...informed the Assembly that he had studied Aristotle, and every other master of the science [of logic]; that he had probably the largest private library of works in that department in the country, and felt prepared to measure swords on that field with any man alive."[92] Hodge cited this self-disclosure of Thornwell as an example of the latter's tactics in argumentation, which were at odds with Hodge's less self-promoting approach to the debate.

At any rate, Thornwell took some issue with the way that Hodge put his five points, especially arguing that he did not insist that all details of church government must be biblical, but that Scripture established substantive matters about governance (thus no boards were lawful), leaving certain details (which he called circumstances of government—numbers of meetings, erecting committees and commissions, etc.) to the discretion of the church.[93] Yet Hodge thought that Thornwell gave away his argument for his version of divine right Presbyterianism by the concessions that

90 Hodge, *Polity*, 118–119.

91 Specifically, Thornwell published articles recapitulating and expanding on his arguments at the 1860 GA ("Debate Touching Church Boards") and responding to Hodge's much shorter article doing the same (in Thornwell's "Church Boards and Presbyterianism"), both cited here from his *Collected Writings*, v. IV—*Ecclesiastical*, 217–295.

92 Hodge, *Polity*, 126.

93 Thornwell, *Writings*, IV, 245.

he made.[94] Still, for Hodge, he regarded as incidental whether the church used an executive committee/commission for publications, which Thornwell did not oppose, or a board of publication, which Thornwell did oppose. Hodge struggled, as he put it, not to see this as a matter of expediency; he could not truly regard it as a matter of lawfulness,[95] and believed that for Thornwell to make the move to call such boards unlawful was "intolerable."[96]

Hodge, both at the 1860 GA and in his article summarizing his views, enumerated three main points of Presbyterianism First, he argued that where the Spirit of God is dwelling in the people of God, there we find all the attributes and prerogatives of the church. Second, he maintained that as the Spirit "dwells not in the clergy only, but in the people of God, all power is, *in sensu primo*, in the people." Third, the church is to be governed "by principles laid down in the Word of God, which determine, within certain limits, her officers and modes of organization." Beyond these prescribed principles, however, "and in fidelity to them, the Church has a wide discretion in the choice of methods, organs, and agencies." Finally, Hodge said:

> That the fundamental principles of our Presbyterian system are first, the parity of the clergy [*presbuteros* and *episkopos* being synonymous and both being different names for ministers]; second, the right of the people to a substantive part in the government of the Church; and third, the unity of the Church, in such sense, that a small part is subject to a larger, and a larger to the whole.[97]

Thornwell roundly criticized, if not castigated, Hodge for this definition of Presbyterianism, calling it "a little of everything but nothing distinctive."[98] Thornwell believed that Hodge's definition of Presbyterianism was wanting, lacking fuller definition of the sort that Thornwell's had; Hodge, however, Hodge believed that his definition captured what he understood the Scripture to teach as to principles of church government and that to insist on more as binding was unconscionable.[99]

Thornwell argued at length for his approach to Presbyterianism. Hodge had set forth the basic tenets of Thornwell's approach, as noted above, as he understood them, especially from Thornwell's address at the 1860 GA, though Thornwell demurred from some of the description. The most basic feature to which Thornwell

94 Hodge, *Polity*, 118–133.
95 Hodge, *Polity*, 120.
96 Hodge, *Polity*, 133.
97 Hodge, *Polity*, 119. As noted above, this is entirely in keeping with what Hodge said a few years earlier in his address to the Presbyterian Historical Society in Philadelphia, *What is Presbyterianism?*
98 Thornwell, *Writings*, IV, 234.
99 Hodge, *Polity*, 131–133.

returned time and again was his insistence that his view set forth and was faithful to *iure divino* Presbyterianism.[100] Hodge claimed that he believed in *iure divino* Presbyterianism, but of a less strict sort, and suspected Thornwell of baptizing all his views with the evocation of *iure divino* and attempting then to coerce the church to comply with his contention that Thornwell's views all enjoyed a "thus saith the Lord."[101] Asserting that one has the corner on what entails divine warrant for any practice is one thing, while proving or demonstrating it is another.

Thornwell argued at length in a number of respects against the wisdom and usefulness of the Boards.[102] However, that the Boards were cumbersome, not maximally accountable, and possessed other defects as then practiced is not quite the same as arguing that they were wrong because they lacked explicit Scriptural warrant. At times Thornwell's argument was against the utility of the Boards and at other times Thornwell's argument was that a proper biblical Presbyterianism forbade the Boards; thus, ultimately, the Boards were not only not the best or most appropriate way to conduct the church's business, according to Thornwell's construction, but were positively a menace, unbiblical, and thus, immoral. His argument was not that the church should not have Boards because of the problems inherent to them, an argument with which Hodge disagreed but with which, as an approach to the Board question, he thought legitimate; as Thornwell saw it, the church must not have Boards because to do so was wrong and a fundamental departure from Presbyterianism.[103]

Hodge resisted Thornwell's arguments against the Boards chiefly because Thornwell offered principled arguments against them, an approach that Hodge could not abide, rather than pragmatic arguments against them, which Hodge viewed as appropriate. This is because Hodge believed that Thornwell's evocation of principle here was a way of insisting on his position without really being able to prove that such a version of divine right Presbyterianism was indeed biblical. Hodge feared that to adopt Thornwell's approach would place the church in the thrall of the minority of men that joined him in support of his "the Boards are contrary to Scripture" approach. Hodge refused, as he put it, to yield to this sort of approach for a moment, believing that to do so would hand over the reins of the church to Thornwell and his comrades, who would bring the church under their control all in the name of their "new" approach to church government.[104]

---

100 Thornwell, *Writings*, IV, 217–241.

101 Hodge, *Polity*, 122.

102 Thornwell, *Writings*, IV, 242–297.

103 Thornwell, *Writings*, IV, 145–296 reflects his fully developed arguments for his conception of divine right Presbyterianism, to which he saw the existence of the boards as fundamentally opposed.

104 Hodge, *Polity*, 130–133.

Hodge said, getting to the heart of the matter in the divine right Presbyterianism debate, as he saw it, "the grand objection urged against this new theory," as Hodge viewed Thornwell's divine right opposition to the boards, is that it is "intolerable…, nothing more or less than a device for clothing human opinions with divine authority." Whereas Hodge believed that the Scriptures themselves, in all their diversity, enjoyed a grand unity, setting forth a system of doctrine that received expression in the doctrinal standards, he did not believe that they set forth with equal binding clarity and fullness a detailed system of church government. To assume that it did and then to proceed to bind everyone's conscience with what does not find a fullness of expression in subordinate doctrinal standards is to "bind her [the church] with fetters which human logic or caprice forges. This she will never submit to."[105]

However, in practice, certainly as American Old School Presbyterians, Thornwell and Hodge were not far apart[106]: both were signally involved in the revision of the PCUSA Book of Discipline, and much of which necessarily included a detailed development of the practices and functions of church courts that was far more detailed than anything that the Bible itself taught, either explicitly or implicitly.[107] Thus, while Thornwell continued to insist on his version of divine right Presbyterianism, meaning that it all came right out of the Bible, the facts on the ground showed otherwise: far more than the mere presence of Boards characterized daily Presbyterian polity. To be sure, Old School Presbyterian polity was arguably harmonious with the Word and was a proper development of it, but to argue that it simply reflected the Bible's teaching on how the church in its detailed workings should proceed was a claim that strained credulity.

7.7 The Ruling Elder as Representative of the Laity in the Courts of the Church

Returning more narrowly to the question of office, Hodge particularly wanted to maintain the distinction between the clergy and those who were the representatives of the people, namely, the ruling eldership. He argued forcefully that if such distinction were not observed, treating the ruling elder as a presbyter of the same order as the minister, then the genius of the lay order (ruling elders) joining with

---

105 Hodge, *Polity*, 133.

106 One might argue, with respect to the Americanism of Hodge and Thornwell, that the national character of their Presbyterianism did not emerge chiefly in the debate over church office and the nature of Presbyterianism but in the development of their views on the spirituality of the church (see Strange, *The Doctrine of the Spirituality of the Church in the Ecclesiology of Charles Hodge*, 250–257).

107 Hodge, *Polity*, 456–507.

the clerical order (ministers) would be eviscerated and Presbyterianism lost. When both ruling elders and ministers are seen as and operate as those of the same order, then a clerical overlordship results by undercutting lay representation. Practically, the minister does not, in such a scenario, become a layman. He continues to be of the clerical order, as to gifting, calling, full-time service, etc. Rather, it renders the lay ruling elder to be of the same order as the minister, and the laity are no longer through the ruling elder seen to be represented in the judicatories of the church.[108]

If such conclusions seem tendentious (certainly Thornwell dismissed it out of hand),[109] they were not so to Hodge. For Hodge, treating both ruling elder and minister as belonging to the same order of office attacked what he viewed as the genius of Presbyterianism, the harmonious working between the ministerium and the other church governors, who were not ministers. Hodge especially thought that such a move impacted the way matters were conducted in judicatories. He thought that there was a particular brilliance in conceiving the ruling elder as someone that the laity saw as a leader among them, much as the elders in the gate were seen in the Old Testament. They joined with the Levites in joint rule. Hodge thought that Presbyterianism was particularly blessed to have in its judicatories such representatives of the people, because of the particular gifts brought by such in debate and administration, as well as the care for the flock, that characterizes the work of the ruling elder.[110] There is a special quality that a ruling elder who works in some aspect of business or accounting can bring, e.g., to budget discussions, something that most clerics, not trained in, and often ill-equipped for, can use to assist the church.

Hodge thought that the church was far better off with the clerical order and the laity working together in the joint government of the church, not by always insisting on what they had in common in terms of office, but by stressing their different gifts and perspectives, all of which were necessary to avoid clericalism, on the one hand, or Congregationalism on the other.[111] To be sure, others invoked this notion of the ruling elder as a representative of the people, a leader among the laity chosen by them to rule over them, as did Hodge, with a particular eye to the American context. For those who might object to conceiving of the ruling elder as a representative of the people, especially with the American republic in view, they would need to remember that the original concept of a representative (as in the U.S. House of Representatives, for instance) was not someone who voted with his

108 Hodge, *Polity*, 262–271.

109 Thornwell, *Writings*, IV, 232–233.

110 Hodge, *Polity*, 264–266.

111 Hodge, *Polity*, 268–271.

finger in the wind, gauging the opinions of his constituency, but a leader among the people who voted righteously and wisely, not bound merely by popular opinion.[112]

Hodge intended no democracy in church government, as it were. Neither was democracy his conception of the American government. Hodge was a committed Federalist (then Whig, Free-Soiler, and Republican) and his idea of the American Republic was one in which the best men were elected to be representatives in the various legislatures at the local, state, and national levels.[113] A good congressman for Hodge was not someone who voted according to the popular opinions of the electorate but who, having been elected, voted as he best understood the issues before him, having ability and opportunity to understand questions of the day far better than those he represented. Similarly, Hodge saw a good ruling elder as one who studied the matters before him, and, arguably knowing more and better than the man in the pew who had elected him (as a spiritual leader recognized by the people), joined with the minister, in the joint rule of the church.

The ruling elder as representative, then, did not mean that the ruling elder looked to the pew-sitter for guidance.[114] He instead, as a recognized leader among those in the pews, acted, coram Deo, on the best evidence before him, with all the gifts God had given him, as did an elder in the gate in the OT who joined with the Levites in the joint governance of the OT church. Now ruling elders, as representatives and acting on behalf of the people, still joined with the New Testament counterpart of the Levite, the evangelical minister, in the joint rule of the church.[115] Hodge could make sense of this on its own Old Testament and New Testament terms. He could also make sense of it in terms of the American Republic, in which a representative was conceived as the best of men, who ruled not as a slave to popular opinion, but acting on their behalf as one trusted and respected by them and free to lead as he saw fit with a conscience captive to the Word of God.

Ministers are customarily educated in seminaries and have, arguably, more in common with each other than do the ruling elders with each other, coming as the latter do from a variety of socio-economic backgrounds, careers (professionals, skilled workers, etc.), life circumstances, etc. It is best to continue to conceive

112 This notion of the American republic and how it was to be governed by its representatives in the first two branches of government are widely attested to, in the writings of both the Federalists and the Anti-Federalists at the time of the adoption of the U.S. Constitution and Bill of Rights (1788–1791).

113 Alan D. Strange, *Spirituality of the Church*, in chapter 2.

114 Hodge's conviction that the ruling elder was a representative of the people was not merely a concomitant of his American republicanism: Gillespie and Rutherford, as stalwart Scotsmen, also believed that the elders were representatives of the people, Powell, *Crisis of British Protestantism*, 50.

115 *The Form of Presbyterial Church Government*, 400–401, viewed the NT office of minister as the evangelical analogue of the OT Levite/priest.

of the ruling elders as representing all the diversity of the congregation as their representatives, joining together with the minister(s) locally in the joint rule of the congregation and in the higher judicatories of the church.

Further, while it is always a plus for a ruling elder to be able to join the minister in counseling or to know as much about a theological matter as the minister ,the best-case scenarios can become enemies of what is ultimately best and most workable. Most elders are not going to be theologians in the same way that their pastors are and that should not be the goal. The goal is good family men who rule well their households and have the graces and gifts needed for service in the eldership. That which is accidental in a ruling elder (he's a great teacher, speaker, counselor, etc.) must not become the requirement for what is essential (a godly lay leader). When that happens, many men who would be good elders are kept out of the office because the requirement for ruling elder has become something too close to "a minister who also happens to work in the world." Hodge wanted the courts to be populated by those of the clerical order joining together with those of the lay order for the most fruitful joint governance of Christ's church.

7.8 Concluding Matters

As noted above, the key difference between Hodge and certain others in the Old School was over the definition of Presbyterianism. Thornwell and others insisted that Scriptures defined Presbyterianism in detail. Hodge and most of the Presbyterian Church demurred from this view, believing that Scripture clearly taught Presbyterianism in its principles and not in detail. Contrariwise, Hodge believed that Scripture determined doctrine in detail, either implicitly or explicitly, as expressed in the church's doctrinal standards. He also believed that Scripture prescribed the elements of worship, as expressed in what came to be called the regulative principle of worship in the twentieth century. Hodge worked on a committee, chaired by Thornwell, revising parts of the Church Order. Hodge thus knew, as did Thornwell, that what constituted the Book of Discipline was a reasoned development of Scripture principles, a sound practical application, from the matters addressed therein.

The government and discipline of the church, in other words, involved a level of discretion that is not present in setting forth the doctrine of the church or the prescriptions for divine worship. Anyone who thinks that the Presbyterian church has ever had, in any of its branches, a form of government and book of discipline that in all its particulars reflects a regulative principle of government and discipline of the same sort that obtains in the secondary standards, or our worship prescriptions, has not attended well to the actual history of the Presbyterian church. Church orders typically contain a sort of pragmatic "what's the best way agreed upon together to carry out this work?" that markedly differs from the doctrinal standards, which give expression to the system of doctrine contained in God's Word or the elements that Presbyterians believe are properly constitutive of divine worship.

Hodge further, to conclude with his view of church office, found ample biblical and historical warrant for his view of the synonymy of bishop and presbyter, with neither referring to what comes to be called "ruling elders." If his warrant, then, for the office of ruling elder is thought to be weak (an understandable conclusion), then the warrant for such throughout the church's history may simply not be as strong for this as many of us would like. That does not mean, however, that we must, like Witherow or Merkle, conclude that the one office of bishop/presbyter includes what we now call ministers and ruling elders. Gillespie, classically, and Thornwell, as Hodge's contemporary, better construct the view that bishop/presbyter encompasses teaching and ruling elders. Given where Witherow and others come down on this, it seems hard to escape Witherow's claim that all elders can preach and administer the sacraments, and that it isa matter of gifting and organization that limits it to the "teaching" elder.[116]

Hodge saw the offices of minister and elder as distinct offices. He was especially concerned that if they are not viewed this way, then the elder will come to be seen in the same light as the minister. For Hodge, if the elder held the same office as the minister, this meant that there would only one governing office in the church, and it defaults in a clerical direction, leaving the people unrepresented in the councils of the church. Hodge believed that if the "one office" of bishop and presbyter defaulted in the direction that the ruling elder is seen as a bishop, then all ecclesiastical rule would be regarded as clerical.

The genius of Presbyterianism as he saw it—the clergy (men called of God to be ministers of Word and Sacrament) joining with the representatives of the laity (the ruling eldership)—would be lost and a functional prelacy would prevail. If it were to move the other way, If the opposite were to prevail—that all church rule was lay not clerical==Hodge would view that t as a functional Congregationalism. He wanted what he regarded to be a proper church government: ministers joining with representatives of the people in the joint government of the church, a rule neither Episcopal nor Congregational, but truly Presbyterian. For Hodge this was *iure divino* Presbyterianism, and he is both a leader in and part of the honored tradition of those who have seen office and Presbyterianism in that same light.

116 Witherow, 132–33.

Works Cited

Bannerman, Douglas. *The Scripture Doctrine of the Church* (Edinburgh: T&T Clark, 1887).

Breckenridge, Robert J. , "Presbyterian Government Not a Hierarchy, But a Commonwealth," *Southern Presbyterian Review.* 33.2 (April 1882).

Breckenridge, Robert J. "Presbyterian Ordination Not a Charm, But an Act of Government," *Southern Presbyterian Review.* 33.3 (July 1882).

Brown, Mark R. *Order in the Offices: Essays Defining the Roles of Church Officers* (Duncansville, PA: Classic Presbyterian Government Resources, 1993).

Burtchaell, James Tunstead. *From Synagogue to Church: Public Services and Offices in the Earliest Christian Communities* (Cambridge: Cambridge University Press, 1992).

Calvin, John. *Institutes of the Christian Religion*, 2 vv., (Battles translation), John T. McNeill, ed. (rpb., Louisville, KY: Westminster John Knox Press, 1960).

Calvin, John. *The Necessity of Reforming the Church* (1536; rpt., Audubon, NJ: Old Path Publications, 1994).

Campbell, Peter Colin. *The Theory of Ruling Eldership or The Position of the Lay Ruler in the Reformed Churches Examined* (Edinburgh and London: William Blackwood and Sons, 1866).

Campbell, R. Alastair. *The Elders: Seniority within Earliest Christianity* (Edinburgh: T&T Clark, 1994).

Clowney, Edmund P. "Answer to the Complaint in re: Laying-on of hands in the Presbytery of New Jersey (OPC)," in *Minutes of the PNJ*, v. 3 (Feb. 23, 1963).

Coffey, John. *Politics, Religion, and the British Revolutions: The Mind of Samuel Rutherford* (Cambridge: Cambridge University Press, 1997).

Dabney, Robert L. *Discussions: Evangelical and Theological, v. 2* (1891; rpt., London: Banner of Truth Trust, 1967).

De Witt, John Richard. *Jus Divinum: The Westminster Assembly and the Divine Right of Church Government* (Kampen: J.H. Kok, 1969).

Edwards, David L. *Christian England*, v. 2., *From the Reformation to the 18th century* (Grand Rapids: Eerdmans, 1983).

The First and Second Books of Discipline (rpt., Dallas: Presbyterian Heritage Publications, 1993).

Form of Government, in *The Book of Church Order of the Orthodox Presbyterian Church* (Willow Grove, PA: Committee on Christian Education of the OPC, 2020).

Form of Presbyterial Church Government in *The Westminster Confession of Faith* (1645; republished, Glasgow: Free Presbyterian Publications, 1994).

The Genevan Ecclesiastical Ordinances in P.E. Hughes, ed., *The Register of the Company of Pastors of Geneva in the Time of Calvin* (Grand Rapids: Eerdmans, 1966).

Gillespie, George. *A Dispute Against the English Popish Ceremonies Obtruded on the Church of Scotland* (1637).

Gillespie, George. *Aaron's Rod Blossoming, or the Divine Ordinance of Church Government Vindicated* (London, 1646).

Gillespie, George. *An Assertion of the Government of the Church of Scotland, in the Points of Ruling Elders, and of the Authority of Presbyteries and Synods* (Edinburgh, 1641).

Grimes, Dee Aleasha. "God's Imposition: The Centrality of Vocation in the Spirituality of William Perkins," Ph.D. diss., The Southern Baptist Theological Seminary, 2021.

Gutjahr, Paul C. *Charles Hodge: Guardian of American Orthodoxy* (New York: Oxford University Press, 2011).

Hart, D.G. and John R. Muether, *Seeking a Better Country: 300 Years of American Presbyterianism* (Phillipsburg, NJ: P&R Publishing, 2007).

Hodge, A. A. *Life of Charles Hodge*, (London: T. Nelson and Sons, 1881).

Hodge, Charles. *The Church and its Polity* (London: Thomas Nelson Sons, 1879).

Hodge, Charles. *The Constitution of the Presbyterian Church in the United States of America*, 1821 ed, rev. 1833 (Philadelphia: Presbyterian Board of Publication, 1839).

Hodge, Charles. *The Name, Nature, and Functions of Ruling Elders* (New York: Wiley and Putnam, 1845).

Hodge, Charles. *What is Presbyterianism?* (Philadelphia: Presbyterian Board of Publication, 1855).

Hodge, J. Aspinwall. *What is Presbyterian Law as Defined by the Church Courts?* (Philadelphia: Presbyterian Board of Education, 1882).

Hoffecker, W. Andrew. *Charles Hodge: The Pride of Princeton* (Phillipsburg, NJ: P&R Publishing, 2011).

Irons, Lee. "Theories of Eldership: A Study in Presbyterian Polity," (unpublished paper).

Isbell, Sherman. *Ordained Servant* vol. 4, no. 4 (October 1995).

Lightfoot, J.B. *St. Paul's Epistle to the Philippians* (1868; republished, Lynn, MA: Hendrickson Publishers Inc., 1981).

Loetscher, Lefferts A. *A Brief History of the Presbyterians*, 4th ed. (Philadelphia: The Westminster Press, 1978).

Macleod, John. *Scottish Theology in Relation to Church History Since the Reformation*, 3rd ed. (Edinburgh: Knox Press, 1973).

McKay, W.D.J. *An Ecclesiastical Republic, Church Government in the Writings of George Gillespie* (Edinburgh: Rutherford House, 1997).

Merkle, Benjamin L. *The Elder and Overseer: One Office in the Early Church* (New York: Peter Lang, 2003).

Miller, Samuel. *The Ruling Elder* (1832; republished, Dallas, TX: Presbyterian Heritage Publications, 1987).

Murray, Iain H. "The Problem of the 'Eldership' and Its Wider Implications," in *The Banner of Truth* (magazine), issue 395–396 (August/September 1996).

Paul, Robert S. *The Assembly of the Lord: Politics and Religion in the Westminster Assembly and the Grand Debate* (Edinburgh: T&T Clark, 1985).

Perkins, William. *The Works of William Perkins*, edited by J. Stephen Yuille, v.10, "Treatise on Vocations" (Grand Rapids, Michigan: Reformation Heritage Books, 2014-).

Powell, Hunter. *The Crisis of British Protestantism: Church Power in the Puritan Revolution, 1638–44* (Manchester: Manchester University Press, 2015).

Rayburn, Robert. "Ministers, Elders, Deacons," in *Order in the Offices*, ed. by Mark Brown (Duncansville, PA: Classic Presbyterian Government Resources, 1993).

Robinson, Stuart. *The Church of God as an Essential Element of the Gospel* (1858; rpt., Willow Grove, PA: Committee on Christian Education of the Orthodox Presbyterian Church, 2009).

Rutherford, Samuel. *A Peaceable and Temperate Plea for Paul's Presbytery in Scotland* (London, 1642).

Rutherford, Samuel. *The Divine Right of Church Government and Excommunication* (London, 1646).

Rutherford, Samuel. *The Due Right of Presbyteries, or a Peaceable Plea for the Government of the Church of Scotland* (London, 1644).

Smith, Thomas. *The Name, Nature, and Functions of Ruling Elders* (New York: Wiley and Putnam, 1845).

Stewart, Alistair C. *The Original Bishops: Office and Order in the First Christian Communities* (Grand Rapids: Baker Academic, 2014).

Strange, Alan D. "Do the Minister and Elder Hold the Same Office?" *Ordained Servant* (Dec. 2013).

Strange, Alan D. *The Doctrine of the Spirituality of the Church in the Ecclesiology of Charles Hodge* (Phillipsburg, NJ: P&R Publishing, 2017).

Strange, Alan D. *The Imputation of the Active Obedience of Christ in the Westminster Standards* (Grand Rapids: Reformation Heritage Books, 2019).

Thornwell, James Henley. *The Collected Writings of James Henley Thornwell, vol. IV: Ecclesiastical* (1875; reprint, Edinburgh: Banner of Truth Trust, 1974).

Torrance, Thomas F. *Scottish Theology: From John Knox to John McLeod* Campbell (Edinburgh: T&T Clark, 1996).

Torrance, T. F. "The Eldership in the Reformed Church," *Scottish Journal of Theology* 37.4 (1984).

Troxel, A. Craig. "Divine Right Presbyterianism and Church Power," PhD. Dissertation, Westminster Theological Seminary, 1998.

Turretin, Francis. *Institutes of Elenctic Theology*, v. 3, translated by George Musgrave Giger, edited by James T. Dennison, Jr (Phillipsburg, NJ: P&R Publishing, 1997).

Van Dixhoorn, *The Minutes and Papers of the Westminster Assembly, 1642–1652*; 5 vv. (Oxford: Oxford University Press, 2012).

Van Dixhoorn, Chad. "Presbyterian Ecclesiologies at the Westminster Assembly," in *Church Polity and Politics in the British Atlantic World, c. 1635–66* (Manchester, GB: Manchester University Press, 2020).

Vance, John Lloyd. "The Ecclesiology of James Henley Thornwell: An Old Southern Presbyterian Theologian," Ph.D. Dissertation, Drew University, 1990.

Wallace, Peter J. "The Bond of Union": The Old School Presbyterian Church and the American Nation" (Ph. Dissertation, University of Notre Dame, 2004).

Wingard, Brian. "As the Lord Puts Words in Her Mouth: The Supremacy of Scripture in the Ecclesiology of James Henley Thornwell and its Influence upon the Presbyterian Church of the South," Ph.D. Dissertation, Westminster Theological Seminary, 1992.

Witherow, Thomas. *The Apostolic Church* in *I Will Build My Church,* ed. by Jonathan Gibson (1869 ed., rpb., Glenside, PA: Westminster Seminary Press, 2021).

Mark Herzer

8. Recasting Baptism: Charles Hodge and the Validity of Roman Catholic Baptism

Many Presbyterians and historians are aware about the baptism debate between Charles Hodge and James Henley Thornwell. Some have formed their own opinions on the debate, either from having read the literature surrounding this controversial issue, or from their own studied convictions. Many recognize that the debate includes historical precedents and, more importantly, that the issue hinges on how we interpret the writings of previous relevant theologians. This essay will focus primarily on Hodge's use of Reformed orthodox writers to support his position on the validity of Roman Catholic baptism, while analyzing his own unique arguments for his position. As the title implies, he did not necessarily follow older Reformed authors slavishly or without some modifications to their arguments. I will argue that though he heavily used Protestant scholastic writers, as well as Calvin and the Reformed symbols, Hodge's own unique ecclesiastical theories served as an important animus for the position he advanced. These observations will enable readers both to understand Hodge's position on Roman Catholic baptism in its context, and provide a broader picture of continuities and discontinuities in Reformed theology up to Hodge's nineteenth century American context.

8.1 Circumstances Surrounding the Debate

In 1845, the PCUSA General Assembly met in Cincinnati, Ohio. One of the motions entertained by that Assembly was, "Shall the inquiry of the Presbytery of Ohio, 'Is baptism in the Church of Rome valid?' be answered in the negative?" The Assembly voted 173 in the affirmative and 8 in the negative. That meant the Assembly affirmed Ohio Presbytery's question by declaring that Rome's baptism was indeed invalid. Included in the majority vote was James Henley Thornwell (1812–1862) who argued for the majority position on the floor.[1]

---

1 For the actual minutes of that Assembly regarding this motion and the count, see C. N. Willborn, "Hodge and Thornwell: 'Princes in Israel'," *The Confessional Presbyterian* 8 (2012): 52 n20. Cf. Andrew W. Hoffecker, *Charles Hodge: The Pride of Princeton*, American Reformed Biographies (Phillipsburg: P & R Publishing, 2011), 248. Hodge stated it was 169–8 and Hoffecker probably mistyped it as 169–68. The error is repeated in A. A. Hodge, *The Life of Charles Hodge, D.D., LL.D., Professor in the Theological*

For some reason, Charles Hodge did not attend the Assembly that year, but he wrote about the General Assembly's decision a few months later. He confessed that he felt "almost overwhelmed" by the vote and, while recognizing the need to respect the decision given such a large majority by which the motion passed, he believed that it "almost imposes silence on all dissentients." Yet he wondered what "new light" had been discovered on this question since the vote would make "Calvin, Luther, and all the men of that generation… to have lived and died unbaptized?"[2] In the end, Hodge chose to take up the pen against the Assembly's decision, believing firmly in the validity of Roman Catholic baptism.

In 1846 Thornwell wrote against Hodge's essay in a series of articles first published in the *Watchman and Observer*.[3] Before Thornwell had finished publishing his position, Charles Hodge wrote another essay that year answering the following question, "Whether the church of Rome is still a portion of the visible church of Christ?"[4] This question intimately relates to the 1845 General Assembly's decision on the validity of Roman Catholic baptism, although they are two distinct questions, because the Assembly had rejected Roman Catholic baptism on the grounds that the Roman Catholic church did not belong to the visible church. While Hodge responded to the Assembly's action in 1845 directly, he addressed a specific author whom he called "Theophilus" in the second article in 1846. Theophilus seems to have been a pen name and Hodge never mentions who he really was, if he even knew. By the time Hodge wrote the second essay, twelve articles had been written by Theophilus, which prompted the topic of Hodge's reply.[5] It appears that the

---

Seminary, Princeton, N. J. (New York: Charles Scribner's Sons, 1880), 340. However, Calhoun rightly noted that it was 173–8, see David B. Calhoun, *Princeton Seminary: Faith and Learning 1812–1868* (Carlisle: Banner of Truth, 1994), 304.

2 Charles Hodge, *Discussions in Church Polity*, ed. William Durant (New York: Charles Scribner's Sons, 1878), 192 (hereafter, *DCP*). This volume reproduced the original article which Hodge wrote, "The General Assembly," *The Biblical Repertory and Princeton Review* 17:3 (July 1845): 428–471 (hereafter, "General Assembly").

3 The same was republished in three parts in *The Southern Presbyterian Review* (July and October of 1851 and January of 1852). Those three essays were finally combined and reproduced into one essay in his collected works. I will be citing from James Henley Thornwell, "The Validity of the Baptism of the Church of Rome," in *The Collected Writings of James Henley Thornwell* (1875; repr., Carlisle, PA: The Banner of Truth Trust, 1986), 3:283–412.

4 "Review of Essays in the Presbyterian by Theophilus on the Question: Is Baptism in the Church of Rome Valid?," *The Biblical Repertory and Princeton Review* 18:3 (July 1846): 320 (hereafter, "Theophilus"). Theophilus had not finish the series of his articles in *The Presbyterian* before Hodge wrote his second essay.

5 Hodge, "Theophilus," 320–321: "After writing ten weeks he is but approaching the subject.… In the meantime the topic discussed by Theophilus in his eleventh and twelfth numbers, is so important in itself and so intimately connected with this whole subject, that we have determined to devote a

pseudonymous author penned at least fourteen articles.[6] The title of the connected articles, presented in fourteen parts, was, "Is Baptism in the Church of Rome Valid?"[7] Hodge's second article interacts predominantly with Theophilus and very little with Thornwell, who was often his major opponent in theological debates such as this one. He knew Thornwell was working on a series of essays on the validity of Roman Catholic baptism, but he chose to not interact with them because Thornwell had not yet completed his series. Hodge wrote, "Our respect for the writer in the Watchman, and for the thoroughness and ability which distinguish his opening numbers, imposes on us the duty of silence as to the main point in dispute, until his series of articles is completed."[8] Hodge never ended up engaging directly with Thornwell's thorough expositions of this topic. The editors of Thornwell's *Collected Writings* made that very point, which many subsequent writers have overlooked, noting that, "No reply appeared from the other side."[9] Hodge, in this 1846 article, interacted with Theophilus extensively (citing him at least seventeen times) and refers to Thornwell only four times, all four with reference to Thornwell's argument

---

few pages to the consideration of the question, Whether the church of Rome is still a portion of the visible church of Christ?"

6 I could not find anything beyond the fourteenth article. No. XIV (April 4, 1846) ends with the author saying "...we want to suspend operations for a time or two. We are tired, and our readers probably more so." He still wanted to answer a "few objections and difficulties." Mark Alan Reynolds lists only thirteen articles in his dissertation, "Charles Hodge's Ecclesiastical Elenctics: His Response to Catholicizing Tendencies in the Churches, 1837–1860" (Ph.D. Dissertation, Saint Louis University, 2000), 104. The first article is not in the January edition as he suggests.

7 These are numbered articles in *The Presbyterian*: No. II (Jan. 3, 1846); No. III (Jan. 10, 1846); No. IV (Jan. 17, 1846); No. V (Jan. 24, 1846); No. VI (Jan. 31, 1846); No. VII (Feb. 7, 1846); No. VIII (Feb. 14, 1846); No. IX (Feb. 21, 1846); No. X (Feb. 28, 1846); No. XI (March 7, 1846); No. XII (March 14, 1846); No. XIII (March 21, 1846); No. XIV (April 4, 1846). I could not find No. I, but there was a short notice entitled "Is the Church of Rome a Church of Christ?" penned by N. E. Puritan [New England? Puritan] on Sept. 6, 1845. I do not know if that was the first article. However, included in *The Presbyterian*, when No. II was published, is an editorial notice entitled "Baptism in the Church of Rome," in which the editor was "gratified" that someone capable was willing to write against "the doctrine of the Biblical Repertory." The editor clearly had in mind Theophilus's articles.

8 Hodge, "Theophilus," 320.

9 Thornwell, *Collected Writings*, 3:279. Fesko stated that Hodge's second article in 1846 was a "rejoiner to Thornwell," but the actual title of the article clearly indicated Hodge was interacting with Theophilus. See J. V. Fesko, *Word, Water and Spirit: A Reformed Perspective on Baptism* (Grand Rapids: Reformation Heritage Books, 2010), 382. Thornwell wrote against Hodge, but Hodge wrote principally against the 1845 General Assembly (which would include Thornwell) and Theophilus. Hodge did not interact with Thornwell's writings on Roman Catholic baptism in 1846 (or any time after). William Shea mistakenly wrote that Thornwell did not respond to Hodge until 1851 and this error complicates his argument, see William M. Shea, *The Lion and the Lamb: Evangelicals and Catholics in America* (Oxford: Oxford University Press, 2004), 127–131.

at the 1845 General Assembly rather than to his more extended treatments of the topic, leaving this large work unanswered for unknown reasons.

By April of 1846, Hodge was well aware of the general response to his 1845 article. In a very understated manner, he began the article with, "It is very plain that our remarks, in our number for July last, in favour of the validity of Romish baptism, have not met the approbation of a large portion of our brethren. This, though a matter of regret, is not a matter of surprise."[10] He knew he represented a very small minority in his church at that time, but he remained unshaken in his position. Part of his confidence stemmed from the conviction that his position aligned with the Reformers and the subsequent generations. He believed the Reformed forefathers taught the same position as his own regarding the question whether Rome belonged to the visible church of Christ. Hodge knew that both questions (the validity of RC baptism and Rome being part of the visible church) had firm historical support, both from the Reformers and other later established Reformed orthodox stalwarts.

We will see that this Princeton theologian ably substantiated his claims regarding historical precedent for his views, but we will also notice that his perspective was unique in some respects, expanding earlier ideas. We have no evidence that the position for which he argued in the mid 1840s changed throughout his life. What became clearer and more pronounced was his unique ecclesiastical theory that undergirded his position.

8.2 Reformed Orthodoxy and Charles Hodge

Was Charles Hodge in any way influenced by Reformed orthodoxy in his theology in relation to the validity of Roman Catholic baptism? Regarding the scholastic influence on Hodge's theology generally, scholars like Richard Muller already addressed this matter. He aptly summarized Charles Hodge's use of Reformed orthodox scholasticism in these words, "The great American system of theology that developed at Princeton Seminary during the mid-nineteenth century around the thought of Charles Hodge was, in its form and method, a revival and modernization of the Reformed orthodox scholasticism of the seventeenth century."[11] Muller noted how Reformed orthodoxy also influenced Hodge's contemporaries, such as R. L. Dabney (1820–1898) and A. A. Hodge (1823–1886). It is well known that Charles Hodge drew heavily on Francis Turretin's (1623–1687) *Institutio Theologiae Elencticae* (1679–1685), and that he attempted "to recast the systematic insights

10 Hodge, "Theophilus," 320.

11 Richard A. Muller, "Giving Direction to Theology: The Scholastic Dimension," *JETS* 28 (1985): 186. Bavinck made a similar observation, *Reformed Dogmatics*, trans. by John Vriend, 4 vols. (Grand Rapids: Baker Academic, 2003–2008), 1:202.

of orthodoxy in a nineteenth-century mold."[12] Hodge's use of Turretin in his *Systematic Theology* cannot be denied, since explicit references to it abound. In fact, he wrote to one of his most accomplished students, William Plumer (1802–1880), that, "Turretine's *Institutes* I regard as incomparably the best book as a whole on systematic theology..."[13] But what about the topic before us? Was he influenced by Turretin, or other Reformed orthodox authors, on this matter of Roman Catholic baptism?

Hodge used Turretin by name in the two articles we will be analyzing, and he wholeheartedly depended on the critical distinctions Turretin made in relation to these questions. Though Hodge carefully utilized him, he did not slavishly follow Turretin when expanding his answers, however. His robust defense of Roman Catholic baptism and Rome's place in the visible church found initial support in Turretin's own arguments, but the final product of his answer did not necessarily look as though Turretin influenced him at every point. One nineteenth-century writer reviewing Hodge's publications criticized him for using the orthodox language of the Westminster Confession of Faith while changing or redefining the meaning of their terms. This anonymous author wrote that Dr. Hodge "retains the words, indeed, but gives a tortuous and uncandid explanation of them."[14] Though the reviewer wrote about a different theological topic, that reviewer's estimate could apply to the subject before us. Hodge indeed used the language and many of the categories of Reformed orthodoxy, but his peculiar ecclesiology stamped a different tincture on the doctrine he defended.

In his first article treating the validity of Roman Catholic baptism, Hodge cited Turretin a few times, as well as the French theologian Benedict Pictet (1655–1724), and the Dutch Bernardinus De Moor (1709–1780), both from the late Reformed orthodoxy period,[15] using them to support the consensus opinion since the Reformation regarding the validity of Roman Catholic baptism. Pictet, referenced by Hodge but not specifically quoted, wrote the following:

---

12 Richard A. Muller, *Post-Reformation Reformed Dogmatics: The Rise and Development of Reformed Orthodoxy, ca. 1520 to ca. 1725*, 4 vols. (Grand Rapids: Baker Academic, 2003), 1:29. See also Paul C. Gutjahr, *Charles Hodge: Guardian of American Orthodoxy* (Oxford: Oxford University Press, 2011), 70, 214.

13 A. A. Hodge, *Life*, 391. For further examples of post-Reformation Reformed and Lutheran authors on whom Hodge relied, see chapter 3 of this present volume.

14 Anon., "Writings of Dr. Charles Hodge of Princeton," *Bibliotheca Sacra* 36 (July 1879): 585. The article reviews Hodge's *Discussions in Church Polity* and the reviewer objected to Hodge's own understanding of what "all mankind sinned in Adam" meant.

15 Hodge, "General Assembly," 447, 457, 459, 466.

> Another question is, whether that baptism is lawful, which is administered by heretics. We reply, that a distinction must be made between those heretics who corrupt the substance of baptism, and omit or alter the form of the institution, and those who retain the essentials, and maintain the true doctrine of the Trinity, though they err in other points of doctrine, as did formerly the Novatians and Donatists, and in the present age, the papists. With respect to the former class of heretics, we say that baptism administered by them is not lawful: for this reason the baptism of those Arians was rejected, who baptized *in the name of the Father, as the true God, of Jesus Christ, as the Saviour, and a creature, and in the Holy Ghost, as the servant of both* ...With respect to the other class of heretics, who retain the essentials of baptism, not changing or corrupting the form, we maintain that baptism administered by these, is valid and lawful: for, although they are not true members of the church, this does not prevent them from lawfully baptizing, provided they retain the essentials of the ordinance; since in the performance of the rite, they merely lend their hand and tongue to the Lord, who himself baptizes, and works through their instrumentality.[16]

Pictet's explanation very closely mirrors Turretin's, both of whom accepted Roman Catholic baptism on these grounds.[17] Both argued that the baptism of heretics could be accepted, provided they retained "the essentials" of the faith. Arian baptism and others were rejected because they denied the full orthodox doctrine of the Trinity, making Trinitarian orthodoxy an essential hinge of the argument for identifying valid baptisms. This perfectly supported Hodge's arguments, since "papists" retained the "essentials" and "maintain the true doctrine of the Trinity." Hodge also cited one of the champions of Lutheran orthodoxy, Johann Gerhard (1582–1637), to add support to his argument along similar lines.[18] From these references and others Hodge drew this conclusion, "It is therefore, the doctrine of the universal church, that baptism administered in the name of the Trinity, by one professing faith in that doctrine, is not void on account of heresy."[19] Thus Trinitarian doctrine was the key identifier of a valid baptism, dwarfing other considerations.

---

16 Benedict Pictet, *Christian Theology*, trans. Frederick Reyroux (Philadelphia: Presbyterian Board of Publication, n.d.), 417–418. It should be noted, the edition of this book being cited has the following bracketed footnote that is of particular interest to the subject at hand: "[The General Assembly of the Presbyterian Church, at their Session in May, 1845, decided the question "Is Baptism in the Church of Rome valid?" in the negative, by a vote of 173 to 8.—*Note by the Editor of the Board of Publication.*]" The vote tally we mentioned above perfectly matches the editorial footnote.

17 Hodge cites Turretin in "General Assembly," 447. See Francis Turretin, *Institutes of Elenctic Theology*, translated by G. M. Giger, 3 vols. (Phillipsburg, NJ: R&R Publishing, 1992–1997), 19.15.3.

18 Hodge, "General Assembly," 447. J. Gerhard ranks as the third most respected theologian within Lutheranism, following Luther and Chemnitz. See Robert D. Preus, *The Theology of Post-Reformation Lutheranism*, 2 vols. (Concordia Publishing House: St. Louis, 1970), 1:52–53, 107–143.

19 Hodge, "General Assembly," 447.

Expanding this idea, Hodge argued that three things were "essential to baptism; the matter, form, and intention." The matter is "the washing with water."[20] Hodge was surprised by Thornwell's charge that Rome mixed water with oil.[21] But Theophilus argued the same and charged that the "Repertory" was "incorrect in point of fact." Even against Hodge's contention that "water with oil… is still water," Theophilus retorted, "Water with sulphuric [sic] acid, or arsenic thrown upon it, is not water."[22] It appears both Thornwell and Theophilus raised this objection as one of the reasons to invalidate Rome's baptism, but Hodge brushed it off as inconsequential. He argued that additions to the water did not change the essence of the washing of water, which was essential to valid baptism.

Secondly, the correct form of a valid baptism required the "washing in the name of the Trinity."[23] Hodge argued that this form "is identical with our own," and that the words and the "avowed sense" of those words were orthodox. No Lutheran or Reformed churches held to the doctrine of the Trinity more "accurately, thoroughly or minutely" than Rome. In fact, Hodge ventured to add, "There is no such thing as baptism in the name of the Trinity in any church, if Romish baptism is not."[24] For Hodge, this point was both unassailable and fundamental with regard to valid baptisms. The above referenced scholastic divines and others like them dealt with this point at length, and Hodge and they thus far agree. Interestingly, however, the writers of *Synopsis Purioris Theologiae* noted that the mere use of the Trinitarian formula must not be accepted in itself, primarily on historical grounds. For example, Paulinists (followers of Paul of Samosata) used the Trinitarian formula in baptism, but the Council of Nicaea (325 AD) invalidated their baptisms due to their heterodox doctrine of the Trinity. Paulinists' baptism came from "a church which is no church."[25] This illustrates that an orthodox theology of the Trinity was more important to the validity of baptism than was the mere use of the Triune name.

Hodge did not utilize orthodox theologians to support the third essential matter of baptism, dealing with "intention" or design in baptism. The Westminster Standards stated that the design of the Sacrament "is to signify, seal and apply to believers the benefits of the new covenant." Hodge added that, "This is the precise

---

20 Hodge, "General Assembly," 448–449.

21 Hodge, "General Assembly," 449.

22 Theophilus, "Is Baptism in the Church of Rome Valid? No. IX," *The Presbyterian* 16 (Feb. 21, 1846). Hodge would have read this essay since he had access up to the twelfth article when he penned his 1846 article.

23 Hodge, "General Assembly," 448.

24 Hodge, "General Assembly," 450. This assertion about Roman Catholic views of the Trinity is interesting in light of his treatment of the Trinity (see chapter 5 of the present volume), where he vigorously rejected medieval views of person as relation of origin or communication of essence.

25 Harm Goris, ed. *Synopsis Purioris Theologiae / Synopsis of a Purer Theology*, trans. Riemer A. Faber, 3 Vols. (Leiden: Brill, 2014–2020), 3:143.

doctrine of the Romanists, so far as this."[26] Yet Theophilus noted that the Council of Trent anathematized precisely this view in the sixth and eighth canon on the sacraments.[27] He added:

> Here we have strong points of contrast. The Bible, and our Confession, say, Baptism is a *sign* and *seal* of grace. Rome says, it is the grace *itself*. The Bible affirms that it is by faith through the working of the Spirit, that the grace results; Rome, that the water hath power to sanctify. The Bible, that the sign and seal are separable from the thing signified — baptism is not necessary to salvation: Rome denies this and affirms it is indispensable to salvation. The Bible makes the essential substance of ordinance to consist, thus, in signifying, representing and sealing to the believer, the righteousness and grace of Christ: but Rome makes it work grace, not by faith, but by its own inherent operation—The baptizer gives, confers, and works grace in the baptized.[28]

Charles Hodge had the above objection within his purview, and yet he never responded to it.[29] The whole intent of baptism differed between the Reformed and Roman Catholic churches, and to this writer, this constitutes a weighty unanswered objection against Hodge's argumentation. Changing the intent of Christ in the sacrament constituted a change in the nature of the sacrament itself, rendering it something other than Christ's command to the church.

Standing behind all three of these matters was the question as to whether or not Rome was a true part of the visible church. Hodge heavily appealed to Turretin when answering the question, is "Rome is a true church?"[30] Turretin wrote that Rome was, in one sense, a Christian church, while in another sense she was not. Hodge believed this lacked the necessary nuanced distinctions he expected from Turretin,

---

26 Hodge, "General Assembly," 450.

27 Theophilus cites the following from the Council of Trent: "Whoever shall affirm that the sacraments of the new law do not contain the grace which they signify, or that they do not confer that grace on those who place no obstacle in the way; as if they were only the external signs of grace, or righteousness received by faith, and marks of Christian profession, whereby the faithful are distinguished from unbelievers; let him be accursed… Whoever shall affirm that grace is not conferred by these sacraments of the new law, by their own power, [*ex opera operato*;] but that faith in the divine promise is all that is necessary to obtain grace; let him be accursed." Cf. Hendricus Denzinger, *The Sources of Catholic Dogma*, translated by Roy J. Deferrari (Fitzwilliam, NH: Loreto Publications, 1955), 263–263.

28 Theophilus, "Is Baptism in the Church of Rome Valid? No. IX."

29 Thornwell had raised the same objection and as noted, Hodge never interacted with Thornwell's position. Thornwell indicated that sacraments were *means* of grace while Rome made them the *causes* of grace. They were not *signs* but *efficient agents* of grace (*Collected Writings*, 3:305–306).

30 Hodge, "General Assembly," 466–467. He appeals to the same passage in Turretin's *Institutes* in the second article.

but nevertheless it conveyed the necessary truth. Hodge observed, "We admit that it is a very unfortunate method of speaking, to say a body is a church secundum quid, and secundum quid is not a church. Still, this is an inconvenience we have to submit to on almost all subjects, and in the present instance, it expresses a great truth."[31] Hodge's point should not be missed. He leaned on the careful theological distinction Turretin made since "it expresses a great truth." Yet Hodge was not satisfied by the question ("What is a church?") because of the infelicitous way of affirming and denying the same proposition. That answer revealed that the question was not well framed. He said, "The necessity of making these distinctions, of affirming and denying the same proposition, show the impropriety of the question."[32] He asked what he believed to be a better question: "Instead of asking, What is a church? we should ask, What is a pure church? All the definitions given in our books, tell us what a pure church is." All Reformed divines, Hodge believed, would state that Rome was not a pure church, but they would also affirm Rome to be a true church *in some sense.*

The General Assembly, Hodge surmised, affirmed that Rome was not a pure church because she could not possibly state that "Rome is in no sense a church" given all that Rome believed. For that reason, Hodge believed that the General Assembly's foundation for their decision was "false" because she assumed what was patently false, namely, "the church of Rome is in no sense a church."[33] Rome may not be a pure church, but she is still a church *in some sense*, Hodge argued. Again, Turretin made this exact point, albeit in a more complex manner, and Hodge deftly incorporated that same point into his own argument.

In this first article, Hodge built on Turretin's distinctions, and Turretin's scholastic influence remains obvious. Hodge had full support of the orthodox divines when it came to validity of Roman Catholic baptism and and the idea that Rome was, in some sense, a true but impure church. However, Hodge brought out a unique element in advancing Rome's inclusion in the church. Not surprisingly, he did not quote any of the orthodox writers to advance this peculiar element. He contended "that baptism does not initiate the recipient into any particular church, but into the church catholic." He argued against the assumption that "baptism is an act of a church; or that the administrator so acts in the name of the organized society

---

31 Hodge, "General Assembly," 467.

32 Hodge, "General Assembly," 467–468. He said the same in the next article: "This distinction is natural and just, though it imposes the necessity of affirming and denying the same proposition… …People will not trouble themselves, however, with such distinctions, though they often unconsciously make them and are forced to act upon them" ("Theophilus," 336).

33 Hodge, "General Assembly," 468.

to which he belongs."[34] This, we will see, raises some interesting problems, but he concludes the point with the following statement:

> It follows from this that the validity of baptism does not depend upon the character of the particular denomination to which the administrator belongs; because he does not act in the name of that denomination, but as a member of the church catholic. And every man who professes saving truth is a member of that church. It matters not therefore whether the Quakers as a society come within the definition of a church; individual Quakers, if they have the faith of God's elect and profess it, are members of his church. And so too it matters not whether the papacy comes within the definition of a church; individual papists, if they profess that Jesus is the Son of God, are within the pale of the church catholic, and, if they have public authority, may baptize in the name of Christ.[35]

The last sentence almost disregards everything for which Hodge had argued thus far. All of sudden accepting Rome's baptism and including her in the visible church seemed irrelevant. Hodge seems to be arguing that as long as the person "professes saving truth," then it does not matter if he or she received baptism in the visible church catholic. He appears to have made his arguments for the validity of Roman Catholic baptism hinge on the doctrine of the Trinity and on Rome's part in the visible church, but then appears to shift to resting its validity on individual faith regardless of church affiliation or status. Two things emerge from Hodge's statement. First of all, the person is baptized into the "church catholic" and not into a visible "organized society" or "into any particular church." Secondly, the one administering the baptism must be a member of the "church catholic" irrespective of denominational or sectarian affiliation. Hodge seems to say that the validity of baptism depends on the "administrator" or the one performing the baptism. Even "individual papists" could baptize if "they profess that Jesus is the Son of God, are within the pale of the church catholic" and "have public authority." That is, the one administering baptism has to be a member of the "church catholic" irrespective of the denomination or even if the church is not part of the visible church. The administrator must be part of the "church catholic," whether or not the church of which they are a part is.[36] Readers should remember that all Reformed orthodox writers had argued consistently that, to be valid, sacraments had to be administered in a

34 Hodge, "General Assembly," 468.

35 Hodge, "General Assembly," 469. We will interact with this more fully below.

36 On Oct. 4, 1845, Thornwell wrote to Dr. Breckinridge about Hodge's argument in the *Biblical Repertory* and, given the principles Hodge used to sustain "Popish baptism," Thornwell demurred, "Just let Tom, Dick, and Harry apply water, in the name of the Trinity, to the first person either shall meet on the street, and intend it to be a Christian baptism; and Christian baptism, according to Princeton, it is and must be." See B. M. Palmer, *The Life and Letters of James Henley Thornwell,*

true branch of the visible church. Though Hodge retained this idea, he appears to have redefined the presence of the visible church in terms of the faith of individual Christians rather than its objective traditional marks. At the very least, this appears to substitute the presence of a visibly professing Christian for a visibly confessing church.

The first point is curious because he makes such a radical distinction between the organized visible church and the universal or catholic church. The WCF 15.3 speaks of the "catholic visible church" with its order and ordinances, but Hodge makes the "church catholic" distinct from any "organized ...particular churches."[37] We will deal with this peculiar point in a different section below, but we need to note that Hodge never appealed to any Reformed authors to establish this point. This did not originate in Reformed scholasticism, constituting a subtle redefinition of the visible church.

Hodge's second point (regarding the one administering the baptism) differed substantially from men like Francis Turretin and Benedict Pictet as well. Turretin argued that a heretic could administer a valid baptism providing he retain the essentials of the ordinance. Turretin stated that even a secret heretic's baptism remained valid, provided that the church "thinks rightly" (i. e., retains orthodox doctrine of the Trinity) and that he used the proper "formula of Christ."[38] Pictet made the exact same point, noting, "But here we must remark, that the question is not concerning baptism administered by a pastor, who is heretical indeed, but secretly, in an orthodox church; for in this case baptism is lawful."[39] It is the church's orthodoxy and her existence in the visible church that matters, and not the administrator's personal and secret faith in the heart. The administrator's status before Christ is subjective, while the church's official standing is objective, as is the administrator's ordination in that church. Unless I am misreading Hodge, this comes close to veering into Donatism (namely, the administrator's own standing - for Hodge, that he be part of the church catholic - determines the validity of the baptism). Hodge already affirmed the truth of Pictet's statement, and yet he seems to undercut what he previously affirmed in this paragraph.[40] At the very least, tensions appear to exist in Hodge's arguments for what constituted valid baptisms.

D.D., LL.D. (Richmond: Whittet & Shepperson, 1875), 288. Thornwell clearly believed Hodge made baptism too easy and common.

37 Hodge, "General Assembly," 468: "After they were baptized, and thus introduced into the church catholic, they associated or organized themselves into particular churches."

38 Turretin, *Institutes*, 19.15.3. Ryan McGraw rightly argued that we should evaluate the church's public confession of faith in regarding a congregation or denomination's claim to be part of the true church, see his review of *Word, Water, and Spirit*, by J. V. Fesko, *The Confessional Presbyterian* 9 (2013): 194.

39 Pictet, *Christian Theology*, 417.

40 Hodge, "General Assembly," 447. We already quoted Hodge to that effect above.

A point I have not touch upon pertains the officers administering the baptism.[41] Should the Reformed church accept Romish priests as ordained ministers? This question is relevant because, in contrast to the Roman Catholic promotion of lay baptisms in cases of emergency, Reformed orthodox church consistently taught that lawfully ordained ministers alone could administer valid baptisms. Before engaging the argument regarding the valid ordination of Roman Catholic priests, Hodge threw in a complaint that stemmed from his understanding of ecclesiology. He wrote that "Christ has not made the ministry essential to the church" and, therefore, making administration by a lawfully ordained minister a condition of a validity of baptism was essentially a popish error, since Roman Catholics made ministry an essential constituting element of the church. He argued emphatically, "The being of a church does not depend upon the ministry, nor the being of the ministry on the rite of ordination. Any man is a minister in the sense of the proposition under consideration, who is recognised as such by a Christian community."[42] Hodge had a distinctive understanding of the "being of a church" and that understanding serves as the initial criticism against those who deny the validity of Romish ordination. He supported this point by offering five separate arguments. In addition, he once again appealed to Turretin and De Moor to prove the validity of Romish priests.[43] He accurately showed that Romish priests were received as valid elders and, therefore, that the baptisms they administered were deemed valid in Reformed churches.[44] Lest readers get lost at this point, it is important to remember that efficacy and validity were two distinct questions in Reformed theology. The Westminster Standards represented a Reformed consensus by stating that the efficacy of the sacraments depended on the blessing of the Christ rather than on the church or the one administering them. However, to be valid, the church identified the sacraments by their administration in a true branch of the visible church by a lawfully ordained minister. Hodge's point that the church did not exist for the ministry, but the ministry for the church, was a common one, yet he appeared to blur the distinction between efficacy and validity here, at least to some extent.

The valid ordination of ministers and the truth or falsehood of a church went hand in hand. When answering the question whether or not the church of Rome was a true church, Hodge began by defining terms, namely, "fixing the meaning of the term" church. We again see his unique ecclesiology in this when he said, "the church, or the called, as such, are not an organized body, though it is their duty to organize." What Hodge emphatically stated here, he would do in other

41 Hodge, "General Assembly," 454–459.

42 Hodge, "General Assembly," 455.

43 Hodge, "General Assembly," 457, 459; Turretin, *Institutes*, 18.25.8. Hodge also cites Gerhard on p. 459.

44 Hodge, "General Assembly," 458.

places as well. The church was not fundamentally an "organization." Herein, he believed, lay the root problem for misunderstanding the nature of the visible church among most people. He wrote, "It seems to us that a large portion of the false reasoning connected with this whole subject, arises from the erroneous assumption that organization enters into the very idea of the church. An organized body may be a church, but it is not their organization that makes them so…" The church, for Hodge, is "a collective term for true believers" without respect to their organization into visible societies. Since we cannot read hearts, we must regard all who make "a credible profession of faith in Christ" as believers.[45] Therefore, we should not exclude Rome from being part of the visible church, even though she might not be a pure church. Hodge develops this quite well in this article, but fleshes it out more broadly in the article that followed less than a year later in 1846, which we will now discuss.

In 1846 Hodge took on Theophilus in the second article in *The Biblical Repertory and Princeton Review*. In the first article, Hodge reacted to the General Assembly's ruling and some of the arguments advanced by the commissioners of that Assembly, but in this article, he addresses Theophilus for the first time. Though the topic of the validity of Roman Catholic baptism was in the forefront of the Thornwell's and Theophilus's writings, Hodge took the opportunity in the 1846 article to further pursue the question of "Whether the church of Rome is still a portion of the visible church of Christ?"[46] The topic actually arose in Theophilus's ongoing articles, and proved to be central to the question, so Hodge used the occasion to expand his response. His approach to this issue is important because of what it suggests. He says, "It is neither by research nor argument the question whether Romanists are members of the visible church is to be answered. It is a simple matter of definition and statement."[47] Could it be said that this is reminiscent of the scholastic *status questionis* and the various distinctions and definitions they made? He stated the question, after all, clearly at the beginning of his article. Mark Noll goes so far as to say that A. A. Hodge drew on Turretin more than Hodge at this juncture because his use of the "question and answer method promoted by Turretin."[48] Though that method is not used in Charles Hodge's *Systematic Theology*, it is at the heart of the two articles. This had the advantage of bringing potential clarity to the matter at the outset.

45 Hodge, "General Assembly," 460–461. Many modern readers no longer would agree with Hodge's understanding of the etymology of *ecclesia* which he argues on these two pages.

46 Hodge, "Theophilus," 321.

47 "Review of Essays in the Presbyterian by Theophilus on the Question: Is Baptism in the Church of Rome Valid?," *The Biblical Repertory and Princeton Review* 18:3 (July 1846): 323.

48 Mark A. Noll, "Introduction," in *The Princeton Theology, 1812–1921*, ed. Mark A. Noll (Grand Rapids: Baker Publishing House, 1983), 29–30.

Another aspect of scholasticism comes later on in the second article when Hodge writes, "This distinction is natural and just, though it imposes the necessity of affirming and denying the same proposition. If by the church of Rome, you mean one thing, it is not a church; if you mean another, it is a church."[49] The distinction comes from Turretin who argued that Rome needed "to be viewed under two aspects."[50] Hodge made use of the same point in the previous article in 1845 and retained the distinction Turretin made (viewing the church under two aspects, that Rome is not a church in one sense not a pure church, but a church in another sense and thus part of the true church). To make these distinctions required specific definitions of terms to which Hodge gave great attention. The whole debate could hinge on definitions. Hodge's full statement of the matter is as follows:

> It is neither by research nor argument the question whether Romanists are members of the visible church is to be answered. It is a simple matter of definition and statement. All that can be done is first to determine what is meant by the word church; and secondly what is meant by Rome, church of Rome, Romanists, or whatever term is used, and then see whether the two agree, whether Rome falls within or without the definition of the church.[51]

Even in his previous article of 1845, he would ask what an "ordained minister" was and see if "the Romish priests come within the definition." In the ensuing answer he wrote that "any man is a minister in the sense of the proposition under consideration" and then offers five proofs.[52] On this matter, Hodge's method is not strictly scholastic but echoes of that can be seen.[53] Nevertheless, we have clearly seen he often resorted to Turretin's arguments.

In the second essay, Hodge challenged Theophilus's interpretation of Francis Turretin. Both Hodge and Theophilus buttressed their positions with Turretin, but Hodge believed that Turretin did not support Theophilus's argument. Hodge wrote, "He quotes largely from Turrettin as sustaining his views on this subject; whereas

---

49 Hodge, "Theophilus," 336.

50 Hodge, "Theophilus," 325. The most recent translation has, "The church of Rome can be regarded under a twofold view (*schesei*) [*sub duplici cesei spectari potest*] …" (Turretin, *Institutes*, 18.14.23).

51 Hodge, "Theophilus," 323. Hodge cites Bernardinus De Moor as Morus. Hodge refers to De Moor's *Commentarius Perpetuus in Johannes Marckii Compendium Theologiae Christianae Didactico-Elenchticum*.

52 Hodge, "General Assembly," 454–457.

53 Regarding the definition of "scholastic" and its wide range of use, see Richard Muller, "The Problem of Protestant Scholasticism—a Review and Definition," in *Reformation and Scholasticism*, ed. Willem J. van Asselt, and Eef Dekker (Grand Rapids: Baker Academic, 2001), 45–64. Cf. Carl R. Trueman and R. S. Clark, eds. *Protestant Scholasticism: Essays in Reassessment* (Carlisle: Paternoster Press, 1999).

Turrettin is on precisely the opposite ground; affirming what Theophilus denies, and denying what Theophilus affirms."[54] Hodge quotes Turretin to show how he actually supports his own contention over against Theophilus's. In fact, the passage cited by both Theophilus and Hodge is the exact same passage in Turretin that Hodge had used in the article a year before.[55] He interacted with Turretin's view only on two pages, but the important distinction made by Turretin regarding the twofold sense of church serves as the basis for Hodge's entire argument against Theophilus.[56] He also alluded to Turretin when he wrote of the subtle distinction made by "the reformers and their successors" between the Papacy and the people under their dominion.[57] The former no longer formally constituted the church, while the latter did, even though they belonged only to what was materially the church in some respects. Hodge thus appeared to reject such scholastic distinctions as too fine, while his argument hinged on them.

In his *Systematic Theology* on the sacraments (or, "Means of Grace") he did not depend upon protestant orthodoxy overtly. Apart from a specific theological debate in which De Moor, Vitringa, and Gomarus are mentioned, Hodge did not engage the thoughts of Turretin and the like.[58] Hodge briefly addressed the subject raised in the two articles and merely repeated what constituted a valid baptism or sacrament.[59] He stayed clear of the debate in this case and cited no one, moving on to his general treatment of the sacraments.

Did Hodge use the scholastic method in his theological construction of the validity of Roman Catholic baptism? Of course it depends on how we define *scholasticus*, but he did state the question (in both articles) and methodically answered each question in the articles though not in his *Systematic Theology*.[60] Hodge's teacher, Dr. Archibald Alexander, regularly used the *Status Quaestionis* in his theological lectures, depending heavily on Turretin, and Hodge himself adopted the same method at key points.[61] More importantly, Hodge depended on Turretin's careful theological distinctions in his two articles. The various questions Turretin raised were the same ones that Hodge pursued generally, though with less detail. Turretin's question in this instance was, "Can the church of Rome of today be called a true

54 Hodge, "Theophilus," 324. Readers can see that Hodge spelled Turretin differently.

55 Turretin, *Institutes*, 18.14.3.

56 Hodge, "Theophilus," 324–325.

57 Hodge, "Theophilus," 336.

58 Charles Hodge, *Systematic Theology* (Grand Rapids: Eerdmans, 1986), 3:562–564.

59 Hodge, *Systematic Theology*, 3:523–525.

60 Hodge, "Theophilus," 321, 323, 326, 327, 330, 333, 336. Specific questions were raised and then methodically answered. He disputes Theophilus in his ongoing answers and definitions.

61 For A. Alexander, see A. A. Hodge, *Life*, 65, 553. Charles Hodge embraced the same method in his theological lectures as he would discuss theological topics "in the form of question and answer" (A. A. Hodge, *Life*, 323).

church of Christ? We deny against the Romanist."[62] Hodge's question was more narrow, "Whether the church of Rome is still a portion of the visible church of Christ?"[63] Hodge answered his question by the answer Turretin gave by stating that Rome is in some sense part of the visible church. In fact, though he cited Calvin within the Reformed circle in the two articles, he more often cited the Protestant scholastics (even a Lutheran orthodox theologian Johann Gerhard) than any other to support his position.[64]

8.3 Some Differences Between Hodge and Reformed Orthodoxy

The three differences Hodge with orthodoxy had to do primarily with a shift in emphasis. Hodge did not directly contradict Turretin or others, but his emphases and tone differed noticeably. In general, Hodge had a more positive attitude towards Rome than Reformation and Reformed orthodox writers did. That does not mean that he by any means diminished the seriousness of Rome's errors, nor did he fail to show how vastly the Reformed view of various essential doctrines differed from theirs.

The first difference related to a consistent Reformed appeal to depart from Rome, and on this point, Hodge seems to have remained virtually mute. Should a believer depart from Rome to a Protestant church, or remain under the Pope? Regarding this, Hodge did not go as far as Turretin.[65] He mentioned this specific issue at the end of the article against Theophilus. Critics like Theophilus had objected to Hodge's view by noting that the people of God were commanded to come out of the church of Rome "which would not be the case were she still a part of the visible church."[66] Hodge responded that we are commanded to leave every church "which either professes error, or which imposes any terms of communion which hurt an enlightened conscience," even if that church is a true, albeit corrupt, branch of the visible church.[67] However, even though Hodge defended that sentiment, he never actually encouraged Catholics to depart from Rome, while Turretin clearly

---

62 Turretin, *Institutes*, 18.14.

63 Hodge, "Theophilus," 321.

64 Again, in his *Systematic Theology*, he did not use Protestant scholastic authors overtly in his treatment of Baptism.

65 In 1873, he talked about respecting each other.

66 Theophilus made that exact point in "Is Baptism in the Church of Rome Valid? No. XIII," *The Presbyterian* 16 (March 21, 1846): "Here it is *assumed* that the Church of Rome is the Babylon—such is the judgment of the entire Protestant world; and we shall not go behind it. Now will it be maintained that the people of God are commanded to separate from the true church?"

67 Hodge, "Theophilus," 343.

did.[68] Had he echoed Turretin's view of separating from Rome in the two articles in question, this could have gone a long way of removing some of the misgivings people have had with his position during his lifetime.[69] I could not find places in which Hodge encouraged separation or departure from Rome in his other writings (though they could be present), but this idea was definitely not present in the two important articles we have surveyed and with which we have interacted.[70]

Another point of disagreement with many Reformed orthodox divines gets at the heart of the issue of Rome's viability. Hodge wrote, "The question, whether the Romish Church is a true church, was admitted to turn on the previous question: Does she retain truth enough to save the soul?"[71] Hodge deduced that if true believers can be found in Rome, then salvation can be gleaned from within her fold and therefore had enough truth to save. That is, Rome is a vehicle for salvation and, therefore, part of the visible church. Hodge believed that Rome professed "saving doctrines" and that she brought forth children unto God.[72] He concluded that "the church of Rome retained truth enough to save the soul, from the fact that true believers… are to be found in that communion."[73] She "still retains the profession of saving doctrines… by those doctrines men are born unto God and nurtured to heaven."[74] In light of the fact that Rome had denied fundamental Protestant doctrines, such as justification by faith in Christ alone, and affirmed other things that infringed on Protestant fundamentals, such as the Papacy, this assertion is somewhat surprising. Hodge seemed to suggest, contra most Protestants, that salvation naturally and easily flowed within the Roman church. This point became more explicit in 1872. Hodge was asked by an editor of *The Presbyterian* to give his opinion about "granting tracts of land" to the Catholics so that they could build

---

68 Turretin, *Institutes*, 18.14.22, 26.

69 Notwithstanding the following, he never encouraged separation from Rome in the two articles, even though he wrote: "Fourthly, it is objected that the people of God are commanded to come out of the church of Rome, which would not be the case were she still a part of the visible church. To this we answer, that the people of God are commanded to come out of every church, which either professes error, or which imposes any terms of communion which hurt an enlightened conscience. The non-conformists in the time of Charles II., were bound to leave the church of England, and yet did not thereby assert that it was no longer a church" (Hodge, "Theophilus," 343).

70 Charles Hodge, "Tracts for the Times," *The Biblical Repertory and Princeton Review* 10:1 (January 1838): 118. In view of the growing influence of the Tractarian movement, Hodge did encourage men to separate from Oxford like the Reformers did from Rome.

71 Hodge, "General Assembly," 463.

72 Hodge, "General Assembly," 467–468.

73 Hodge, "General Assembly," 465.

74 Hodge, "Theophilus," 341. He says, "Papists of course hold the truth of natural religion; and many of the distinguishing doctrines of the Gospel…Protestants can… joyfully admit that there are among Romanists such godly men as St. Bernard, Fénélon, and Pascal, and doubtless thousands more known only unto God" (*Systematic Theology*, 3:817n1).

churches. Hodge responded by writing that the "Roman Catholic Church teaches truth enough to save the souls of men" and that "it is unspeakably better than no church at all. And, therefore, when the choice is between that and none, it is wise and right to encourage the establishment of churches under the control of Catholic priests."[75] He admitted that he dreaded Rome's influence on Protestant society, but nevertheless taught that Roman Catholics were better than "infidels or atheists." In his view, they taught people "to worship Christ and to regard and acknowledge him as the Salvator Hominum."[76] Hodge essentially concluded that Rome was better than nothing and he believed this church did good to the souls of men.

Hodge's idea differed drastically from what Turretin taught. Turretin did not believe that "salvation can be obtained" in the corrupt Papal church. Fundamentals might remain in the papacy, but that did not mean "that the Roman church is a true church in which salvation can be obtained" and he and others would urge secession "from her as a thing of the highest necessity for salvation."[77] While this did not mean that people could not be saved in the Roman Catholic church through the Bible and faith in Jesus Christ, it meant that such people were saved in spite of the official teaching of the church rather than because of it. This earnest plea for secession for the purpose of salvation differed widely from Hodge's more moderate assessment of the danger that Rome presented to people's souls. Again, Hodge did fight against their errors with vigor, though he also never condoned them theologically. Yet if salvation remained in the heart of Rome, then why depart from her?

Thornwell's blistering attack against Hodge on this point seems insurmountable and better in accord with earlier Reformed thinking. He summarized the issue at hand differently: "The question then is, not, as the Reviewer [Hodge] intimates, whether Rome teaches truth enough to save the soul, but whether she teaches error enough to damn the soul.... not whether her systems falls short of the Gospel stand by defect, but whether it is inconsistent with it by error…"[78] Let me add an illustration to further illustrate Thornwell's point. One could have a bottle of pure water with several drops of poison in it, which may or may not be fatal, or one could have a bottle of water with enough poison that would, more often than not, lead to death. Hodge argued for the former view concerning Rome, while Thornwell the latter. Thornwell's viewpoint coheres with the notion that believers in the Roman Catholic Church could be saved in spite of her official teaching rather than because of it.

Hodge argued further that Rome's ecumenical creeds proved Rome to be part of the visible church. In response to the criticism that Rome "vitiates" the truth of those

75 A. A. Hodge, *Life of Charles Hodge*, 342.

76 "Dr. Hodge on the Roman Catholic Church," *The Presbyterian* (August 10, 1872).

77 Turretin, *Institutes*, 18.14.26.

78 Thornwell, *Collected Writings*, 3:337.

creeds "by her explanations," he argued that the words of the creeds essentially spoke for themselves, and that people should take them at face value. He even admitted that "Romish theologians do explain away most of the saving doctrines of her ancient creeds," but still "she retains saving truth" in its essential components. This, of course, raises the question regarding Hodge's views of the fundamental doctrines of the faith, to which Turretin and others devoted careful attention. Next, Hodge stated that the creed without the interpretation was what mattered, "Because it is the creeds and not the explanations, that constitute the profession of the people."[79] The only way to come to terms with this statement is Hodge's penchant for self-evident truths rooted in his foundationalist common sense realism.[80] He seems to have believed that the propositions of creeds were some sort of brute facts that could be "adopted" with "no explanations" given. Propositions must be interpreted and explained, and no one approaches statements without presuppositions and prior commitments. Thornwell essentially argued that one could not isolate the truths of these creeds from the errors espoused by Rome and imposed upon them.

Lastly, Hodge believed that it was a sin not to acknowledge that true believers remained within Roman Catholicism, "there are, and ever have been, many Romanists who are the true children of God."[81] His very robust view of the salvation held forth in Rome, coupled with what seemed to be a great many of true believers among the Romanists easily enabled him view Rome as part of the church. Reformed orthodox divines admitted that true believers could be found with the corrupt Romish church but they never wrote of such a fact in the more positive and affirming terms that Charles Hodge did. For Turretin, it was a bare admission that true believers may be present in Rome, but he was quick to point out how and why the Roman church was not a true church in spite of this fact. In other words, the marks of the church constituted a true branch of the visible church rather than the mere presence of true believers. Why, then, would Hodge admonish his readers about the sin of not loving the brothers within Catholicism? Hodge readily admitted that the General Assembly of 1845, along with the Reformed churches previously, all acknowledged that believers existed within Catholicism. Yet he concluded that since the Spirit gave birth to some within Catholicism, we must recognize that Rome is part of the visible church, though Turretin and earlier authors rejected this fact as a decisive mark of the visible church. Thornwell believed that Hodge begged the very question in dispute: "If these true believers reject, in their hearts, the complicated system of the

79 Hodge, "Theophilus," 342.

80 See the second and fourth chapters of this present volume regarding Scottish Common Sense Realism.

81 Hodge, *Systematic Theology*, 3:822. "We shall not less sin against God and our own best interests, if we reject as reprobates any of the real followers of Christ, no matter in what external communion they may be found" ("General Assembly," 465).

Pope, and were instrumentally converted by a different Gospel from that of Trent, the truth of their piety is no proof that the Romish creed is saving."[82] That is, they are believers despite the heresies present inimical to the gospel, and God's grace to them no way establishes the fact that Rome is a Christian church. Believers may be found within her walls *in spite* of her apostate status and not *because* of it[83] Therein lies the fundamental difference between the positions of these two men on the visible church: Hodge believed that the church was present where believers were, while Thornwell taught that we should identify the visible church by her traditional Protestant marks of the church. No doubt Thornwell would have concurred with the words of the editor of *The Presbyterian* who lauded Theophilus's contributions, writing: "We do not pretend to say that all included visibly in this communion will be lost; but we do say, that if any are saved, it must be by a departure from the received doctrines of that church."[84] That is, true believers can only arise in the walls of the Romish church if they *depart from* and *not embrace* her received doctrines. Thornwell declared succinctly, "They are saved in spite of her creed."[85] All of this illustrates that while Hodge's reception of Roman Catholic baptism cohered with earlier Reformed thinking, the grounds on which he did so constituted a significant redefinition of the marks and definition of the visible church.

8.4 An American Context: Hodge's "Catholic Sympathies"

Hodge's minority position, at least in 19th century American Presbyterianism, on the validity of Roman Catholic baptism was rooted in his understanding of the historic church, especially the Reformers and the protestant scholastics. He held his ground firmly and exhibited broad charity toward Rome while being firmly critical of her theological errors. What made his stance even more heroic in light of the current opinion of his church had to do with the general antipathy against Roman Catholicism that swept through North American and within the American Presbyterian church. Paul C. Gutjahr placed this baptism debate within the context of some of the social reactions to Catholicism in America in the early 1800s. Catholic immigrants from Germany and Ireland in the 1830s ended up changing the demographics in America, and many American Protestants became

82 Thornwell, *Collected Writings*, 3:341.

83 N. E. Puritan says that true believers may be found in the "Romish Church… *in spite of* all the proper tendencies of her institutions…" (emphasis added). See "Is the Church of Rome a Church of Christ?," *The Presbyterian* 15 (Sept. 6, 1845).

84 "Baptism in the Church of Rome," *The Presbyterian*, January 3, 1846.

85 Thornwell, *Collected Writings*, 3:342.

paranoid against Catholics and their allegiance to the Pope. Gutjahr believes that this Presbyterian animosity "was but a reflection of American culture at large."[86]

In the midst of this context, Hodge seemed to show "Catholic sympathies" in his writings, especially in his reaction to the 1845 General Assembly. His "Catholic sympathies" drew "some of the most pointed and aggressive criticisms of his career."[87] Even as early as 1838 Hodge was astonished that the high-church movement (e. g., the Oxford Movement, and Tractarianism) unchurched Presbyterians and other Protestants. Even though he did not agree much with Tractarianism, he could not unchurch them in return.[88] That "spirit of tolerance" (Gutjahr's description) would prevail in 1845 and to his later years. One could hardly read a few pages in *The Presbyterian* in 1845 and 1846 without running into frequent references to the dangers of "Papism." Reports from oversea missions in Germany, Ireland, and other places detailed the pernicious influence of Rome.[89] J. V. Fesko mentions Lyman Beecher's warning to the Protestants at the time about the dangers of Roman Catholic influence in America.[90]

David Calhoun has helpfully documented one thing missed by Paul Gutjahr and W. Andrew Hoffecker in their biographies of Hodge in relation to the debate over Roman Catholic baptism. Though all three authors offered some very insightful perspectives on this debate, Calhoun drew attention to some of the decisions made by the previous PCUSA General Assemblies, which shed greater light on the context of the debate.[91] Ten years before the baptism issue arose, the General Assembly of 1835 had already adopted the following resolution moved by Dr. James Hoge (1784–1863): "Resolved, that it is the deliberate and decided judgment of this Assembly, that the Roman Catholic Church has essentially apostatized from the

---

86 Gutjahr, *Charles Hodge*, 235.

87 Gutjahr, *Charles Hodge*, 235–236; Andrew W. Hoffecker, *Charles Hodge: The Pride of Princeton*, American Reformed Biographies (Phillipsburg: P & R Publishing, 2011), 248.

88 Charles Hodge, "Tracts for the Times," *The Biblical Repertory and Princeton Review* 10:1 (1838): 97. He said of the Tractarians, "We prefer our own form, but we do not denounce theirs. We shrink from the idea of renouncing communion with the Holy Catholic church, the congregation of Christian people dispersed throughout the whole world." Gutjahr seems to imply Hodge wrote this in view of Roman Catholics but it is clear from the context he wrote this for those in the Church of England who were unchurching other Protestants. See Gutjahr, *Charles Hodge*, 237. On the Tractarian movement, see Peter Toon, *Evangelical Theology, 1833–1856— A Response to Tractarianism*, New Foundations Theological Library (Atlanta: John Knox Press, 1979).

89 A simple perusal of *The Presbyterian* will amply bear this out. There was one curious notice in the periodical in which the writer was cautiously optimistic that a group of German Catholics in America had declared their repudiation of Romish doctrines, see "German Roman Catholic Movement," *The Presbyterian* 16 (Dec. 19, 1846).

90 Fesko, "Rejoiner by J. V. Fesko," *The Confessional Presbyterian* 9 (2013): 198.

91 Calhoun, *Princeton Seminary*, 304.

religion of our Lord Jesus Christ, and therefore cannot be recognized as a Christian church."[92] The judgment of the church had already been rendered on a key issue Charles Hodge would wrestle against in 1845 and in 1846. Furthermore, the General Assembly in 1840 voted to annually deliver a sermon on the evils of popery, and Robert J. Breckinridge (1800–1871) was appointed to give the first sermon.[93] Even before these events, the 1831 General Assembly sought to address the question of Roman Catholic baptism, though no final report resulted at the time (both Archibald Alexander and Samuel Miller (1769–1850) were appointed to look into this question).[94] The 1845 General Assembly decision, therefore, did not originate without some precedent. Anti-Roman sentiment had been growing in nineteenth century American Presbyterianism, and the church's rejection of Roman Catholic baptism appears to have been a natural step in this progression.

With the growing civil and religious antagonism against Catholicism at the time, and the consistent opposition within the American Presbyterian church, it should not surprise us to see how easily the 1845 General Assembly passed the motion related to Ohio presbytery's overture respecting the validity of Roman Catholic baptism. During that same Assembly, the Board of Domestic Missions spoke of the crisis rising from "the rapid increase of Popery and other heresies." They warned, "The Valley of the Mississippi has especially been selected as the great field in which Popery has declared her design to fight the battle for empire in this Republic."[95] The 1845 General Assembly unmistakably revealed their adamant opposition to Roman Catholicism by rejecting Roman Catholic baptism as a public statement that Rome was a false and dangerous church. The vote of 173–8, therefore, was hardly surprising or unexpected in light of current events.

After the 1845 General Assembly and Hodge's rebuttal in the *Biblical Repertory*, the weekly periodical, *The Presbyterian,* published at least three series of articles against Roman Catholic baptism. Theophilus's lengthy series against Hodge was not the only one occupied with the issue in the Old School ecclesiastical periodical. The Presbytery of Carlisle, for example, felt it necessary to have their position paper

92 Charles Hodge, "The General Assembly of 1835," *The Biblical Repertory and Princeton Review* 7:3 (1835): 475. Dr. Hoge was most likely the Rev. James Hoge, D.D. (1784–1863) of the First Church of Columbus, Ohio.

93 Calhoun, *Princeton Seminary*, 304, 478n32. The sermons were delivered until 1852 when they were indefinitely postponed.

94 Calhoun, *Princeton Seminary*, 303–304. Calhoun cites Samuel Miller, Jr., *The Life of Samuel Miller*, 2 vols. (Philadelphia: Claxton, Remsen & Haffelfinger, 1869), 2:198–200. In 1830, Samuel Miller chaired the Assembly's committee appointed to give a report on the validity of "Popish baptisms, a subject introduced by overture from the Synod of New York" (198). By 1833, Dr. Alexander told the Assembly that the committee was not prepared to submit a report and did not think allowing the committee to continue would yield a "favorable result" (199).

95 "General Assembly" [1845], 435–436.

published in *The Presbyterian* during this period,[96] which was a scathing repudiation of the validity of Roman Catholic baptism. Of course, men like Thornwell ably defended the General Assembly's decision as well, though he published his material in a different journal.[97] The periodical also published a short single piece written by the pseudonymous N. E. Puritan, entitled, "Is the Church of Rome a Church of Christ?"[98] However, near the end of Theophilus's series, someone by the name of "Frederick" published a four-part series entitled, "Is Baptism in the Church of Rome Valid?"[99] This was a measured article supporting Hodge's position without specifically mentioning him. Though Frederick's was the minority position in the periodical, his contribute illustrates the persistence of both views in the church at the time.

Charles Hodge most certainly sensed and understood the results of the generally harsh and prevalent sentiment against Rome in his church. Writing as he did in defense of Roman Catholic baptism must have taken courage in light of this fact. One of his own professors, Samuel Miller, had made his position known almost fifteen years before and his view corresponded with Hodge's.[100] Whether Hodge took encouragement from the fact we do not know, but we know he firmly held his convictions and ably argued that his position, aligned as he was with the Reformers and elder Protestant theologians on the validity of Rome's baptism in spite of her apostasy from the gospel. For the same reason, his son, A. A. Hodge, labeled the General Assembly's ruling as "anti-Protestant"[101] because it deviated from Protestant orthodoxy and historic practice.

Some within the Presbyterian church were disturbed by Hodge's Catholic sympathies. Thornwell privately wrote that Hodge was "an apologist for Rome." He believed Princeton "had pursued a disastrous course…on the Romish question" and needed "to be checked" by "strengthening the hands of other Seminaries." He wanted to "break the charm" Princeton had over the Presbyterian church.[102] Therefore, many old school men were alarmed by Hodge's Catholic sympathies and

96 "Presbytery of Carlisle," *The Presbyterian* 16 (May 2, 1846). The Presbytery's report stretched into three weeks, May 2, 9 and 16. The Presbytery passed this resolution: "*Resolved*, that the report of the committee on Romish Baptism, be published in the Presbyterian." The report added, "The question before us is one of great practical moment, and demands a prayerful and deliberate answer.... We hold baptism in the church of Rome to be invalid…" (May 2, 1846).

97 As mentioned above, they were first published in the *Watchman and Observer* in 1846.

98 See above for the reference.

99 Frederick, "Is Baptism in the Church of Rome Valid? I," *The Presbyterian* 16 (April 4, 1846). Also, No. II (April 11, 1846); No. III (April 18, 1846); and No. IV (April 25, 1846).

100 Miller, *Samuel Miller*, 2:200.

101 A. A. Hodge, *Life*, 340.

102 Palmer, *Thornwell*, 288–290.

vigorously countered it.[103] Hodge's 1845 article defending Rome's baptism ended up coloring Princeton as the seminary that defended Rome.

Maintaining the validity of Rome's baptism and viewing Rome as part of the visible church, at least in some sense, indicated that Hodge stood with our Reformed forefathers, though he defended this position based on revised parameters delineating the visible church. Though he held the same conclusions of our forefathers, he infused his own peculiar ecclesiology into them and thus broke with them with his understanding of ecclesiology. Regardless of what readers think about Hodge's arguments, they should recognize a certain consistency in them. Where the true church and true ministers exist, valid sacraments followed. Most of the American Presbyterian church at the time believed that Rome was not a church and thus had no ministers or sacraments, while Hodge believed that Rome was a true church and had both. In the end, the crux of the matter devolved into debates over Rome's status as a true church of Christ rather than resting on the Trinitarian formula of baptism.

8.5 "Without External Organized Union:" Hodge's "Idea of the Church"[104]

Hodge's unique "idea" of the church dominated and regulated his defense of the validity of Roman Catholic baptism, hinging as it did on how and why Rome remained within the pale of the visible church. In this area his creativity (or idiosyncrasy) became clear. His ecclesiology can be found in a collection of his articles which was formed into a book (*Discussions in Church Polity*), which supplemented the omission of ecclesiology in his *Systematic Theology*.[105] Some of the themes we have already seen in his two articles on Rome and baptism resurface in this collection, which expanded upon the ideas already expressed in the articles.

For example, Hodge's essay entitled, "Idea of the Church," explains in one coherent article how he could view Rome the way he did.[106] The essence of the church was not, in his view, something visibly organized: "the Church may continue under any external organization, or without any visible organization whatever." She is not

103 As mentioned above, an editor of *The Presbyterian* was happy that Theophilus rose to the challenge of combatting "the doctrine of the Biblical Repertory."

104 Hodge, "Idea of the Church," in *DCP*, 5.

105 For a good explanation on this lacuna in Hodge's *Systematic Theology*, see Alan D. Strange, *The Doctrine of the Spirituality of the Church in the Ecclesiology of Charles Hodge*, Reformed Academic Dissertations (Phillipsburg: P&R Publishing, 2017), 162ff.

106 It was originally published in the *Princeton Review* in 1853 and wisely placed as the first chapter in *Discussions in Church Polity.*

"essentially a visible society" and there may be "communion without external organized union." The church "consists of saints" and in communion with each other.[107] The Holy Spirit indwells the body and unites them. This requires no specific external organization. Hodge believed it was ritualism to include an organized society into the definition or idea of church. He would call this a "catholicizing" tendency.[108] More harshly, he wrote, "It is the parent of bigotry, religious pride combined with malignity."[109] In fact, Hodge charged the men of the General Assembly with the "spirit of Popery" because of this issue.[110] He maintained a minimalist definition of the church because the "only essential mark of a true church… is the profession of the true religion."[111] While Protestants generally agreed that the polity of the church did not constitute its essence, Hodge went further by arguing that a church could exist without distinct organization into a tangible society of believers bearing the marks of the visible church. How this affected his view of Roman Catholic baptism will become apparent after fleshing out his idea of the church further below.

Hodge concerned himself greatly with the essence of the church. This Common Sense Realist almost sounds like an idealist when he says, "The object of inquiry is not the usage of a word [i. e. church], but the true idea of a thing; not how the word church is employed, but what the Church itself is."[112] He recognized that the word "church" had been variously used in history, but he concerned himself with the true idea of the church as he saw it. In short, Hodge's interesting, logical, and forceful article argued that the church essentially "consists of saints… and that the essential bond of their union is not external organization, but the indwelling of the Holy Ghost."[113] On the surface, this assertion appears to conflate the visible and invisible aspects of the church, broadening the definition of the visible church to the presence of elect regenerate believers. Therefore, no visible churches in any form fully encapsulates all that the Scripture teaches about the church. Only his "idea of the church" meets the description and teaching of the Bible by defining the church in terms of the presence of believers rather than their visible society and common public confession of the gospel. These salient points regarding the church are present in the two articles we have dealt with above as well. Alan Strange described

---

107 Hodge, "Idea of the Church," 5–6.

108 See Mark Alan Reynolds, "Charles Hodge's Ecclesiastical Elenctics: His Response to Catholicizing Tendencies in the Churches, 1837–1860" (Ph.D. Dissertation, Saint Louis University, 2000).

109 Hodge, "Idea of the Church," 34.

110 Hodge, "The General Assembly," 452.

111 Hodge, "Theories of the Church," in *DCP*, 45, cf. 138. Also, Reynolds, "Charles Hodge's Ecclesiastical Elenctics," 25ff.

112 Hodge, "Idea of the Church," 7.

113 Hodge, "Idea of the Church," 8.

Hodge's definition in this way, "This is a quintessentially 'spiritual' conception of the church."[114]

Hodge went on to draw out some of the implications of his "idea" of the church. All the promises, protection, discipline, etc. of the church apply not to the visible, but to the invisible church, which is the communion of saints united by the indwelling of the Holy Spirit. For example, when Christ promised to ratify the church's decisions in matters of discipline (cf. Matt. 18:15–20), He said this is for "the Church considered as the communion of saints." The prerogative of the keys belongs not to the visible church with her officers, but only to true believers.[115] The attributes, titles, descriptions, etc. of the church apply only to the communion of elect regenerate saints. Hodge thus seems to diminish the value of the tangible objective marks of the visible church. Whether a person is a Baptist, Methodist, Anglican, Presbyterian, etc. matters little since what counts is being a true saint. If there are true saints in that particular external organized union, then she can easily be deemed to be part of the visible church. Since the members of the General Assembly of 1845 admitted that true believers existed in the church of Rome, it only made sense for Hodge to view Rome as part of the visible church. This appears to neglect the fact that WCF 25.2 asserted that while membership in the visible church was ordinarily necessary for salvation, some rare cases existed in which people, like the thief on the cross, could be members of the invisible church without having opportunity to join the visible church. Similarly, Turretin explained the presence of believers in the Roman Catholic church in this manner.

Since Hodge prioritized the church catholic over any and all external organized groups and denominations, we can understand another aspect of his view of baptism. He very specifically and unmistakably argued that a person is baptized into the "church catholic" and not to any organized denomination.[116] Since all the promises and ordinances truly apply to the church catholic, it only follows that those baptized are baptized into the church catholic, argued Hodge. But Turretin said that exact opposite. Hodge said baptism placed the person into the church catholic, while Turretin taught it placed the person into the visible church. It was true that the catholicity of the church preceded its locality, but it was equally true that people could be baptized into the visible church catholic only through its local expressions. Turretin insisted that the "sacrament is the property of the church, which is administered in her name and in her faith."[117] Notice the last clause, the person is baptized in the church's name and "in her faith (*in ejus fide*)," i. e., in the church's confession,

---

114 Strange, *The Doctrine of the Spirituality of the Church in the Ecclesiology of Charles Hodge*, 165.

115 Hodge, "Idea of the Church," 35–36.

116 Hodge, "General Assembly," 468–469. See the discussion above.

117 Turretin, *Institutes*, 19.15.3: "Quia Sacramentum est peculium Ecclesiae, quod Ecclesiae nomine dispensator, & in ejus fide."

in what she believes.[118] The context makes it clear that Turretin did not have in mind merely the universal church in abstraction from the local church because he was answering the question of the validity of a heretic administering baptism. Even the heretic's error does not nullify the baptism if done in the right manner and in the context of an orthodox church. He concluded, "Undoubtedly, the public faith of the church is here to be considered, into which he (who is baptized) is introduced and the promises made to him by Christ."[119] The "public faith of the church" referred to the doctrinal position of the particular church or denomination, and not to some intangible universal church's public faith. Theophilus likewise said that baptism makes the person "a member of the visible church."[120] Hodge seems to have overlooked the definition of baptism in the Larger Catechism which stated that "the parties baptized are solemnly admitted into the visible church" (Q. 165). The Westminster Confession teaches that "Baptism is… not only for the solemn admission of the party baptized into the visible church…" The definition of baptism includes being baptized *into* the visible church. In the end, all of this reflected the first mark of the visible church, namely the church's public confession of the true doctrine of the gospel. This point made confessional affirmations of the gospel primary, which from a Protestant perspective, Rome had denied in creeds like Trent.

This is the only way to validate a baptism for the visible church, viz., by the "public faith of the church." Of course, a true believer is indeed baptized into the church catholic ultimately, but that is Christ's doing through the ordained ministry in local visible churches. We judge by sense and use visible ordinances in the visible church knowing our Savior alone knows who are truly His. These are Christ's visible ordinances to His true church; He did not give invisible ordinances to an undefined individual collection of believers. Hodge's "idea" of the church appears to diminish the objectively identifiable nature of Christ's ordinances in the context of the church as a society of those who professed the true religion, together with their children. How does one practically utilize the sacraments and orders Christ gave to His church? Hodge wrote, "It is not organization, but evocation, the actual calling out and separating from others, that makes the Church."[121] It is hard to grasp how ministry and sacraments could remain essential to the definition of the true visible church, both of which rested on the validity of that church's public confession of faith. But how could they not be since Christ instituted those visible ordinances for

---

118 Harm Goris, ed., *Synopsis Purioris Theologiae/Synopsis of a Purer Theology*, 3:157.

119 Turretin, *Institutes*, 19.15.3. Thornwell demonstrates that those who received Rome's baptism became her disciple: "that he who requests baptism from Rome declares by the act that he is a Romanist" (*Collected Writings*, 3:335–336).

120 Theophilus, "Is Baptism in the Church of Rome Valid? No. IX," *The Presbyterian* 16 (Feb. 21, 1846).

121 Hodge, "Idea of the Church," 10.

His church? Can the instituted sacraments and orders exist without an organization? Christ required both. To appoint elders and call pastors, to order worship, exercise discipline, administer the sacraments, etc. all require some visible organization because God is not a God of confusion, and all things should be done decently and in order. Furthermore, Christ gave the sacraments and order to His church, to His true church (using Hodge's argument). Therefore, some external elements have always been present within the definition of the church among Protestant churches. These sacraments and orders cannot and should not be viewed as accidents, but essential to the being of the church on this side of heaven. This did not mean that the truth or falsehood of the church rested for Protestants on a particular form of church polity, but rather that believers should identify the visible church and valid sacraments in the context of a church professing sound doctrine with lawfully ordained ministers. Hodge conceded this point, after all, when he argued for the validity of Roman Catholic baptism from the idea that Rome was a true branch of the visible church and that Roman Catholic priests were true ministers of the gospel. He seems to have argued his case by including Rome in the church by excluding a society of believers under a common confession from the definition of the church.

Theophilus tackled Hodge's rejection of external organization in the definition of the church in his second article, and he elaborated upon this subject in the third. He took Hodge to task for stating that "the church …is not an organization."[122] Later on he declared, "Who, in all the world, ever heard of a church without officers? No, the idea is unscriptural; it is anti-Genevan; it is anti-presbyterian."[123] The background of this argument is that one cannot have officers without an external organization. Theophilus quoted Calvin on how one can recognize the church: "For, wherever we find the word of God purely preached and heard, and the sacraments administered according to the institution of Christ; there, it is not to be doubted, is church of God: for his promise can never deceive: 'Where two or three are gathered together, in my name, there am I in the midst of them.'"[124] The Belgic Confession added to this list a third mark of the right administration of church discipline. Applying the logic of Hodge's view, Theophilus taunted Hodge by exclaiming,

> O! John Calvin, how Puseyistic you are. You are become a real Ritualist, says Princeton. You make organization necessary to the existence of a church; you deny that the called without a ministry are a church; you hold 'the erroneous assumption that organization enters into the very idea of the church;' and 'any number of the called,' without a ministry,

122 Theophilus, "Is Baptism in the Church of Rome Valid? No. II" *The Presbyterian* 16 (Jan. 3, 1846).

123 Theophilus, "Is Baptism in the Church of Rome Valid? No. VII" *The Presbyterian* 16 (Feb. 7, 1846).

124 Theophilus, "Is Baptism in the Church of Rome Valid? No. V" *The Presbyterian* 16 (Jan. 24, 1846). He is quoting Calvin's *Institutes*, 4.1.9.

> without preaching of the word, without sacraments, are not a church; that repudiation, or absence of a ministry, of government, disorganizes the church, rather subverts and destroys it altogether. Why, John, you are extravagant; you affirm the existence of the ministry to be even more necessary to the church, than food is to the life of our body, or than light and heat are to the sun.[125]

Because Calvin made the organization necessary to the church (as explained by Theophilus), he would, under Hodge's definition, be a Ritualist. Theophilus pointed out other matters on which he believed Hodge had erred, though some of his criticisms were uncharitable, since he understood the implications of Hodge's words in the worst possible light. To Theophilus's credit, though, his main argued zeroed in on Hodge's definition or idea of the church, as being broader than the common conception of Protestantism.

Hodge prioritized the invisible church over against the visible in a way that made the visible church exist everywhere its invisible members existed. He affirmed the visibility of the church, but his strong emphasis on the invisible church tended to collapse the two, at least to an extent.[126] Alan Strange suggested Hodge's New Side sympathies were coming into play on this matter.[127] Yet New Side men never conceived of the church in this manner.[128] Furthermore, when defining the church in his first essay, he never appealed to Reformed orthodox divines on this modified definition.[129] Neither did he refer to them in his article, "Idea of the Church." Hodge declares that his is the Protestant view, but it is difficult to find a notable theologian who taught as Hodge did.[130] His historic Reformed precedent is not readily apparent in light of the evidence.

Hodge needed to explain his view on the visible church given his predilection for the invisible, which he did in 1853. He took issue with those who charged him of holding to "a chimera, a Platonic idea" of the visible church, transforming it

---

125 Theophilus, "Is Baptism in the Church of Rome Valid? No. VII."

126 Hodge gave a whole essay on the "Visibility of the Church" (originally published in the *Presbyterian Review*, 1853). See "Visibility of the Church," in *DCP*, 55–67.

127 Strange, *The Doctrine of the Spirituality of the Church in the Ecclesiology of Charles Hodge*, 166–167.

128 For example, even the New Side Gilbert Tennent (1703–1764) spoke of the necessity of the "*Order* and *Government* in the *Church* of Christ", of the visible Church with her ordinances, etc. See *Irenicum Ecclesiasticum* (Philadelphia, 1749), pp. v, 11–12, etc. One can read of baptism being "the *Door* of Entrance into the visible *Church*" (26), the "Officers of the Church" (28), the discipline in the visible church (81–82), the "Essentials of that *Order* and *Government* which CHRIST has appointed in his Word" (98), etc. Tennent's understanding of the Visible Church did not differ from the general Reformed position.

129 Hodge, "General Assembly," 460ff.

130 Hodge, "General Assembly," 468; "Visibility of the Church," in *DCP*, 60.

into an ideal rather than a real society.[131] The Princeton professor did not follow the traditional distinctions regarding the visible church, but he instead offered his peculiar definition and, which becomes apparent from the title of the essay itself, "The Visibility of the Church." Hodge used a noun and not the adjective "visible." This, I will explain, was deliberate and fit into his "Idea of the Church." In explaining the visibility of the true church, he said that "the true Church is always visible."[132] Why? Because we are not ghosts and members of the true church have bodies: "Protestants admit that the Church on earth consists of visible men and women, and not of invisible spirits."[133] He rightly insisted that "…the Church is no more invisible than believers are."[134] This admission enabled him to clarify where he intended to go with his arguments in that he expanded the visible church to the presence of true believers wherever they might be found.

He argued that the visibility of the church did not belong to the "external society" because it belongs "to true believers, or the communion of saints."[135] In short, the true church possessed visibility because the members of the true church consisted of true visible believers, who often, though not always, existed in external organizations. He added, "An external society, therefore, may properly be called a Church, without implying that the visibility of the true Church consists in outward organization."[136] The true church exists within "an external society" or in an "outward organization," but the true church was not itself an outward organization, she merely lives within it. On the visibility element of the church, A. Craig Troxel suggested that Hodge was "contradictory" on this point, and John Jey Deifell argued that the Princetonian was "inconsistent and almost contradictory."[137] Yet I submit Hodge was remarkably consistent and purposely so.

As mentioned, Hodge deliberately chose to use the noun "visibility" and not the adjective "visible." The two are not the same because the adjective would mix or confuse Hodge's conception of the idea of the church as being the communion of saints, the true believers, the invisible church; the visible church is never the true church. This stands in contrast to the standard Protestant idea that visible and

---

131 Hodge, "Visibility of the Church," in *DCP*, 57. One cannot help but see an element of truth in this charge which Hodge rejected. I was led to this exact same assessment after my reading of his first chapter in his *DCP* ("Idea of the Church") not knowing his contemporaries had made similar charges.

132 Hodge, "Visibility of the Church," 65.

133 Hodge, "Visibility of the Church," 56.

134 Hodge, "Visibility of the Church," 65.

135 Hodge, "Visibility of the Church," 60.

136 Hodge, "Visibility of the Church," 63.

137 A. Craig Troxel, "'Divine Right' Presbyterianism and Church Power" (Ph.D. Dissertation, Westminster Theological Seminary, 1998), 200; John Jey Deifell, Jr., "The Ecclesiology of Charles Hodge" (Ph.D. Dissertation, University of Edinburgh, 1969), 388.

invisible are not two churches, one true and one false, but rather two aspects of a single church. An organized external group of professing believers with officers (word, sacrament, ministry, etc.) may have visible members of the true church, but this organized external group is not the true church. The visible church (as an external organized union) can never be the true church because she is mixed, but the visible church would include the true church and she would be visible within the organized church, hence, the visibility of the church. That is, when one speaks of the "visible church", he uses the word "church" to mean that she is a mixed visible society. Yet Hodge preferred to use the word "church" in a way that corresponded to her essential being, namely the communion of saints, or the body of true believers. By speaking of the "visibility" of the church, he retained his definition of the idea of the true church (the communion of true saints) while denoting her visibility. Speaking of the visible church (which he did earlier and continued to do) could easily lead the reader to equate an external organized group or denomination with the church, which is something Hodge sought to avoid. So, he argued that the "true Church is visible in the external Church, just as the soul is visible in the body."[138]

Hodge's essay on the visibility of the church, therefore, circles back to his original understanding of the "Idea of the Church." The only element which the article ("Visibility of the Church") adds is that the true church actually had physical visible members, which meant that there is an element of visibility in the definition of the truth church catholic. Once that is grasped, the reader can see how the essay easily dovetails into his seminal essay, "Idea of the Church." The visibility of the church meant the true church could be seen in the visible church and defining it this way enables him to loop back to his definition of what the church is.

Though nothing is wrong *per se* in emphasizing the priority of the invisible church, Hodge painted all of ecclesiology with it in a way that redefined the visible church in terms of catholicity to the potential exclusion of its locality. His "Idea of the Church" was essential to his argument for the validity of Roman Catholic baptism, going beyond Turretin and other scholastic divines in their arguments for the validity of Rome's baptism. This became clearer in relation to the weightier issue over Rome being "a true church of Christ," since this would affect the character of her sacraments. On this he weighs the whole issue on the definition of the word church.[139] "It seems to us that a large portion of the false reasoning connected with this whole subject, arises from the erroneous assumption that organization enters into the very idea of the church."[140] He said the same thing in his first article against the Assembly's ruling on Roman Catholic baptism he would say later in 1853 (in his

138 Hodge, "Visibility of the Church," 57.

139 Hodge, "General Assembly," 459ff.

140 Hodge, "General Assembly," 460.

essay on the idea of the church). He insists that the church "is not an organization" because "organization does not make … a church."[141] This definition of the church would enable him to make Rome part of the church because true believers existed within the organized society of Rome.

Several problems could be raised against Hodge's view of the church and baptism. But what stands out is how he brought his idea of the church to the baptism debate. Since the true church is not an "organized society" it does not matter if the papacy fits within the definition of a church. Given Hodge's definition, Rome is definitively part of the church because she has the true believers within her. She also has within her saving doctrines by which "men are born unto God and nurtured for heaven" and therefore, Hodge concludes, "we dare not deny that she is still part of the visible church."[142] Hodge's idea of the church enabled him minimize differences among denominations. Though he argued cogently for the validity of Rome's baptism using the scholastic divines, his idea of the church would have easily cleared the way for its validity irrespective of their support. Since true believers exist in Rome's organized society, she is part of the visible church and, therefore, her baptism must remain valid. Hodge has recast the baptism issue into his "Idea of the Church." The existence of true believers meant something of the true church existed in Rome.

In one sense, his ecclesiology compelled him to justify Roman Catholic baptism. The effect required a cause; the existence of true believers within her walls, meant she possessed enough truth to be a church. This meant that her sacrament of baptism had to be valid because she was part of the visible church. Hodge could not see how we could refuse the sacraments and orders of Rome because they had genuine believers within her walls. He concluded his first article saying, "And if they [the Romanists] are in the church [i. e. true church], their baptism being a washing with water in the name of the Trinity, is Christian baptism…"[143]

8.6 Conclusion

As late as 1873, five years before Charles Hodge's death, he held to his conviction regarding the validity of Roman Catholic baptism and to his modified idea of the visible church. In speaking to a large conference of Evangelicals, he delivered a lecture on the unity of the Church. In it, he reiterated his definition and view of his idea of the church clearly: "The idea of the Church, therefore, as presented in the Bible, is that believers scattered over the world are a band of brethren, children of

141 Hodge, "General Assembly," 460. He again says, "the church Catholic is not an organized society" (468).

142 Hodge, "Theophilus," 341. We have quoted this before.

143 Hodge, "General Assembly," 471.

the same Father, subjects of the same Lord, forming one body by the indwelling of the Holy Ghost, uniting all to Christ as their living head."[144] He also encouraged Christians to recognize each other's sacraments and orders. Though he did not mention Rome by name, one could easily see implied applications in that direction because the argument echoed what he had already argued regarding the validity of Rome's baptism.[145]

Due to his idea of the church, he recognized true believers existed in all the various denominations, among which he included the Roman Catholic Church. In that lecture, he said something that greatly offended many in the audience. The editor explained that Hodge's view was his own and did not represent the Alliance when he wrote,

> Dr. Hodge was called upon to express his view on the Unity of the Church. This he did freely, although fully aware that many Episcopalians, Presbyterians, Congregationalists, and Baptists dissented more or less from some of the principles which he advanced.... It is with surprise, therefore, as well as with regret, that he learns that some of his brethren were grieved by what he said, especially on the subject of Christian communion.[146]

This ecumenical spirit Hodge espoused in his lecture was rooted in his idea of the visible church existing wherever individual believers existed. Because true believers exist all denominations and various external organizations, there should be "intercommunion" between them: "No particular church has the right to require any thing as a term of communion which Christ has not made a condition of salvation."[147] Hodge tended to *include* rather than *exclude* and this animus stemmed from his idea of the church. Where true believers were found in any external organization, including Rome, baptism in the Triune name was valid. Thus, Hodge's views of the validity of Roman Catholic baptism illustrate continuities and discontinuities with Reformed orthodoxy, as American controversies served as the backdrop for his teaching. In his own way, he sought to make arguments for Roman Catholic baptism more consistent by including Rome in the visible church through broadening the definition of the visible church beyond the traditional marks found in Reformed theology.

---

144 Charles Hodge, "The Unity of the Church Based on Personal Union with Christ," in *History, Essays, Orations, and Other Documents of the Sixth General Conference of the Evangelical Alliance*, ed. Philip Schaff, and S. Irenaeus Prime (New York: Harper & Brothers, 1874), 142, cf. 143.

145 Hodge, "The Unity of the Church Based on Personal Union with Christ," 144.

146 Hodge, "The Unity of the Church Based on Personal Union with Christ," 144 (see footnote).

147 Hodge, "The Unity of the Church Based on Personal Union with Christ," 143. One wonders if this statement was not the cause of the grief among the auditors.

Works Cited

Bavinck, Herman. *Reformed Dogmatics*. Translated by John Vriend. 4 vols. Grand Rapids: Baker Academic, 2003–2008.

Calhoun, David B. *Princeton Seminary: Faith and Learning, 1812–1868*. Carlisle: Banner of Truth, 1994.

Deifell Jr., John Jey. "The Ecclesiology of Charles Hodge." Ph.D. Dissertation, University of Edinburgh, 1969.

Denzinger, Hendricus. *The Sources of Catholic Dogma*. Translated by Roy J. Deferrari. Fitzwilliam, NH: Loreto Publications, 1955.

"Dr. Hodge on the Roman Catholic Church," *The Presbyterian* (August 10, 1872).

Editor. "Baptism in the Church of Rome." *The Presbyterian* 16 (Jan. 3, 1846).

Fesko, J. V. "Rejoiner by J. V. Fesko." *The Confessional Presbyterian* 9 (2013): 197–199.

———. *Word, Water and Spirit - A Reformed Perspective on Baptism*. Grand Rapids: Reformation Heritage Books, 2010.

Frederick. "Is Baptism in the Church of Rome Valid? I." *The Presbyterian* 16 (April 4, 1846).

———. "Is Baptism in the Church of Rome Valid? II." *The Presbyterian* 16 (April 11, 1846).

———. "Is Baptism in the Church of Rome Valid? III." *The Presbyterian* 16 (April 18, 1846).

———. "Is Baptism in the Church of Rome Valid? IV." *The Presbyterian* 16 (April 25, 1846).

"German Roman Catholic Movement," *The Presbyterian* 16 (Dec. 19, 1846).

Goris, Harm, ed. *Synopsis Purioris Theologiae / Synopsis of a Purer Theology*. Translated by Riemer A. Faber. 3 Vols. Leiden: Brill, 2014–2020.

Gutjahr, Paul C. *Charles Hodge: Guardian of American Orthodoxy*. Oxford: Oxford University Press, 2011.

Hodge, A. A. *The Life of Charles Hodge, D.D., LL.D., Professor in the Theological Seminary, Princeton, N. J.* New York: Charles Scribner's Sons, 1880.

Hodge, Charles. *Discussions in Church Polity*, Edited by William Durant. New York: Charles Scribner's Sons, 1878.

———. "The General Assembly of 1835." *The Biblical Repertory and Princeton Review* 7:3 (July 1835): 440–482.

———. "The General Assembly." *The Biblical Repertory and Princeton Review* 17:3 (July 1845): 428–471.

———. "Review of Essays in the Presbyterian by Theophilus on the Question: Is Baptism in the Church of Rome Valid?" *The Biblical Repertory and Princeton Review* 18:2 (1846): 320–344.

———. *Systematic Theology.* 3 vols. Grand Rapids: Eerdmans, 1986.

———. "Tracts for the Times." *The Biblical Repertory and Princeton Review* 10:1 (January 1838): 84–119.

———. "The Unity of the Church Based on Personal Union with Christ." In *History, Essays, Orations, and Other Documents of the Sixth General Conference of the Evangelical Alliance*, edited by Philip Schaff and S. Irenaeus Prime. New York: Harper & Brothers, 1874.

Hoffecker, Andrew W. *Charles Hodge: The Pride of Princeton*. American Reformed Biographies. Phillipsburg: P & R Publishing, 2011.

McGraw, Ryan. Review of *Word, Water, and Spirit*, by J. V. Fesko. *The Confessional Presbyterian* 9 (2013): 190–197.

Miller Jr., Samuel. *The Life of Samuel Miller*, 2 vols. Philadelphia: Claxton, Remsen & Haffelfinger, 1869.

Muller, Richard A. "Giving Direction to Theology: The Scholastic Dimension." *Journal of Evangelical Theological Society* 28:2 (June 1985): 183–193.

———. "The Problem of Protestant Scholasticism—a Review and Definition." In *Reformation and Scholasticism*, edited by Willem J. van Asselt and Eef Dekker. Grand Rapids: Baker Academic, 2001.

———. *Post-Reformation Reformed Dogmatics: The Rise and Development of Reformed Orthodoxy, ca. 1520 to ca. 1725*. 4 vols. Grand Rapids: Baker Academic, 2003.

N. E. Puritan. "Is the Church of Rome a Church of Christ?" *The Presbyterian* 15 (Sept. 6, 1845).

Noll, Mark A. "Introduction." In *The Princeton Theology, 1812–1921*, edited by Mark A. Noll. Grand Rapids: Baker Publishing House, 1983.

Palmer, B. M. *The Life and Letters of James Henley Thornwell, D.D., LL.D.* Richmond: Whittet & Shepperson, 1875.

Pictet, Benedict. *Christian Theology*. Translated by Frederick Reyroux. Philadelphia: Presbyterian Board of Publication, n.d.

"Presbytery of Carlisle." *The Presbyterian* 16 (May 2, 1846).

"Presbytery of Carlisle." *The Presbyterian* 16 (May 9, 1846).

"Presbytery of Carlisle." *The Presbyterian* 16 (May 16, 1846).

Preus, Robert D. *The Theology of Post-Reformation Lutheranism*. 2 vols. Concordia Publishing House: St. Louis, 1970.

Reynolds, Mark Alan. "Charles Hodge's Ecclesiastical Elenctics: His Response to Catholicizing Tendencies in the Churches, 1837–1860." Ph.D. Dissertation, Saint Louis University, 2000.

Shea, William M. *The Lion and the Lamb: Evangelicals and Catholics in America*. Oxford: Oxford University Press, 2004.

Strange, Alan D. *The Doctrine of the Spirituality of the Church in the Ecclesiology of Charles Hodge*. Reformed Academic Dissertations. Phillipsburg: P&R Publishing, 2017.

Tennent, Gilbert. *Irenicum Ecclesiasticum*. Philadelphia, 1749.

Theophilus. "Is Baptism in the Church of Rome Valid? No. II." *The Presbyterian* 16 (Jan. 3, 1846).

———. "Is Baptism in the Church of Rome Valid? No. III." *The Presbyterian* 16 (Jan. 10, 1846).

———. "Is Baptism in the Church of Rome Valid? No. IV." *The Presbyterian* 16 (Jan. 17, 1846).

———. "Is Baptism in the Church of Rome Valid? No. V." *The Presbyterian* 16 (Jan. 24, 1846).

———. "Is Baptism in the Church of Rome Valid? No. VI." *The Presbyterian* 16 (Jan. 31, 1846).
———. "Is Baptism in the Church of Rome Valid? No. VII." *The Presbyterian* 16 (Feb. 7, 1846).
———. "Is Baptism in the Church of Rome Valid? No. VIII." *The Presbyterian* 16 (Feb. 14, 1846).
———. "Is Baptism in the Church of Rome Valid? No. IX." *The Presbyterian* 16 (Feb. 21, 1846).
———. "Is Baptism in the Church of Rome Valid? No. X." *The Presbyterian* 16 (Feb. 28, 1846).
———. "Is Baptism in the Church of Rome Valid? No. XI." *The Presbyterian* 16 (March 7, 1846).
———. "Is Baptism in the Church of Rome Valid? No. XII." *The Presbyterian* 16 (March 14, 1846).
———. "Is Baptism in the Church of Rome Valid? No. XIII." *The Presbyterian* 16 (March 21, 1846).
———. "Is Baptism in the Church of Rome Valid? No. XIV." *The Presbyterian* 16 (April 4, 1846).
Thornwell, James Henley. "The Validity of the Baptism of the Church of Rome." In *The Collected Writings of James Henley Thornwell*. 4 Vols. Carlisle, PA: The Banner of Truth Trust, 1986.
Toon, Peter. *Evangelical Theology, 1833–1856— A Response to Tractarianism*. New Foundations Theological Library. Atlanta: John Knox Press, 1979.
Troxel, Craig A. "'Divine Right' Presbyterianism and Church Power." Ph.D. Dissertation, Westminster Theological Seminary, 1998.
Trueman, Carl R. and R. S. Clark, ed. *Protestant Scholasticism: Essays in Reassessment*. Carlisle: Paternoster Press, 1999.
Turretin, Francis. *Institutes of Elenctic Theology*. Translated by G. M. Giger. 3 vols. Phillipsburg, NJ: R&R Publishing, 1992–1997.
Willborn, C. N. "Hodge and Thornwell: 'Princes in Israel.'" *The Confessional Presbyterian* 8 (2012): 44–54.
"Writings of Dr. Charles Hodge of Princeton." *Bibliotheca Sacra* 36 (July 1879): 584–588.

Stefan Lindholm

9. Charles Hodge on Christ's Presence in the Eucharist

9.1 Introduction

Among the many theological battles Charles Hodge fought in his distinguished career as theological educator at Princeton Theological Seminary, the most taxing one was perhaps his debate over the presence of Christ in the Eucharist with John Williamson Nevin (1803–1886). Nevin was professor at the German Reformed Seminary in Mercersburg. He had written a scholarly work on the Eucharist entitled, *Mystical Presence: A Vindication of the Reformed or Calvinistic Doctrine of the Holy Eucharist* in 1846[1]. In this book, he argued that Hodge and other divines in North America had deviated from Calvin's rich view of eucharistic presence – for the Eucharist "forms the very heart of the whole Christian worship."[2] Hodge wrote a rather negative review of the book, which motivated Nevin to write a thorough point-by-point refutation of it in the *Mercersburg Review*.[3] Nevin was not, however, the only one who raised objections to Hodge's review. For instance, the Princeton graduate and Church Historian at Columbia Seminary in South Carolina, John Adger, wrote a review of the whole debate between the two and came down in

1 John Williamson Nevin, *The Mystical Presence: And the Doctrine of the Reformed Church on the Lord's Supper*, ed. Linden J DeBie, vol. 1, The Merceburg Theology Study Series (Eugene: Wipf & Stock Publishers, 2012). Hereafter abbreviated as MTSS I. It has been lauded by modern reformation scholars such as Brian Gerrish as a forerunner of the historical studies in reformed theology that would appear in the 20th century.

2 MTSS I:11

3 Hodge's hesitated to get involved in a debate with Nevin is clear from the way he began his review: "We have had Dr. Nevins' work on the *Mystical Presence* on our table since its publication, some two years ago, but have never really read it, until within a fortnight." in John Williamson Nevin and Charles Hodge, *Coena Mystica: Debating Reformed Eucharistic Theology*, ed. Linden J DeBie, vol. 2, The Merceburg Theology Study Series (Eugene: Wipf & Stock Publishers, 2013). Hereafter abbreviated as MTSS II. The quote is from MTSS II: 2. During Hodge's study period in Europe, none other than John W. Nevin had been his supplement teacher at Princeton. It is understandable that it took two years for Hodge to write his review of *Mystical Presence* and that the battle against German mediating theology became one of his main apologetic concerns. (Originaly in Charles Hodge, "Doctrine of the Reformed Church on the Lord's Supper", *The Biblical Repertory and the Princeton Review*, 20 (April 1848): 227–77.) See Linde J. LeBie bibliographical essay in MTSS II; E. Brooks Holifield, *Sacramental Theology in America: Seventeenth–Nineteenth Centuries*, ed. Hans Boersma and Matthew Levering (Oxford: Oxford University Press, 2015): 389.

Nevin's favor.[4] Although Hodge did not respond at that time to Nevin's rebuttal, is clear that the issues stemming from their exchange in the 1840s stayed with him for his entire career as we will see. Indeed, the debate over the Eucharist was an expression of two rather different sets of theological sensibilities at Princeton and Mercersburg, which arguably have repercussions in American protestant church life to this day.

Several scholars have analyzed the exchange between Nevin and Hodge and the majority view may be summed in the words of Robert Letham:

> When, in in the 1840's, John Nevin of Mercersburg expounded the classic Reformed teaching on the Lord's Supper, he was trenchantly opposed by some of the appointed guardians of that very theology, such as Charles Hodge. The verdict of history has been that Nevin was right and that Hodge had failed to grasp his own theological tradition.[5]

Although, Hodge's exposition and defense had a more immediate influence in his contemporary context, late 19th and 20th century scholars have judged that Nevin's work was of a higher quality regarding the historical and theological grounds for the Reformed view of Eucharist. I will discuss relevant aspects the Nevin-Hodge debate but my main focus is Hodge's view of Christ's presence in the Eucharist and the reasons for it in his 19th century American context as well as in relation to the Reformed historic heritage he wanted to claim his own.

I will, in section 9.2, deal with the diverging historiographical and philosophical aspects of Nevin's and Hodge's approaches to the Reformed tradition on eucharistic presence. In section 9.3, I shall look closer at Hodge's attempt to avoid both Zwingli's and Calvin's views of eucharistic presence and show that (although there are some tendencies in the late Hodge toward a more complete view of the Eucharist) he was not successful in upholding a stable and coherent intermediate position, but wavered between memorialism and parallelism. In section 9.4, I compare Hodge with some representative Reformed orthodox theologians, since he held the Reformed theologians of the 17th century in high regard. I conclude briefly in section 9.5, that Hodge's view of the Eucharist is marked by conflicting ideas and tensions, much due to his own ecclesial as well theological and philosophical presuppositions.

---

4 John Adger, "Calvin Defended Against Drs. Cunningham and Hodge", *The Southern Presbyterian Review* vol 27 (1876): 133–166. See also E. Brooks Holifield, "Mercersburg, Princeton, and the South: The Sacramental Controversy in the Nineteenth Century", *Journal of Presbyterian History* 54, no 2 (1976): 238–57.

5 Robert Letham, *The Lord's Supper: Eternal Word in Broken Bread* (Phillipsburg: P&R Publishing Company, 2001): 2.

9.2 Hodge and Nevin on the Development of the Reformed Doctrine of the Eucharist

In his review of *The Mystical Presence*, Hodge expressed admiration of Nevin's collection of historic material from confessions and theologians, although he complained that the interpretation of them was one sided. Hodge readily acknowledged that it is difficult getting to grips with the the magisterial teaching on Christ's presence in the Eucharist since "The subject itself is mysterious."[6] Despite that, he declared that he essentially disagreed with Nevin on "the whole subject" – what the real doctrine of the Eucharist in the Reformed tradition is, both on historical and dogmatic grounds. In large part their differences played out in the way they approached the major Reformed confessional documents on the Eucharist, especially the Heidelberg Catechism and the Westminster standards.[7] In the exchange between Nevin and Hodge, we see two opposed schools of thought, both driven by theological (and philosophical) concerns although both profess to present the matter in strict historical and academic terms.

Hodge's approach to the Reformed confessional tradition was exemplified, by a document that never received an official of status as a pan-Reformed confession, the *Consensus Tigurinus* (1549).[8] For Hodge, the Consensus was a precursor to the

6 MTSS II: 3

7 George Hunsinger's comment captures the gist of the opposition of Hodge's and Nevin's views: "Both the Heidelberg Catechism and the Westminster standards were in play. Neither Nevin nor Hodge wanted to reject either of these venerable Reformed symbols. Nevertheless, it seems fair to say that Nevin read Westminster through the lens of the Heidelberg Catechism, while Hodge did much the reverse by reading Heidelberg through the lens of the Westminster standards." George Hunsinger, "The Heidelberg Catechism in America: A Snapshot from the History of Its Reception", *Theology Today* 70, no. 3 (October 2013): 256–68, quote at 263.

8 See "Mutual Consent As to the Sacraments" in *Calvin's Tracts and Letters* (Edinburgh: Banner of Truth, 2009) vol II: 199–244. Here I quote from the more recent translation of the Consensus in Torrance Kirby, "3. *Consensus Tigurinus* , 1549", *Reformation & Renaissance Review* 18, No 1 (January 2016): 34–44. See also, R. Ward Holder, "The Pain of Agreement: Calvin and the *Consensus Tigurinus*", *Reformation & Renaissance Review* 18, No 1 (January 2016): 85–94; K. J. Drake, *The Flesh of the Word: The Extra Calvinisticum from Zwingli to Early Orthodoxy*, Oxford study in historical theology series (New York, NY, United States of America: Oxford University Press, 2021); Randall C. Zachman, "Did the Zurich Consensus Create the Possibility of Future Dialogue with Wittenberg?", *Reformation & Renaissance Review* 18, No 1 (January 2016): 59–71; Emidio Campi, "The *Consensus Tigurinus* : Origins, Assessment, and Impact", *Reformation & Renaissance Review* 18, no 1 (January 2016): 5–24 and Richard A. Muller, "Calvin on Sacramental Presence, in the Shadow of Marburg and Zurich," in *Lutheran Quarterly*, 23 (2009): 147–167. Due to the lack of recognition of the Consensus in the sixteenth century, Nevin did not even bother to include it in his list of authoritative confessional statements in *Mystical Presence*. Neither had his colleague, the great church historian Philip Schaff in *Creeds of Christendom*, 6th ed. revised and enlarged (New York: Harper and Brothers, Franklin Square, 1983 [1931]).

mature 17th century Reformed eucharistic theology enshrined in the Westminster standards. For this reason, he unreservedly praised the Consensus: [T]here is not a word [in the Consensus], which any of the evangelical churches of the present day would desire to alter. We should like to print them all as the confession of our own faith on this whole subject."[9]

The aim of the Consensus was to bring concord between the pro-Zwinglian and the pro-calvinist in the Swiss churches.[10] There was a fear among the Zwinglian wing that, although Calvin agreed with Zwingli on central negative claims concerning the Eucharist (e. g. that there is no physical or physical presence or a sacrifice of Christ in the Eucharist), he had given in too much to Luther's notion of eucharistic presence. Prior to signing the Consensus, Calvin had for a couple of years corresponded and met with Heinrich Bullinger (1504–1575), who enjoyed great respect in the Swiss churches among the pro-Zwinglians, with the view to drafting a eucharistic Confession on the Eucharist that would unite the Swiss churches. Although Bullinger's eucharistic theology has similarities with Zwingli's it is arguably closer to that of Calvin in many respects as both rejected memorialism and affirmed a Spiritual presence.[11] Brian Gerrish ascribes a kind of parallelism to Bullinger, a position midway view between Calvin's instrumentalism and Zwingli's memorialism.[12] In May 1549 the two men met (together with William Farrell and

---

9 MTSS II: 17–19. This evaluation was consistent through his life – in *Systematic Theology* 3 vol. (Grand Rapids: Baker Bookshouse, 1988 [1871–73]) III: 517, Hodge praised the Consensus as "the most considered and cautiously worded exposition of the Reformed in relation to the sacraments." And later on: "No document […] can have a higher claim to represent the true doctrine of the Reformed Church than this "Consensus". *Systematic Theology* III: 632.

10 There was also political pressure. For instance, Emperor Charles V (1500–1558) had defeated the Lutheran princes, the Schmalkaldic league, in 1547 and imposed a settlement, the so-called Augsburg *interim*, which reduced the effects of the protestant reformation in an attempt to more or less restore Roman Catholic practices. The need to united under one confession among the protestants became acute.

11 See, Joseph C. McLelland, "Meta-Zwingli or Anti-Zwingli? Bullinger and Calvin in Eucharistic Concord" in *Huldrych Zwingli: 1484–1451: A Legacy of Radical Reformation*, ed. Edward J. Furcha (Montreal: FRC/ARC, 1985).

12 The sacramental sign and the reality they signify differs in these three typologies (borrowed from Brian Gerrish) – according to memorialism, the eucharistic elements signify a past event, according to parallelism a simultaneous operation of the Spirit in the believer and according to instrumentalism grace is brought to the believer via the elements, in some sense. See Gerrish, "Sign and Reality: The Lord's Supper in the Reformed Confession" in *The Old Protestantism and the New: Essays on the Reformation Heritage* (Edinburgh: T&T Clarke, 1982): ch 7. In this chapter I use these typologies as an incomplete but still useful heuristic tool. Some of their limitations are pointed out in section 9.4 below. Emidio Campis has remarked, "It is questionable, for example, whether the well–known classification of Brian G. Gerrish […] sheds light on the actual development of their eucharistic thought in each respective phase of their career – or if it instead imposes on them static categories which in reality are not as neat." ("The *Consensus Tigurinus*": 17, fn 64.) However, in *Grace and*

delegates from the city council) in Zurich, trying to settle the matter.[13] The final version of the Consensus contained 26 articles and was signed by both Bullinger and Calvin in the summer.[14] Naturally, the language and concerns of both Bullinger and Calvin are detectible in the text. For instance, when the Confession describes the sacraments as "marks and tokens" of the fellowship with God (art 7) it has a clear bullingerian or even Zwinglian tenor. The calvinian emphasis is also evident, when it says that sign and the thing signified are "distinct but not disjoined" (art 8) and that they are "instruments, by which God acts efficaciously when so he pleases" (art 13). Both agree that the instruments alone do not have any "intrinsic virtue" but that God "uses them as supporting instruments, albeit the whole power of acting remains with him alone" (art 12).[15]

From these examples we may gather that there is an inbuilt ambiguity in the formulations of the Consensus that allows for instrumental as well as parallelist interpretations. This interpretive ambiguity was exploited by both Hodge and Nevin. Nevin read the document as consistently affirming the same notion of presence that Calvin had taught before (and after) the meeting with Bullinger[16] and accused

---

Gratitude: The Eucharistic Theology of John Calvin (Eugene, Or: Wipf and Stock Publ, 2002) Gerrish acknowledges the development of all the three reformers during their career.

13 The text for discussion was then actually a text Calvin had drafted for the Bern pastors around the same time, the Genevan Confession, and expressed more or Calvin's richer view.

14 Calvin had in 1548 drawn up 24 articles on the Eucharist with annotations, which were circulated in the Swiss churches. Here Calvin had distanced himself from both transubstantiation of the Roman Catholics and the consubstantiation of the Lutherans, yet he retained an idea of real or mystical presence and talked of the eucharistic elements as sacramental signs, organs or instruments of Grace the power of the Holy Spirit. Bullinger wrote to Calvin that he rather preferred the term "seal" for "instrument" but could settle for "organ" when talking about the sacrament. However, he emphasized that the signs are not empty and that Christ is by the power of the Spirit truly communicated to us what the signs seal or signify. For an illuminating account of the context and interpretation of the document, see Emidio Campi, "The *Consensus Tigurinus*": 13.

15 "The Consensus could fairly be described as a compromise document, which its reception history is a witness to – instead of bringing concord it drove the parties it sought to bring together further apart . "...the grave irony of Calvin's efforts here were that instead of becoming the glue that would hold various Protestant confessions together, they became a wedge that would drive them further apart." (Holder, "The Pain of Agreement", 86) This is not to say that minimalist and compromise document cannot be received as confessions for large parts of the church. The most obvious example is perhaps the Augsburg Confession (1530), drawn up by Philip Melanchthon, which can be described in the same way as the Consensus, a compromise document, yet in its *invariata*-version is a confession of high standing in most protestant churches.

16 ""...it is a most violent assumption, on the part of Dr. Hodge, that [Calvin's] plain, unequivocal declarations on the subject of his own faith, a hundred times repeated throughout his works, are to be overruled by the authority of this one document, of most questionable sense, instead of allowing it to be interpreted rather by the hundred authorities that are explicit and clear." MTSS, II: 23. See also. MTSS, II: 69–70. See also, "It is Bullinger that rises above his old position...in free obedience

Hodge of reading his modern suppositions into the texts so that Calvin's doctrine was distorted.[17] Nevin also accused him of not taking the time to go back to the sources of the sacramental debate and Calvin's defences in the following years, that certainly strengthens Calvin's "dynamic presence" – one of Nevin's many ways of talking of a the bodily presence of Christ due to the holy Spirit that bridged the local distance between the exalted body of Christ and the faithful communicant.[18]

Behind Hodge's and Nevin's differences lurked the deeper issue of how they received Calvin's teaching on the Eucharist. Calvin had frequently and publicly said, in addition to the Eucharist being a seal of the covenant to the believer (as expressed in the Consensus and elsewhere), that Christ's glorified human body also exerted a kind of influence on the communicants of the Eucharist.[19] An early instance is Calvin's found in "Confession of Faith Concerning the Eucharist" (1537):

> We confess that the spiritual life which Christ bestows upon us does not rest on the fact that he vivifies us with his Spirit, but that his Spirit makes us participants in the virtue of his vivifying body, by which participation we are fed on eternal life. Hence when we speak of the communion which we have with Christ, we understand the faithful to communicate not less in his body and blood than in his Spirit, so that thus they possess the whole Christ.[20]

---

to the superior mind of Calvin; not Calvin that descends as the *Princeton Review* would seem to imagine.....Every such supposition as this last is unhistorical in the extreme. It turns Calvin into either a fool or a knave.... It comes to this then, that he played a false game either at Strasburg or Zurich", MTSS I: 265.

17 He said that Hodge read the Consensus "down to a full level, with the sacramental faith of our modern American churches generally" MTSS, II, 63 and that though Hodge was "perfectly honest" he had spoken "from a very different consciousness, from that which reigned in the Reformed Church in the sixteenth century" (idem, 65). Nevin tried not to distrust Hodge's sincerity but must have wondered at times since to Nevin's mind Hodge simply did not bother to go to the sources.

18 See MTSS, II, 65–70.

19 In fact, Calvin sometimes talks about this as if it is the Spirit's power and sometimes as it is a power in the glorified body of Christ and sometimes a combination of both. See, e. g. John Calvin, *Institutes of the Christian Religion*, ed. John Thomas McNeill, The Library of Christian Classics (Louisville, Ky. London: Westminster John Knox Press, 1960): 4.17.10: "Even though it seems unbelievable that Christ's flesh, separated from us by such great distance, penetrates to us, so that it becomes our food, let us remember how far the secret power of the Holy Spirit towers above all our senses, and how foolish it is to wish to measure his immeasurableness by our measure. What then, our mind does not comprehend, let faith conceive: that the Spirit truly unites things separated in space."

20 in *Calvin: Theological Treatises*. The Library of Christian Classics. Edited and Translated by J.K.S. Reid (Louisville: Westminster John Know Press, 1954): 168. Quoted in MTSS II: 57 who translates vivifying body closer to the Latin as "life-giving flesh" (*carnis suae vivificae*). In other places, Calvin is more careful about this kind of language, like in *Institutes*, 4.17.9: "The flesh of Christ, however, *has not such power in itself as to make us live*, seeing that by its own first condition it was subject to mortality, and even now, when endued with immortality, lives not by itself. Still it is properly said

Hodge, throughout his career, found that Calvin's idea of our partaking in Christ's "vivifying body"[21] deeply problematic and in his review he judge that it was an "uncongenial foreign element" in the reformer's thinking.[22] He understood Calvin as positing a kind of power of effluence radiating from the glorified body of Christ in heaven to the communicants.[23] However, Hodge did not think that the view was unique to Calvin, though, as he admitted that the Gallican, the Belgian and the early Scottish confessions "most nearly conform to the peculiar view of Calvin."[24] In *Systematic Theology* Hodge seemingly tried to downplay the apparent embarrassment by saying that only "at times" did Calvin teach this doctrine and that "unless we are willing to accuse the illustrious Calvin of inconsistency, his meaning must be made to harmonize with what he says elsewhere" (and then goes on to quote the Consensus as proof).[25]

---

to be life-giving, as it is pervaded with the fulness of life for the purpose of transmitting it to us." (Emphasis mine)

21 Calvin was by far not the first who talked about Christ's human nature in this manner. A standard patristic instance of this kind of language is found in Cyril's third letter to Nestorius, read at the Council of Ephesus (431): "This we receive not as ordinary flesh, heaven forbid, nor as that of a man who has been made holy and joined to the Word by union of honour, or who had a divine indwelling, but as truly the life-giving and *real flesh of the Word* [*ut vere vivificatricem et ipsius Verbi propriam factam.*]. For being life by nature as God, when he became one with his own flesh, he made it also to be life-giving, as also he said to us: "Amen I say to you, unless you eat the flesh of the Son of man and drink his blood" . For we must not think that it is the flesh of a man like us (for how can the flesh of man be life-giving by its own nature?), but as being made the *true flesh* [*vere proprium eius factam*] of the one who for our sake became the son of man and was called so." Emphasis mine.

22 MTSS II: 36. William B. Evans comments, however, that Hodge's evaluation of Calvin differs in the *Systematic Theology* from his review of Nevin. In the review, Hodge says that Calvin's concern was to placate the Lutherans. In *Systematic Theology* he is, according to Evans judgement, "more kind to the Reformer," since Hodge seems to acknowledge Calvin's emphasis on the unity of the substance of the Old and New Testaments. Evans refer to *Systematic Theology* III: 647. See Evans, *Imputation and Impartation*: 223 fn 123.

23 As I have pointed out in footnote 20, it should be noted here that Calvin's language wavers between the view Hodge attributes to him and that it is the power of the Holy Spirit that makes Christ's body and blood really present to the communicants, despite the spatial distance. Both of these notions are sometimes seen together. I will not pursue this ambiguity here. It seems to me, however, that a contributing reason to Hodge's rejection of Calvin's notion of "spiritual presence" is that these two notions were not made distinct in the Reformer. As I will discuss later, the reformed orthodox retained Calvin's notion of spiritual presence but did not, as far as I know, employ an explicit terminology that, at least not without certain qualifications, would yield the idea of a vivifying body of Christ. Had these notions been between distinguished in Calvin, as well as his later interpreters, perhaps, Hodge would have been less willing to judge his eucharistic theology as uncongenial.

24 *Systematic Theology* III: 630.

25 *Systematic Theology* III: 646. See also "To preserve the consistency of the great Reformed his language must be interpreted as to harmonize with the two facts for which he so earnestly contends; first, that believers receive elsewhere by faith all they receive at the Lord's table; and secondly, that we

Although this assessment of Calvin may appear odd for a calvinist of Hodge's caliber, it had among 19th century American Reformed theologians become common place to view Calvin's teaching on the eucharist as extreme.[26] A strong kind of memorialism was widespread at the time, which explicitly rejected the notion of Christ's real presence or communication of Christ's body and blood. As an example, Nevin quotes John Dick's popular, *Lectures on Theology*:

> The doctrine of [Christ's] presence I would not found, as others do, upon the words of institution which, when justly interpreted, merely import that the elements are signs of his body and blood. Now, a sign is very far from implying that the thing signified is present. It is rather understood to represent an *absent object* and is put in its place to remind us of it because it is removed to a distance from us. Instead of being a fair conclusion from the Words of the Institution, that there is a peculiar, mysterious presence of our Saviour which can be accounted for only by the miraculous power of the Spirit, *it might rather be inferred that he is not present at all and that the design of the symbols is him to remembrance in his absence.*[27]

Nevin also, anecdotally, relates that Hodge's review was an expression of a wider culturally engrained fear that encouraged believers in the churches "not to think more of such monumental force in the institution [of the Eucharist], lest they should be guilty of popish superstition; and as far as this [review] article goes, Dr. Hodge would seem to have precisely this view."[28] In other words, Nevin thought that Hodge represented this widespread bent towards reducing the Lord's Supper to Zwinglian memorialism.

Hodge himself did not think that he expressed the sort of Zwinglian memorialism Nevin accused him of.[29] Instead he sought for a middle ground or "intermediate form", between Zwingli and Calvin, which he thought became the dominant view

---

Christians receive nothing above or beyond that which was received by the saint under the Old Testament, before the glorified body of Christ had any existence" (idem, 647).

26 The Scottish theologian, William Cunningham (1805–1861) found Calvin's idea of: "...a real influence exerted by Christ's human nature upon the souls of believers...altogether unsuccessful, and resulted only in what was about as unintelligible as Luther's consubstantiation. This is, perhaps, the greatest blot in the history of Calvin's labours as a public instructor." William Cunningham, *The Reformers and the Theology of the Reformation* (Edinburgh: Banner of Truth Trust, 1989 [1862]): 240. Similar sentiments were voiced by Robert Dabney. See, Ralph Cunnington, "Calvin's Doctrine of the Lord's Supper: A Blot upon His Labours as a Public Instructor?", *Westminster Theological Journal* 73 (2011): 215–236.

27 As quoted in MTSS I: 317. Emphasis mine.

28 MTSS II: 111

29 *Systematic Theology* III: 627, "It was the tendency of the Zwinglian element of the Reformed Church, to make less of the supernatural aspect of the sacraments than their associates did." See also, Jonathan

as the Reformed tradition matured.[30] Hodge favorably cited the Second Helvetic Confession (1562), penned by Bullinger.[31] Bullinger had also tried to find a middle way between Zwingli and Calvin but, as will become clear, Bullinger's position is not exactly or at least not consistently that of Hodge. Bullinger parallelism insists on a spiritual communication that is *simultaneous* with the eucharistic eating, although not "caused" by the external signs of bread and wine.[32] Hodge sometimes expressed a similar view and sometimes a view that emphasizes the past sacrificial event of Christ that the communicants are to commemorate.[33]

Hodge evaluation and reading of the Reformed teaching on the Eucharist is explained by his view of doctrinal development, [34] in part based on the notions of

---

G Bonomo, *Incarnation and Sacrament: The Eucharistic Controversy between Charles Hodge and John Williamson Nevin* (Eugene, OR: Wipf & Stock, 2010): 57.

30 *Systematic Theology* III: 627 "There are three distinct types of [eucharistic] doctrine among [the reformed], the Zwinglian, the Calvinist, and an intermediate form, which ultimately became symbolical, being adopted in the authoritative standards of the Church."

31 He claimed that the Helvetic Confession "on some accounts" is to be "regarded as the most authoritative symbol of the Reformed Church, as it was more generally received than any other, and was sanctioned by all parties" (*Systematic Theology* III: 624.) However, later on he asserts that the truest of symbols to his mind was the Westminster standards.

32 *Second Helvetic Confession* (https://www.creeds.net/helvetic/c21.htm): ch XXI: "… the faithful receive what is given by the ministers of the Lord, and they eat the bread of the Lord and drink of the Lord's cup. *At the same time* by the work of Christ through the Holy Spirit they also inwardly receive the flesh and blood of the Lord, and are thereby nourished unto life eternal." It should be noted that there is also an expression in the Second Helvetic Confession that comes closer to Calvin's vivific view: "…Christ, although in his body he is absent from us in heaven, present with us, not corporeally, but spiritually, by his vivfying operation, and as he himself explained at his Last Supper that he world be present with us" (idem.) Hodge is right that one may find support a symbolic, a parallelist as well as an instrumentalist view of the eucharist in the reformed confessions and theologians of the 16th. Sometimes we find a language and implicit or explicit theory that suggests a combination of these views within one and the same corpus, passage or writer. A rather clear movement is, after all, the move away from commemoration alone to include some sort of communication of Christ to the believer in, with or through the sacraments. For instance, commenting on the Second Helvetic Confession, Gerrish notes that "it is not so much anti-Calvinistic as timidly Calvinistic: all the leading confessions place the emphasis on communication rather than commemoration, but some reflect a certain synthesis toward the idea of the means of grace." Gerrish, *The Old Protestantism*: 128.

33 It should, perhaps be added the trivial point, that memorialism and parallelism are not contradictory as interpretations of the eucharistic presence but rather complementary so that it would only be natural to find parallelism if there is memorialism. The problem is when parallelist language is reduced to memoralist language. Arguably, a full orbed eucharistic theology should include all of Gerrish's three types.

34 Thus, Hodge denied doctrinal development as a growth in doctrinal content, in the sense that Nevin allowed. The kind of development in view for Hodge is rather not that something new is added to doctrine but a process of purification of original or biblical doctrine from "uncongenial" elements.

deduction and internal consistency.[35] Doctrinal or systematic theology should seek to deduce from the biblical material a consistent whole. However, the doctrine of the Eucharist is a difficult subject that easily lend itself to error. Thus, Hodge thinks, a consistent set of principles of Reformed theology in general was to be found first in the confessional consolidation in the 17th century:

> The truth [of theology] is usually elicited by conflict; agreement is the result of comparison and adjustment of divergences. We accordingly find in the history of Protestant theology much more of inconsistency and confusion during the sixteenth than during the seventeenth century. It was not until one principle had been allowed to modify another, that the scheme of doctrine came to adjust itself to the consistent and moderate form in which it is presented in the writings of Turretin and Gerhard. [36]

The mature confessional standards, primarily the *Westminster Confession of Faith*, affirmed, the sort of the middle position concerning the presence in the Eucharist that Hodge considered orthodox due to its consistency and moderation. Thus, he thought that the "uncongenial" calvinian idea of a life-giving influence from Christ's glorified body died out in the 17th century – it was either omitted or understood figuratively.[37]

On the basis of Hodge's view of doctrinal development, we seem to have been provided with a criterion by which we can evaluate his eucharistic theology and be justified in making comparisons between Hodge and 17th century Reformed theology. Here I will only make some observations about the eucharistic language in the *Westminster Confession of Faith*, which indeed admits a kind of parallelism that

---

35 This relates to his view on scientific theology. See, *Systematic Theology* I: 1–2: "So the Bible contains the truths which the theologian has to collect, authenticate, arrange, and exhibit in their internal relation to each other. This constitutes the difference between biblical and systematic theology. The office of the former is to ascertain and state the facts of Scripture. The office of [the systematic theologian] is to take those facts, determine their relation to each other and to other cognate truths, as well as to vindicate them and show their harmony and consistency." See also, Annette G. Aubert, *The German Roots of Nineteenth-Century American Theology* (Oxford: Oxford University Press, 2013): ch 7.

36 "The first and Second Adam. The Elohim revealed in the Creation and Redemption of Man", The Biblical Repertory and Princeton Review 32 (1860): 335–376 (quote at 338). See also Hodge in MTSS II: 37. For an analysis of the historiographical issues, consult, Peter J Wallace, "History and Sacrament: John Williamson Nevin and Charles Hodge on the Lord's Supper", *Mid-America Journal of Theology* 11 (2000): 171–201.

37 "What is present, according to Calvin, is [...] a supernatural life-giving influence emanating from his glorified body in heaven and conveyed to the believer by the power of the Holy Ghost. According to the Reformed in general, it is not this supernatural power of the glorified body of Christ that is present and received, but the sacrificial efficacy of his body broken and his blood shed for the remission of sins." *Systematic Theology* III: 666–667.

Hodge could approve of – Christ is present spiritually "to the faith of the believer in that ordinance, as the elements themselves are to their outward senses."[38] But in other places the language seems to at least implicitly affirm a kind of instrumentalism when it is said that grace is "exhibited" (*exhibetur*) in the sacraments, in the sense of "holding forth" and not merely "displaying" Christ.[39] Gerrish judgement seems to be pointing in the right direction, although slightly overstated, that some of the statements in the Westminster Confession could be "understood in a purely Zwinglian sense."[40] In other words, the Westminster Confession of Faith had precisely the variety of ways of expressions that Hodge denied that it did. His own theological agenda and ecclesial context drove him to reduce the variety of expression that the actual text seems to allow.

Hodge's reading the Reformed confessional tradition is very different from Nevin's. His understanding of doctrinal development derives in large part from German mediating theology (*Vermittlungstheologie*).[41] This is seen in Nevin's view the "organic law", adapted from ideas found in George F. Hegel (1770–1831) and Friedrich D. Schleiermacher (1768–1834), according to which Truth reveals itself in the process of history. For the mediating theologians, the truths of Christian doctrine are not simply recorded facts or abstract ideas but the life of the church.[42] Nevin frequently employed organic analogies to express a developmental view of

---

38 *Westminster Confession of Faith* (https://www.ligonier.org/learn/articles/westminster-confession-faith) 29.7: "Worthy receivers, outwardly partaking of the visible elements in this sacrament, do then also inwardly by faith, really and indeed yet not carnally and corporally, but spiritually, receive and feed upon Christ crucified, and all benefits of His death: the body and blood of Christ being then not corporally or carnally in, with, or under the bread and wine; yet as really, but spiritually, present to the faith of believers in that ordinance, *as the elements themselves are to their outward senses*." Emphasis mine. See also *Westminster Confession of Faith* 27.2 "There is in every sacrament a spiritual relation, or sacramental union, between the sign and the thing signified; whence it comes to pass that the names and effects of the one are attributed to the other."

39 *Westminster Confession of Faith* 27.3.

40 *Westminster Confession of Faith* 29.7. See also Gerrish, *The Old Protestantism*: 126 f for his evaluation of the Westminster Catechisms.

41 Mediating theology is a broad term encompassing a range of themes current in 19th century German theology (by such as Friedrich D. Schleiermacher and Isac A. Dorner) not always internally consistent, like the idea of a central motif or dogma Christ as the central principle or idea for theology, the identification of Christian doctrine with "Christian consciousness" (Schleiermacher) and the organic growth of doctrine through history's unfolding of the Christ-idea. Several of these themes are clearly exemplified in Nevin and the Mercersburg theologians, adopted for his American readers. For more, see Aubert, *The German Roots of Nineteenth-Century American Theology*: ch 5–6. Se See also David R. Bains and Theodore Louis Trost, "Philip Schaff: The Flow of Church History and the Development of Protestantism", *Theology Today* 71, no 4 (January 2015): 416–28.

42 Typically, Nevin would insist that Christianity is not about primarily doctrine but about "life", "because Christianity is a new life, that it must work like leaven into our whole existence, generating a theology or theoretical religion in its own form, as well as a religion of mere feeling and practice.

doctrine: The incarnate and resurrected Lord Jesus Christ like an acorn that that causes the church grow and develop into a tree. What he called the "modern puritan" view of Christianity (which Hodge embraced according to Nevin) is characterized as "outward", "mechanical" and "abstract" in contrast to Nevin's understanding which is "inward, "organic" and "concrete".[43] For the church's life becomes visible in history as through its struggles against heresies and is nourished by its inward principle, the life of Christ.

This affords Nevin to be optimistic about the process and direction of historical and doctrinal development.[44] The contemporary church can expect an organic growth in its theological understanding of the central mystery, born out of that seed in early Christian church. Even if the historical process of growth is not without ups and downs, Nevin's Christocentrism allows him to think of the theologian's job as one of discerning the mystery in the life of the church. Such an organic and developmental view of doctrine stands in contrast to Hodge's view, which primarily strove to deduce and systematize the "facts" of the bible.[45] Accordingly, instead of being "uncongenial", Calvin's eucharistic theology represents to Nevin just the kind of organic maturation that has the deepest roots in ancient Christianity.[46] Besides Calvin's writings, Nevin sought to show this from a number of, almost exclusively 16th century, Reformed Confessions, notably the Heidelberg Confession, and some leading theologians.[47]

Thus, we have two sedimented narratives, one according to which the 17th century represents the mature Reformed theology (Hodge) and one its decline (Nevin). For all their differences, there are at least three general features that are common for Hodge and Nevin. First, a drive towards harmonization of the sources from a

---

43 This way of talking has a foundation in Calvin, see MTSS I: 280 ff for Nevin's exposition. See Evans, *Imputation and Impartation*: 156 ff.

44 MTSS I: 138–145.

45 Following the leading mediating theologians, and his colleague at Mercerburg, the German born Church Historian, Philipp Schaff, Nevin replaced Scripture as the *pricipium cognoscendi* (the cognitive foundation) for theology with Christ as an "organic law".

46 Nevin's suggestion was therefore that: "Religion must at once be objective and subjective, churchly and experimental [sic.], in one word Catholic as well as Puritan. This calls precisely for the restitution of the old idea of Christ's life, to the place original assigned to it in the Protestant creeds. What God had joined together, the sacrifice of Christ namely and his life, justification by faith and sacramental grace, let no man put asunder." (MTSS II:113)

47 E. g. in MTSS I:159. Commenting on the Heidelberg Catechism the idea of "life communication with Christ in the Holy Supper" is "solemnly proclaimed". In MTSS I: 304 ff., (referring to questions 75–77 and 79–80) Also, "...we are made to participate not orally and outwardly, but mystically, dynamically and substantially in the inmost soul-centre of our being, in the divine life that spring up perpetually through the fountain of his humanity as Calvin has it, for the use of our dreary nature." (idem, 306) Nevin also quotes the Westminster shorter catechism when expositing the eucharistic doctrine. MTSS I:158–9.

certain hermeneutical horizon, second that the 17th century sources generally did not keep the "Calvinistic doctrine" of the Lord's supper and, third, a desire to point to exemplary sources of (the Heidelberg and Westminster standards, respectively), reflecting their interpretive framework. Let us now turn our attention Hodge's view of the Eucharist in more detail.

9.3 Hodge's Intermediate Position

Since Hodge sought to articulate an intermediate position, between Zwingli and Calvin, we may be justified (as I have pointed out above) in expecting that he defends a kind of parallelism akin to that of Bullinger.[48] However, modern scholars have argued that Hodge did not manage to consistently hold to parallelism. William B. Evans concludes that Hodge's eucharistic theology, "in the final analysis," seems to be "nothing more than a mental exercise of remembrance and reflection that may be used by the Spirit from time to time to deepen the recipient's faith and commitment."[49] Similarly, Di Puccino thinks that this view collapses into mere memorialism, concluding that "The signs are thus reduced to nominalistic abstractions."[50]

One reason for this is that is that Hodge's use of sacramental language is not consistent (and perhaps that is an expression of his finding the doctrine "mysterious" and the confessional documents of the 16th century somewhat bewildering). Nevin complains that "Dr Hodge plays between the objective and subjective scheme of sacramental grace, in such a way that while he appears at times to accept the language of the first, it is only to fall in reality into the common-place sense of the second."[51] As an example of such a passage Nevin quotes the following rather typical summary statement of Hodge:

48 Or at least something more than mere memorialism As suggested in passing by Linden J. DeBie and W. Bradford Littlejohn, "Reformed Eucharistic Theology and the Case for Real Presence", *Theology Today* 71, no 4 (January 2015): 429–39, on page 434.

49 Evans, *Imputation and Impartation:* 224.

50 *The Interior Senses of Scriptures: The Sacred Hermeneutics of John W, Nevin* (Georgia: Mercer University Press, 1998): 73–7. But he admits within parenthesis "(Hodge, of course, did see it this way.) Although he argues that Hodge is a mere memorialist, DiPuccini qualifies these charges by saying that: "Hodge's theology of the Lord's Supper was not out-and-out memorialism. Despite all appearances, Hodge was not about to reduce faith to rationalism. In his view, faith includes both knowledge and assent as well as a "real appropriation of Christ." Nevin may well have exaggerated the degree of Hodge's subjectivity. But altogether with his other nominalistic tendencies, the Mercersburg doctor was more than justified in questioning the direction of his theology." (idem.)

51 MTSS II: 100.

> Christ is really present to his people in this sacrament, not bodily, but in spirit; not in the sense of local nearness, but of efficacious operation. They receive Him, not with the mouth but by faith; they receive his flesh and blood, not as flesh, not as material particles, not its human life, not the supernatural influence of his glorified body in heaven; but his body as broken and his blood as shed. The union thus signified and effected is not a corporeal union, not a mixture of substances, but a spiritual and mystical union due to the indwelling of the Holy Spirit. The efficacy of this sacrament, as a means of grace, is not in the signs, nor in the service, nor in the minister, nor in the word, but in the attending influence of the Holy Ghost.[52]

Hodge used the term "real presence" but the crux is how it is to be understood. Hodge follows the Reformed tradition in rejecting heretical articulations of Christ's "real presence" (Lutheran and Roman Catholic). However, when he affirms a spiritual and mystical union it seems to tend towards memorialism, for what is said to be present is Christ's sacrificed body and blood "as shed", i. e. as a *past* event and the efficacy is brought "by the attending influences of the Holy Ghost."

Hodge would only allow two kinds of presence in general. A thing can either be present to the sense faculties or to the mind's apprehension. Christ is not physically present in the Eucharist. Therefore, the only kind of presence left is a presence to the believer's mind.[53] Expressions like "sacrificial efficacy" and "virtue and efficacy", are translated as an "…intellectual cognition and apprehension, believing appropriation, and spiritual operation. The body and blood are present to us when they fill our thoughts, are apprehended by faith as broken and shed for our salvation, and exert upon us their proper effect."[54] (The term "proper effect" refers to the intellectual apprehension of the believing participant in the Eucharist.) And again, perhaps more clearly: "…presence [in the Eucharist] is to the mind, the object is not presented to the senses, but apprehended by faith. It is a presence of virtue

52 MTSS II:103. As evidence of Hodge's consistent understanding of the Eucharist over the years, these words are reproduced in *Systematic Theology* III: 650. Nevin comments in his review on this passage in bold letters Hodge's assertion that it is the mystical union is due to the indwelling of the Spirit: "NOT AS A PROXY ONLY OF AN ABSENT CHRIST, BUT AS THE SUPERNATURAL BOND OF OF A TRUE LIFE CONNECTION, BY WHICH HIS VERY FLESH IS JOINED TO OURS, MORE INTIMATELY FAR THAN THE TRUNK TO ITS BRANCHES, OR THE HEAD TO ITS MEMBERS, IN THE NATURAL WORLD." (MTSS II: 109) We may note that here is typical example of Nevin's idealist hermeneutics.

53 This is clear for instance, when he says: "A thing is present where it is perceived and where it acts. The nature of that presence varies with the nature of the object of which it is affirmed. A body is present where it is perceived but the senses or acts upon them. The soul is present where it perceives and acts. It is somewhere, and not everywhere. God is present everywhere, as He fills immensity." Hodge *Systematic Theology* III: 670. See also MTSS II: 27.

54 *Systematic Theology* III: 638

and efficacy, not of propinquity."[55] Such explanations of sacramental terminology certainly seem to underscore Nevin's charge of memorialism.

We may point out a few theological ideas that will help us to understand the motivations and ideas behind Hodge's position. First, the particular formulation of physical presence/absence just mentioned is connected with a less salient presupposition in Hodge theology. For Calvin and his generation, and their pre-Copernican cosmology, the problem of spatial distance undergirds the whole eucharistic discussion. Christ is neither locally nor physically present in the Eucharist but in heaven, at a distant physical place whence he shall return.[56] The Reformed (in contrast to say the Lutherans who argued for various notions of ubiquity) therefore argued that the spatial distance is overcome supernaturally by the Holy Spirit's making Christ's body and blood, his human nature, present in the Eucharist.[57] Calvin's acceptance of this view is, of course understandable, but it is striking that the 19th century Hodge accepted a similar spatial presupposition.[58] The reason I bring this up is that the kind of physical absence discussed in the 16th century eucharistic debate was also a presupposition for Hodge for what seems to be the same sort of reason: Christ's body can only be in one place at the same time and is "in" heaven. Assuming that even a glorified body like Christ's cannot act at a distance the only kind of presence left is mental presence, it seems. Nevin rejects out of hand that the human nature of Christ was merely a body in a distant place and argued that Christ incarnate is the very life principle of the humanity and truly communicated in the Eucharist.[59]

Second, the role of the Holy Spirit is important in Hodge's theology. In the quote above, Hodge talked about real presence of Christ in the Eucharist as "efficacious

55 MTSS II: 28.

56 For a discussion of these matters, see, Stefan Lindholm, *Jerome Zanchi (1516–90) and the Analysis of Reformed Scholastic Christology*, Reformed Historical Theology, Volume 37 (Göttingen: Vandenhoeck & Ruprecht, 2016): ch 6.

57 See, Drake, *The Flesh of the Word*, chs 2–3 and Cees Leijenhorst, "Place, Space and Matter in Calvinist Physics", *The Monist* 84, no. 4 (2001): 520–41. This presupposition is not, as far as I have seen, treated by Nevin supposedly because his found it less of a problem due to his idealist metaphysics.

58 Speaking of the ascension, he reports two common historical views: "The seat of [Christ's] kingdom is not clearly revealed. Some suppose that it is to be on this earth regenerated and fitted for this new order of things. Others understand the Scripture to teach that heaven as indicating an entirely different locality, is to be the final home of the redeemed." *Systematic Theology* II: 608.

59 Peter J. Wallace's comment is worth taking note of: "…the two theologians were simply talking past one another. Both conceived of spiritual presence in opposition to physical presence, but while Hodge thought of this as a presence to the mind, or soul, Nevin eliminated the dualism and spoke of it as a presence to the whole person, spiritually, and therefore saw Hodge's doctrine as mere intellectual apprehension (Calvin probably would have found both views unappealing, Hodge's for being too simplistic in its conception of mind, and Nevin's for its Hegelian notion of generic persons.)" Wallace, "History and Sacrament": 197–198.

operation" which is to be understood in terms of the believer's union with Christ through the Holy Spirit's operation (which is "spiritual and mystical due to the indwelling of the Holy Spirit"). However, a recuring concern for Hodge is that the Spirit's operations should be seen as *free*. Thus, in Hodge's talk of an attending power of the Spirit, the emphasis is not on the promise and permanence of the Spirit's action, but on the Spirit's freedom and spontaneity. Since the Spirit is a person or agent he is "acting when and where He pleases; more at one time than another, sometimes in one way and sometimes in another."[60] Any language that suggests that the Spirit is "tied" to the elements or ritual circumstances in the eucharistic offering appeared to Hodge as a threat to the Spirit's freedom.

A third and related factor may be gleaned from Hodge's treatment of the "spirituality of the church" in his attempt to discern the proper relationship between the church's spiritual power and the secular or worldly powers. He sought a moderate view of the spirituality of the church, avoiding the Scylla of emotionalist separatism and the Charybdis of dead formalism,[61] contending that the church is a mystical union of individual believers who are filled with the Holy Spirit. Therefore, the true identity of the church is not dependent upon any visible institution. The relation between the visible and the invisible church, are like the relation between the body and the soul – the latter can exist without the former. Therefore, the church may exist without external structures or means since it ultimately consists of the elect in and united with Christ.[62] Hodge said that:

> …union with the visible church, and participation in the sacraments, are not indispensable conditions for our union with Christ, neither are they the means of communicating, in the first instance, his benefits and grace, but rather the appointed means by which our union with Christ is acknowledged, and from time to time strengthened.[63]

60 "It is not however the influence of a uniformly acting force cooperating with the truth; but that of a person, acting when and where He pleases; more at one time than another, sometimes in one way and sometimes in another. He is a "Helper" who can be invoked, or who can be grieved and resisted." (*Systematic Theology* III: 474) Hodge also makes a striking opposition between "law" and "agent". The Spirit special actions in the world in its "potentia absoluta" is untamed by law and "does not act continuously or in any one way; [sic.] but just as He sees fit…every Christian feels his dependence not upon law, but on the good-will of a person." (Idem.)

61 See, Wallace, "History and Sacrament".

62 See Hodge "Theories of the Church" *The Biblical Repertory and Princeton Review* 18 (1846),:137–158 and "The Visibility of the Church" *The Biblical Repertory and Princeton Review* 25 (1853): 670–685. See also Alan Strange, *The Doctrine of the Spirituality of the Church in the Ecclesiology of Charles Hodge* (Philipsburg: Presbyterian & Reformed Publishing, 2017) and William B. Evans, *Imputation and Impartation*: 215–227.

63 "The Idea of the Church", *The Biblical Repertory and Princeton Review* 25 (1853): 249–290 and 339–389; quote at 343.

Here it seems that Hodge comes close to denying the Eucharist or the sacraments as means of grace for the sacraments are not "the means of communicating, in the first place...but the appointed means."[64] This suggests something less permanent than Bullinger's parallelism according to which there is an inward parallel eating when the outward sign is held forth. Hodge says that the sacraments can "from time to time" become means of a real communication to the believer depending on the movement of the Spirit.

The overall impression is that Hodge's intermediate position is based on an opposition that makes the inward or intellectual take an absolute precedence over the outward and physical. The result is a fragile bond between visible signs and the invisible grace they signify. Although this fragility was meant to safeguard the freedom of the Spirit and the invisibility of the church it had the unfortunate effect that the presence of grace in the Eucharist is rendered less trustworthy for communicants, or at any rate relativizing the connection to the eucharistic elements and the ritual. It is therefore understandable that Nevin accused Hodge of fostering a "mere occasional piety",[65] making the eucharistic offering a mere mental exercise with no causal connection to the visible signs. Brian Gerrish, echoing Nevin, argues that Hodge's view of the Eucharist implies a sort of "radical occasionalism". Gerrish sums up the problem:

---

64 The same is clear from Hodge's general definition of the means of grace (The Word, the Sacraments and Prayer), "those institutions which God has ordained to be the ordinary channels of grace, i. e., of the supernatural influences of the Holy Spirit to the souls of men." *Systematic Theology* III: 467. He also says that the sacraments are "real means of grace" but not "the exclusive channels; but they are channels. A promise is made to those who rightly receive the sacraments that they shall thereby and therein be made partakers of the blessings of which the sacraments are the divinely appointed signs and seals." The word grace in "means of grace" include three things: "1st. An unmerited gift such, such as the remission of sin. 2nd. The Supernatural influence of the Holy Spirit, 3d. The subjective effects of that influence on the soul." (*Systematic Theology* III: 499) Thus, on this rendition, he emphasis of the doctrine of the means of grace is pneumatic and subjective and not on the objectively given promise.

65 MTSS II:107. Nevin says that the reformed on sacramental grace, "depends of course on the Holy Ghost but still bound to the ordinance, was supposed to accompany the outwards signs, as a celestial side joined to the earthly side of one and the same transition. But this Dr. Hodge denies, allowing no other connection between the visible and invisible here, than in any other case where an outward object or event may be employed by God's Spirit as an occasion for calling forth pious thoughts and feelings." (MTSS II: 110) At the most, according to Nevin, Hodge admits a "moral objective power" in the recipient but that is not due to "any specific virtue in the [sacraments] themselves for the ends they propose to reach." (ibid) But the "Old doctrine", says Nevin, "involves for the believer a mystical participation of the flesh and blood and Christ [...] of his veritable human life now glorified in heaven" (ibid.)

> …there is no antecedent guarantee, not even a divine pledge, that the reality will be united with the sign, but only the expectation that, at least sometimes, the Spirit may choose to act upon the elect concurrently with the administration of the sacrament. [66]

Hodge's intermediate position is not a stable parallelist position between memorialism and instrumentalism, but often leans toward the former due to the weak connection with and function of the sacramental signs. However, there is another side to Hodge's eucharistic theology that we have not considered yet, one that potentially places him more firmly between Zwingli and Calvin as he desired.

By the time Hodge wrote the third volume of his *Systematic Theology*, there are some hints of a "a softening [of] Hodge's rugged extrinsic piety"[67] which Nevin thought was characteristic of his eucharistic theology. In other words, it appears that he may recognize the need for more than an "occasional piety". First, in the following passage:

> The reason why believers receive so little by their attendance on this ordinance [the Eucharist] is, that they expect so little. They expect to have their affections somewhat stirred, and their faith somewhat strengthened; but they perhaps rarely expect so to receive Christ as to be filled with all the fulness of God. Yet Christ in offering Himself to us in this ordinance, offers us all of God we are capable of receiving. For we are complete (πεπληρωμένοι) filled, i. e., filled with the fulness of God in Him. (Col. ii.10.)[68]

This seems to speak against occasionalism on God's part; God is always willing to "fill" the recipient in the Eucharist and no qualifications about the "freedom" of the Holy Spirit are added. Instead, the possibility of occasionalism is on part of the recipients due their lack of expectation on God's willingness to fill them. However, by "expectation," Hodge does not seem to mean strong faith as a condition to receive the blessings that is offered, for, he says, the Eucharist is a mean to strengthen faith. Thus, the presupposition is that Christ himself is offered in the ordinance to the believer and *that* this is the reason for the lament for the lack of expectancy

---

66 Brian Gerrish, *Tradition and the Modern World: Reformed Theology in the Nineteenth Century* (Eugene, Or: Wipf & Stock, 1978): 62. Hodge here may be said to express an "Augustinian" tendency in his theological anthropology: knowledge of divine things is contingent upon God's illuminating us subjectively about what has been objectively reveled; it requires more than a mere presentation of "facts" or "signs", it also requires an illumination of the Spirit to rightly apprehend the facts due the darkness of our minds. In its most extreme version, knowledge does not come from sensible impressions but from divine illumination of the intellect directly.

67 William B Evans, *Imputation and Impartation: Union with Christ in American Reformed Theology* (Eugene: Wipf & Stock, 2009): 226.

68 *Systematic Theology* III: 624

among attendees. If we read Hodge's comments about the Spirit's freedom in light of these remarks, it seems that the Spirit is always willing to make Christ present and communicated to the recipient. Here Hodge's view of the offering of Christ in the Eucharist is rendered more trustworthy, and less occasional, than what we saw in the debate with Nevin. For the kind of presence presupposed is certainly more than mere memorialist and more clearly parallelist.[69]

Second, Hodge affirms in another lengthy passage that Christ in his human nature is close to believers in a way that is "different from what it is to any other order of being in the universe."[70] Christ's body and soul in heaven nature can "sympathsie [sic] with his people on earth" in a way that is inexplicably mysterious but nevertheless "remains a fact of both Scripture and experience." Hodge language seems to go beyond what we have seen previously when he says that "it may be said that wherever the divinity of Christ is, there is his humanity, and as, by common consent, He is present at his table, He is there in the fulness of his human sympathy and love." Although Hodge was very careful to avoid the notion that Christ's heavenly flesh possesses a vivificatory power, he shares some central features with Calvin's eucharistic theology here.[71]

William B. Evans suggests that Hodge here expresses "a personalistic communication of the believer with the incarnate humanity by virtue of its union with

---

69 I would not read this passage in any way as instrumentalist for the focus is not on what the signs exhibit or confer to the communicant but on the spiritual experience in Eucharist. Perhaps we may want to add that Hodge here focuses on the Eucharist as an whole event (including the signs), rather than on the nature of signs in the meal.

70 The passage I am quoting from reads: "Christ is a person; a divine person with a human nature; that is with a true body and a reasonable soul. It is that person who is present with us. This again does not mean, that Christ's human nature, his body and soul are ubiquitous; but it does mean that a divine person with human affections and sympathies is near us and within us. We have now a high-priest who can be touched with a sense of our infirmities. (Heb. iv. 15.) [….] The prayers and hymns of the Church addressed to Christ all assume that He has human sympathies and affections which make his relation to us entirely different from what it is to any other order of beings in the universe. If anyone asks, How the humanity of Christ, his body and soul in heaven, can sympathize with his people on earth? the answer is, that it is in personal union with the Logos. If this answer be deemed insufficient, then the questioner may be asked, How the dust of which the human body is formed can sympathize with the immortal spirit with which it is united? Whether the mystery of this human sympathy of Christ can be explained or not, it remains a fact both of Scripture and of experience. In this sense, and not in a sense which implies any relation to space, it may be said that wherever the divinity of Christ is, there is his humanity, and as, by common consent, He is present at his table, He is there in the fulness of his human sympathy and love." *Systematic Theology* III: 653–654.

71 E. g. as in in *Institutes* IV.17.10.: "Even though it seems unbelievable that Christ's flesh, separated from us by such great distance, penetrate to us, so that it becomes our food, let us remember how far the secret power of the Holy Spirit towers above all our sense, and how foolish it is to wish to measure his immeasurableness by our measure. What, then, our mind does not comprehend, let faith conceive: that the Spirit truly unites things separated in space."

the Logos".[72] I think a more precise way of understanding Hodge's language is in terms of a *theoanthropic* (God-man) presence – that is, the recipient's communion with the person of the Logos *ensarkos* (en-fleshed) and not the merely the divine personal Logos *asarkos* (non-fleshed).[73] It is as incarnate, in both natures, that Christ is present and not merely as a divine person. So much is evident from Hodge phrase, "wherever the divinity of Christ is, there is his humanity". By that Hodge not only echoes the Chalcedonian adjectives of "indivisibility" and "inseparability" but also makes connection to ecclesiology and sacramentology in a way that is rare in his writings.

Another thing to note is that, while Hodge affirms that it is the *theanthropic* person, with body and soul, that is present at the table he does not depend on any theoretical explanation (like Calvin's vivification theory). He is apparently not worried about the seeming lack of rational explanation for this assertion, since it is "a fact of both Scripture and experience." The only rationale he gives is from the analogy of the union of soul and body in human nature that he sees as equally mysterious yet evident in our common experience.[74] Neither does he express the worries we have seen elsewhere about the Spirit's being "tied" to the elements in the Eucharist.

Whatever we make of these passages, at least they give us some reason to think that he at some level was struggling with the implications of his theological presuppositions. Taken together, it would appear that these fragments indicate a changing or widening of Hodge's mind. On the down side, rather than completing his view of the Eucharist, these fragments deepen the tension or inconsistency in his view of the Eucharist since they exist alongside the same basic position he held in the 1840s. I leave the final judgement to the reader. As I have tried to explicate some aspect Hodge's eucharistic doctrine, I will end this article with making some suggestions about his relation to the Reformed orthodox theologians on the Eucharist.

---

72 *Imputation and Impartation*: 225–226.

73 This view is through and through Reformed in its emphasis on Christ mediatorial role as the God-man with the focus on the person. In fact, Calvin (in)famously had emphasized the mediatorial role of Christ before the incarnation (although in an infralapsarian manner) and it is at least possible that this is what is in the background of Hodge's thinking. See, David E. Willis, *Calvin's Catholic Christology: The Function of the so-called Extra Calvinisticum in Calvin's Theology* (Leiden: Brill, 1966)

74 The soul-body relationship in Hodge's thinking is another thorny issue that sometimes leans towards separation and sometimes towards integration. In his use of it in the analogy here, we may be content with noting that it is integration that is the emphasis.

9.4 Hodge and Some Reformed Orthodox Theologians

Since Hodge did not bring up the Reformed orthodox theologians of the 16th and 17th century at any length in his treatment of the Eucharist, we are not able to make any certain judgement about the level of his dependence on or independence from them. Having teased out some threads from Hodge's rather conflicted eucharistic tapestry we can still make some relevant comparisons between a representative selection of Reformed scholastic theologians and Hodge, although refraining from making any ultimate judgement about influence. We may thus begin with some general remarks. First, there is a significant agreement between Hodge and the Reformed orthodox theologians about the kinds of apologetic or "elenctic theology" issues that a eucharistic theology should focus on. Hodge follows the Reformed orthodox in refuting the Lutheran and Roman doctrine of real presence (e. g. of ubiquity, transubstantiation, the eating of the flesh.)[75] Such intricate arguments of the 16th to 17th century debate between Lutheran, Reformed, and Roman Catholic theologians over Christology and the Lord's Supper were staple food in Francis Turretin's *Institutio Theologiae Elencticae*[76] which was the textbook Hodge required his students to read (in Latin), until he made his own *Systematic Theology* the primary textbook in the 1870s. However, the width and depth of Turretin's exegetical, historical and dogmatic treatments are lacking in Hodge's treatment.[77]

Second, the rather sketchy structure and seemingly *ad hoc* priority of issues of the eucharistic doctrine in *Systematic Theology* differs from the sober scholasticism of Turretin's *Institute* as well as the works of other Reformed orthodox theologians. Hodge abbreviated and appropriated Turretin's scholastic text, not only for the class room, but for the polemical context he was in. He, who had spent two years in German universities in order to better understand the alien theology and philosophy he saw coming to America, had gained a sensibility that was rare among seminary professors in America in the mid 19th century. An example of this the concern is the exposition of the Eucharist in *Systematic Theology*, contains inordinately long sections arguing against idealism.[78]

Third, although Hodge repeats the arguments against the "ubiquitarians", "Romanists" (and to some extent the Socinians) he rarely does so with explicit reference

---

75 *Systematic Theology* III: 661–670 and 677–692.

76 3 vol. (Geneva, 1687–9).

77 See, Paul C Gutjahr, *Charles Hodge: Guardian of American Orthodoxy* (Oxford: Oxford University Press, 2011): ch 11 and Nicholas A. Cummings, *Francis Turretin (1623– 87) and the Reformed Tradition* (Leiden: Brill, 2021): ch 8.

78 *Systematic Theology* III: 650–661 and 673–677. Nevin is mentioned in a lengthy footnote (655) in which Hodge expresses lament over the theological and philosophical path Nevin and others like him had taken.

to Turretin and the other Reformed orthodox theologians. But according to Hodge's historiography the mature Reformed theology emerged in the 17th century authors and documents and thus we would have expected that Turretin and other Reformed orthodox theologians should could be consulted. True, in his debate with Nevin, he turns to the Westminster confessional documents, claiming that they were only preceded by Tigurinus (and the Second Helvetic Confession) in balance. Nevertheless, it remains a curious fact that Turretin and other Reformed orthodox theologians were not explicitly quoted or referred to in the eucharistic context. One explanation for this omission is that Hodge's review was written as a response to *The Mystical Presence* in which almost no 17th century texts, besides the Westminster confessional documents, are treated or quoted.[79] Yet this literary limitation of his review does not explain why Hodge did not include references to Reformed orthodox theologians in his subsequent writings, especially in his *Systematic Theology*.

There are certain difficulties in determining Hodge's relation to the Reformed orthodox theologians, primarily, because there are some variations in the eucharistic language among the Reformed scholastics in the late 16th and the 17th centuries – such variations are more or less muted in Nevin's as well as Hodge's treatment. A more nuanced approach to these variations would require typologies broader (or other) than those of Gerrish, on which I have largely depended in my analysis. I will indicate what I think is lacking but only in so far as it is relevant to the topic at hand. With these caveats, I offer a brief comparative analysis of Hodge's relation to some representative Reformed orthodox theologians on the Eucharist.

Let us come back then to the question of whether the Reformed orthodox theologians eventually eliminated Calvin's instrumentalism. I have found little or no evidence that the kind of *explicit* vivification language that we have seen in Calvin survived or was prevalent.[80] So Hodge's claim that this aspect of Calvin's instru-

79 Nevin includes the English puritan divine, John Owen 1616–1683) which he the one hand thinks "falls short altogether of the firm, clear utterances of Calvin and the Church of the sixteenth century." Yet, on the other he says that in Owen "…we have at least in strong terms, the sense of an objective force, a true exhibition of the thing signified in the sacrament. The communion, moreover, is specific, mystical, bound to the ordinance as its medium and instrument. Then it involves a real incorporation into Christ; and it is plainly felt that this includes a special respect to his human nature, his flesh and blood, given for the life of the world. But just at this point the representation is found to waver. The truth that struggles for utterance is still embarrassed by the abstractions of the understanding and is not permitted to come to a full, unfaltering expression." MTSS I: 91. Nevin's omission of explicit treatment Turretin and other 17th century orthodox theologians thus seems to be indicative of his mixed evaluation of Owen's eucharistic theology. However, it remains a curious fact of Hodge's review that not only does he not take the opportunity to fill this gap in Nevin's presentation neither does bother to respond to Nevin's comments on Owen.

80 Of similar importance, it seems, is the realistic language of 'participation' and of being 'grafted in' in Christ through the Eucharist. This is more explicit, for instance, in Zacharias Ursinus talks of a

mentalism either died out or was interpreted metaphorically in the 17th century was not completely misguided.[81] Nevin's lack of attention to 17th century Reformed theology in both *The Mystical Presence* and subsequent articles, confirms Hodge's view indirectly.

However, things are not quite as tidy as that. We may discern a sort of instrumentalism that neither depends on the vivification-view nor is reducible to parallelism.[82] According to this view, the sacramental sign is an external instrument of a mystical or sacramental communication of the body and blood of Christ to the believer in the Supper by the power of the Holy Spirit – and not merely an external indication (or "seal") of an inward movement in the recipient at the time of the Eucharist. For instance, Gulielmus Bucanus (-1603) claims Christ does:

> not merely [communicate] by affection, love agreement and concord, not to communicate merely in Christ's merits. It is to have Christ abiding and living in and for us to abide and live in Christ [...] to be united and joined to Christ also by the actual communication of Christ's human nature.[83]

Theodore Beza (1519–1605) at Colloquy of Worms (1557) continued the language of substance, found in Calvin, and explicitly rejects memorialism in favor of real presence:

---

mutual indwell of the believer and Christ through the power of the Holy Spirit so that we are joined to the "true essential body" of Christ, as limbs to the head or branches to the vine. In vivid language, Ursinus says that the Spirit establishes a "...living, eternal and incomprehensible bond between him and us, by which our moral flesh is incorporated and knit to the living flesh of Christ a thousand times more closely, firmly, and stronger than all the members of our body are joined by their veins and fleshly bands to our head." Zacharias Ursinus, *Grundlicher Bericht vom Heiligen Abendmal* (c. 1564), quoted in MTSS I: 308.

81 I have obviously not looked at all the aspects of Calvin's eucharistic theology that would be relevant for a fuller assessment of the continuity and discontinuity between Calvin and the Reformed orthodoxy. Brian Gerrish has neatly summarized them in *Grace and Gratitude,* 134–145. The central points are (i) The supper is a divine gift and not merely a reminder, (ii) Christ is the gift, (iii) the gift is communicated and guaranteed through signs, (iv) The gift is given through the Holy Spirit, which is what Calvin means by "spiritual presence", (v), the gift is given to all but without condemnation on those who receive it in faith, (vi) the gift evokes gratitude and praise. I would argue that most, if not all, of these aspects are exemplified in the Reformed orthodox theologians.

82 A special case, among the English divines, is Richard Hooker (1554–1600), who argued that the sacraments as "morall instrumentes" in a way that seemed to converge with medieval sacramental causality more than other Reformed orthodox theologians. See, T. L. Holtzen, "Sacramental Causality in Hooker's Eucharistic Theology", *The Journal of Theological Studies* 62, no 2 (Oct 2011): 607–48.

83 Heinrich Heppe, *Reformed Dogmatics: Set out and Illustrated from the Sources.* Revised and Edited by Ernst Bizer. English translation by G.T. Thomson (London, 1950): 646. Do note the present tense of the language here.

> We confess that in the Supper of the Lord not only the benefits of Christ, but the very substance itself of the Son of Man; that is, the same true flesh which the Word assumed into perpetual personal union ... are not only signified, or set forth symbolically, typically, or in figure, like the memory of something absent, but are truly and really represented, exhibited, and offered for use.[84]

Beza expresses a sense of instrumentalism, but without explicit recourse to the effluence doctrine of Calvin. Examples from the 16th century can be multiplied from the sources quoted in *The Mystical Presence*.

A particularly instructive example from the 16th century is Peter Vermigli (1499–1562), especially because of his application of scholastic notions. Reformed theologians insist that eucharistic theology should uphold a distinction (against Lutherans and Roman Catholics) and resist a separation (against Zwingli) of sign and grace. Thus, by detailing the mode of signification of the outward signs, Vermigli argued for a dynamic or sacramental relationship with the believing communicant.[85] He employed causal notions when he called the elements "instrumental causes",[86] saying that the efficient cause is not in the elements as such but comes from God's power, using instruments to communicate and signify grace.[87] Of course, the sacramental signs, are only functioning as sacraments on the condition of faith in the believer and the concomitant work of the Holy Spirit in the communicant – for the signs do not become sacraments out of mere use (*ex operere operato*). Thus faith makes believers able to use the elements correctly whereas unbelieves do not and drink and eat what they signify.[88] On this basis, Vermigli is willing to acknowledge that believers who are rightly instructed and

---

84 As quoted in Nevin, MTSS I: 65.

85 A general note: Vermigli seemed to share with Peter Lombard that the whole world is a sacrament, in the sense that it signifies the Creator. There is, thus, an inherently teleological character in the natural world that the eucharistic signification can piggy back on. This teological or sacramental character of creation itself was gradually lost with the introduction of the empirical method and the mechanical view of matter in 17th century intellectual life. Teleology became external to the natural world and not an explanatory inherent principle, i. e. formal and final causes. It is within the nexus of such a teleology that pre-moderns like Aquinas but also the Reformed scholastics as much, formulated their theology. In the Eucharist it takes on a special character but still builds on these objective features of the world.

86 *Dialogue on the Two Natures in Christ*. The Peter Martyr Library vol 2. (Kirksville, Mo: Sixteenth Century Journal Publishers, 1995): 190.

87 "Sacraments are not the cause of grace, but the means which God uses while he sanctifies his own through them." Vermigli in *Early Writing: Creed, Scripture and Church*. Peter Martyr Library. Vol 1 (Kirksville: Sixteenth Century Studies & Essays, 1994): 107.

88 For a lucid assessment of Vermigli's eucharistic theology in context, see Jason Zuidema, *Peter Martyr Vermigli (1499–1562) and the Outward Instruments of Divine Grace*. Reformed Historical Theology, volume 4 (Göttingen, Vandenhoeck & Ruprecht, 2008), especially chs 5–6.

therefore able to discern what the elements signify and not fall prey to idolatry, may adore, bend the knee and even prostrate before the elements.[89] Here, he employs Augustine's distinction between *usus* and *frui* (use and enjoyment) so that he may identify a proper use of the sacramental elements.[90] This openness to material and ritual aspects of the sacraments follows from the careful distinctions Vermigli employed.[91] It is clear that without such distinctions, the claim that the elements, rightly used and by the power of the Holy Spirit, who always uses these external means truly communicate Christ's body and blood to us, was obscured in Hodge due to a lack of such detailed distinctions.[92]

Looking beyond the group of Reformed theologians brought up by Nevin, we may mention some late 16th and 17th century theologians,[93] such as Amandus Polanus (1561–1610) who says:

> Christ's body is absent from us locally. But he is most present to us by our union with him, through Christ's Spirit dwelling in him and in us. So there is present in the Supper not only bread and wine and not only Christ's deity and not only Christ's power and efficacy but also his actual body and blood are there in the Holy Supper.[94]

---

89 "I consider it profitable to abstain from outward adoration, namely prostration or kneeling, until they can be instructed. Indeed, worship may be used without risk, nor would the outward be evil in itself. For many kneel and worship devoutly when they hear those words of the gospel. 'And the word became flesh,' yet the words themselves are not said to be worshipped, but rather their signification." *Oxford Treaties and Disputation on the Eucharist*. Peter Martyr Library. Vol 7 (Kirksville: Sixteenth Century Studies & Essays, 2000): 87

90 "But just was Augustine warned us not to settle on the flesh but to go on to the godhead, so here concerning worship I advise us when receiving the Eucharist not to stick with the symbols but in spirit and truth to adore Christ sitting in heaven at the Father's right hand." *Oxford Treaties and Disputations*: 87.

91 It should also be noted that Vermigli worked within the early Anglican context which remained more open to liturgical action than other Reformed contexts in Europe at the time.

92 It may safely be said that this was so because the notion of signification and also the sacramental character of the physical world is a loss in other areas of his theology or his theology as a whole. Maybe this is due to his tacit acceptance of a modern view of matter and the cosmos; although resisting Darwinism, he ends up affirming a dualism of a spiritual subject and a largely mechanical material cosmos.

93 Ludwig Crocius: "Christ's body and blood are things present in the Supper neither locally nor in any physical way, but truly and really, without any fiction, united with the bread and wine by a sacramental union, on a mystical analogy and relation which is not fictitious but the true and real conjunction of the pact. Crocius, *Syntagma Sacrae Theologiae* (Bremen, 1636), 1164. Quoted in Heppe, *Reformed Dogmatics*: 641.

94 Amandus Polanus, *Syntagma Theologiae Christianae* (Hanover, 1624), VI.56. Quoted in Heppe, *Reformed Dogmatics*: 637

Polanus' statement can be interpreted as compatible with the effluence doctrine but can also be read as a version of parallelism and/or instrumentalism *sans* the vivification doctrine. His language was shared with many Reformed orthodox theologians indicate that Hodge's claim that central aspects of Calvin's view died out in the orthodox period is neither explicitly nor unequivocally supported from leading Reformed theologians.

To take another example, Johannes Wollebius (1589–1629) distinguished between three different (but overlapping) senses of presence: (i) symbolic by word or image, (ii) spiritual by faith and (iii) in "power, when what is remotely spatially is present in efficacy, as the sun" claiming that all these three senses of presence apply to the sacraments. The first sense is common to unbelievers whereas the second and the third only to believers. He adds: "Thus although Christ's body in local presence is as remote from the sign as heaven from earth, yet the sacramental presence remains. The presence is opposed not to distance but to absence."[95] A fuller statement to the same effect is found in Francis Turretin, who wrote:

> presence is not to be confounded with propinquity. What is near is not always present, and what is present is not always near. For example, the sun is present to us (although it is situated far off) when it shines upon us with its rays and nothing intervenes between it and the eye [....] Presence is not opposed to distance, but to absence. The latter, not the former, intercepts the use and enjoyment of the object.[96]

Again, here is a notion of presence that claims something more than the conflicted position of Hodge – and much more so than Hodge's memorialist contemporaries, such as Dick.

Keith A. Mathison, however, claims that Turretin (and Wollebius) held to a form of memorialism since Turretin replaces Calvin's notion of "Spiritual presence" with "mental presence" and adds that it "...seems to be one of the key ideas that have influenced Reformed sacramentology to this day."[97] The central problem is that the "connection between the sings and the thing signified is a connection that *occurs in our minds*. Just as words are signs that bring to mind the things signified, so the

95 Heppe, *Reformed Dogmatics*: 641–642. Keith A. Mathison's treatment of Wollebius, omits this last phrase in the quote and thus makes a memoralist out of him. He interprets "spiritual presence" in a sense that is more or less identical to we have seen in Hodge. He says that presence in power, means the effect of a thing and not the thing itself. See Mathison, *Given for You: Reclaiming Calvin's Doctrine of the Lord's Supper* (Philipsburg: Reformed and Presbyterian Publishing, 2002): 111–113.

96 Francis Turrettin, *Institutes of Elenctic Theology*. Translated by James T Dennison (Philippsburg, NJ: P & R Publishing, 1997) III: 506.

97 *Given for You*, 119. Here is apparently taking his cue from Nevin and Gerrish.

sacraments are signs that make reality signified present in our minds."[98] There are, however, aspects in Turretin that Mathison overlooked, who is worth quoting at length:

> They are not formal signs, which mark the species itself received by cognitive faculty, to which the sign is proposed. Rather they are instrumental, which represent themselves to the senses and a thing different from themselves to the intellect. *In their own way, they make it present because God uses them as organs and instruments for offering and conferring grace upon us in their own way*. But the formal of the sign ought not to be confounded with the formal sign; for another thing is opposed to the sign materially considered, as in the Supper the bread is the material of the sacramental sign; but if it is considered as a sign, it is of the body of Christ. This pertains to the formality of that, which is considered reduplicatively as a sign of the body of Christ. But the formal sign distinctly (not from the material, but from the instrumental) is the intelligible species itself excited by the sign in its formality in the mind.[99]

That sacramental signs "in their own way" surely make the thing signified present to the intellect is not quite the mere "mental presence" which Mathison suggests. Rather it reflects an understanding of signification that is analyzed in terms of scholastic view of causality and semantics. It belongs to the nature of signs of signify other thing, both in natural matters and in supernatural matters. In the Eucharist, the thing signified can in faith be perceived and made present through the sacramental signs by the Holy Spirit's work as efficient cause.[100] Turretin's expression "conferring grace" indicates a communication via external signs, not as efficient cause but as organs and instruments. His language in some respect has a resonance in Aquinas' and other medieval theologians' talk of sacramental causality, who used the notion of 'instrument' in a broad sense, for secondary causes

---

98 *Given for You*, 115. Emphasis mine.

99 *Institutes*, III: 347.

100 See e. g., *Institutes* III: 353: "Although the word and Holy Spirit testify of the grace of God and also seal it in their own way, it does not follow that this also does not belong to the sacraments. These are subordinates, not opposites. The effect is common to both causes, but the manner of effecting is diverse; there verbal, here symbolic; there by hearing, here by the sight and other senses. The Spirit is the internal seal, which seals from its own nature; but the sacraments are external seals, which seal only from their institution; the Spirit as the principal and efficacious cause who uses the word and sacraments as instruments." Turretin is (maybe too) careful not to imply any "physical" causation in the sacramentals signs as he thought that the Romanist reduced the sacramental signs to an inherent power, thus obscuring the distinction between sign and grace.

of various kinds as well as the human nature of Christ as "the organ of divinity" (*organum divinitatis*).[101]

Hodge by contrast, as I have showed, held to an epistemology that was more limited than scholastic epistemology tended to be. According to Hodge, our knowledge boils down to either intellectual apprehension (of immaterial things), or to sense perception (of material things), allowing only a limited, or occasional, function for material signs but rather different from the instrumental and sacramental character of the scholastics.[102] For, as we also have seen, according to the dominant strand in Hodge eucharistic theology, the Spirit works directly on the mind (by "filling", bring Christ's benefits to the mind etc.), but not always concurrently with the physical eating of the consecrated elements in the liturgy.[103] What I labelled *theanthropic* presence above seems to transcend these epistemic principles and perhaps moves his eucharistic theology closer to Calvin and at least to some of the Reformed orthodox theologians I have cited. On the downside, this feature remains an exception to the rule in Hodge's case.

9.5 Concluding Remarks

To sum up: I have showed that, Hodge tried to uphold a kind of parallelism and also struggled to avoid the memorialism that was prevalent in his day. He did not fully succeed in formulating a coherent or stable view of Christ's presence but vacillated

---

101 For a good overview of Aquinas' view of signification and causality, see John P. Yocum "Aristotle in Aquinas Sacramental Theology" in *Aristotle in Aquinas's Theology*, eds. Matthew and Giles Emery Levering O.P. (Oxford: Oxford University Press, 2015). Thanks to Dr McGraw for this reference. As a side note, Hodge's common-sense realism and Aquinas' realism are not necessarily worlds apart, as some commentators have suggested. For this, see Seán M. Connolly, "The Reality of Knowing: The Status of Ideas in Aquinas and Reid" (Proquest, Umi Dissertation Publishing, 2011). A related problem is *how* Hodge came to apply (or not) common-sense philosophy to theology.

102 Since the scholastic terminology was often simplified in Hodge's writing on the Eucharist, he would perhaps may even misinterpreted Turretin if he had actually consulted him on the complex issue of sacramental causality

103 This is close to the way Mathison reads the majority of the Reformed orthodox theologians. Perhaps, what is at work here is an imagined opposition between the humanist (Calvin) and scholastic (Vermigli) strands of early modern thought. Calvin depended on a different kind of prose style and conceptualities but was accepted by his scholastic trained Reformed colleagues. These differences have been blown up by modern commentators and it seems to me that this is also a tacit presupposition in treatments such as Mathison's. For some insightful comments, see Bradford Littlejohns unpublished paper, "The Real Presence and the Presence of Reality: A Fresh Look at Reformed Sacramentology" (https://www.academia.edu/35002362/The_Real_Presence_and_the_Presence_of_Reality_A_Fresh_Look_at_Reformed_Sacramentology)

between memorialist and parallelist interpretations of the Eucharist. Toward the end of his life, he seems to have gestured towards a sort of *theanthropic* presence. However, since this idea cannot clearly be distinguished as a development in his thinking, and is found alongside the views he held since the 1840s, it does not help to make his view more coherent in the end. Rather, what we are left with are various tendencies pulling him in different directions. Finally, it remains a curious fact that, he almost never referred explicitly to Reformed orthodox theologians on the topic. For had he done so, he would ideally have had to acknowledge that there is more width in the Reformed orthodox theologians than he admitted.[104]

Works Cited

Adger, John. "Calvin Defended Against Drs. Cunningham and Hodge." *The Southern Presbyterian Review*, no 27 (1876): 133–166.

Aubert, Annette G. *The German Roots of Nineteenth-Century American Theology*. Oxford: Oxford University Press, 2013.

Bains, David R. and Theodore Louis Trost. "Philip Schaff: The Flow of Church History and the Development of Protestantism." *Theology Today* 71, no 4 (January 2015): 416–28.

Bonomo, Jonathan G. *Incarnation and Sacrament: The Eucharistic Controversy between Charles Hodge and John Williamson Nevin*. Eugene OR: Wipf & Stock, 2010.

Campi, Emidio. "The *Consensus Tigurinus* : Origins, Assessment, and Impact." *Reformation & Renaissance Review* 18, no 1 (January 2016): 5–24.

Calvin, John. *Calvin's Tracts and Letters*. Edinburgh: Banner of Truth, 2009.

------. *Institutes of the Christian Religion*, edited by John Thomas McNeill, The Library of Christian Classics. Louisville, Ky. London: Westminster John Knox Press, 1960.

------. *Calvin: Theological Treatises*. The Library of Christian Classics, edited and translated by J.K.S. Reid. Louisville: Westminster John Know Press, 1954.

Cunningham, William. *The Reformers and the Theology of the Reformation*. Edinburgh: Banner of Truth Trust, 1989 [1862].

Cunnington, Ralph. "Calvin's Doctrine of the Lord's Supper: A Blot upon His Labours as a Public Instructor?" *Westminster Theological Journal* 73 (2011): 215–236.

Cummings, Nicholas A. *Francis Turretin (1623–87) and the Reformed Tradition*. Leiden: Brill, 2021.

Connolly, Seán M. "The Reality of Knowing: The Status of Ideas in Aquinas and Reid." Proquest, Umi Dissertation Publishing, 2011.

Crocius, Ludwig. *Syntagma Sacrae Theologiae*. Bremen, 1636.

DeBie, Linden J. and Bradford Littlejohn. "Reformed Eucharistic Theology and the Case for Real Presence." *Theology Today* 71, no 4 (January 2015): 429–39.

104 Thanks to Tomas Nygren, Leif Svensson and especially Ryan McGnaw for valuable comments on an earlier version of this text.

DiPuccino, William. *The Interior Senses of Scriptures: The Sacred Hermeneutics of John W, Nevin*. Georgia: Mercer University Press, 1998.

Drake, K. J. *The Flesh of the Word: The Extra Calvinisticum from Zwingli to Early Orthodoxy*, Oxford Study in Historical Theology Series. New York, NY, United States of America: Oxford University Press, 2021.

Evans, William B. *Imputation and Impartation: Union with Christ in American Reformed Theology*. Eugene: Wipf & Stock, 2009.

Gerrish, Brian A. *Grace and Gratitude: The Eucharistic Theology of John Calvin*. Eugene, Or: Wipf and Stock Publ, 2002.

------. *The Old Protestantism and the New: Essays on the Reformation Heritage*. Edinburgh: T&T Clarke, 1982.

------. *Tradition and the Modern World: Reformed Theology in the Nineteenth Century*. Eugene, Or: Wipf & Stock, 1978.

Gutjahr, Paul C. *Charles Hodge: Guardian of American Orthodoxy*. Oxford: Oxford University Press, 2011.

Heppe, Heinrich. *Reformed Dogmatics: Set out and Illustrated from the Sources*, revised and edited by Ernst Bizer. English translation by G.T. Thomson. Grand Rapids: Baker Book House, 1950).

Hodge, Charles. "Theories of the Church." *The Biblical Repertory and Princeton Review* 18 (1846): 137–158.

------. "Doctrine of the Reformed Church on the Lord's Supper." *The Biblical Repertory and the Princeton Review*, 20 (April 1848): 227–77.

------. "The Visibility of the Church." *The Biblical Repertory and Princeton Review* 25 (1853): 670–685.

------. "The Idea of the Church." *The Biblical Repertory and Princeton Review* 25 (1853): 249–290 and 339–389.

------. "The first and Second Adam. The Elohim revealed in the Creation and Redemption of Man." *The Biblical Repertory and Princeton Review* 32 (1860): 335 376.

------. *Systematic Theology* 3 vol. Grand Rapids: Baker Bookshouse, 1988 [1871–73].

Holder, R. Ward. "The Pain of Agreement: Calvin and the *Consensus Tigurinus*." *Reformation & Renaissance Review* 18, no 1 (January 2016): 85–94.

Holifield, E. Brooks. "Mercersburg, Princeton, and the South: The Sacramental Controversy in the Nineteenth Century." *Journal of Presbyterian History* 54, no 2 (1976): 238–57.

------. *Sacramental Theology in America: Seventeenth-Nineteenth Centuries*, edited by Hans Boersma and Matthew Levering. Oxford: Oxford University Press, 2015.

Holtzen, T. L. "Sacramental Causality in Hooker's Eucharistic Theology." *The Journal of Theological Studies* 62, no 2 (October 2011): 607–48.

Hunsinger, George. "The Heidelberg Catechism in America: A Snapshot from the History of Its Reception.", *Theology Today* 70, no 3 (October 2013): 256–68.

Kirby, Torrance. "3. *Consensus Tigurinus* , 1549", *Reformation & Renaissance Review* vol 18, No 1 (January 2016): 34–44.

Leijenhorst, Cees. "Place, Space and Matter in Calvinist Physics." *The Monist* 84, no 4 (2001): 520–41.

Letham, Robert. *The Lord's Supper: Eternal Word in Broken Bread*. Phillipsburg.: P&R Publishing Company, 2001.

Lindholm, Stefan. *Jerome Zanchi (1516–90) and the Analysis of Reformed Scholastic Christology*, Reformed Historical Theology, Volume 37. Göttingen: Vandenhoeck & Ruprecht, 2016.

Littlejohn, Bradford. "The Real Presence and the Presence of Reality: A Fresh Look at Reformed Sacramentology." (https://www.academia.edu/35002362/The_Real_Presence_and_the_Presence_of_Reality_A_Fresh_Look_at_Reformed_Sacramentology)

Mathison, Keith A. *Given for You: Reclaiming Calvin's Doctrine of the Lord's Supper*. Philipsburg: Reformed and Presbyterian Publishing, 2002.

McLelland, Joseph C. "Meta-Zwingli or Anti-Zwingli? Bullinger and Calvin in Eucharistic Concord." In *Huldrych Zwingli: 1484–1451: A Legacy of Radical Reformation*, edited by Edward J. Furcha. Montreal: FRC/ARC, 1985.

Muller, Richard A. "Calvin on Sacramental Presence, in the Shadow of Marburg and Zurich." *Lutheran Quarterly*, 23 (2009): 147–167.

Nevin, John Williamson and Charles Hodge. *Coena Mystica: Debating Reformed Eucharistic Theology*, edited by Linden J DeBie, vol. 2, The Merceburg Theology Study Series. Eugene: Wipf & Stock Publishers, 2013.

Polanus, Amandus. *Syntagma Theologiae Christianae*. Hanover, 1624.

Schaff, Philipp. *Creeds of Christendom*, 6th ed. revised and enlarged. New York: Harper and Brothers, 1983 [1931].

Strange, Alan. *The Doctrine of the Spirituality of the Church in the Ecclesiology of Charles Hodge*. Philipsburg: Presbyterian & Reformed Publishing, 2017.

The Council of Ephesus (431). https://www.papalencyclicals.net/councils/ecum03.htm.

The Second Helvetic Confession (1562). https://www.creeds.net/helvetic/c21.htm

Turretin, Francis. *Institutio Theologiae Elencticae* 3 vol. Geneva, 1687–9.

Turretin, Francis. *Institutes of Elenctic Theology*, translated by James T Dennison. Philippsburg, NJ: P & R Publishing, 1997.

Vermigli, Peter. *Early Writing: Creed, Scripture and Church*. Peter Martyr Library. Vol 1. Kirksville: Sixteenth Century Studies & Essays, 1994.

------. *Dialogue on the Two Natures in Christ*. The Peter Martyr Library vol 2. Kirksville, Mo: Sixteenth Century Journal Publishers, 1995.

------. *Oxford Treaties and Disputation on the Eucharist*. Peter Martyr Library. Vol 7. Kirksville: Sixteenth Century Studies & Essays, 2000.

Yocum, John P. "Aristotle in Aquinas Sacramental Theology" in *Aristotle in Aquinas's Theology*, edited by Matthew and Giles Emery Levering O.P. Oxford: Oxford University Press, 2015.

Zachman, Randall C. "Did the Zurich Consensus Create the Possibility of Future Dialogue with Wittenberg?" *Reformation & Renaissance Review* 18, No 1 (January 2016): 59–71.

Zuidema, Jason. *Peter Martyr Vermigli (1499–1562) and the Outward Instruments of Divine Grace.* Reformed Historical Theology, volume 4. Göttingen: Vandenhoeck & Ruprecht, 2008.

Wallace, Peter J. "History and Sacrament: John Williamson Nevin and Charles Hodge on the Lord's Supper." *Mid-America Journal of Theology* 11 (2000): 171–201.

Westminster Confession of Faith (1646) (https://www.ligonier.org/learn/articles/westminster-confession-faith

Willis, David E. *Calvin's Catholic Christology: The Function of the so-called Extra Calvinisticum in Calvin's Theology*. Leiden: Brill, 1966.

Name and Subject Index